LEARNING WITH PROFESSIONALS
Selected Works from the Joint Military Intelligence College

A collection of previously published works by students and members of the faculty of the Joint Military Intelligence College

CENTER FOR STRATEGIC INTELLIGENCE RESEARCH

JOINT MILITARY INTELLIGENCE COLLEGE

Washington, DC

July 2005

*The views expressed in this book are those of the authors
and do not reflect the official policy or position of the
Department of Defense or the U.S. Government*

CONTENTS

The History of Intelligence

The Applications of Intelligence

LEARNING WITH PROFESSIONALS

Selected Works from the
Joint Military Intelligence College

INTRODUCTION

The University of Maryland's July 2005 conference on "Teaching Intelligence in America's Universities" marks the turning of a significant page in the history of American academia. The history, the role, and the contributions of intelligence are now recognized in growing numbers of institutions of higher learning across the land as important fields of academic study and research.

If intelligence was first formally declared an instrument of U.S. national security in the National Security Act of 1947, it did not enter the mainstream of American thinking and discourse until the terrorist attacks of 2001 and their aftermath. Now, with the benefit of commission studies and recommendations and executive and legislative actions culminating in the passage of the Intelligence Reform and Terrorism Prevention Act of 2004, good, timely, relevant intelligence is recognized as "the air the nation breathes." Soccer moms discuss intelligence. College students' interest in intelligence extends beyond the work of the classroom to the prospect of intelligence as a career.

The Joint Military Intelligence College has the privilege and the trust of serving as the Federal Government's center of excellence for intelligence education and research. With teaching and research at both the classified and unclassified levels, the College awards the Master of Science of Strategic Intelligence degree and the Bachelor of Science in Intelligence degree. The College's degrees are authorized by the Congress. The College is accredited by the Middle States Commission on Higher Education and is a member of the Consortium of Universities of the Washington Metropolitan Area.

The research and publications of the College's students, faculty, and research fellows are contributing to the work of intelligence and the security of the nation. They are creating the literature of intelligence. This book of readings taken from such research and writings offers a window on the incredible history and evolving work of intelligence and the contributions it is making in the early 21st century. The different chapters underscore the importance of the emergence of intelligence as a sought-after academic discipline.

A. Denis Clift
President,
Joint Military Intelligence College

THE WORK OF INTELLIGENCE

MEETING THE COMMUNITY'S CONTINUING NEED FOR AN INTELLIGENCE LITERATURE

Russell G. Swenson

(Originally Published in the Defense Intelligence Journal; 11-2 (2002), 87-98.)

Intelligence today is not merely a profession, but like most professions it has taken on the aspects of a discipline: it has developed a recognized methodology; it has developed a vocabulary; it has developed a body of theory and doctrine; it has elaborate and refined techniques. It now has a large professional following. What it lacks is a literature.[1]

Sherman Kent's argument, published in 1955, bears re-examination. On the same page with the passage above, he noted that "The sort of literature I am talking about is of the nature of house organ literature, but much more. You might call it the institutional mind and memory of our discipline." Over the years, the journal *Studies in Intelligence*, published by the Center for the Study of Intelligence, has brought to light the insights of government intelligence practitioners. Featured articles, for example, have addressed Kent's concern that the professional literature address questions of mission and method. His other concerns, that the literature promote a shared definition of terms, and that it elevate the level of debate of all these issues, have certainly been accomplished in the training and especially the education classrooms of the Intelligence Community.[2] However, active debate over the principles and practices of intelligence remains confined largely to those classrooms. How can a more mature literature be drawn from these obscure debates, so as to expose arguments to the sometimes humbling yet clarifying light that comes with their publication as a permanent record? How can those of us who feel responsible for capturing institutional knowledge accommodate ourselves to the maxim that, as earlier generations might have put it: *Litera scripta manet* — [It is] the written word [that] remains — and that provides a literature on which an applied (field-tested) academic discipline may develop.

As Kent acknowledges, this literature must at times bear a classification to protect sensitive information. However, he also suggests that a surprising share of the literature can be produced without controls that shield it from "outsiders." Academically oriented publication of Intelligence Community literature on collection, analysis and presentation methods, and published explorations of such topics as the intelligence-policy relationship and international intelligence sharing, if presented on a Community website, could broadcast

---

[1] Sherman Kent, "The Need for an Intelligence Literature," *Studies in Intelligence* 1, no. 1 (September 1955): 3. Reproduced in 45th Anniversary, Special Unclassified Edition (Fall 2000): 1-11.

[2] The two continuing venues where national-level, practitioner-oriented intelligence issues are commonly debated are the CIA's Sherman Kent School, founded in May 2000, and the Joint Military Intelligence College, established in 1962, since1980 operating as the Community's de facto academic center, focused around its accredited graduate program.

carefully considered positions on these issues and offer a platform for the "elevated debate" he envisioned. These prospects beg the question of where this original literature will come from: Who will conceive of important questions, and who will engage in an impartial examination of those questions?

Since 1980, when the JMIC was first authorized to confer a master of science of strategic intelligence degree, some 1,600 master's theses and 400 master's-level seminar papers have been completed.[3] Now, 120-140 theses are completed each year, most by full-time students in the one-year program, who are in the main from the military services. Significantly, a growing proportion of the total is by civilians (now 38 percent of all the College's students), who are employees of the spectrum of Community organizations. Naturally, this database offers a starting point for an "applied" intelligence literature. Theses do reflect classroom learning, and their validity as additions to the professional literature does benefit greatly from the productive interaction among well-experienced students, which is promoted by their work throughout the year within a small but diverse group of fellow students through a "track" system. However, exigencies stemming from intense course requirements and limited time for data gathering and analysis often do not allow even these written arguments to be as thoroughly presented as warranted by the seriousness of many topics.

The academic journals that support the profession offer exposure mainly to "retrospective" analyses of intelligence questions, although a few items in these fora do examine the tensions that characterize contemporary government intelligence practices.[4] Some of these periodicals also publish exchanges between readers and authors (see the "Correspondence" section of *Intelligence and National Security* and the "Reader's Forum" of the *International Journal of Intelligence and Counterintelligence*). Nonetheless, the give-and-take does not reach the frequency or intensity of that encountered in JMIC classrooms.

OPERATIONAL INTELLIGENCE: PROFESSIONALS ON STAGE

The intelligence activities of peacetime, no less than those of wartime, are a vast bureaucratic and intellectual exercise in international epistemology. ...on the issue of policy implementation, an egregiously neglected subject by international relations scholars, intelligence studies may well be in the lead.[5]

---

[3] A searchable index to this student work is available on the Community's web-based Intelink system at *http://diacovweb.dia.ic.gov/jmic/mssipapers.nsf*. The two-seminar-paper option for meeting the non-course degree requirement was dropped in 1993; since then the requirement has been for each graduate student to complete a thesis — a sustained argument — of about 100 pages.

[4] Besides *Studies in Intelligence*, The English-language journals most closely associated with the government intelligence profession are the *International Journal of Intelligence and Counterintelligence, Intelligence and National Security*, the *American Intelligence Journal* (from the National Military Intelligence Association), the Intelligencer (of the Association of Former Intelligence Officers) and the *Defense Intelligence Journal* (published by the JMIC Foundation). Other, military service-oriented journals that occasionally publish articles of value to national intelligence scholars are the Army's *Military Intelligence* and the *Naval Intelligence Professional's Quarterly*.

Professional and academic journals, as well as issue panels, such as those sponsored by the Intelligence Studies section at meetings of the International Studies Association, provide a forum for incipient intelligence literature. At the same time, the crucible of operational or "strategic" intelligence production at national agencies, Combatant Command headquarters, executive branch Departments, and within U.S. embassies, yields a continuous stream of raw material suitable for reflection and refinement into principles that emerge from professional practice. The term "operational intelligence" may usefully be joined with another term of practice, "actionable intelligence," to accommodate the idea that, at least in large intelligence bureaucracies, information can become so fine-grained and attuned to immediate needs that strategic "big ideas" default to, or become the preserve of public policy participants mediated through the press, think tanks, and popular civic organizations such as the Council on Foreign Relations, and occasionally even individual university professors.[6] Of course, this situation supports the ideals of democratic governance.

In the bureaucratized, national intelligence environment, the concept of strategic intelligence is represented by substantive discussions found in National Intelligence Estimates, as well as putative "strategic warning" documents. However an "intelligence literature" at the national level, at least as generated by active intelligence professionals, may best be described as concerned with "operational" phenomena.[7] Thus, the continued development of an intelligence literature appears to depend on our ability to capture the protean "challenge and response" scenes experienced by intelligence careerists, including those who rise to become leaders of agencies, as well as those who remain in the rank and file. Among U.S. federal government "house organs," the publications of the Center for the Study of Intelligence offer reflections by individual careerists on signal historical developments in international relations episodes, and occasionally on some continuing questions of the mission of the national intelligence establishment.[8] In doing so, CSI car-

---

[5] Michael G. Fry and Miles Hochstein, "Epistemic Communities: Intelligence Studies and International Relations," *Intelligence and National Security* 8, no. 3 (July 1993): 18, 25.

[6] For example, the National Intelligence Council's *Global Trends 2015*, after being released to the public in January 2001, has been the subject of constructive criticism by numerous scholars. A number of their observations are reproduced in the Woodrow Wilson Center's *Environmental Change and Security Project Report*, no. 7 (Summer 2001): 59-99.

[7] Definitions of strategic intelligence wear well. Influential ones include "high-level, foreign positive intelligence," — Sherman Kent, *Strategic Intelligence for American World Policy* (Princeton, NJ: Princeton University Press, 1949, 3); "knowledge pertaining to the capabilities, vulnerabilities and probable courses of action of foreign nations," — Washington Platt, *Strategic Intelligence Production: Basic Principles* (New York: Frederick A. Praeger, Publishers, 1957) and that which is "designed to provide officials with the 'big picture' and long-range forecasts they need in order to plan for the future," — Bruce D. Berkowitz and Allan E. Goodman, *Strategic Intelligence for American National Security* (Princeton, NJ: Princeton University Press, 1989), 4. Notably, the last authors do not acknowledge the existence of "operational intelligence," which suggests a recent origin of the term, in the sense used in the present paper. In fact, though, Sherman Kent himself long ago alluded to the same concept (1949: 9) when he noted how "men who work in the world of affairs...turn out, as by-products of their main jobs, large amounts of material which is the subject matter of strategic intelligence." In this framework, then, professional intelligence literature is concerned mainly with the theory and practice, or operationalization, of the "main job."

[8] For a sample of CSI publications, see their web site at *http://www.cia.gov/csi/*.

ries out a significant part of Sherman Kent's vision for an intelligence literature. The *Defense Intelligence Journal* also frequently gives voice to Community leaders and senior analysts on an inclusive menu of topics and issues. In neither of these media, though, are rebuttals or counter-rebuttals published. Any debates that may arise in pre-publication review remain hidden from readers.

It does appear that only in Community schools, such as the Kent school and the JMIC, do debates occur among those whose views may not yet have been hardened by solitary experience. Commenting on the Kent school and its promise for "socializing" new hires and exploring ways to capture CIA DI corporate knowledge, Stephen Marrin expresses a hope for the emergence of a "CIA University." [9] The JMIC, as suggested above, already exists as the Community's College, and is recognized as the core for at least a virtual university.[10] Only here are students and faculty from CIA, State, NSA, NRO, DIA, as well as all the military and law enforcement intelligence organizations and congressional oversight staff able to put on display, for discussion, their personal interpretations without themselves being viewed through the lens of their organization's reputed culture.

JMIC classroom debates over intelligence processes, salient issues in international relations and domestic intelligence and law enforcement applications, and the developing environment of international intelligence cooperation all put on display student and faculty experience in operational intelligence practice. From these debates, principles of intelligence practice are each day further defined and subjected to peer criticism. At the same time, JMIC students try their hand at applying research and writing that rest on time-tested scientific method.

INTELLIGENCE LITERATURE FOR THE COMMUNITY

As Sherman Kent notes, although "'security' and the advancement of knowledge are in fundamental conflict...many of the most important contributions to this literature need not be classified at all."[11] From the typical, free-wheeling challenge of debate in its classrooms, the College has begun to add a dimension to the literature on government intelligence. Thus far, this contribution focuses on *process* and *organization*. This new Community literature resource, some of it classified and some not, now preserves a portion of the institutional knowledge generated in the school environment. Since 1996, the

---

[9] Stephen Marrin, ""The CIA's Kent School: A Step in the Right Direction," *Intelligencer: Journal of U.S. Intelligence Studies* (Winter 2000): 56.

[10] Lloyd Salvetti, Director of CSI, "Teaching Intelligence: Working Together to Build a Discipline," in *Teaching Intelligence at Colleges and Universities,* Conference Proceedings, 18 June 1999 (Washington, DC: JMIC, 1999): 18.

[11] Kent, 1955: 9. A recent argument for carefully limiting the openness of national intelligence services is in a Commentary article by Thomas Patrick Carroll, "The Case Against Intelligence Openness," in *International Journal of Intelligence and Counterintelligence* 14, no. 4 (Winter 2001-2002): 559-574. However, his premise sees intelligence only as information (p. 561) — or "knowledge," in Kent's terminology — rather than as *process* (activity) or *organization*. For Kent, all three terms are equally valid labels for the phenomenon of government intelligence. Further, intelligence *process* need not be equated with intelligence *methods*, particularly in the usual, collection-oriented sense of "sources and methods."

College has published Discussion Papers, Occasional Papers and books, all contributing to the Community's operational intelligence literature. This literature is available in its entirety on Intelink at *http://www/dia.ic.gov/proj/JMIC/Publications.htm*, much of it is available to the public through the National Technical Information Service, and some through the U.S. Government Printing Office.

Figure 1 and Figure 2.

To illustrate the fulfillment of Kent's recommendations for the development of a literature by and for active professionals, the variety of recent JMIC publications (see examples in accompanying illustrations) addresses his idea that it deal with "first principles" and that it provide for a definition of terms. The condition that this professional literature be for the benefit of active intelligence professionals is readily met, given that several of these publications are used in Community training and education settings, from the National Drug Intelligence Center to various Department of Defense senior educational institutions, as well as by instructors in various colleges and universities across the U.S. where intelligence studies is part of the curriculum. It should be noted, too, that JMIC courses count on publications from the Center for the Study of Intelligence (such as Richards J. Heuer, Jr.'s *Psychology of Intelligence Analysis,* published in 1999) to acquaint students with non-JMIC professional literature. JMIC publications undergo pre-publication review by Community experts and by academics and other security professionals in the private sector. The one Kent recommendation that has not yet been adopted in the College's publication program is provision for a post-publication "elevated debate" of issues addressed in this literature. In part, this is because these publications, not being journals or regularly appearing "periodicals" in the strict sense, offer no mechanism for commentary and rebuttal. The College is now about to embark on an endeavor to raise the level of debate on prominent issues in the intelligence profession.

CENTER FOR STRATEGIC INTELLIGENCE RESEARCH

To capture the spirit of debate in JMIC classrooms, and to elevate it to a level commensurate with the best professional literature, the College in late 2002 will inaugurate a Center for Strategic Intelligence Research. The Center's Office of Research Fellows will sponsor and publish the investigative and practical work of a few "Fellows" from across the Community who will tackle a single research theme each year. The Center's Applied Research Office will support JMIC faculty as they distill and reproduce their classroom insights in the continuing series of Discussion and Occasional Papers. Community Research Fellows will be senior analysts or operatives who can be freed from their regular duties for a full year. Their work will be presented for comment and advice in periodic workshops. Some potential research themes include: adapting new and powerful but practical analytic tools for use by Community analysts; identifying terms, conditions and opportunities for effective multilateral intelligence sharing; developing mechanisms for building the professional resources of law enforcement intelligence offices and the integration of these offices into the Intelligence Community.

The problem of how the Community can best develop a useful, professional literature, free of self-congratulatory excesses, and able to stir interest among harried practitioners, remains unresolved. However, the combined efforts of the Center for the Study of Intelligence and the Center for Strategic Intelligence Research represent a commitment to continue production of that literature and to expand its value.

THE BASIC TOOLS OF WRITING WITH INTELLIGENCE

James S. Major

(Originally Published as Chapter 2 in his textbook, Writing With Intelligence.)

SUMMARY

Writing is a basic skill required of intelligence professionals. We learn to write by writing, observing, and learning from our own mistakes and the mistakes of others. All writing, including intelligence writing, should **communicate** something.

- The basic principles of **all** writing are clarity, conciseness, and correctness. **Clarity** ensures that you are understood. To be **concise** in intelligence writing, say what you need to say in as few words as possible, then stop. **Correctness** includes both precision and mechanical correctness. The most common errors are misspellings, usage, punctuation, and subject-verb agreement.
- Other important considerations in your writing include appropriateness, completeness, and coherence. **Appropriateness** means considering your audience and their needs. To be **complete**, be sure you've said everything you need to say. A **coherent** paper is a unified whole, focused on a central theme.
- There is no magic formula for becoming a good writer. Common components of most good intelligence writing are hard work and perseverance.

Writing is an interesting and challenging part of the intelligence profession. Master the basic skills of writing with intelligence, and you will be a step closer to mastering the tools of your trade. Commanders, warfighters, decisionmakers, planners, and force developers depend on intelligence. The way you communicate that intelligence to them in writing may be the key to success in accomplishing the mission.

WHY WRITE?

The most basic skill required of the intelligence professional is the ability to write. Some students claim they can't write because they "just weren't born with the ability." Are we to infer, then, that the capacity to write well is genetically transmitted? Don't you believe it! Look in the reference section of any library or book store and you'll find scores of "How To" books dealing with writing. Obviously a lot of writers out there believe they can help aspiring authors do a better job. My aim is to help you do a better job disseminating the results of your research and analysis. A basic way to disseminate intelligence is via the written word.

This chapter is illustrated with examples of student writing that have felt the stroke of my pen over the last 10 years. Having examined thousands of papers, I found no shortage of material. Examples are quoted verbatim, warts and all, with no editing except the deletions shown by ellipsis periods (. . .), mainly due to the length of the sentence. In no case have I taken any example out of context. What you see is what we got from a mid-level intelligence professional in the postgraduate or undergraduate program at the Joint Military Intelligence College.

We learn from our mistakes, and from observing the mistakes of others as well. We learn to write better by noting shortcomings and avoiding them the next time we write. In writing this material, I benefited from the counsel and critiques of my colleagues and my students. I hope that you will find something of use to you somewhere in this chapter.

The reason for all writing is to communicate something: ideas, emotions, or information, for example. This tenet should be immediately obvious to the writer of an intelligence product; yet too many publications of the Intelligence Community leave the reader puzzled as to what the author was trying to say. For instance, after Operation DESERT STORM, when General H. Norman Schwarzkopf testified before the Senate Armed Services Committee on 12 June 1991, he said: "[B]y the time you got done reading many of the intelligence estimates you received, no matter what happened they would have been right. . . . [T]hat's not helpful to the guy in the field."[12]

Intelligence writers either violate or ignore the simplest, most straightforward principles of writing that they learned when they graduated from finger paint to pencil and pen, and finally, to the word processor. These are, for the most part, intelligent people who genuinely want to share their knowledge or their analytical product with an audience. They fall short not from ignorance, but from their failure to consider those basic principles of all writing.

THE BASICS: CLARITY, CONCISENESS, AND CORRECTNESS

Like skilled carpenters with their toolboxes, ready to tackle a construction project, students must equip themselves with the tools of their trade before tackling a writing project. Writing is hard work. There's nothing more intimidating than a blank piece of paper in front of your face — or, in this computer and word-processing age, a blank *screen*. (Why do you think they call that blinking dot on the screen a "cursor"?) But you can win the standoff and break the ominous "writer's block" by keeping in mind a few basic principles to make your writing smoother, easier to read, and more informative to your reader.

Clarity

Clarity, clarity, clarity. When you become hopelessly mired in a sentence, it is best to start fresh; do not try to fight your way through against the terrible odds of syntax. Usually what is wrong is that the construction has become too involved at some point; the sentence needs to be broken apart and replaced by two or more shorter sentences.

— Strunk and White
The Elements of Style

---

[12] Quoted in Gen. Frederick J. Kroesen, "Intelligence: Now a Two-Way Street?" *Army*, September 1994, 7.

Robert Louis Stevenson said it clearly: "Don't write merely to be understood. Write so you cannot possibly be misunderstood." Do that and you'll never have a problem with your papers. What's crystal clear to you may be unintelligible to a reader without your experience or background. One person's "simple" is another person's "huh?" Have someone else read your writing — a classmate, your spouse, or a friend. Ask them for constructive and objective criticism. Don't be thin-skinned. Your masterpiece may be maligned or murdered, but you'll learn more that way.

If you can't have a second set of eyes on your work, reread it yourself. Put it aside first, for as long as you can. Try hard to be objective, and read it as though you have no prior knowledge of the subject. Ask yourself, as often as possible while you read: "Is this clear? Does it make sense?"

After I bought a condo in 1992, I tried to find out how much insurance I needed for my unit. In the documents from the association, I found the following 128-word sentence:

Each Unit Owner or any tenant of such Unit Owner should, at his own expense, obtain additional insurance for his own Unit and for his own benefit and to obtain insurance coverage upon his personal property, for any "betterments and improvements" made to the Unit and for his personal liability, provided that no Unit Owner or tenant shall acquire or maintain such additional insurance coverage so as to decrease the amount which the Board of Directors, on behalf of all Unit Owners, may realize under any insurance policy which it may have in force on the property at any particular time or to cause any insurance coverage maintained by the Board of Directors to be brought into contribution with such additional insurance coverage obtained by the Unit Owner. (Can anyone tell me how much insurance I should have bought?)

In February 1990 a member of Congress described his position on abortion. As reported by the *Washington Times* on 13 February 1990, he said: "I have come to the conclusion that I must, and have modified my position and that the position that grants choice is, upon fresh examination, not at all inconsistent with my overall philosophy." (Was he for or against?)

A suburban Washington, DC apartment complex sent a letter to its residents warning of the likelihood of increased crime during the holidays: "We are sure that you are aware that during the Christmas Season the Police Department is plagued by shoplifting, breaking and entering, and a general overall increase in crime." (It's no wonder crime is so bad in the streets. We can't even keep the criminals out of the *Police Department!*)

Speaking of crime, how about this item from the Durham, NC *Morning Herald*? "Durham police detectives say [the victim] was stabbed repeatedly during an apparent struggle between her car and the side kitchen door." (What a sight that must have been: a car and a kitchen door locked in mortal combat!)

We've all seen our own government's bureaucratic writing. Imagine the drought-stricken farmer who read the following and tried to apply for aid under Public Law 100-387:

Effective only for producers on a farm who elected to participate in the production adjustment program established under the Agricultural Act of 1949 for the 1988 crop of wheat, feed grains, upland cotton, extra long staple cotton, or rice, except as otherwise provided in this subsection, if the Secretary of Agriculture determines that, because of drought, hail, excessive moisture, or related conditions in 1988, the total quantity of the 1988 crop of the commodity that such producers are able to harvest on the farm is less than the result of multiplying 65 percent of the farm program payment yield established by the Secretary for such crop by the sum of acreage planted for harvest and the acreage prevented from being planted (because of drought, hail, excessive moisture, or related condition in 1988, as determined by the Secretary) for such crop, the Secretary shall make a disaster payment available to the producers. (I wonder if the writer of that 145-word sentence was paid for a disaster?)

An article in a 1989 business journal was entitled "Tips for Improving Absenteeism." (Did the article *really* purport to tell us ways we could get better with our absenteeism? On the contrary, it dealt with methods of *reducing* absenteeism.)

In a writing journal I spotted an item entitled "Composition Theory in the Eighties." Anticipating an article that might help me do a better job of teaching that theory, I quickly turned to the piece. Then I read its subtitle: "Axiological Consensus and Paradigmatic Diversity." I read no further. Unclear titles will discourage your reader from proceeding.

Look at the student writing examples that follow. (The snide remarks in parentheses are mine.) Do you think these students reread what they had written?

"The cities of Paris, Rome, London, Brussels and Bonn are on daily alert due to the new term 'Euroterrorism' being practiced throughout the continent." (No they're not! Those cities are nervous because of the *threat* of Euroterrorism, not the *term*. Try this instead: "The threat of Euroterrorism is spreading, and daily alerts are common in Paris, Rome, London, Brussels, and Bonn." Notice also that I didn't say "the cities of. . .," because most people who can read will know that those are cities.)

"Something has to be said for the quality of an individual which is my personal goal although contrary to any career goals." (Something has to be said for the complete lack of clarity in that sentence.)

"The fact that it is hard to *continue* to impress the public and terrorist is not cheap is evident." (Is that a fact? Emphasis was the author's, although I don't know why.)

"Coordinating actions and attacks leads to the other question raised by the original one but is directly tied to the first part." (Does this student hate his reader? Why else would he force the reader to decipher a complex sentence like that one? I suspect that even the *writer* of that sentence would not have understood what he was trying to say.)

I could cite many other examples of similarly convoluted sentences and phrases from my collection. But I suspect that by now you've had enough of this offal. The point is this: In intelligence writing, clarity is second only to accuracy in importance. (I'll say more about accuracy later in this chapter.) Even if you have all the facts, the writing must be clear if you are to get your point across. A reader who spots inaccuracies may lose faith in the writer or question the author's sources; but if the writing is not clear, the reader will be lost. Often the reader will simply discard the publication. So be reader-friendly. Be **clear**.

Conciseness

> *Omit needless words. Vigorous writing is concise. A sentence should contain no unnecessary words, a paragraph no unnecessary sentences, for the same reason that a drawing should have no unnecessary lines and a machine no unnecessary parts. This requires not that the writer make all his sentences short, or that he avoid all detail and treat his subjects only in outline, but that every word tell.*

> *— Strunk and White*
> ***The Elements of Style***

If I were more concise, this chapter would have been completed by now! Henry David Thoreau, while he was "Pond-" ering at Walden, said: "Not that the story need be long, but it will take a long while to make it short." How true it is. There's work involved in achieving a concise product. But that work will prove its worth in the reader's satisfaction with your writing.

Don't confuse conciseness with brevity. In *Hamlet*, Polonius said to the King and Queen, "Brevity is the soul of wit." Then he proceeded to ramble on and on, prompting Gertrude to reply, "More matter, with less art." That's what we need in intelligence writing: more matter — the essence of the words — and less art, the "fluff" of saying the words.

Some long pieces of writing are nonetheless concise because they say what needs to be said without repeating, then quit. That's the key to being concise. Each time you write a paper, prune the deadwood from your phrases and sentences. Cut unneeded verbiage from paragraphs. Be merciless.

The short quotation from Strunk and White's *The Elements of Style* that opened this section is loaded with meaning, especially the last five words: "but that every word tell." The papers that we write in the Intelligence Community would mean so much more to our audience if we took the time to ensure that every word is needed to convey the meaning. Of course, we don't have time to linger over every single word in our writing; but we can and should be sensitive to the most obvious troublemakers, like the ones that follow.

Look at the phrases below, all from student papers. The highlighted portions are deadwood, unnecessary to the meaning of the sentence. They do nothing but fill white space and waste the reader's time. Avoid the use of these and similar phrases in your own writing:

"...*the month of* February..."   "...*the city of* Munich..."

"...the 1980-81 *period*..."   "...whether *or not*..."

"...*a distance of* 20 miles..."   "...at *the hour of* noon..."

There may be occasions when, for the sake of clarity, you need a few extra words. For example, you might want to be sure that your reader understands you mean *the state of* Washington, not Washington, *DC*. Let the principle of clarity guide you in each case.

Being concise means saying what you need to say in as few words as possible. The two writing examples that follow illustrate clearly that these students had no concern for conciseness. Parenthetically after each example, I've included my rewrite. Compare the two and see if you think the point is still made in the shorter version.

"By way of presentation and because of the instructor it was to me, the most successfully presented, also." (The instructor's presentation succeeded.)

"What has been the impact of the tax cuts on the average U.S. citizen, myself included? Although not an expert in this field, I will attempt to answer this question in subsequent paragraphs. In as few words as possible, I feel that very little was gained by the tax cuts." (The impact of tax cuts on the average U.S. citizen has been minimal.)

The 50-word student dissertation above falls into a common trap: repeating the question and overstating the obvious. The student was asked to write a brief essay on the impact of President Reagan's tax cuts. Many students start out answering a question by rephrasing or simply repeating it. That's the old trick of trying to use as many pages in the examination blue book as possible, to impress the professor with your depth of knowledge. But believe me, the professor knows the question, and doesn't need it parroted back. If anything, do some redefinition of the problem and restate the question in another form — the form in which you intend to answer it. And do it with **conciseness**.

> *That writer does the most, who gives the reader the most information, and takes from him the least time.*
>
> — *Charles C. Colton*

Correctness

Perhaps you are a gifted writer. You may write the clearest, most concise, coherent, appropriate, and complete paper ever to flow from a word processor; but if it is not *correct,* you will offend your reader. I could devote a separate book to this principle alone, but I hope that the brief summary here and the exercises later in the book will help you avoid some of the more common pitfalls.

Correctness in intelligence writing has two facets: factual precision and mechanical correctness. Neither is more important than the other. They complement each other by providing an edge of finesse that makes one person's writing better than another's.

Precision. Precision is a cornerstone of the intelligence profession. The term itself is synonymous with *exactness*. Mark Twain said: "The difference between the right word and the nearly right word is the same as that between lightning and the lightning bug." Say precisely what you mean. Go for the lightning. Don't use the all-too-familiar "weasel words" that disguise your intent.

If you're writing about the FIZZLE fighter, and no one in the Intelligence Community has any idea of the aircraft's combat radius, don't write: "The FIZZLE is believed to have a substantial combat radius." What in the wide world of wonder does that mean? (Yet you've seen intelligence writing like that, haven't you?) Instead, make a positive and precise statement for your reader: "The combat radius of the FIZZLE is unknown." Is it such a sin to admit an intelligence gap? Not at all. The most serious intelligence gap we have is the space between analysts' ears when they try to cover up a dearth of knowledge by "writing around it." By admitting the unknown, you may get someone's attention and initiate some seriously needed collection action.

Students have unwittingly provided scores of examples of imprecise writing. Four are shown below.

One student wrote of the importance of geographic intelligence to a commander in the field, saying that "it must keep the commander abreast of weather and climatic conditions which can change drastically within a few minutes." (We've all seen wide swings in weather, but *climate* takes more than a few minutes to change.)

"The Soviets rely on their command structure for strict control of their aircraft and SAMs. This is implemented by communications activity." (*What* is implemented? "Command," "control," or "aircraft and SAMs"? By *what* kind of communications activity? Introducing a sentence with the word "this" is an invitation to imprecision. Watch out, too, for other vague openings like "there is" or "it is.")

"Political power is one of eight components of strategic intelligence used to quantify aspects of foreign governments." (Have you ever tried to quantify an aspect? What is this writer trying to say?)

"Barron contends that the Soviets realize the value of even uncontrolable [sic] terrorist groups and is offering clandestine aid." (Besides the uncontrolable speling, this student implies that author John Barron is offering aid to terrorists!)

Mechanical correctness. The final touch a good writer adds to ensure readability is a check for mechanical correctness. Proofreading and editing involve more than "dotting i's and crossing t's." Proofread for correctness and edit for style. Go back over your paper from top to bottom for misspellings, errors in punctuation, agreement of subject and verb, and other common errors. If you have trouble detecting spelling errors in your own writing, welcome to the club! Most people tend too overlook there own misteaks. (Yes, I did that on purpose.) If you belong to that Misstep Majority, try proofing your paper by reading backwards. By scanning words out of context, your mind will catch more mistakes. It really does work. A good alternative, of course, is to have someone else proofread your paper — preferably a disinterested observer with little knowledge of your topic. If all else fails, then read your words aloud. The mind's "ear" will catch many errors and problem areas for you.

If you are fortunate enough to have access to a word processor, try one of the many software programs that check for spelling. Keep in mind, though, that most of these programs still do not recognize the difference between *form* and *from*, between *complement* and *compliment*, or between *too, to*, and *two*. You'll still need to check for usage errors.

Adeptness at proofreading and editing may be acquired, but only through practice, practice, and more practice. Try different techniques to see what works best for you. For example, proofread once from the big picture working down to the individual words: Start by looking at form and format for coherence and conformity; then check pages for appearance; next, read paragraphs for coherence and unity, one main idea per paragraph; look at sentences next for completeness and correctness; and finally, check individual words for usage and spelling. It won't take you as long as it sounds. If you're uncomfortable with that approach, next time try it the other way around — from the words, working up to the form and format.

Some errors are more serious than others. We all misuse the most frequently abused punctuation mark, the comma. It's one thing to omit the comma before "and" in a series (experts can't agree on that one, but I prefer to use it); it's quite another matter to use a comma between two complete sentences with no joining word like "and" or "but." (GASP! A comma splice!)

The most common mistakes I encounter in papers at the Joint Military Intelligence College are misspellings, usage and punctuation errors, and agreement of subject and verb. These errors are illustrated by the student writing examples below.

Misspellings. Some misspellings completely change the meaning of a sentence, while others leave the reader gazing quizzically into space. Look at the following examples from our students (which also show errors in usage).

"At the operational level of war, intelligence concentrates on the collection, identification, location, and analysis of strategic and operational centers of gravy." (Isn't a center of gravy in the middle of mashed potatoes?)

"In realty, an integrated Euroterrorist front would stand little ... chance of success." (Then what about some other business besides real estate? This student strayed from "reality.")

"One serious ommission [sic] from the orientation program was a lack of information on what is currently going on at the DIAC." (Ommit that spelling! Precision is at fault here, too. Do you think the student really was complaining about our omitting a lack of information?)

"In Europe this is relected clearly by the small groups who use terrorism and revolution as a means of political change." (That sentence is a clerar relection of the student's proofreading prowess.)

Proofread carefully to see if you any words out.

—William Safire, in Fumblerules

Usage of words in the English language is dynamic. Words and phrases are in use today that were unknown to our grandparents. According to self-proclaimed "verbivore" Richard Lederer, about 450 new words are coined every year in our dynamic language. One need only listen to the younger generation to learn that "bad" may mean "good," that "rad" has nothing to do with nuclear radiation, and that the admonition to "chill out" doesn't involve refrigeration. While usage rules change over the years, the basic conventions of the language remain intact, providing a framework upon which to build "correct" writing. The better dictionaries in print have usage panels. These august bodies don't lay down rules and tell the population how to write; rather, they advise on the language as it is being used.

Even the usage panels don't always agree. (See, for example, the entry under "data" *in The American Heritage Dictionary of the English Language*, Fourth Edition, 2000.) The most common usage errors are often clear-cut: affect — effect, it's — its, principal — principle. Four more are cited below, courtesy of students.

". . . the public has more disposal income." (We're buying more disposals? "Disposable" is the intended word here.)

"I am very weary about speed reading. I feel that I will miss a great deal of information." (The student missed something else here. Maybe he **was** tired of speed reading, but the second sentence led me to believe that he was guarded or cautious — "wary.")

"[Terrorist groups] are small, secretive and extremely security conscience." (And I always thought they didn't have a conscience!)

"On 1 June 1992, the U.S. Strategic Command's Joint Intelligence Center (STRATJIC) was formally established from the ruminants of the 544th Intelligence Wing." (Now there's something to chew on! He meant to say "remnants," meaning "remains.")

Spell checkers are grate, butt they wont sea awl yore errors!

Punctuation is difficult. Many "grammar guides" give you 72 rules for use of the comma, tack on 144 exceptions to those rules, then tell you to use the comma any time you want your reader to pause briefly. Few writers have problems with the question mark or the period; but the comma, colon, and semicolon are bugaboos.

"Negative results have occurred also, such as; record trade imbalances." (Don't use a semicolon to introduce a list; that's the job of the colon. Note one common use of the semicolon, as I employed it in the previous sentence. It is used to separate closely related sentences — like a supercomma or a semiperiod. Remember that a semicolon separates, and a colon anticipates.)

"Much the same can be said of the classes that I attended however the instructor made a big difference." (Many students have problems punctuating the word **however**. If there are **complete sentences** on both sides of the "however" — as there are in the example — it must be preceded by a semicolon and followed by a comma. If the "however" is followed by a phrase or dependent clause — not a complete sentence — then it is set off by commas on both sides; for example: "Much the same can be said of the classes that I attended, however, **in which** the instructor made a big difference.")

> *Anyone who can improve a sentence of mine by the omission or placing of a comma is looked upon as my dearest friend.*
>
> *— George Moore*

Subject-Verb Agreement. The subject of a sentence should agree in number with its verb. If you have a singular subject, then your verb must also be singular. Writers seem to have the most problems with this principle when their subject is separated by a lot of words from their verb, or when there is a vague subject. Witness the following:

"The amount of funds available have had an enormous impact." (Because of that definite article, "*the*," the verb must be "has." If it had been "*an* amount," the verb would be correct, although the sentence would sound awkward.)

"The media has focused more on the negative effects." (***Media*** — like ***data, phenomena***, and ***criteria*** — is a plural word. "The media ***have***" or "The medium of television ***has***.")

"I think the issue of tax raises and cuts are clouded with too much emotion." (I think it are, too. Note that the subject is ***issue***, but the writer used the plural verb to match the ***raises and cuts***.)

"Each of these areas were administered in a professional manner." (The singular word ***each*** is the subject of the sentence, not the plural ***areas***.)

> *Verbs has to agree with their subjects.*
>
> *— William Safire, in Fumblerules*

OTHER IMPORTANT CONSIDERATIONS: APPROPRIATENESS, COMPLETENESS, AND COHERENCE

Appropriateness

If you haven't already done so by now, you need to consider your reader. You seldom know precisely who will be reading your work, but you can generally make a pretty good guess. If you're an analyst and you've been tasked to write a paper for the Director of your agency or for your commander, you can bet that everyone between you and the intended recipient will read it. But if you're doing a thesis or a study that will receive wide dissemination, you may be less certain. At least you can get your hands on the proposed distribution list for your product and try to gear it toward that audience.

To help you determine whether your writing is appropriate for the intended audience, ask yourself the following questions: **Who** will read my product? **Why** will they read it? **How** will they use the information? It's unlikely that you'll be able to answer those questions every time, but the mere act of asking them may prove useful.

Another important consideration in appropriateness is the use of jargon. The "shop talk" of our trade saves us a lot of time in daily dealings with our colleagues. The Joint Military Intelligence Training Center, for example, may talk about the DLOs in the IMP for ANA325 satisfying the needs of the UGIP. If they were writing something about that, and they knew it was going outside the Center, they might write that the Desired Learning Objectives (DLOs) in the Instructional Management Plan (IMP) for the Intelligence Analysis Course (ANA325) satisfy the requirements of the Undergraduate Intelligence Program (UGIP).

Always try to consider whether your paper will be read by someone without a clear understanding of the jargon you use. If you must use an abbreviation or acronym, that's no problem; just spell it out first, and follow it parenthetically with the abbreviation, like I did above. Then, when you use the term again, use the abbreviation. If you write more than a page or so without using the term again, spell it out one more time for your reader. When in doubt, spell it out.

These techniques of considering your reader and avoiding jargon will make your writing more **appropriate** for your intended audience. And they will appreciate your efforts on their behalf.

Easy reading is damned hard writing.

— Nathaniel Hawthorne

Completeness

The flip side of the conciseness coin is the consideration of completeness in your writing. When you write concisely, you want to ensure that you've said what you need to say in as few words as possible. With completeness, you want to be sure that you haven't left anything unsaid. Prewriting helps a lot.

Go back and review your outline or mind-map, and compare it to your first draft. Have you covered everything you wanted to cover? Are your main points all there? Is there any point you've raised that hasn't been fully resolved, either by answering all the questions or by stating that there are still some unknowns or gaps in information? If you can answer those questions appropriately, then your product is probably complete.

Look at completeness from several angles. The review process I've just addressed provides a "big picture" of whether your product is complete with respect to all the major points to be covered. But you should conduct a more detailed review of your work to ensure that the individual paragraphs and sentences are complete.

Look for the *topic sentence* in each paragraph and see if all the other sentences relate to it and complete the thought it introduced. Remember that the topic sentence is the main idea or central assertion of the paragraph; but without substantiating evidence in the form of follow-on sentences to expand upon or clarify the assertion it makes, the paragraph may be incomplete. The reader will be confused if the topic sentence introduces a thought and the remainder of the paragraph fails to carry that thought to completion. It's like starting your car, revving the engine, and then just letting it idle. The engine warms up, but you don't go anywhere.

Carry your search for completeness down to the individual sentence. There is a fine line between completeness and correctness in the student writing examples that follow. They could have been used to illustrate incorrect usages, but I chose to use them here in conjunction with the principle of completeness because they are, in fact, incomplete sentences.

"The 1985 killing of French General Rene Audran on January 25th and the killing of German arms executive Ernst Zimmermann on February 1st by members of Direct Action and the RAF." (That sentence started out going somewhere, but it never got there. It is an incomplete sentence because there's **no verb**. The most common form of incomplete sentence we notice in student papers is the lengthy one without a verb. One of your most basic tasks in reviewing your paper for completeness should be to double-check each sentence for its subject and verb.)

"If cuts provided a badly needed boost in public confidence in this country and slowly seem to be succeeding." (Watch out for the demon sentence that begins with a word like "if," "because," or "although." It introduces what is called a "dependent clause," meaning that it depends on something else for its existence as a sentence. The "if" clause above needed a "then" clause to follow, such as "then the cuts would have been worthwhile." The easiest fix, though, is simply to omit the "if." Read the example again without the "if," and you'll see that it makes perfect sense.)

"Utilizing the assumption that military deception at the strategic and tactical level has been and may again be an effective and efficient technique in armed conflict, one that repays handsomely the minimal investment of resources it usually requires." (This excerpt from a graduate thesis uses lots of big words, but it goes nowhere. There's no verb for the subject.)

Coherence

"The assessment additionally need to be based on human perceptions and assessment of the problem. Combining the two above factors, the determination of terrorist responsibility may be expedited. Monitoring of the terrorist problem must be continuous and thorough, as well."

The student who wrote that short paragraph wasn't thinking about coherence. There are at least three major ideas: 1) assessing the terrorism problem; 2) determination of the responsibility for terrorism; 3) keeping track of the problem. It may be easier to keep track of shadowy terrorist groups than the main idea of that paragraph.

Think of coherence as a plan, a blueprint for logical continuity in your paragraphs. *Merriam Webster's Collegiate Dictionary*, 11th edition (2003) defines coherence as a "systematic or logical connection or consistency." Our minds have a natural tendency to think logically, always trying to connect one thing to another and make sense of them in terms of things we've experienced in our lifetime. When we encounter something incoherent, our minds immediately say "Whoa!" and shift into neutral, grinding and crunching what we've encountered, trying to bring it into focus. Failing our ability to understand, the inevitable result is frustration.

You don't want your readers to be frustrated because you failed to follow a coherent organizational scheme in your writing. That's why the topic sentence is so important to intelligence writing. The topic sentence, usually the first sentence of your paragraph, says to the reader: "Hi, there. Welcome to a new paragraph. I'm the main idea here and I'll be your guide through the next few sentences." Pick your controlling idea — your central assertion for each paragraph — and stick to it. When you change controlling ideas, move to a new paragraph with a smooth transition. In that way, you'll ensure a more **coherent** product for your reader.

USING THE BASIC TOOLS

Having reviewed the basic tools of writing an intelligence paper, you're now ready to proceed with the writing itself. Don't be overwhelmed with rules and regulations to the extent that you shy away from writing. Just try to remember those six basic principles, and review your papers with them in mind. Keep your writing *clear* and understandable; be *concise*, saying only what you need to say in order to get the point across; watch for *coherence* throughout the process, sticking to an orderly, logical procedure; be sure your writing is *appropriate* for your intended audience, as nearly as you can determine that audience; check the final product to ensure that you've said everything you needed to say about the subject — that your paper is **complete**; and finally, edit and proofread as many times as possible to ensure **correctness**.

If you seem to have particular trouble with one or two of the principles, spend extra time on the most troublesome. It's easy for me to tell you these things, but the proof comes when the boss tells you to write a fact sheet and have it on his desk the next morning. You can never anticipate all the variables that may occur, but you can be sure that there will be some short suspenses and deadly deadlines you'll have to cope with in your writing.

Keep in mind that there's no magic formula for writing, and that the ability to write well is not something you're born with. While some writers seem to have a "natural" ability, most of the authors who have written anything about writing have admitted that it's hard work, and they have to struggle with words even after years of successful writing.

If people only knew how hard I work to gain my mastery, it wouldn't seem so wonderful at all.

— Michelangelo

SOME FINAL THOUGHTS ABOUT THE BASICS

Four Levels of Knowledge

1) Know what you know; 2) Know what you don't know; 3) Don't know what you know; 4) Don't know what you don't know.

To be precise as an intelligence writer, you must know the limits of your information and where gaps in the data lie (that is, know what you know and what you don't know). If you know neither of those essential elements, then don't try to disguise that fact by writing imprecisely.

What We Write, Others Don't Always Read

I wrote a draft description for a new course offering to be placed in the College Catalog. My intention was to write that it was based on "an *existing* course," but instead I typed *exiting* course on my word processor. The spellchecker read that as a perfectly good word, but my boss caught the typographical error. I had left for a two-week trip; so he corrected it to read the way *he* thought it should: ". . . based on an *exciting* course."

INTELLIGENCE ESSENTIALS FOR EVERYONE

Lisa Krizan

(Originally Published as JMIC Occasional Paper Number Six, June 1999.)

PROLOGUE:
INTELLIGENCE SHARING IN A NEW LIGHT

Education is the cheapest defense of a nation.

— Edmund Burke, 18th-century British philosopher

National Intelligence Meets Business Intelligence

This intelligence primer reflects the author's examination of dozens of unclassified government documents on the practice of intelligence over a period of nearly seven years. For the national security Intelligence Community (IC), it represents a concise distillation and clarification of the national intelligence function. To the private sector, it offers an unprecedented translation into lay terms of national intelligence principles and their application within and potentially outside of government.[13] Whereas "intelligence sharing" has traditionally been a government-to-government transaction, the environment is now receptive to government-private sector interaction.

The widespread trend toward incorporating government intelligence methodology into commerce and education was a primary impetus for publishing this document. As economic competition accelerates around the world, private businesses are initiating their own "business intelligence" (BI) or "competitive intelligence" services to advise their decisionmakers. Educators in business and academia are following suit, inserting BI concepts into professional training and college curricula.[14]

Whereas businesses in the past have concentrated on knowing the market and making the best product, they are shifting their focus to include knowing, and staying ahead of, competitors. This emphasis on competitiveness requires the sophisticated production and use of carefully analyzed information tailored to specific users; in other words, intelli-

---

[13] For the purpose of this study, the author includes in national security intelligence those analogous activities conducted by law enforcement personnel at the federal, state, and local levels. Readers seeking further information on law enforcement applications of intelligence may wish to read Marilyn Peterson, *Applications in Criminal Analysis* (Westport, Connecticut: Greenwood Press, 1994). An additional resource is the International Association of Law Enforcement Intelligence Analysts. Local IALEIA chapters are listed on the Association's web site: http://www.ialeia.org.

[14] An authoritative guide to business intelligence practices is found in Larry Kahaner, *Competitive Intelligence: From Black Ops to Boardrooms — How Businesses Gather, Analyze and Use Information to Succeed in the Global Marketplace* (New York, NY: Simon and Schuster, 1996).

gence. But the use of intelligence as a strategic planning tool, common in government, is a skill that few companies have perfected.[15]

Although BI practitioners refer to the national security model of intelligence, they do not seek to conduct secret intelligence operations, which are limited by law to government authorities. The Society of Competitive Intelligence Professionals (SCIP), headquartered in the Washington, DC area, is an international organization founded in 1986 to "assist members in enhancing their firms' competitiveness through a greater... understanding of competitor behaviors and future strategies as well as the market dynamics in which they do business."[16] SCIP's code of conduct specifically promotes ethical and legal BI practices.[17] The main focus of "collection" is on exploiting on-line and open-source information services, and the theme of "analysis" is to go beyond mere numerical and factual information, to interpretation of events for strategic decisionmaking.[18]

Large corporations are creating their own intelligence units, and a few are successful at performing analysis in support of strategic decisionmaking. Others are hiring BI contractors, or "out-sourcing" this function. However, the majority of businesses having some familiarity with BI are not able to conduct rigorous research and analysis for value-added reporting. According to University of Pittsburgh professor of Business Administration John Prescott, no theoretical framework exists for BI. He believes that most studies done lack the rigor that would come with following sound research-design principles. By his estimate, only one percent of companies have a research-design capability exploitable for BI applications.[19] At the same time, companies are increasingly opting to establish their own intelligence units rather than purchasing services from BI specialists. The implication of this trend is that BI professionals should be skilled in both intelligence and in a business discipline of value to the company.[20]

On the other hand, as businesses come to appreciate the value of intelligence about their competitors, they are increasingly realizing their own vulnerability to similar scrutiny. The private sector can therefore benefit from IC expertise in disciplines complementary to active intelligence production, namely defensive measures. The whole concept of openness regarding intelligence practices may hinge upon the counter-balancing effect of self-defense, particularly as practiced through information systems security (INFOSEC) and operations security (OPSEC).[21] Because the IC seeks to be a world leader in INFOSEC and OPSEC as well as intelligence production, defensive measures are an appropriate topic for dialogue between the public and private sectors.

---

[15] Richard D'Aveni, "Hypercompetition," briefing to SCIP Conference, Alexandria, VA, 28 March 1996.

[16] SCIP, *Competitive Intelligence Review*, 8, No. 3 (Fall 1997), unnumbered 8th page.

[17] SCIP, *1995 SCIP Membership Directory* (Alexandria, VA: SCIP, 1995), xxvii.

[18] Leila Kight, "Elements of CI Success," briefing to SCIP Conference, Alexandria, VA, 28 March, 1996.

[19] John Prescott, Professor of Business Administration, University of Pittsburgh, "Research," briefing to SCIP conference, Alexandria, VA, 28 March 1996.

[20] Jan Herring, "Strides in Institutionalizing BI in Businesses," briefing to SCIP Conference, Alexandria, VA, 28 March 1996.

[21] These concepts are addressed in Part IX.

The U.S. government INFOSEC Manual sums up the relationship between offense and defense in a comprehensive intelligence strategy in this way:

> In today's information age environment, control of information and information technology is vital. As the nation daily becomes more dependent on networked information systems to conduct essential business, including military operations, government functions, and national and international economic enterprises, information infrastructures are assuming increased strategic importance. This has, in turn, given rise to the concept of information warfare (INFOWAR) — a new form of warfare directed toward attacking (offensive) or defending (defensive) such infrastructures.[22]

Giving citizens the tools they need to survive INFOWAR is one of the IC's explicit missions. This intelligence primer can assist that mission by offering a conceptual and practical "common operating environment" for business and government alike.[23]

Assessing and Exchanging Best Practices

In documenting the essentials of intelligence, this primer is an example of *benchmarking*, a widely used process for achieving quality in organizations, the use of which is a criterion for the business world's Malcolm Baldrige National Quality Award.[24] Benchmarking normally assesses best professional practices, developed and refined through experience, for carrying out an organization's core tasks.[25] An additional aim of benchmarking is to establish reciprocal relationships among best-in-class parties for the exchange of mutually beneficial information.[26] Because the IC is the *de facto* functional leader in the intelligence profession, and is publicly funded, it is obligated to lead both the government and private sector toward a greater understanding of the intelligence discipline.

In the mid-1990s, as national intelligence agencies began to participate in international benchmarking forums, individuals from the private sector began to request practical information on the intelligence process from IC representatives. The requestors were often participants in the growing BI movement and apparently sought to adapt IC methods to their own purposes. Their circumspect counterparts in the government were not prepared to respond to these requests, preferring instead to limit benchmarking relationships to common business topics, such as resource management.[27] Concurrently, the annual SCIP

---

[22] National Security Agency, *1995 INFOSEC Manual* (Ft. Meade, MD: NSA, 1995), para. C.1.

[23] Readers in doubt of the need for INFOSEC in the private sector may wish to study the real-world examples of INFOWAR battles and their implications for economic and personal security that author Winn Schwartau reveals in *Information Warfare: Chaos on the Electronic Superhighway* (New York: Thunder's Mouth Press, 1994).

[24] A useful reference to benchmarking within the U.S. government is Jerry Frankenfield and Melissie Rumizen, *A Guide to Benchmarking* (Fort Meade, MD: National Security Agency (NSA), 12 July 1995). An overview of benchmarking in the private sector can be found in Dean Elmuti, Hanus Kathawaia, and Scott J. Lloyed, "The Benchmarking Process: Assessing Its Value and Limitations," *Industrial Management* 39, No. 4 (July/August 1997): 12-19.

[25] Elmuti, Kathawaia and Lloyed, 12.

[26] Elmuti, Kathawaia and Lloyed, 13.

international conference highlighted the needs and capabilities of intelligence departments in the private sector.

Demand in the private sector for intelligence skills can be met through the application of validated intelligence practices presented in this document. Conversely, the business-oriented perspective on intelligence can be highly useful to government intelligence professionals. As a BI practitioner explains, every activity in the intelligence process must be related to a requirement, otherwise it is irrelevant.[28] Government personnel would benefit from this practical reminder in every training course and every work center. In the private sector, straying from this principle means wasting money and losing a competitive edge. The consequences of inefficient national intelligence can be costly on an even larger scale.

The basis for an IC benchmarking exchange with the private sector continues to grow. The Society of Competitive Intelligence Professionals is a clearinghouse for the review of private business intelligence practices, and therefore a champion of information sharing. Leading colleges and universities are beginning to offer coursework in intelligence methods, and in many cases intend to expand their offerings. Curriculum exchanges between private sector educators and the IC are encouraged by legislation and by Congressional Commission recommendations,[29] yet little such formal exchange has taken place.

Whereas government practitioners are the acknowledged subject-matter experts in intelligence methodology, the private sector offers a wealth of expertise in particular areas such as business management, technology, the global marketplace, and skills training. Each has valuable knowledge to share with the other, and experience gaps to fill. On the basis of these unique needs and capabilities, the public and private sectors can forge a new partnership in understanding their common responsibilities, and this primer may make a modest contribution toward the exchange of ideas.

The following chapters outline validated steps to operating an intelligence service for both the government and the private sector. In either setting, this document should prove useful as a basic curriculum for students, an on-the-job working aid for practitioners, and a reference tool for experienced professionals, especially those teaching or mentoring others. Although the primer does not exhaustively describe procedures for quality intelligence production or defensive measures, it does offer the business community fundamental concepts that can transfer readily from national intelligence to commercial applications, including competitive analysis, strategic planning and the protection of proprietary information. Universities may incorporate these ideas into their business, political science, and intelligence studies curricula to encourage and prepare students to

---

[27] Melissie C. Rumizen, Ph.D., Benchmarking Manager, National Security Agency, interview with the author, 2 April 1996.

[28] David Harkleroad, "Actionable CI," briefing to SCIP Conference, Alexandria, VA, 28 March 1996.

[29] For example, the 1991 National Security Education Act (P.L. 102-183), the 1993 Government Performance and Results Act (P.L. 103-62), and the Congressional Report of the Commission on the Roles and Capabilities of the U.S. Intelligence Community, *Preparing for the 21st Century: An Appraisal of U.S. Intelligence* (Washington, DC: GPO, 1 March 1996), 87.

become intelligence practitioners in commerce or government. For anyone outside of the national security apparatus, this intelligence primer will shed light on why and how the government spends federal tax dollars on national intelligence.

Independent Agency   DoD Element   Non-DoD   OSD/DCI Agency

Source: Based on a Department of Defense publication.

Figure 3. The National Intelligence Community.

PART I
INTELLIGENCE PROCESS

[I]ntelligence is more than information. It is knowledge that has been specially prepared for a customer's unique circumstances. The word *knowledge* highlights the need for human involvement. Intelligence collection systems produce... data, not intelligence; only the human mind can provide that special touch that makes sense of data for different customers' requirements. The special processing that partially defines intelligence is the continual collection, verification, and analysis of information that allows us to understand the problem or situation in actionable terms and then tailor a product in the context of the customer's circumstances. If any of these essential attributes is missing, then the product remains information rather than intelligence.[30]

The intelligence profession, already well established within government, is growing in the private sector. Intelligence is traditionally a function of government organizations serving the decisionmaking needs of national security authorities. But innovative private firms are increasingly adapting the national security intelligence model to the business world to aid their own strategic planning. Although business professionals may prefer the term "information" over "intelligence," the author will use the latter term to highlight the importance of adding value to information. According to government convention, the author will use the term "customer" to refer to the intended recipient of an intelligence product — either a fellow intelligence service member, or a policy official or decisionmaker. The process of converting raw information into actionable intelligence can serve government and business equally well in their respective domains.

The Intelligence Process in Government and Business

Production of intelligence follows a cyclical *process*, a series of repeated and interrelated steps that add value to original inputs and create a substantially transformed product. That transformation is what distinguishes intelligence from a simple cyclical activity.[31] In government and private sector alike, analysis is the catalyst that converts information into intelligence for planners and decisionmakers.

Although the intelligence process is complex and dynamic, several component functions may be distinguished from the whole. In this primer, components are identified as Intelligence Needs, Collection Activities, Processing of Collected Information, Analysis and Production. To highlight the components, each is accorded a separate Part in this study. These labels, and the illustration below, should not be interpreted to mean that intelligence is a uni-

---

[30] Captain William S. Brei, *Getting Intelligence Right: The Power of Logical Procedure*, Occasional Paper Number Two (Washington, DC: Joint Military Intelligence College, January 1996), 4.

[31] Melissie C. Rumizen, Benchmarking Manager at the National Security Agency, interview by author, 4 January 1996.

dimensional and unidirectional process. "[I]n fact, the [process] is multidimensional, multi-directional, and — most importantly — interactive and iterative."[32]

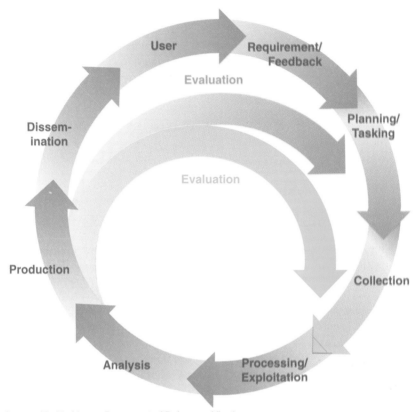

Source: Modified from a Department of Defense publication.

Figure 4. Process of Intelligence Creation and Use.

The purpose of this process is for the intelligence service to provide decisionmakers with tools, or "products" that assist them in identifying key decision factors. Such

---

[32] Douglas H. Dearth, "National Intelligence: Profession and Process," in *Strategic Intelligence: Theory and Application*, eds. Douglas H. Dearth and R. Thomas Goodden, 2d ed. (Washington, DC: Joint Military Intelligence Training Center, 1995), 17.

intelligence products may be described both in terms of their subject content and their intended use.[33]

Table 1. Types of Intelligence Product Categories
Source: adapted from Garst, "Components of Intelligence"

By Subject	By Use
Biographic	Research
Economic	Current
Geographic	Estimative
Military	Operational
Political	Scientific and Technical
Sociological	Warning
Scientific and Technical	
Transportation and Communications	

Any or all of these categories may be relevant to the private sector, depending upon the particular firm's product line and objectives in a given industry, market environment, and geographic area.

A nation's power or a firm's success results from a combination of factors, so intelligence producers and customers should examine potential adversaries and competitive situations from as many relevant viewpoints as possible. A competitor's economic resources, political alignments, the number, education and health of its people, and apparent objectives are all important in determining the ability of a country or a business to exert influence on others. The eight subject categories of intelligence are exhaustive, but they are not mutually exclusive. Although dividing intelligence into subject areas is useful for analyzing information and administering production, it should not become a rigid formula. Some intelligence services structure production into geographic subject areas when their responsibilities warrant a broader perspective than topical divisions would allow.[34]

Similarly, characterization of intelligence by intended use applies to both government and enterprise, and the categories again are exhaustive, but not mutually exclusive. The production of basic research intelligence yields structured summaries of topics such as geographic, demographic, and political studies, presented in handbooks, charts, maps, and the like. Current intelligence addresses day-to-day events to apprise decisionmakers of new developments and assess their significance. Estimative intelligence deals with what might

---

[33] Ronald D. Garst, "Components of Intelligence," in *A Handbook of Intelligence Analysis*, ed. Ronald D. Garst, 2d ed. (Washington, DC: Defense Intelligence College, January 1989), 1; Central Intelligence Agency, *A Consumer's Guide to Intelligence* (Washington, DC: Public Affairs Staff, July 1995), 5-7.

[34] Garst, *Components of Intelligence*, 2,3.

be or what might happen; it may help policymakers fill in gaps between available facts, or assess the range and likelihood of possible outcomes in a threat or "opportunity" scenario. Operational support intelligence incorporates all types of intelligence by use, but is produced in a tailored, focused, and timely manner for planners and operators of the supported activity. Scientific and Technical intelligence typically comes to life in in-depth, focused assessments stemming from detailed physical or functional examination of objects, events, or processes, such as equipment manufacturing techniques.[35] Warning intelligence sounds an alarm, connoting urgency, and implies the potential need for policy action in response.

How government and business leaders define their needs for these types of intelligence affects the intelligence service's organization and operating procedures. Managers of this intricate process, whether in government or business, need to decide whether to make one intelligence unit responsible for all the component parts of the process or to create several specialized organizations for particular sub-processes. This question is explored briefly below, and more fully in Part VII.

Functional Organization of Intelligence

The national Intelligence Community comprises Executive Branch agencies that produce classified and unclassified studies on selected foreign developments as a prelude to decisions and actions by the president, military leaders, and other senior authorities. Some of this intelligence is developed from special sources to which few individuals have access except on a strictly controlled "need-to-know" basis.[36] The four categories of special intelligence are Human Resources (HUMINT), Signals (SIGINT), Imagery (IMINT) and Measurement and Signatures (MASINT). The four corresponding national authorities for these categories are the Central Intelligence Agency (CIA), the National Security Agency (NSA), the National Imagery and Mapping Agency (NIMA) and the Defense Intelligence Agency (DIA). DIA shares authority for HUMINT, being responsible for Department of Defense HUMINT management. Along with these four agencies, other members of the Intelligence Community use and produce intelligence by integrating all available and relevant collected information into reports tailored to the needs of individual customers.

Private sector organizations use open-source information to produce intelligence in a fashion similar to national authorities. By mimicking the government process of translating customer needs into production requirements, and particularly by performing rigorous analysis on gathered information, private organizations can produce assessments that aid their leaders in planning and carrying out decisions to increase their competitiveness in the global economy. This primer will point out why private entities may desire to transfer into their domain some well-honed proficiencies developed in the national Intelligence Community. At the same time, the Intelligence Community self-examination conducted in these pages may allow government managers to reflect on any unique capabilities worthy of further development and protection.

---

[35] CIA, *Consumer's Guide*, 5-7.
[36] CIA, *Consumer's Guide*, vii.

Human Source Intelligence (HUMINT)

- Agents *(Controlled Sources)*
- Informants *(Willing Sources)*
- Observers *(Attaches)*

Imagery Intelligence (IMINT)

- Photo/Digital
- Electro-Optical
- Multispectral
- Infrared
- Radar

Open Source Intelligence (OSINT)

- Public Documents
- Newspapers
- Television and Radio
- Books and Journals

Signals Intelligence

- COMINT *(Communications)*
- ELINT *(Electronic)*
- FISINT *(Telemetry)*

Measurement and Signatures Intelligence (MASINT)

- ACINT *(Acoustic)*
- RADINT *(Radiation)*

Source: Modified from a Department of Defense publication.

Figure 5. National Intelligence Production Resources.

PART II
CONVERTING CUSTOMER NEEDS INTO
INTELLIGENCE REQUIREMENTS

The articulation of the requirement is the most important part of the process, and it seldom is as simple as it might seem. There should be a dialogue concerning the requirement, rather than a simple assertion of need. Perhaps the customer knows precisely what is needed and what the product should look like. Perhaps... not. Interaction is required: discussion between ultimate user and principal producer. This is often difficult due to time, distance, and bureaucratic impediments, not to mention disparities of rank, personality, perspectives, and functions.[37]

Defining the Intelligence Problem

Customer demands, or "needs," particularly if they are complex and time-sensitive, require interpretation or analysis by the intelligence service before being expressed as intelligence requirements that drive the production process.[38] This dialog between intelligence producer and customer may begin with a simple set of questions, and if appropriate, progress to a more sophisticated analysis of the intelligence problem being addressed.

The "Five Ws" — *Who, What, When, Where,* and *Why* — are a good starting point for translating intelligence needs into requirements. A sixth related question, *How,* may also be considered. In both government and business, these questions form the basic framework for decisionmakers and intelligence practitioners to follow in formulating intelligence requirements and devising a strategy to satisfy them. Typically, government intelligence requirements are expressed in terms of foreign threats to national or international security. In business, requirements may be expressed in terms of the competitor's standing in the marketplace in comparison to one's own posture. Representative examples from each sector follow:

---

[37] Dearth, "National Intelligence," 17-18.
[38] Dearth, "National Intelligence," 18.

Table 2. Illustrative Definitions of Intelligence Problems and Customer Needs

Source: Author

A Government Scenario

The Intelligence Problem

Who	What	When	Where	Why	How
A foreign president	Refusing to allow weapons sites to be inspected	Now; for several months	Country X	Unknown, possibly to hide illegal weapons	Barring access, destroying monitoring equipment

The Intelligence Need

Who	What	When	Where	Why	How
U.S. President	Wants info on Country X President	Now, and update	White House	Determine power base and intent	All-source collection & analysis

A Business Scenario

The Intelligence Problem

Who	What	When	Where	Why	How
Company X	Reorganizes production department	Sudden	Saturated market	Unknown	Unknown

The Intelligence Need

Who	What	When	Where	Why	How
CEO of similar Company Y	Wants to know why and how Company X changed	ASAP	CEO's office	Determine if new structure gives advantage	Open source analysis; tailored, confidential report

Examination of these basic scenarios should inspire further development of the concept of determining customer needs in specific situations. The thoughtful researcher may propose, for example, ways to gather information on additional aspects of the problem (Who, What) and on customers (Who), as well as on the attendant motivations (Why) and strategies (How) of the target and the customer. Defining the intelligence problem in this manner paves the way for the next step in the intelligence process — the development of intelligence collection, analysis, and production *requirements*, explained later in this chapter.

Another, more complex model for defining intelligence scenarios employs the Taxonomy of Problem Types.[39] The table below illustrates the factors that customers and producers may take into account in articulating the nature of the intelligence problem and selecting a strategy for resolving it.

Table 3. Taxonomy of Problem Types

Source: Analysis course material, Joint Military Intelligence College, 1991

Characteristics	Problem Types				
	Simplistic	Deterministic	Moderately Random	Severely Random	Indeterminate
What is the question?	Obtain information	How much? How many	Identify and rank all outcomes	Identify outcomes in unbounded situation	Predict future events/ situations
Role of facts	Highest	High	Moderate	Low	Lowest
Role of judgment	Lowest	Low	Moderate	High	Highest
Analytical task	Find information	Find/create formula	Generate all outcomes	Define potential outcomes	Define futures factors
Analytical method	Search sources	Match data to formula	Decision theory; utility analysis	Role playing and gaming	Analyze models and scenarios
Analytical instrument	Matching	Mathematical formula	Influence diagram, utility, probability	Subjective evaluation of outcomes	Use of experts
Analytic output	Fact	Specific value or number	Weighted alternative outcomes	Plausible outcomes	Elaboration on expected future
Probability of error	Lowest	Very low	Dependent on data quality	High to very high	Highest
Follow-up task	None	None	Monitor for change	Repeated testing to determine true state	Exhaustive learning

---

[39] Morgan D. Jones, *The Thinker's Toolkit* (New York: Random House, 1995), 44-46, as elaborated by Thomas H. Murray, Sequoia Associates, Inc., Arlington, VA., in coursework at the Joint Military Intelligence College.

As with the "Five Ws," this model enables decisionmakers and analysts to assess their needs and capabilities in relation to a particular intelligence scenario. This ability to establish a baseline and set in motion a collection and production strategy is crucial to conducting a successful intelligence effort. Too often, both producers and customers waste valuable time and effort struggling to characterize for themselves a given situation, or perhaps worse, they hastily embark upon an action plan without determining its appropriateness to the problem. Employing a structured approach as outlined in the Taxonomy of Problem Types can help the players avoid these inefficiencies and take the first step toward generating clear intelligence requirements by defining both the intelligence problem and the requisite components to its solution. Following are example scenarios. The reader is encouraged to follow the scenarios down the columns of the taxonomy table, then generate new scenarios in similar fashion.

INTELLIGENCE PROBLEM DEFINITION
A GOVERNMENT SCENARIO

The Severely Random problem type is one frequently encountered by the military in planning an operational strategy. This is the realm of wargaming. The initial intelligence problem is to identify all possible outcomes in an unbounded situation, so that commanders can generate plans for every contingency. The role of valid data is relatively minor, while the role of judgment is great, as history and current statistics may shed little light on how the adversary will behave in a hypothetical situation, and the progress and outcome of an operation against that adversary cannot be predicted with absolute accuracy. Therefore, the analytical task is to define and prepare for all potential outcomes. The analytical method is role playing and wargaming: placing oneself mentally in the imagined situation, and experiencing it in advance, even to the point of acting it out in a realistic setting. After experiencing the various scenarios, the players subjectively evaluate the outcomes of the games, assessing which ones may be plausible or expected to occur in the real world. The probability of error in judgment here is inherently high, as no one can be certain that the future will occur exactly as events unfolded in the game. However, repeated exercises can help to establish a measure of confidence, for practice in living out these scenarios may enable the players to more quickly identify and execute desired behaviors, and avoid mistakes in a similar real situation.

A Business Scenario

The Indeterminate problem type is one facing the entrepreneur in the modern telecommunications market. Predicting the future for a given proposed new technology or product is an extremely imprecise task fraught with potentially dire, or rewarding, consequences. The role of valid data is extremely minor here, whereas analytical judgments about the buying public's future — and changing — needs and desires are crucial. Defining the key factors influencing the future market is the analytical task, to be approached via the analytical method of setting up models and scenarios: the if/then/else process. Experts in the proposed technology or market are then employed to analyze these possibilities. Their output is a synthesized assessment of how the future will look under various conditions with regard to the proposed new product. The probability of error in judgment is extremely high, as the decision is based entirely on mental models rather than experience; after all, neither the new product nor the future environment exists yet. Continual reassessment of the changing factors influencing the future can help the analysts adjust their conclusions and better advise decisionmakers on whether, and how, to proceed with the new product.

Generating Intelligence Requirements

Once they have agreed upon the nature of the intelligence problem at hand, the intelligence service and the customer together can next generate intelligence *requirements* to drive the production process. The intelligence requirement translates customer needs into an intelligence action plan. A good working relationship between the two parties at this stage will determine whether the intelligence produced in subsequent stages actually meets customer needs. However, the differing perspectives that each side brings to the negotiation process can make cooperation between them a difficult feat.[40]

Customers want intelligence to guide them clearly in making policy and operational decisions. They may have little understanding of the intelligence process, and little patience for the subjectivity and conditionality of intelligence judgments. For customers, intelligence can be just one of many influences on their decisionmaking, and may be given little weight in comparison to other, more readily digested, familiar, or policy-oriented inputs. However, intelligence is neither designed nor equipped to meet these customer expectations.[41]

As a discipline, intelligence seeks to remain an independent, objective advisor to the decisionmaker. The realm of intelligence is that of "fact," considered judgment, and probability, but not prescription. It does not tell the customer what to do to meet an agenda, but rather, identifies the factors at play, and how various actions may affect outcomes. Intelligence tends to be packaged in standard formats and, because of its methodical approach, may not be delivered within the user's ideal timeframe. For all these reasons, the customer may not see intelligence as a useful service.[42]

Yet, somehow the intelligence producer and customer must reconcile their differing perspectives in order to agree on intelligence requirements and make the production process work. Understanding each other's views on intelligence is the first step toward improving the relationship between them. The next step is communication. Free interaction among the players will foster agreement on intelligence priorities and result in products that decisionmakers recognize as meaningful to their agendas, yet balanced by rigorous analysis.[43] In addition, as discussed below, customer feedback on production quality will lead to better definition of future intelligence problems and requirements.

---

[40] Arthur S. Hulnick, "The Intelligence Producer-Policy Consumer Linkage: A Theoretical Approach," *Intelligence and National Security*, 1, No. 2, (May 1986): 214-216.

[41] Hulnick, "Producer-Policy Consumer Linkage," 215-216.

[42] Hulnick, "Producer-Policy Consumer Linkage," 216.

[43] Adapted from Michael A. Turner, "Setting Analytical Priorities in U.S. Intelligence," *International Journal of Intelligence and CounterIntelligence*, 9, No. 3, (Fall 1996): 320-322.

Types of Intelligence Requirements

Having thus developed an understanding of customer needs, the intelligence service may proactively and continuously generate intelligence collection and production requirements to maintain customer-focused operations. Examples of such internally generated specifications include analyst-driven, events-driven, and scheduled requirements. The table below briefly describes them.[44]

Table 4. Types of Producer-Generated Intelligence Collection and Production Requirements

Source: Hulnick

Analyst-driven	Based on knowledge of customer and issues
Events-driven	In response to time-sensitive relevant events
Scheduled	Periodic activities to document and update target status

Further distinctions among intelligence requirements include timeliness and scope, or level, of intended use. Timeliness of requirements is established to meet standing (long-term) and *ad hoc* (short-term) needs. When the customer and intelligence service agree to define certain topics as long-term intelligence issues, they generate a standing requirement to ensure that a regular production effort can, and will, be maintained against that target. The customer will initiate an *ad hoc* requirement upon realizing a sudden short-term need for a specific type of intelligence, and will specify the target of interest, the coverage timeframe, and the type of output desired.

The scope or level of intended use of the intelligence may be characterized as strategic or tactical. Strategic intelligence is geared to a policymaker dealing with big-picture issues affecting the mission and future of an organization: the U.S. President, corporate executives, high-level diplomats, or military commanders of major commands or fleets. Tactical intelligence serves players and decisionmakers "on the ground" engaged in current operations: trade negotiators, marketing and sales representatives, deployed military units, or product developers.

Table 5. Types of Customer-Defined Intelligence Requirements

Source: Author

Timeliness	Short-term *(ad hoc)*	Long-term (standing)
Scope	Broad (strategic)	Narrow (tactical)

---

[44] Adapted from Arthur S. Hulnick, "Managing Intelligence Analysis: Strategies for Playing the End Game," *International Journal of Intelligence and CounterIntelligence* 2, No. 3 (Fall 1988): 327.

Ensuring that Requirements Meet Customer Needs

Even when they follow this method of formulating intelligence requirements together, decisionmakers and their intelligence units in the public and private sectors may still have an incomplete grasp of how to define their needs and capabilities — until they have evaluated the resultant products. Thus, customer feedback, production planning and tasking, as well as any internal product evaluation, all become part of the process of defining needs and creating intelligence requirements. However, when intelligence producers and users are not in nearly direct, daily contact, this process can consume a good deal of time. This is why the national Intelligence Community is experimenting with compressing both the accustomed time and spatial dimensions of the intelligence process through remote electronic collaboration and production methods.[45]

Whether in business or government, six fundamental values or attributes underlie the core principles from which all the essential intelligence functions are derived. The corollary is that intelligence customers' needs may be defined and engaged by intelligence professionals using these same values. Table 6 offers a brief explanation of how both intelligence customers and producers may use these values to evaluate how well they have translated needs into requirements that will result in useful products.[46]

Interpretation of these values turns a customer's need into a collection and production requirement that the intelligence service understands in the context of its own functions. However, illustrating the complexity of the intelligence process, once this is done, the next step is not necessarily collection.

Rather, the next stage is analysis. Perhaps the requirement is simply and readily answered — by an existing product, by ready extrapolation from files or data bases, or by a simple phone call or short desk note based on an analyst's or manager's knowledge. On the other hand, the requirement might necessitate laborious effort — extrapolation, collation, analysis, integration, and production — but still the product can be constructed and sent directly to the requester. Case closed; next problem.... Preliminary analysis might well show, however, that while much data exists, because the issue at hand is not a new one, gaps in information must be filled... Obviously, this calls for collection. This brings up an essential point: consumers do not drive collection *per se*; analysts do — or should.[47] Part III explores this next step in the intelligence process.

---

[45] The U.S. military has pioneered the concept of an electronic intelligence operating environment that transcends organizational boundaries. Congress has recommended that the IC adopt this *Joint Intelligence Virtual Architecture* model to take advantage of technological developments, reduce bureaucratic barriers, and thereby provide policymakers with timely, objective, and useful intelligence. See U.S. Congress Staff Study, House Permanent Select Committee on Intelligence, *IC21: The Intelligence Community in the 21st Century*, (April 1996): Section III, "Intelligence Requirements Process."

[46] The six values are adapted by Brei from an earlier version of U.S. Department of Defense, Joint Chiefs of Staff, Joint Pub 2-0, *Joint Doctrine for Intelligence Support to Operations* (Washington, DC: GPO, 5 May 1995), IV-15.

[47] Dearth, "National Intelligence," 18-19.

Table 6. Intelligence Values

Source: Brei

Accuracy: All sources and data must be evaluated for the possibility of technical error, misperception, and hostile efforts to mislead.

Objectivity: All judgments must be evaluated for the possibility of deliberate distortions and manipulations due to self-interest.

Usability: All intelligence communications must be in a form that facilitates ready comprehension and immediate application. Intelligence products must be compatible with a customer's capabilities for receiving, manipulating, protecting, and storing the product.

Relevance: Information must be selected and organized for its applicability to a customer's requirements, with potential consequences and significance of the information made explicit to the customer's circumstances.

Readiness: Intelligence systems must be responsive to the existing and contingent intelligence requirements of customers at all levels of command.

Timeliness: Intelligence must be delivered while the content is still actionable under the customer's circumstances.

ON BECOMING AN INTELLIGENCE ANALYST

Ronald D. Garst and Max L. Gross

(Originally published in the Defense Intelligence Journal 6, no. 2 (1997): 47-59.)

Intelligence analysis is the most sophisticated and intellectually demanding activity in the Intelligence Community. One does not become an analyst solely by being appointed to an analytical position nor develop into an analyst after only a few days or even weeks of training. Rather, becoming an effective all-source analyst requires years of rigorous education and on-the-job experience. Even after years of appropriate education and experience, many people fail to make the grade. The competent intelligence analyst must have a unique combination of talents, technical skills, intellectual curiosity, and a keen sense of what the customer needs.

This article describes that set of talents, skills and personal characteristics required of the successful all-source intelligence analyst. If the reader comes away with an understanding of the extraordinary effort and commitment required to develop into a capable analyst, then we will have succeeded in our task.

SOME GENERAL THOUGHTS

Analysis, in the first instance, is the ability to see patterns. In a world of information overload, the mark of the capable analyst is the ability to separate the wheat from the chaff, the important from the less important or even the trivial, and to conceptualize a degree of order out of apparent chaos. Such capability is not automatic, and the effort to conduct analysis is subject to many pitfalls-biases, stereotypes, mirror-imaging, simplistic thinking, confusion between cause and effect, bureaucratic politics, group-think, and a host of other human failings. Even the best analyst, moreover, will sometimes run afoul of one of these pitfalls. But, at least, the capable analyst knows what the pitfalls are and strives for objective analysis and assessment. Despite the expectation of the consumer, absolute perfection is impossible.

The hallmark of the capable analyst is the breadth and depth of knowledge that the individual brings to the task of assessing the meaning of some particular event or series of events. The acquisition of such knowledge requires years of rigorous education and experience. But even, then, such preparation is insufficient, as the experience of many PhDs in the Intelligence Community has shown. In addition to a strong knowledge base, the capable analyst must have adopted certain skills and patterns of thinking that virtually become part of one's personality:

- First, the individual must not only start from a strong knowledge base but must possess and retain a continuing passion to add to that knowledge in order to keep abreast of an ever-changing world.
- In addition, the aspiring analyst must enjoy research and be skilled in obtaining the information required to analyze and assess a particular issue or situation.

- Thirdly, the skilled analyst must be able to apply a variety of analytical techniques that students of analysis have developed over the years.
- Finally, the capable analyst must be competent and experienced in presenting analysis, both orally and in writing.

The following sections examine these four requirements in more detail.

The Knowledge Base

Analysts concentrate their efforts on a region, a set of activities, and often, physical systems.

A truly accomplished area analyst will have studied a region, probably will have lived there and will speak one or more of the languages of the region. A first-rate analyst will know about the political systems, the biographies of pertinent players, the economy, sociology, and the transportation and telecommunications systems of the region. For the all-source military intelligence analyst, however, in-depth knowledge of a region or a particular topic is not sufficient. The analyst must also know about those issues of importance to the military intelligence consumer. Under the rubric of geography, for example, the analyst must know how to do terrain analysis, be familiar with the questions of trafficability and choke points, know about the climate and how it influences military operations, and so on.

Not all analytical tasks are geographically based. Some, such as counternarcotics or counterterrorism analysis, are transnational. Despite the global nature of these issues, the competent analyst must also have considerable regional knowledge.

Since military commanders are a principal customer, military capabilities analysis is one of the critical analytical skills. As a first step, the analyst must have a working knowledge of order of battle databases. Beyond that, knowledge of foreign military doctrine, organization, command and control, communications systems, equipment, training, manpower, and political-military relations are required.

Another important component in the analysis of foreign militaries is weapons system analysis, a subset of scientific and technical intelligence (S&TI) analysis. The competent S&TI analyst will probably have a degree in engineering or physics.

Without a solid knowledge base concerning the region or issue to which an analyst is assigned, especially with regard to those aspects of the region having military significance, the individual will not even know what question to ask. That is, the person will not really be qualified to be called an "analyst." In addition, if lacking a sense of what is needed by the consumer, even the person labeled "analyst" is limited to reporting on a series of facts that may or may not be relevant to the needs of the commander or other intelligence consumers.

Analytic capability is only to some degree fungible. While a competent analyst assigned to the Middle East who has no experience or academic background in that region cannot be expected to become an expert quickly, the thirst for knowledge, analytic skills and logical procedures of the dedicated analyst, can, over time, assisting in developing the required expertise. Furthermore, a good North Korean missile analyst may be able to make some useful statements about missiles in the Middle East — having dealt with the same missiles in North Korea. But the level of capability is sharply reduced when the analyst is working outside the area of his or her specialized knowledge. The North Korean missile analyst, for example, may be limited in assessing the doctrine and method of employing those missiles in the Middle East or in understanding the geopolitical environment in which Middle Eastern decisionmaking takes place.

Information: The Raw Material of Analysis

Intelligence analysts have a wide array of classified and unclassified information sources available. Unfortunately, the mediocre analyst is often trapped in the so-called "inbox syndrome."

That is, the only information considered is that which is delivered to the analyst's desk, or today, to the analyst's computer. That is not enough; active information searching is critical. Thus, first, the analyst needs to have a full array of information sources available. Poor analysis, in an organization with meager information sources, is not the fault of the analyst, but the fault of the manager who has failed to provide the information resources needed.

Assuming the information systems are available, the experienced analyst will not only know how to use them, but will be a facile user, able to quickly ferret out information. Systems that should be available include, at a minimum, Intelink, specialized data systems, and the Internet. In addition, the analyst needs to be intimately familiar with the intelligence organization's library.

Information comes in a variety of qualities. Thus, the skilled analyst is a shrewd evaluator of information. According to an old axiom, a reliable source does not always yield reliable information, while a marginally reliable source sometimes provides accurate information. A correct evaluation of the accuracy of information requires a mental database against which the new information is compared, and multiple sources to verify it. Unfortunately, the inexperienced analyst is more likely to accept all information as accurate, sometimes with tragic consequences.

The use of multiple sources to ensure accuracy is critical to useful and actionable analysis. Verification through the use of information from more than one intelligence source is at the heart of all-source analysis. Increasingly, the competent analyst will ensure that unclassified sources are added to the mix. Or, perhaps, it might be better to say that the competent analyst will ensure that classified sources will be effectively integrated with his or her overall unclassified database of knowledge about the subject under consideration.

Intelligence analysis is more difficult than academic analysis because the target of intelligence interest frequently is taking active measures to hide the information, or to deceive the analyst. Thus, multiple sources are a must. At times, however, the analyst may be forced to rely on only one source, because no others are available. In such cases it is necessary to tell the consumer what is known, what is not known, and the reliability of the known.

Coping with all these problems requires the analyst to be a dyed-in-the-wool researcher. The person should enjoy the rather lonely process of conducting research. More importantly, the individual must have learned, through education as well as experience, how to do research. Research differs significantly from learning in that it employs an active mind, bent on searching various data sources that will likely help the analyst assess a certain problem. Research is narrow, focused and specific, unlike learning which tends to be broad, comprehensive and general.

Military intelligence, in recent years, has become a less congenial environment for the conduct of such research than once was the case. The pressures of budget reduction and the resulting "downsizing" have put a premium on bureaucratic or operational flexibility. Individuals are required to take on a variety of functions to response to rapidly changing requirements, thereby limiting their time and attention for research. Failure to maintain such a congenial environment over the long run, however, will tend to undermine the very analytical capabilities that make military intelligence effective.

Analytical Skills

Armed with knowledge of the area or topic, and in possession of a mass of information, the analyst must make sense out of information that is often fragmentary, ambiguous, contradictory and subject to deception. Moreover, the information is about events that have already occurred, but the analysis must look into the future.

Analysts can do four things: describe, explain, evaluate, or forecast. A description on an area, issue or weapon system may be used by military commanders for operations planning. In addition, description serves as the introduction to analysis. An issue must be described before it can be explained and evaluated. Explanation tells the consumer why something happened — for example, why a group of military officers staged a coup. Evaluation, then, can examine the implications of the coup for the political system of that nation. Evaluation can also proceed directly from description as when it examines the effectiveness of something such as a military force or an individual weapon system. Forecasting, looking into the future — for example, concerning the future stability of the nation that has just suffered a coup or the future development of the weapon system — is the core of intelligence estimating and the most sophisticated of the analytic arts.

For whatever type of analysis one is undertaking, the analyst must possess an extensive toolkit of different analytical approaches in order to work effectively with different kinds of data. At a minimum, a good analyst must be skilled at the use of logic, statistical inference, the analysis of cause and effect, probability, and decisionmaking models. The set of analytical skills needed by the transnational specialist includes some of those used in law enforcement — for example, link analysis and time-event charting.

All of these tools require lengthy education to master. Statistics, for example, can be introduced in a single, rigorous ten-week academic quarter in which thirty hours of class time is augmented by at least 150 hours of homework. A five-day training course would provide sufficient class time — 40 hours — but insufficient homework time. A ten-week academic quarter is a minimum; preferably statistics should be learned over two quarters of this length. If the person assigned as an analyst does not possess the required analytic tools, the organization must provide appropriate education or training.

Presentation Skills

Good analysis poorly presented is useless. Analysts must be able to write clearly, concisely, and accurately. Unfortunately, most high school graduates, and many college graduates, are unable to write effectively. Therefore, improvement of writing skills, basic though they may be, is often required as part of becoming a competent intelligence analyst.

In addition to writing, today, due to downsizing and the elimination of graphics shops, the analysts must be skilled at graphic presentation. This requires the ability to use computer software such as Harvard Graphics or Power Point. While few analysts will be skilled at computer-based mapping — in fact few will have access to such software—they need to know where to get appropriate maps and how to import them into reports and studies they are preparing.

Increasingly, analysts are required to brief consumers. Routine, daily briefings are usually provided by a briefing team but, often, the analyst is expected to provide a specialized briefing. While many people are uncomfortable with briefing — for a surprisingly high portion of the population, public speaking is a source of considerable anxiety — it is a skill that all can learn.

ON EDUCATING THE ANALYST

A sophisticated intelligence analyst is one who is steeped in the history and culture of a region, has a lifelong interest in an area, and approaches the study of the region as a professional responsibility, and probably as an avocation as well. Such an analyst will read a wide array of non-fiction about the region: novels set in the region, novels by authors from the region, and personally subscribe to newspapers, magazines and journals from the region.

It is clear from the foregoing, however, that these qualities, though fundamental, do not yet describe the properly educated and effective military intelligence analyst. Knowledge of a great variety of military-related topics; of primary research skills; of analytic methods; of computer systems, databases, and computer graphics software; and of basic writing and speaking techniques are all part of the toolbox of the skilled intelligence analyst.

At the Joint Military Intelligence College, the undergraduate and postgraduate programs are aimed at educating analysts familiar with regions, skilled at actively acquiring information, adept at analysis, and well-practiced in writing and presentation. It is impossible to produce an analyst with a week of training — in fact, a year of education is only an introduction. At the end of the academic year, the graduate has been introduced to the skills needed, but it is up to the individual to practice the trade of analysis on-the-job to hone those skills.

Comparison of JMIC Past and Present Core Curricula.

Joint Military Intelligence College Core Curriculum		
1998-2003	*1998-2003*	*2003-present*
The Intelligence Community		
Intelligence Organization and Resource Management	National Security Structure and Policy	National Security Structure and Policy
Intelligence and National Security Policy		
Intelligence Process		
Management of Intelligence Collection	Management of Intelligence Collection	Intelligence Collection: Evidence for Analysis
Strategic Warning and Threat Management	Strategic Warning and Threat Management	Strategic Warning and Intelligence Analysis
Research, Analysis and Writing	Thesis Writing Seminar	MSSI Thesis Research and Writing
Intelligence Analysis	Intelligence Analysis	Information Operations
	Intelligence Research and Analytic Methods	
	Intelligence Systems in the Cyberspace Era	
The Subject(s) of Analysis		
International Security Environment	Intelligence in the 21st Century: Future International Security Environment	Intelligence in the 21st Century: Future International Security Environment
The Users of Intelligence		
Intelligence and National Military Strategy	Intelligence and 21st Century National Military Strategy	Intelligence and 21st Century National Military Strategy

Comparison of JMIC Past and Present Core Curricula.

Source: authors. This table is an update (May 2005) of the material originally published in the DIJ.

The graduate core curriculum at the College recognizes the centrality of analysis, but also recognizes the wider context in which the analyst operates. The curriculum has been under review for the past two years, and certain changes are planned for introduction during Academic Year 1998-99 (See Table).

The core curriculum is supplemented by a number of elective courses which enable the student to examine each of these core areas more deeply and to gain a basic introduction into the various specialty areas — regional, transnational, S&T — in which intelligence analysts typically work. Because of the long years required to acquire the in-depth knowledge, including languages, in these various specialty areas, the Intelligence Community must rely on other academic institutions, highly-focused recruitment policies, and well-structured on-the-job development to obtain the specialized knowledge bases required for the effective accomplishment of its mission.

INTELLIGENCE TRAINING

Training is also a useful means of introducing an increased number of intelligence professionals to some of the skills required by analysts. Mobile training teams are often used, because it costs less to send two instructors to the field than to send thirty people to Washington, DC. But a week of analytical training, though of value, is clearly inadequate. It needs to be supplemented by an ongoing, structured program of required readings and writing. Using old-fashioned technology, that could be done by correspondence courses. Using more modern communications technology, computer-based instruction could be provided via Intelink. Such a program is not without cost, for computer-based instruction is very expensive to develop; each hour of instruction takes several hundred hours of development time. Instructors of intelligence analysis would have to be trained in the development of computer-based instruction, and then they would have to be free from teaching to develop the programs. Once developed, computer-based instruction has to be maintained and updated, and the instructors must have time to interact with students over Intelink. At the receiving end, students would need the time to complete time-consuming courses, Improving analytical instruction by this means is feasible, but the cost is not inconsequential.

FINALLY: THE NEED TO MAINTAIN A
COMMITMENT TO THE ANALYST

Beyond education and training, there always needs to be bureaucratic incentives to become and remain an analyst. Some analysts may be drawn into management sectors of the Intelligence Community. Indeed, such movement should be encouraged, because having former analysts serving in leadership positions — leaders who know the world of analysis — can only benefit the overall intelligence effort. Those who do flourish in analytical capacities, however, should be assured that they can have full and rewarding careers helping their agencies succeed in achieving the national security objectives of the nation's policymakers.

GETTING INTELLIGENCE RIGHT: THE POWER OF LOGICAL PROCEDURE

William F. Brei

(Originally published as JMIC Occasional Paper Two, Getting Intelligence Right: The Power of Logical Procedure, January 1996.)

INTUITION OR REASON?

The challenges facing the Intelligence Community are formidable. Continual budget and manpower cuts degrade managerial continuity, experience levels, and technical expertise. Yet, the international arena and issues that we monitor are becoming more complex. Learning to work smarter has become imperative.

The purpose of this paper is to help intelligence professionals view their work in an entirely new way: through the lens of doctrine. Why doctrine? Simply put, doctrine leads us away from over-reliance on intuition and toward a sharper focus on reasoning.

The Old Intelligence Cycle Model

In its current state of development, intelligence doctrine is based on a model that represents intelligence as a data collection-analysis-production-dissemination cycle. Visualized as a set of gears, the cogs on each gear represent functions and activities necessary for the purpose of each gear. Although this seems to be a sensible model for how we produce intelligence, it does not address the cognitive dimension behind the process. In addition, the model tends to segment each gear into functionally distinct identities. People assigned to work in a cog on a gear lose their sense of involvement in the end product and in the final customer. People who are cogs on one wheel tend to pay close attention to the movement of their assigned wheel and disregard the value that the other gears add to the overall system.

Intuition Over Reason

Further exacerbating the problems that come with segmentation, the perception that doctrine would become an undesirable mental straight-jacket has hindered full acceptance of new joint intelligence doctrine. The potential value of the new doctrine is weakened because it actually promotes intuition over reason, as no emphasis is placed on analytical skills. Technical training is based on doctrine, and the technical training for intelligence personnel therefore includes little in managerial, reasoning, and critical thinking skills.

Intelligence professionals have much in common with Yoda, a fictional character in the movie The Empire Strikes Back. Yoda was a gnarlish, troll-like creature who lived in a dank underground cubicle, surviving by the "force" of his intuition. Intelligence customers would be better served by Mr. Spock, the fictional Vulcan character from Star Trek.

Spock represents the contrast between intuition and logic; Spock presents a formidable figure of authority, respected for his logical judgment and strict adherence to principle. Spock respected the power of intuition, but demonstrated its limits. Intuition that is not grounded in principles leads to unnecessary mistakes and unsupportable conclusions. Intuition that has developed as a natural outgrowth of rigorous training and adherence to basic principles results in a greater chance for success.

While intuition can be an asset, intelligence professionals need a foundation of knowledge and experience upon which to base our judgment. Doctrine provides this common baseline. Personnel who are educated in the language and knowledge of their profession are indoctrinated. Indoctrinated personnel propagate this common baseline of knowledge and language throughout the professional community. Doctrine establishes the common vision. Fundamental principles set the common focus. Ultimately, properly developed and propagated doctrine nurtures consistency of thought and action across diverse bureaucratic empires.

The doctrine of any profession is more than a statement of purpose and a set of rules-of-thumb which prescribe how one goes about one's business. Doctrine's most important role is to define and explain the subject's fundamental principles. The fundamental principles of any service-oriented discipline must be based on what its customers' value. Intelligence personnel must understand what it is about their service that customers consider valuable, and then translate these values into mandates — or principles — for everyday use.

Doctrine also establishes consistency and coherence in the evaluation of intelligence policy, programs, processes, and products. Any study of intelligence successes will show that fundamental principles have been honored; conversely, studies of intelligence failures reveal the lack of principle-based management and leadership.

FPI Forces the Issue

DoD and the Intelligence Community are meeting drawdown challenges head-on by developing doctrine and implementing the Functional Process Improvement (FPI) Program. FPI encompasses a multi-tiered approach, starting with a low-risk, workshop-level focus on quality improvement to high-risk, enterprise-wide Business Process Reengineering (BPR). While full-blown process reengineering efforts may not need to be performed at every echelon of command, the results must be felt at every level. FPI's natural niche, however, is at the Command and Service echelons, where long-range planning functions are performed. The most effective way to maximize the impact of FPI and other such initiatives is through doctrine.

Work process analyses such as FPI should not only influence doctrine, they should challenge and reshape it. Indeed, work process analyses and doctrine are equally necessary and mutually supporting: doctrine provides the context that process analysis requires — the "As-is" view of work processes and the values that drive them. Process analysis helps us identify work processes that should be refined or eliminated — thus reshaping doctrine. In this manner, process improvement initiatives and doctrine exist in a symbiotic relationship that leads to the same ultimate goal: people working smarter, not harder.

This paper presents what I propose as simple, distinct, and coherent definitions for intelligence and its fundamental principles. This step leads to the realization that these principles serve as our doctrinal criteria for success. The actions of process re-engineering, or of linking work activities and processes to fundamental principles, focuses us on what an intelligence customer values. In addition, the effort of linking work activities to principles may expose tasks that do not support any fundamental principles, and hence, do not add value to the intelligence service. Unless non-value added tasks are required by law, such tasks should be de-emphasized or terminated.

Finally, principle-based management provides for simple self-evaluations that will be consistent with customer comments. Intelligence personnel will understand what the customer expects, and will know which activities support those expectations. The neglect of processes that are necessary for honoring a doctrinal principle will probably result in an intelligence failure. This study thus establishes the practical and mutually supporting relationship between doctrine, day-to-day management, and functional process improvement.

THE MEANING OF INTELLIGENCE

The first step in developing doctrine is to define and limit the problem. This naturally leads to an examination of the definition of intelligence:

> the product resulting from the collection, processing, integration, analysis, evaluation, and interpretation of available information concerning foreign countries or areas.[48]

Although this definition reiterates Sherman Kent's view that *intelligence* is a "product of many steps in a complicated, demanding process,"[49] it obscures the substance of the product and includes the publishers of *The World Almanac* and the *Encyclopedia Britannica* as intelligence producers. This definition is clearly too ambiguous and broad. These weaknesses are well-known, but persistent. One researcher reports that

> The [1955] Hoover Commission's Task Force on Intelligence Activities sought "an acceptable definition" of intelligence, [but] it was surprised to discover that each agency had its own pet definition. It was dismayed to note that many of the definitions were "lengthy" and "requiring additional interpretation or delimitations to get at their precise application." What the investigators sought was a definition "as simple and clear as possible," which, of course, is what a definition is ideally supposed to be.[50]

---

[48] Department of Defense, Joint Chiefs of Staff, *Dictionary of Military and Associated Terms* (Joint Pub 1-02) (Washington, DC: GPO, 1 December 1989), under the word "intelligence."

[49] Thomas F. Troy, "The Correct Definition of Intelligence," *International Journal of Intelligence and Counterintelligence* (Winter 1991-1992): 442.

Indeed, more recently, an author of a 1990 dictionary of intelligence terms emphasized this problem by entering 127 definitions under the word *intelligence* — an effort that consumed 17 pages of the dictionary.[51]

Advancing past this ambiguity requires the adoption of a more suitable definition for intelligence. For the remainder of this paper, *Intelligence* means

> "knowledge of the enemy"[52] and the operational environment, both of which are processed and packaged for a specific customer's requirements for making decisions in matters of national security and operational execution.

With this definition, *intelligence* is more specific than information about foreign countries. International law considers intelligence activities to be hostile acts; hence, the focus must be on our adversaries — not foreign nations in general. Secondly, intelligence is more than information. It is *knowledge* that has been specially prepared for a customer's unique circumstances.

The word *knowledge* highlights the need for human involvement. Intelligence collection systems produce sensory data, not intelligence; only the human mind can provide that special touch that makes sense of data for different customers' requirements.

The special processing that partially defines *intelligence* is the continual collection, verification, and analysis of information that allows us to understand the problem or situation in actionable terms and then tailor a product in the context of the customer's circumstances. If any of these essential attributes is missing, then the product remains *information* rather than *intelligence*.

The line between *information* and this definition of intelligence is consistent with the U.S. Army's distinction of combat information from intelligence. According to the Intelligence and Electronic Warfare Operations Field Manual (FM) 34-1, combat information is:

> Unevaluated data, gathered by or provided directly to the . . . commander which, due to its highly perishable nature or the criticality of the situation, cannot be processed into tactical intelligence in time to satisfy the user's tactical intelligence requirements.[53]

Only after data are verified for accuracy and analyzed for their significance to a specific customer's situation can they become the substance of intelligence.

---

[50] U.S. Commission on Organization of the Executive Branch of the Government (1953-1955), Intelligence Activities, A Report to the Congress, 84th Cong., 1st sess., June 1955, H. Doc 201. 25-26. Quoted by Troy, 437-38.

[51] Leo D. Carl, "The International Dictionary of Intelligence" (McLean, VA: International Defense Consultant Services, Inc., 1990), under the word "intelligence," 178-195.

[52] Constantine FitzGibbon, Secret Intelligence for the Twentieth Century (New York: Stein and Day, 1977), 56; quoted in Troy, 433.

[53] Headquarters, Department of the Army, Intelligence and Electronic Warfare Operations FM-34-1 (Washington, DC: GPO, July 1987), 2-13.

FUNDAMENTAL PRINCIPLES OF INTELLIGENCE

With an acceptable definition of "intelligence" in view, the next requirement becomes the identification of its fundamental principles. Fundamental principles are the underlying ideas or core values from which essential work processes are derived. Customers dictate our core values, defining what our service provides that is valuable to them. Although customers often require help in defining their intelligence requirements, determining what our customers value is simple: listen to their complaints.

After rigorous analyses of current doctrinal publications and over ten years of direct customer liaison, I propose a set of six fundamental principles: Accuracy, Objectivity, Usability, Relevance, Readiness, and Timeliness.[54] These principles are defined in tonebox below.

OVERVIEW OF THE PRINCIPLES OF INTELLIGENCE

ACCURACY: All sources and data must be evaluated for the possibility of technical error, misperception, and hostile efforts to mislead.

OBJECTIVITY: All judgments must be evaluated for the possibility of deliberate distortions and manipulations due to self-interest.

USABILITY: All intelligence communications be in a form that facilitates ready comprehension and immediate application. Intelligence products must be compatible with the customer's capabilities for receiving, manipulating, protecting, and storing the product.

RELEVANCE: Information must be selected and organized for its applicability to a consumer's requirements, with potential consequences and significance of the information made explicit to the consumer's circumstances.

READINESS: Intelligence systems must be responsive to the existing and contingent intelligence requirements of customers at all levels of command.

TIMELINESS: Intelligence must be delivered while the content is still actionable under the customer's circumstances.

To understand the efficacy of this set of principles, consider our customers' point of view. Our customers need information that is relevant and timely. When customers com-

---

[54] These principles are similar to the Attributes of Intelligence Quality in Joint Doctrine for Intelligence Support to Operations (Joint Pub 2-0), suffer from poor definitional rigor, circular error and gross ambiguity. In addition, the authors of Joint Pub 2-0 overlooked the basic significance of the Principles of Intelligence, specifying rules-of-thumb for intelligence actions rather than the basic values that the actions support. See Captain William S. Brei, Assessing Intelligence by Principles of Quality: The Case Study of Imagery Intelligence Support to Operation PROVIDE COMFORT, Unpublished thesis, Washington DC: Defense Intelligence College, July 1993.

plain about a lack of relevance, the fault may be with inaccurate data, a lack of objectivity, or an unusable product format. The Principles of Accuracy, Objectivity, and Usability are attributes of the more general Principle of Relevance. In a similar manner, timeliness depends upon — and customers value — the vigilance and responsiveness that result from readiness. This set of principles is sensible from the points of view of both the intelligence professional and the customer.

These principles apply across all intelligence specialties, disciplines, and organizational boundaries. Each principle encompasses specific goals, or performance standards, achieved by specific work processes and tasks.[55] In this manner, fundamental principles provide specific qualitative objectives for managers and leaders, and a framework for standards against which intelligence services should be judged.

Logically, the principles of Readiness and Timeliness are distinct in nature from the principles of Accuracy, Objectivity, Usability, and Relevance. Readiness and Timeliness embody the constraints of the operational environment in which intelligence processes are performed. An intelligence organization's readiness — the state of its responsiveness to changes — provides the capacity to achieve a timely intelligence product. Readiness and Timeliness are limiting factors affecting what we can do to achieve accurate data, objective judgments, usable formats, and relevant products.

The Principles of Accuracy, Objectivity, and Usability are principles that partially support the principle of Relevance. Together, Relevance and its supporting principles address the form and substance of an intelligence product. In essence, accurate data provide the foundation for subsequent objective judgments, and the expression of objective judgments in a usable form provides much of the basis of a relevant product. Thus, unverified data can not only cost an intelligence product its Accuracy, but also damage its Relevance to the customer.

Accuracy, Objectivity, Usability, and Relevancy govern the value-adding processes that culminate in the delivery of intelligence to a customer. Figure 2 illustrates this point with a filtering process analogy: we filter raw data for Accuracy and analytical judgments for Objectivity. Accurate data and acceptably objective judgments are then filtered through the customer's product format requirements, and the result is filtered to ensure relevancy to the customers' requirements.

Assuming that high-quality intelligence provision does not happen by magic or accident, the ability to honor these principles must result from deliberate processes. During the development and refinement of an intelligence product, processes employed to address one or more of these principles may be revisited any number of times and are likely to occur in parallel. To prevent a loss of focus on the principles as the intelligence

---

[55] Performance standards are "specific criteria, goals, or objectives against which performance....is judged." Glenn Hastedt, "Intelligence and U.S. Foreign Policy: How to Measure Success," *International Journal of Intelligence and Counterintelligence*, (Spring 1991): 51.

product is shaped, analysts and managers must clearly understand the essential attributes of each principle and where the lines between them are drawn.

The following sections of this paper explain what is meant by each principle, to include an explanation of vital concepts, the pitfalls that limit success, and some actions intelligence professionals can take to honor each principle.

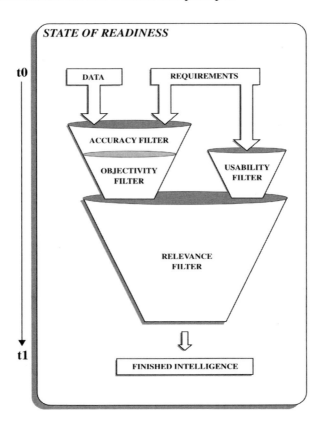

Figure 2. Principles Viewed as Process Filters.

THE PRINCIPLE OF ACCURACY

What is Accuracy?

All intelligence products must be based on data that have been evaluated for technical error, misperception, and hostile efforts to deceive. All data must be accepted as *fact*, meaning "true statements."[56] To understand what we mean by fact, we must clarify the meaning of *true*, or *truth*. Without digressing through the many schools of thought on the subject of truth, let us pragmatically combine Bertrand Russell's view that truth is the "correspondence of thought to the external world"[57] with William James' view that "true ideas are useful leadings; in that they lead us through experiences in ways that provide consistency, orderliness, and predictability."[58] This definition of truth is sufficiently practical.

The data useful to intelligence production, therefore, must qualify as useful leadings; consistent with what we expect from a predictable and orderly world. Since human perception and mechanical precision are both imperfect, some degree of variation is acceptable. Any determination of Accuracy must consider the data available and where the data fell within established limits of acceptability.

Importantly, the interpretation of data on an intelligence target is the responsibility of the intelligence staff. The data attributes of consistency, orderliness, and predictability are separately (and perhaps distinctly) defined by intelligence personnel as they process (analyze and synthesize) the data. This does not, of course, mean that intelligence will have a monopoly on truth; a commander, with even more sources of information, may perceive another truth. But the most useful attributes of Accuracy, in doctrinal terms, are consistency, orderliness, and predictability.

Limit Accuracy to Facts

Many scholars and critics mistakenly apply Accuracy to predictive estimates, usually when espousing the so-called *warning paradox* to prove the inevitability of intelligence failure.[59] The warning paradox occurs when analysts predict an attack and the attacker cancels his plans to attack after learning that surprise has been lost. Rather than considering the warning given by the intelligence service a success, it is argued that the absence of the attack falsifies the prediction.[60] Aside from the fallacy of requiring accurate judgments

---

[56] Monroe C. Beardsley, *Practical Logic* (New York: Prentice-Hall, 1950), 5.

[57] Shirley R. Letwin, "Certainty Since the Seventh Century," *Dictionary of the History of Ideas: Studies of Selected Pivotal Ideas*, Vol 1 (New York: Charles Scribner's Sons, 1973), 319.

[58] *Academic American Encyclopedia*, Online Edition, under the word "Pragmatism," downloaded from Prodigy (Rockville, MD: Grolier Electronic Publishing, 1993), 12 July 1993.

[59] Avi Shlaim, "Failure in National Intelligence Estimates: The Case of the Yom Kippur War," *World Politics* 28, no. 3 (April 1976): 378; also quoted by Richard K. Betts, "Analysis, War and Decision: Why Intelligence Failures are Inevitable," *World Politics* 31, no. 1 (October 1978): 61-89.

[60] Shlaim, 378; also see Richard Brody, "The Limits of Warning," *The Washington Quarterly* 6, no. 3 (Summer 1983): 46.

from an inductive reasoning process, the issue over the warning paradox is disingenuous because it ignores the purpose of the warning function.[61] The purpose of warning predictions is to prevent surprise and *influence* the future. The actual objective in military intelligence is not so much to be right as it is to ensure safety by producing the most reasonable prediction while there is still time to prevent the worst. Judging whether a prediction came true offers nothing meaningful to the evaluation of intelligence, although it may have some applicability to assessing our national clout in the international arena.

Predictions are nothing more than hypotheses that have been "accepted" as the most likely of many competing hypotheses, given the accuracy of the data available:

When we come to accept a hypothesis, we are not saying it is an inescapable or accurate conclusion from the evidence, but that it is the most acceptable conclusion. We can never exhaustively verify a hypothesis. A hypothesis, like a generalization, always has a kind of provisional character: it is acceptable until further notice.[62]

Although the difference between accurate and acceptable may be derided as merely a matter of semantics, one of the major challenges to establishing useful doctrine lies in the elimination of semantic confusion.

The Pitfalls to Accuracy

Achieving Accuracy is a daunting challenge that forces us to be aware of and overcome many hurdles. The first hurdle is environmental: the data we gather are often inconclusive, contradictory, and deliberately deceptive. The second hurdle is internal: the mental capabilities that we rely upon for accepting and processing large amounts of data tend to act as bias filters that lead to misperception.

Inconclusive, Contradictory, and Deceptive Data. Without direct, conclusive evidence, intelligence analysts must develop judgments through an inferential line of reasoning that generates probabilities rather than conclusiveness. Thus, "squishiness" of data is an occupational hazard that actually provides the Intelligence Community's *raison d'etre:* Decision-makers need someone to make sense of the volumes of ambiguous, contradictory, incomplete, and deceptive information that would otherwise drive them to distraction.[63]

Clever adversaries use deception to condition opponents to overlook attack signals and dull the sensitivity of the warning system. One common technique creates an illusory pattern of normal activity by conducting routine military exercises that trigger the target's warning system. Over time, the target simply gets used to the attacker's heightened mili-

---

[61] Accuracy applies to data, not estimates. Inductive reasoning requires we show only "reasonable" judgment; not accurate judgment. Inferential reasoning is applied when needed data are not available or trustworthy.

[62] Beardsley, 225-226.

[63] If handled poorly, "squishy" evidence leads to "squishy" conclusions that customers detest. After Operation DESERT STORM, General Schwarzkopf charged that intelligence assessments were so "caveated, footnoted and watered down" that the information was worthless. "Schwarzkopf Faults Gulf Intelligence," *Facts on File*, 18 July 1991, 535.

tary activity level. In this way, the Soviet Union successfully surprised the world with its invasion of Czechoslovakia in 1968, and Egypt, too, achieved surprise when its "routine" border exercise turned into an invasion of the Sinai in October 1973. The Argentine invasion of the Falkland Islands provides an excellent example of effective operational security and deception:

It is clear that [Argentina's] plans were made in utmost secrecy, and that most ministers, diplomats, and senior officers were unaware of them until the very last moment. The army's Director of Military Intelligence failed to identify his country's preparations for war and was innocently abroad when it started. . . . On both the military and political fronts, there was an effective policy of disinformation, misrepresentation, and deception.[64]

Misperception: Our Intellectual Frailties. The Agranat Committee concluded that the most significant problem in the warning failure of the 1973 Yom Kippur War was "incorrectly interpreted data due to intrinsic faults in the mind's handling of information."[65] These "intrinsic faults" are cognitive biases, and their influence leads to consistent and predictable patterns of error in judgment.[66]

Cognitive biases help the mind filter and organize information, and then create a tendency to discount information that runs against its organizational scheme. These patterns of error may be inescapable, as researchers believe they arise from the way people think rather than from self-interest (the conscious bias that conflicts with objectivity).[67]

The main difference between professional scholars or intelligence officers on the one hand, and all other people on the other hand, is that the former are supposed to have had more training in the techniques of guarding against their own intellectual frailties.

—Sherman Kent

Our thinking processes follow patterns of behavior that control how we assimilate and accommodate information from the environment and recall information from memory. Assimilation refers to the mental "modification and elaboration of information to fit prior conceptions or hypotheses," and accommodation refers to the "modification of the existing contents of memory to accept new or inconsistent information."[68]

---

[64] David E. King, "Intelligence Failures and the Falklands War: A Reassessment," *Intelligence and National Security*, 2, no. 2 (April 1987): 337.

[65] Ytzhak Katz and Ygal Vardi, "Strategies for Data Gathering and Evaluation in the Intelligence Community," *International Journal of Intelligence and Counterintelligence*, 5 no. 3 (Fall 1991): 313. The Agranat Committee was established after the Yom Kippur War to examine the events preceding the war, the failures in evaluation, and the first stages of the war.

[66] Richards J. Heuer, Jr., "Cognitive Biases: Problems in Hindsight Analysis," *Studies in Intelligence*, 22, no. 2 (Summer 1989): 21.

[67] Heuer, 21.

[68] J.R. Thompson, R. Hopf-Weichel, and R.E. Geiselman, "The Cognitive Bases of Intelligence Analysis." Unpublished research paper funded by the US Army Intelligence and Threat Analysis Center, Arlington Hall Station, Arlington, VA. Contract no. MDA 903-82-C-0409, OSD Report No.: R83-039C. 30 July 1983, 2-9.

Information assimilation, the fitting of data into preconceived patterns, encompasses the functions of selectivity and generalization. Selectivity entails the filtering of raw data, selection of those aspects that are significant to preconceptions, and the dismissal of details that do not fit the preconceptions. Selectivity is "tuned" by expectations, which, once established, also "increases the accessibility of memory contents related to that expectation."[69] Generalization is another type of filtering mechanism that determines the "types and degrees of similarities required to recognize things as members of well-known categories."[70] Selectivity and generalization are fundamental and necessary processes for accepting large amounts of data and organizing large numbers of unique experiences into a manageable form. All people are influenced by bias, and these patterns of thinking can lead to consistent error in judgment.

When assimilation is carried to the extreme, a bias toward confirming preconceived hypotheses is in evidence; whereas when accommodation is carried to the extreme, the analyst may disregard the probabilistic nature of intelligence data and exhibit a bias toward switching hypotheses upon receipt of minimally conflicting information. Both of these extreme tendencies are more likely to occur under conditions of stress.[71]

The balance between assimilation and accommodation of data dictates the type and severity of a person's cognitive bias. The answer for intelligence professionals is that we need to understand bias, develop more self-awareness of our own cognitive patterns, and recognize the appearance of bias in the work of others.

Overconfidence. An example of assimilation carried to the extreme was Israel's "failure" on the eve of the 1973 Yom Kippur War. Israeli intelligence overrated its nation's superiority and "drastically underrated" Egypt's military strength, ability to learn from previous military setbacks, and capacity for deception.[72]

Mirror-Imaging. Bias sometimes appears as a phenomenon known as "mirror-imaging." This bias occurs when someone with little understanding of how someone else thinks or acts expects parallel thinking and behavior.[73] An example of this problem occurred when British military intelligence tried to infer how Nazi Germany would use its air power. According to Robert Jervis, British military intelligence mirror-imaged in the assumption that the Luftwaffe's thinking was like that of the Royal Air Force and the Germans would thereby concentrate their attacks on British and French cities. As a result, the British overestimated the threat that German air power posed to their civilians and underestimated its utility in supporting German ground forces. When they examined the structure of the German

---

[69] Thompson and others, 2-4.

[70] Thompson and others, 2-5.

[71] Thompson and others, 2-3.

[72] Walter Laqueur, *A World Of Secrets: The Uses and Limits of Intelligence* (New York: Twentieth Century Fund, 1985), 281.

[73] Robert Jervis, "Puzzle and Paradox: Strategic Intelligence and Effective Policy," 33, no. 4 *Studies in Intelligence* (Winter 1989): 24.

air force in more detail, they continued to use their own experience as a template and thus misjudged the pace and purpose of the buildup.[74]

Empathy. The obverse side of mirror-imaging is a lack of empathy. This occurs when an analyst is unable to place himself in another person's position, and instead, "assume[s] that the other's behavior is driven by unusual, and frequently malign, internal characteristics."[75]

Although too much empathy obviously might lead to error associated with sympathy, researchers generally assert that too little rather than too much empathy is the more common problem.

Intelligence — and still more, statesmen — usually do not see others, especially adversaries, as like themselves. Furthermore, they underestimate the extent to which the other's behavior is to be explained by the situation the other faces and correspondingly overweigh the importance of the other's peculiar goals and beliefs.[76]

This pattern of inference ascribes an adversary's actions to goals and beliefs rather than operational realities. This creates expectations that decisions and behavior will be more consistent than will be the case, rather than allowing for creative responses to changing circumstances.[77]

Assumed Rationality. Another bias occurs when we grant unwarranted rationality to decision-making and behavior. Henry Kissinger once commented that "all intelligence services congenitally overestimate the rationality of the decision-making process they are analyzing."[78] Further complicating this problem is that people in other cultures, especially non-Western, tend to employ thought processes that appear irrational and illogical to us— but are entirely sensible in their own cultural context. Intelligence analysts, therefore, must ensure their set of competing hypotheses account for cultural context, as well as the possibility of irrationality, mistakes, and accidents.

The combined effects of "squishy" data and cognitive biases, and the failure to manage their influences, may result in serious problems. One such problem is the "Cry-Wolf Syndrome." Admiral Stark used this phrase to explain why he stopped sending Admiral Kimmel warnings about Japanese military movements. According to Admiral Stark, Admiral Kimmel and his staff grew weary of checking out reports of Japanese submarines in the vicinity of Pearl Harbor — they had checked out seven reports in the week preceding the Japanese attack, all of which were false.[79]

---

[74] Jervis, 24.

[75] Jervis, 24.

[76] Jervis, 24.

[77] Jervis, 24.

[78] Henry Kissinger, For the Record: Selected Statements, 1977-1980 (Boston: Little, Brown, 1981), quoted by Helene L. Boatner, "The Evaluation of Intelligence," *Studies in Intelligence*, 28, no. 2 (Summer 1984): 68.

[79] Roberta Wohlstetter, "Cuba and Pearl Harbor: Hindsight and Foresight," *Foreign Affairs* 43 (July 1965): 699.

Man is not rational, merely capable of it.

— Jonathan Swift

Processes that Help Achieve Accuracy

Processes that can help to achieve Accuracy include data verification, authentication of sources, and systematic analytical methods.

Source and Data Verification. Thoughtful people normally respond to new information with several questions. The initial reaction asks "Is it true or false?" and is followed by "Is it likely, doubtful, or unlikely?"[80] These questions mark the beginning of the verification process, and the answers come from a combination of knowledge, common sense, skepticism, faith, and guesswork.[81] With the development of these facilities, people tend to handle rumor (unverified information), by doing at least one of the following:

(1) they accept it because it came from a trusted source, (2) they reject it because it does not square with what they think to be likely, (3) they suspend judgment until more information comes out, or (4) they ignore the information altogether.[82]

If intelligence professionals, as Sherman Kent suggested, are trained "in the techniques of guarding against their own intellectual frailties," this training would prompt them to suspend judgment (choice 3) until more information becomes available.[83]

The other choices, (1), (2), and (4), do not compel analysts to perform the deliberate and methodical actions necessary to reach conclusions that are rationally convincing, not only to themselves, but to others.[84] These actions constitute the process of verification, and hence, comprise the most important processes that support the achievement of Accuracy.

The data on which a judgment or conclusion may be based, or by which probability may be established, begins with evidence:

A datum becomes evidence in some analytic problem when its relevance to one or more hypotheses being considered is established. Evidence is relevant to a hypothesis if it either increases or decreases the likelihood of that hypothesis. Without hypotheses, the relevance of no datum could be established.[85]

---

[80] Jacques Barzun and Henry F. Graff, *The Modern Researcher* (New York: Harcourt Brace Jovanovich College Publishers, 1985), 96.

[81] Barzun and Graff, 96.

[82] Barzun and Graff, 96.

[83] Sherman Kent, *Strategic Intelligence for American World Policy*, revised ed. (Princeton University Press, 1966), 199, as quoted by Harold P. Ford in "A Tribute to Sherman Kent," Studies in Intelligence, 24, no. 3 (Fall 1980): 3.

[84] Barzun and Graff, 99.

[85] David A. Schum, *Evidence and Inference for the Intelligence Analyst* (Lanham, MD: University Press of America, 1987), 1:16.

Regardless of its use, "no piece of evidence can be used in the state in which it is found."[86] Whenever an analyst considers new evidence, the critical mind must follow a systematic interrogatory:

Are these data genuine?
How do I know?
What does this evidence state or imply?
Who is its author or maker and what degree of access does he have?[87]
What is the relation in time and space between the author and the information, overt or implied, that is conveyed by the information?
How does the statement compare with other statements on the same point?
What do we know independently about the author and his credibility?[88]

The product of critical inquiry is a judgment about the credibility and reliability of the evidence and its source.[89] Credibility (a measure of confidence) is only partly based on reliability (a measure of consistency), since past performance is never perfectly repeated.

Pertinent data may not be available when an analyst begins to verify a piece of evidence. Under these circumstances, common sense and educated guesswork may be the only means of answering the questions asked in the evaluation of evidence. The specific basis of the answers is important and must be recorded. In this way, resort to intuition as the basis for decisionmaking is avoided. The key to the process is not that all of the answers to the inquiry are based on fully verified facts; rather, that the process is systematic and each answer is documented.

Systematic Analytical Method. When an analyst systematically verifies data, authenticates a source, or accepts the likelihood of a hypothesis, important benefits ensue if the details of the process are recorded. Aside from serving as a paper trail that proves an evaluation was accomplished, documentation will hold crucially important information: the degree of rigor involved, what was known and unknown, what the analyst had confidence or doubts in, and a level of plausibility or acceptability of the evidence. A record of the manner in which the analyst evaluated the evidence also exposes the analyst's assumptions and values for consistent application when other evidence arises. Finally, these records can be available for periodic review and reassessment by both the analyst and others who need to understand the analyst's line of reasoning to evaluate the acceptability of the conclusions.

---

[86] Barzun and Graff, 156.

[87] There are four levels of verifiability: personal observations, reports, inferences, and assumptions. These levels correspond to the directness of the source to the information being reported. Karl Albrecht, *Brain Power: Learn to Improve Your Thinking Skills* (Englewood Cliffs, New Jersey: Prentice-Hall, 1980), 121.

[88] Barzun and Graff, 157-158.

[89] Credibility is a level of confidence in someone's or something's credit-worthiness. Reliability refers to the repeatability, including intrasubjective replicability, of observation. Suppose a technical surveillance system or human source produces approximately the same set of responses on repeated trials (and with different analysts or debriefers), we can say that the observational technique/source has high reliability, regardless of the actual validity of the findings. Pertti J. Pelto, *Anthropological Research: The Structure of Inquiry* (New York: Harper and Row, 1970), 42.

Documentation also helps minimize bias in analysis:

The question is not whether one's prior assumptions and expectations influence analysis, but only whether this influence is made explicit or remains unconscious. Objectivity is gained by making assumptions explicit so that they may be examined and challenged.[90]

Human cognitive biases tend to pattern information into existing frames of reference, and unless an external analytical method is used, the mind will do a poor job of simultaneously evaluating multiple hypotheses. The mind seeks to simplify the data and fit them into the first satisfactory model; the use of a systematic and documented analytical method helps keep competing hypotheses under full consideration.[91] Further, there is evidence that some external analytical procedures "force the analysts' judgments to come faster and farther away from their starting point [initial mindset] than would otherwise be the case."[92]

Toward Performance Standards for Accuracy

With a comprehensive understanding of the issues underlying Accuracy, we now identify some of the fundamental activities that directly support honoring this principle. Each of these fundamental activities may also serve as performance standards from an evaluative perspective. This effort will not be exhaustive; the only need is to identify sufficient processes to demonstrate the concept of matching basic intelligence tasks to the principle they support.

1. Employ a systematic source authentication and data verification method; record assumptions and doubts.

2. Authenticate sources of information for motive and the degree of access; establish a credibility rating.

3. Verify all data: establish probabilities or likelihood; document all assumptions and doubts about each datum, and do not accept the source's inferences uncritically as if they have the weight of directly observed facts.

4. Review documentation before release of intelligence product to customer; identify all facts used in the line of reasoning and ensure they were challenged and verified to a probability that is appropriate to the degree of influence they exert in the analytical product.

---

[90] Richards J. Heuer, Jr., "Strategies for Analytical Judgment," *Studies in Intelligence* 25, no. 2 (Summer 1981): 83.

[91] Herbert Simon identified a less-than-optimal analytical strategy used by analysts facing incomplete information. He called this strategy "satisficing," in which the first satisfactory hypothesis is selected, rather than examining all alternatives for the optimal solution. Heuer, "Strategies for Analytical Judgment," 75.

[92] "Analysts' overall intuitive evaluation of probabilities usually lags behind events, and the Bayesian procedure compensates for this" by asking the question, "Given the truth of this hypotheses, what is the probability of seeing this evidence?" This reverses the "normal" way of evaluating evidence, which asks, "Given this evidence, what is the probability of the various hypotheses?"

5. Review the documentation of assumptions and doubts expressed during the verification and authentication processes for evidence of unconscious and emotional bias patterns.

THE PRINCIPLE OF OBJECTIVITY

What is Objectivity?

Objectivity pertains to how our judgment correlates to the external world, as it actually exists, regardless of our desires. Written in the context of intelligence doctrine, Objectivity requires us to evaluate all judgments for the deliberate distortions and manipulations due to self-interest.

To understand Objectivity, we must define "external world." The external world is *existence* apart from one's self. Unfortunately, *Existence*, a metaphysical axiom, completely resists objective definition. With the exception of concepts referring to sensations and metaphysical axioms, every concept can be objectively defined and communicated in terms of other concepts.[93] The exceptions, sensations and metaphysical axioms, require ostensive definitions:

To define the meaning of the color "blue," for instance, one must point to some blue objects to signify, in effect: "I mean this." . . . To define "existence," one would have to sweep one's arms around and say: I mean this."[94]

The Principle of Objectivity requires us to be the honest broker and messenger of that which exists and may occur.

Get your facts first, and then you can distort them as much as you please.

—Mark Twain

Pitfalls that Limit Objectivity

Both Accuracy and Objectivity are influenced and shaped by biases. Many people use the term Objectivity to mean freedom from bias.[95] This is incorrect; no judgments can ever be truly unbiased. Biases are inescapable, but their influence may be recognized and managed.[96] I will establish a clear line between the two principles by declaring that biases which limit accuracy are unconscious and the biases which limit objectivity are conscious and deliberate. Unconscious biases lead to misperceived data — a limiting factor of Accuracy, while conscious biases lead to the deliberate manipulation of data to support a pre-determined outcome — the limiting factor of Objectivity.

---

[93] Ayn Rand, *Introduction to Objectivist Epistemology* (New York: Mentor, 1979), 52-53.
[94] Rand, 53.
[95] Barzun and Graff, 174.
[96] Jack Davis, "Combating Mindset," *Studies in Intelligence*, 35, no. 4 (Winter 1991): 13-18.

Politicization. The Principle of Objectivity highlights the ambivalent relationship between the intelligence profession and its customers. On one hand, customers fear the possibility of politically "tainted" intelligence and adamantly support the primacy of independent and honest analyses. On the other hand, many customers also dislike their intelligence support because it has the potential to undercut policies, provoke public controversy, and reduce a decision-maker's options.[97]

Objectivity is a matter of integrity. Integrity dictates that intelligence professionals not pander to customers who want reinforcement of their beliefs and policies. Integrity also dictates that intelligence professionals freely and openly adjust assessments as new evidence provides additional pieces of the puzzle. Conclusions and hypotheses are always provisional, based on the best information available at the time.

Institutionalization. Any hypothesis that provides the basis for a management decision becomes institutionalized, and as such, directly influences how new data are perceived. Expectations tend to replace detached observation, shape official policies, and draw bureaucratic supporters. Roberta Wohlstetter, Amos Perlmutter, and Abraham Ben-Zvi point to instances when analysts have creatively interpreted data so that they would not "rock-the-boat." In the case of Japan's surprise attack on Pearl Harbor, U.S. Army and Navy planners focused their efforts on Atlantic and European affairs and tended to ignore signals from the Far East.[98] In a slightly different twist, the failure to predict Egypt's attack on Israel in October 1973 "was largely due to the intelligence community's disregard for warning indicators because they contradicted finished intelligence that minimized the possibility of war."[99]

Toward Performance Standards for Objectivity

Attaining a consistently acceptable level of Objectivity requires the disciplined use of a systematic method. Much of what we do to attain Accuracy also applies to Objectivity. The key is to focus on the judgments that arise during analysis.

The following is a list of fundamental activities that can lead to honoring the Principle of Objectivity.

1. Employ a systematic and documented analytical method to establish consistency of judgment.

2. Develop and record a list of competitive hypotheses that explain the target's behavior and decisions as viewed from the available evidence.

---

[97]Hans Heymann, Jr, "The Intelligence-Policy Relationship," *Studies in Intelligence*, 28, no. 4 (Winter 1984): 61-64.

[98] Wohlstetter, 701.

[99]Abraham Ben-Zvi, "Hindsight and Foresight: A Conceptual Framework for the Analysis of Surprise Attacks," *World Politics* 28 (April 1976): 386; Amos Perlmutter, "Israel's Fourth War, October 1973: Political and Military Misperceptions," *Orbis 19*, no. 2 (Summer 1975): 453.

3. Hypothesize the possibility of mistakes, accidents, and uncharacteristic irrationality.

4. List all evidence under the hypotheses that makes the appearance of the evidence plausible.

5. Record analysts' assumptions and values for consistent application when other evidence arises.

6. Review and reassess the documented line of reasoning to evaluate the acceptability of the conclusions after the receipt of new evidence.

7. Review documented assumptions and values for signs of conscious biased distortion due to personal or institutional self-interest.

THE PRINCIPLE OF USABILITY

What is Usability?

Usability pertains to product form rather than content. The form in which intelligence is communicated must render it ready for easy comprehension and immediate application. Intelligence is Usable if it is compatible with the customer's capabilities for receiving, manipulating, protecting, and storing the product. The intelligence service is responsible for knowing and working within the customer's format requirements. The Principle of Usability is a pre-requisite for addressing the Principle of Relevance.

Pitfalls that Limit Usability

Ignorance of the customer's needs, circumstances, and capabilities results in unusable products. This ignorance begins in the requirements definition stage, when we fail to ask several critical questions:

What level of classification can the customer handle?

Are control and storage requirements for compartmented information difficult to meet under the customer's circumstances?

Does the customer have the physical space available to secure the material?

What are the customer's data storage media capabilities and requirements? Are our products compatible with the customer's system and format?

What type of map is the customer using and what kind of coordinates do they work with?

What is the exact purpose of the product and how does this purpose affect our choice of presentation media?

Classic errors in format include the delivery of target coordinates in a format that is different from the customer's maps, and the delivery of imagery with annotations that block or obscure terrain that the customer needs to see. These problems would be avoided if the intelligence provider were to actively seek a fuller understanding of the customer's circumstances.

Pitfalls that Support Usability

Intelligence Writing. Intelligence must be in a format that directs the customer to the most significant information in the product without requiring additional manipulation or analysis. Unlike academic writing, intelligence presents the most important conclusions first, followed by a brief, but clear, concise, and coherent line of reasoning.[100] The language used and units of measure must be tailored to the customer and his use of the product.

Selection of Presentation Media. The presentation media greatly influence the usability of an intelligence product. Presentation media, to include the printed word, audio, television and film, and computers, are not neutral transmitters of information.

Through the filter of its technical and formal characteristics, a medium transforms information while communicating it, emphasizing particular aspects of events and ideas, deemphasizing others. As a consequence, each medium presents certain types of information easily and well, other types with difficulty or relatively poorly.[101]

Each medium has its own strong suit. In relation to the other media, the printed word is "extremely good at presenting a person's inner reflections;" audio increases information recall of dialogue and figurative language; television and film is "strong in presenting action, three-dimensional space, and several items of information at once;" and computer technology "has a great strength in allowing users to interact with complex systems having multiple, interacting, dynamic variables."[102] On the other hand, visual images distract attention from dialogue, leading to recall of the image but not of the dialogue. These influences shape what people learn and recall with regard to the particular sorts of information being presented. Intelligence organizations must consider these influences as the customer develops and refines intelligence requirements, so intelligence information is presented in the most understandable manner.

---

[100] Coherent writing "does not say one thing one place and something contradictory elsewhere, "and the conclusions logically follow from the data presented." Karl Pieragostini, Defense Intelligence College faculty member, "Assessing Intelligence," unpublished paper, 6.

[101] Patricia M. Greenfield, "Electronic Technologies, Education, and Cognitive Development," *Applications of Cognitive Psychology: Problem Solving, Education, and Computing,* Ed. Dale E. Berger and others (Hillsdale, New Jersey: Lawrence Erlbaum Associates, Publishers, 1987), 18.

[102] Greenfield, 18-19.

Toward Performance Standards for Usability

The following activities support the ability of intelligence professionals to honor the Principle of Usability:

1. Ask the customer for specific product form requirements, such as the presentation media, electronic data storage format, appropriate language and units of measure, and reference annotations.

2. Negotiate with the customer over the most appropriate product medium, instilling awareness of possible biases that spring from specific media characteristics.

3. Communicate the customer's specific product form requirements to all supporting intelligence production elements.

4. Provide, with the product, information that reminds the customer why he asked for the product.

5. Review all products before release to ensure product form meets the customer's specifications; proofread for simple mistakes, and ensure the writing is clear, concise, and coherent.

6. Provide classification, releasibility, and sanitization procedures.

THE PRINCIPLE OF RELEVANCE

What is Relevance?

Relevance is the "big-picture" principle; the fusion of customer requirements with the appropriate data and judgments about that data. To understand what makes intelligence relevant as opposed to merely accurate, objective, and usable, consider once again the process filter model illustrated in Figure 2. Before reaching the relevance filter, data and requirements are verified for accuracy and every attempt has been made to weed out deliberate attempts to skew judgment of that data. Furthermore, the product has been formatted in a manner consistent with the requirements of the customer. The relevance filter is the final screen, where all of the information that passed through the Accuracy, Objectivity, and Usability filters is tailored specifically for its applicability to the customer's requirements. At this point, potential consequences and the significance of the information are made explicit to the customer's circumstances.

Although all intelligence activities are conducted to answer documented requirements, analysts who understand the customer's circumstances may find it possible to increase the product's relevance by answering unstated — or unforeseen — questions that present themselves in the data and in the analysis. The attribute that Relevance brings to this discussion is pertinence.

Pitfalls that Limit Relevance

Processes and tasks that contribute to Relevance include those that ensure the Accuracy of data, the Objectivity of analysis, and the Usability of product format. All of the obstacles to these principles also limit the Relevance of the intelligence product.

Relevance has a vulnerability above and beyond those that affect Accuracy, Objectivity, and Usability. This vulnerability is the question of the analyst's ability to understand the nuances of the customer's circumstances. Distances between a supporting intelligence organization and the customer could literally be "worlds apart." Distance also could be a matter of culture, such as between uniformed services or between civilian and military agencies.

Unfortunately, we typically fail to ensure all of the customer's requirements are known in every office and activity that supports the satisfaction of a requirement. This failure begins at the point where a customer's need for intelligence is accepted; we fail to clarify and capture the nuances of the request — the customers' circumstances, language, and intentions.

Activities that Support Relevance

The nuances of customer circumstances, language, and intentions must be available at every point along the intelligence production cycle, driving every action we take. The clarified customer requirements also must be delivered with the product. This point is important — many customers forget the context behind their request for intelligence. In addition, providing the customer's requirement turns the customer into an active participant in the process, improving cooperation and communication between the customer and intelligence provider.

Toward Performance Standards for Relevance

The following activities support the ability of intelligence professionals to honor the Principle of Usability:

1. Highlight evidence and inferences that pertain to the customer's circumstances and intended use of the product.

2. Identify the significant consequences for the most acceptable and troubling hypotheses, in the context of operations and in relation to the customer's circumstances.

THE PRINCIPLE OF READINESS

What is Readiness?

Whether due to military contingencies or political challenges, sudden changes in customer requirements allow little reaction and recovery time. Maintaining our responsiveness under such circumstances requires considerable vigilance and foresight. We must anticipate not only the future decisions of our adversaries, but of our customers as well. Readiness is achieved only by prior and continuous preparation; the processes that help attain readiness have long lead times. Intelligence fails if it faces a new situation with a blank slate: We must develop competency with the prior investment of technical training and professional education, we must staff organizations with people who possess the appropriate mix of skills, and we must employ automated data handling and communication systems that facilitate our exploitation of data and its seamless delivery to our customers. None of this can be done overnight.

Intelligence managers continually assess what must be done to support potential requirements, craft concepts of operations, and adjust resources. Readiness requires anticipation and flexibility, but for the most part, intelligence organizations should be managed as if they were already "at war" — staffed, equipped, and delivering the type of services that operational customers value and need to maintain their own state of readiness.

Pitfalls that Limit Readiness

Bureaucratic competition for resources not only reduces what intelligence could provide; it also inhibits full cooperation among organizations that see themselves as competitors rather than teammates. Readiness-enhancing decisions inspire resistance when they entail the reorganization, reprioritization, or re-justification of resources. Achieving readiness is a fundamentally long-term project that requires a principled commitment on the part of senior leadership, and an accurate vision of future requirements.

Finally, bureaucracies influence Readiness through education and training standards. The quality of any intellectual product is a direct reflection of the education and training of the personnel that produced it. Education and training, therefore, are vital aspects of personnel preparation, and must be addressed by intelligence doctrine. The intellectual demands on intelligence analysis justify stringent personnel screening and selection standards, and subsequent education and training demands a considerable investment of time.

Students of tactical intelligence point to two problems with the preparation of military intelligence personnel that directly stems from specialization training. First, service-conducted training tends to prepare personnel for service-specific threats and activities. Second, military intelligence training concentrates on foreign or "red" threat information.[103]

---

[103] Colonel John Macartney, "Intelligence and Bureaucratic Politics," *Studies in Intelligence*, 33, No. 1 (Spring 1989): 20

To the dismay of their customers, military intelligence personnel are often ignorant of U.S., or "blue," information. This deficiency tends to spoil the credibility of intelligence personnel when, for example, an air analyst expresses ignorance of his or her own air force. Also, customers are increasingly demanding comparative assessments, "red versus blue."[104] Demands for comparative assessments significantly increase the amount of education and training that intelligence specialists need, and present a major obstacle to attaining Readiness.

Toward Performance Standards for Readiness

Managers of intelligence organizations support Readiness by performing the following verifiable actions:

1. Participate from the initial point when operations are contemplated or directed to identify appropriate intelligence capabilities and help the commander develop intelligence requirements.

2. Form intelligence infrastructure before assembly of forces; establish a Joint or Combined Intelligence Center with a single director of intelligence activities to unify intelligence efforts.

3. Provide mobility requirements to the mobility management system for all intelligence capabilities that may require movement.

   a. Ensure components, service elements, and supporting agencies provide Unified Command intelligence planners with the requisite movement data for capabilities that might deploy in a contingency or crisis situation.

   b. Review operational plans and update Unit Line Numbers and Type Unit Data Files so the movement of intelligence resources is integrated into the general deployment flow.

   c. Insert place holders in operations plans to reflect available non-organic intelligence capabilities.

4. Periodically exercise continuous operations by implementing 24-hour, 7-days-per-week, operational schedules.

5. Reprogram collection requirements for operational support at the onset of operational planning.

6. Employ intelligence systems that can receive and exchange intelligence information with supported and supporting organizations.

7. Conduct exercises of skills and operations that are not routinely performed.

8. Maintain intelligence liaison among supported and supporting organizations to bridge culture and language barriers between Services and allies.

---

[104] Macartney, 20.

9. Exercise routine arrangements for sharing intelligence with allies.

10. Ensure all intelligence centers are on the distribution list for operational reporting.

11. Encourage tactical reporting by distributing updated list of Essential Elements of Information (EEIs) and procedures for reporting on those EEIs in a timely manner.

12. Establish requirements for dedicated, standardized, and inter-operable communications circuits that can support the frequency, baud rate, and bandwidth requirements of the information systems that have been identified for movement.

THE PRINCIPLE OF TIMELINESS

What is Timeliness?

Philosophically, the consciousness of time is inseparable from that of change, and it is the element of change that gives time its significance.[105] Applied to intelligence, the significance of information is greatest when someone may act on it. Current information aids in the understanding of changes as they occur or as they may occur in the actionable future, allowing for the identification of opportunities for influence. The continual stream of change, however, ends earlier moments of opportunity and erodes the relevancy of intelligence products. Intelligence is not considered timely unless it is delivered when the information is still applicable to the decisions needed to resolve the operational problem.

Time inherently limits the effort that can be expended to achieve Accuracy, Objectivity, Usability, and Relevance. Timeliness dictates that intelligence must produce a product with the best available information, in full realization that the product may be considerably different if time permitted more data collection, verification, analysis, and formatting. Timeliness relates to Relevance in two ways: intelligence that cannot be delivered when the content is actionable loses relevancy to the customer. In addition, an increase in timeliness inherently increases the relevance of a product's content. The intelligence industry thus can legitimately operate on a "just-in-time" basis to deliver its products as the customer needs them.

Timeliness implies more than whether people and systems can produce and deliver before a requirement is overtaken by changing events. Timeliness requirements, based on the rate of change in the situation, define the upper limits of effort that can be spent in honoring the other Principles at any moment. Judgments regarding the quality of service, therefore, have meaning only when evaluated in light of the timeliness requirements that existed at the time the customer needed the intelligence product. Using a

---

[105] Milic Capek, "Time," *Dictionary of the History of Ideas: Studies in Selected Pivotal Ideas*, Vol IV, Ed. by Philip P. Wiener (New York: Charles Scribner's and Sons, 1973), 389.

motion picture analogy, time serves as the film that continuously runs, as we work frame-by-frame.

Figure 3 illustrates how the element of change gives Timeliness its significance in relation to the other principles. Within each frame (State of Readiness), a t0 and t1 mark the moment a requirement is levied to the moment a product is disseminated. The value (t1-t0) represents the amount of time that an intelligence organization at a specific state of readiness requires to deliver a product. This time value establishes what is technically and humanly possible under that frame's specific state of readiness. T1, T2, . . . Tn represent changing circumstances.

Toward Performance Standards for Timeliness

Activities for which performance may be verified:

1. Establish direct lines of communication with customers for developing and clarifying intelligence requirements.

2. Electrically communicate products when possible.

3. Minimize distance between production elements and the customer: Deploy a liaison intelligence/ communications element. This liaison element must be dedicated to the coordination of intelligence requirements and operation of transportable production capabilities.

4. Employ reconnaissance and surveillance systems whose operational, production, and dissemination processes can satisfy the timeliness requirements.

5. Establish courier network systems, with selected personnel and dedicated transportation, between production elements and customers to hand-deliver products that cannot be electronically communicated.

6. Inform customers of production and dissemination time for specific intelligence materials — help the customer factor intelligence production time into his or her own planning cycle.

7. Implement continuous operational schedules and plan for long-term resources sustainment.

8. Clarify the commander's view of operational requirements and activities needing intelligence support.

9. Assume that the commanders' requirements are valid.

10. Establish a Joint or Combined Intelligence Center to serve as the tasking control point.

11. Prioritize intelligence production by immediacy of objectives.

12. Establish liaison elements in each supporting and supported echelon.

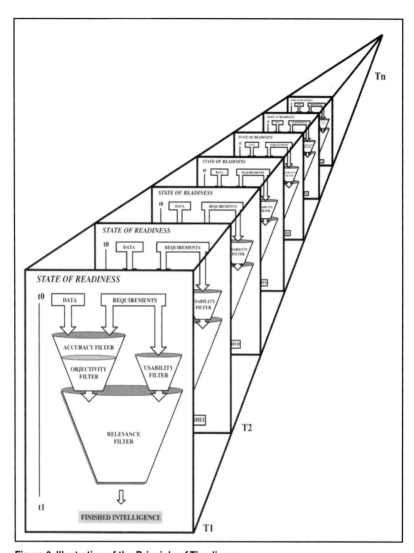

Figure 3. Illustration of the Principle of Timeliness.

THE FRAMEWORK FOR RELATING PROCESS TO PRINCIPLE

What is Timeliness?

Figures 4 and 5 group related questions that lead toward performance standards in the context of the principle that they support. With the ease of a checklist, this framework presents a big-picture view of the intelligence provision mission. From these lists, an intelligence provider can quickly identify and resolve potential problems without becoming distracted by a larger group of irrelevant issues. As a doctrine-based tool, this framework is extensible, universally open to continual development and refinement of processes within specific offices.

This framework provides a simple and direct method for resolving customer complaints and fixing problems before they contribute to an intelligence failure. An example of the manner in which an intelligence provider may use the framework for resolving customer complaints may be illustrated by a simple scenario: suppose several customers complain that their intelligence products were not relevant. The first step for the intelligence manager is to ask why the intelligence products were not relevant. In this case, the customers, who happen to be pilots, may declare that the scale of the imagery was too large for use in studying their ingress and egress routes to their assigned targets.[106] At this point, the intelligence provider would refer to the Usability list for actions that could have prevented this problem. In this case, the intelligence manager should recognize that several processes need attention not only to correct the pilot's complaint, but also to ensure that customers with similar format requirements are properly supported. For example, additional emphasis must be placed on asking the customer for specific product form requirements, communicating the customers' product form requirements to all supporting production elements, and reviewing the products before dissemination to ensure they meet the customers' stated requirements.

---

[106] This incident occurred, in the author's experience, during Operation PROVIDE COMFORT and demonstrated the value of deploying a liaison officer from the production facility to work directly with the consumers.

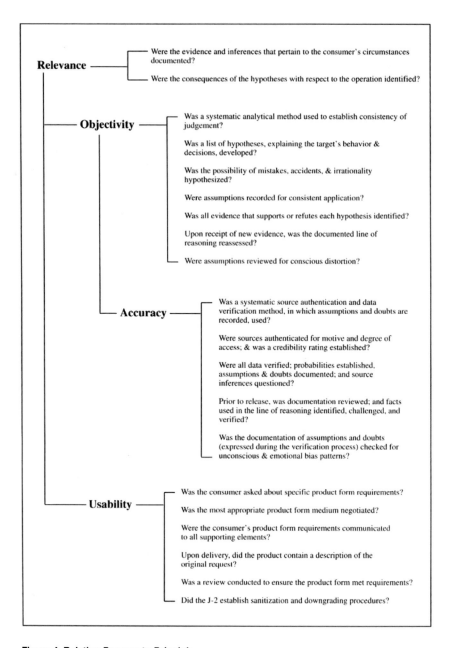

Relevance
- Were the evidence and inferences that pertain to the consumer's circumstances documented?
- Were the consequences of the hypotheses with respect to the operation identified?

Objectivity
- Was a systematic analytical method used to establish consistency of judgement?
- Was a list of hypotheses, explaining the target's behavior & decisions, developed?
- Was the possibility of mistakes, accidents, & irrationality hypothesized?
- Were assumptions recorded for consistent application?
- Was all evidence that supports or refutes each hypothesis identified?
- Upon receipt of new evidence, was the documented line of reasoning reassessed?
- Were assumptions reviewed for conscious distortion?

Accuracy
- Was a systematic source authentication and data verification method, in which assumptions and doubts are recorded, used?
- Were sources authenticated for motive and degree of access; & was a credibility rating established?
- Were all data verified; probabilities established, assumptions & doubts documented; and source inferences questioned?
- Prior to release, was documentation reviewed; and facts used in the line of reasoning identified, challenged, and verified?
- Was the documentation of assumptions and doubts (expressed during the verification process) checked for unconscious & emotional bias patterns?

Usability
- Was the consumer asked about specific product form requirements?
- Was the most appropriate product form medium negotiated?
- Were the consumer's product form requirements communicated to all supporting elements?
- Upon delivery, did the product contain a description of the original request?
- Was a review conducted to ensure the product form met requirements?
- Did the J-2 establish sanitization and downgrading procedures?

Figure 4. Relating Process to Principle.

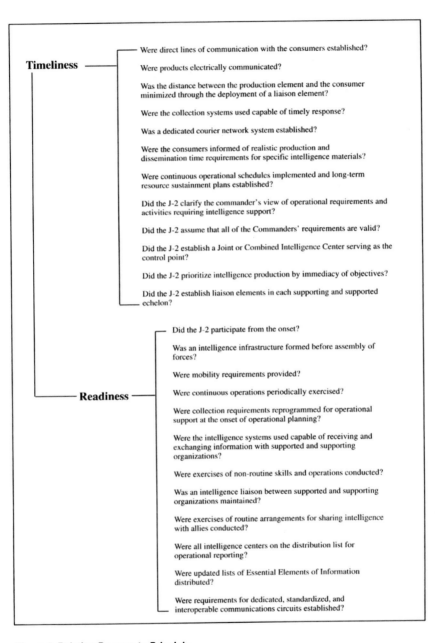

Timeliness

- Were direct lines of communication with the consumers established?
- Were products electrically communicated?
- Was the distance between the production element and the consumer minimized through the deployment of a liaison element?
- Were the collection systems used capable of timely response?
- Was a dedicated courier network system established?
- Were the consumers informed of realistic production and dissemination time requirements for specific intelligence materials?
- Were continuous operational schedules implemented and long-term resource sustainment plans established?
- Did the J-2 clarify the commander's view of operational requirements and activities requiring intelligence support?
- Did the J-2 assume that all of the Commanders' requirements are valid?
- Did the J-2 establish a Joint or Combined Intelligence Center serving as the control point?
- Did the J-2 prioritize intelligence production by immediacy of objectives?
- Did the J-2 establish liaison elements in each supporting and supported echelon?

Readiness

- Did the J-2 participate from the onset?
- Was an intelligence infrastructure formed before assembly of forces?
- Were mobility requirements provided?
- Were continuous operations periodically exercised?
- Were collection requirements reprogrammed for operational support at the onset of operational planning?
- Were the intelligence systems used capable of receiving and exchanging information with supported and supporting organizations?
- Were exercises of non-routine skills and operations conducted?
- Was an intelligence liaison between supported and supporting organizations maintained?
- Were exercises of routine arrangements for sharing intelligence with allies conducted?
- Were all intelligence centers on the distribution list for operational reporting?
- Were updated lists of Essential Elements of Information distributed?
- Were requirements for dedicated, standardized, and interoperable communications circuits established?

Figure 5. Relating Process to Principle.

SUMMARY AND CONCLUSIONS

Process improvement efforts have had limited success within the intelligence service. Many people attribute this failure to cultural resistance — the belief that government bureaucracies insulate themselves from the consequences of poor management. Certainly, the Intelligence Community is susceptible to this charge: it restricts information flow with stringent security compartmentation, lacks pressure from stockholders and competition, and fails to provide meaningful incentives for conscientious resource management. In addition, intelligence products are not commodities that can be objectively weighed and measured for quality or value. Many managers of intelligence activities consider the judgment of quality is simply beyond their control, having learned to accept that there will be as many measures of quality as there are customers.

The goal of this paper has been to demonstrate that it is possible to define an unambiguous, logical model for intelligence provision, and that such a model, or doctrine, would sharpen our focus on what our customers value. Our customers' values must be our values; doctrine built on these values provides the basis of principled leadership and service. The systematic value-based focus, with the help of a simple process-to-principle framework, should help us identify and overcome specific preventable weaknesses in intelligence support.

The illustrative performance standards identified in this paper encompass the vast breadth of activities needed to conduct an intelligence support service. The benefits of a doctrinal framework for performance standards would be magnified greatly if intelligence providers tailor the standards in the framework to the responsibilities and goals of their own offices. In this manner, doctrine becomes a managerial tool relevant for day-to-day use and a systematic path for process improvement initiatives.

OPENING WINDOWS OF OPPORTUNITY:
THE NEED FOR OPPORTUNITY-BASED WARNING

Stewart C. Eales

(Originally published in Jan Goldman's compiled JMIC Occasional Paper Number Eight, Dangerous Assumption: Preparing the U.S. Intelligence Warning System for the New Millennium June 2000.)

The young woman gazed attentively across the table at the old lady hovering over a crystal ball. The elderly gypsy looked up slowly and in a hushed, mysterious, tone said, you will meet a tall, dark stranger who will change your life. The young woman, a member of the U.S. warning community, instantly perceived a potential threat and decided she would purchase a gun.

—Anonymous DoD employee

The U.S. strategic warning community concentrates its efforts entirely on threat-based warnings, and ignores the more positive form of the process: opportunity-based warning. Living with the legacy of Pearl Harbor, the community dedicates extensive collection and analytical resources to the identification of potential enemies who demonstrate the capability and intent to harm American citizens or interests. This tendency to focus entirely on the dangers of the world warps the way in which warning analysts evaluate the future. Their preconception with the U.S. as a victim shapes their warnings to evoke a deterrent response, thus condemning decisionmakers to a reactive policymaking process.

The consequences of this mentality are manifest in the likely reaction of the woman in the story to any encounter with a tall, dark man. Because she is primed by her perceptions to see only the potential threat, and fails to recognize an opportunity which may change her life for the better, she will probably greet the man with a gun in her hand. If the U.S. warning community is to remain relevant in a rapidly changing world it must pursue a more balanced approach to warning analysis, expanding its efforts to include responsible strategic warning of opportunity.

Warning, as it is employed today, is a negatively oriented process practiced within a system populated by cynics. It is defined as "a process of communicating judgments about threats to U.S. security or policy interests to decisionmakers."[107] The objectives of the warning process, as implied by this definition, are (1) to prevent strategic surprise and (2) to insure timely, accurate action by decisionmakers which facilitates the "deterrence, avoidance, or containment of harm."[108] A review of the terminology used in these and other professional commentaries on the subject — words like "threat," "danger," "harm,"

---

[107] Mary McCarthy, "The National Warning System: Striving for an Elusive Goal," *Defense Intelligence Journal* 3, no. 1 (Spring1994): 5.

[108] John F. McCreary, "Warning Cycles," *Studies in Intelligence* 27, no. 3 (Fall 1983): 7.

"war," "prevent," "avoid," "limit" and "deter" — reveals the fundamentally negative nature of warning in its current form. One standard textbook used to teach military professionals about the missions, methods, and structure of the national Intelligence Community uses the word "threat" fourteen times in the first three pages of its chapter on warning intelligence. The text's single, fleeting reference to the Intelligence Community s role in "promoting a positive social and economic environment for all people in the world," is symptomatic of its fundamental message that warning is about being safe.[109]

The strategic warning system was meant to insure the nation's safety, and was specifically designed to identify and close windows of vulnerability. Its threat-based orientation was established on the foundation of Pearl Harbor, [which] drove the idea of surprise attack so deeply into the national psyche that 'Pearl Harbor' became almost a generic term for any sneak attack.... After World War II, it was generally agreed that any future attack almost certainly would be in the nature of a surprise. Therefore the nation must be alert.[110]

This mentality was reinforced by experiences such as the Berlin Blockade, the North Korean invasion of South Korea, and the Tet Offensive by the Viet Cong. All involved some unpleasant strategic surprise with significant, harmful consequences for American citizens or interests, and implied some failure of the U.S. intelligence system.

The Warning Community's initial charter, influenced by these memories, was limited to monitoring for the indications of military mobilization which would presage an armed confrontation.[111] This charter was drafted in a bipolar world, where every conflict between a communist and non-communist nation had potential Great-Power implications. For this reason the original warning structure was not tailored to identify threats, (or opportunities) which had no direct correlation to the Cold War. As a result, U.S. decisionmakers were unprepared to deal with a series of adverse incidents over the next three decades.

Each of the Congressional committees assigned to review these warning "failures" (among them the 1973 Arab-Israeli War, India's first nuclear test, and the fall of the Shah in Iran), raised serious questions about the system's ability to provide leaders with adequate warning of potential threats to U.S. interests. What usually followed was a reorganization of the system to "address deficiencies, create structures, and channel resources to better position intelligence agencies to provide timely strategic warning."[112] Such changes were purely institutional in nature, addressing the forms of warning without adequately considering its comprehensive substance. One of the more recent "review and revise" processes, initiated by Director of Central Intelligence Robert Gates in 1992, was no different in this respect. Its contribution was the enactment of "the most comprehensive plan to date for restructuring the Community to enhance its ability to warn."[113] As a result,

---

[109] Defense Intelligence Agency, *National Foreign Intelligence Community* (NFIC) *Course Textbook* (Washington, DC: Joint Military Intelligence Training Center, September 1996), 12/1-12/3).

[110] Harold P. Ford, *Estimative Intelligence: The Purpose and Problems of National Intelligence Estimating*, (Lanham, MD: University Press of America Inc., 1993), 26.

[111] McCarthy, 6.

[112] McCarthy, 6.

today's strategic warning network, while very different in structure from its original form, is still conceptually tied to its initial Cold War charter. It remains a relatively skeptical, threat-oriented system dedicated to the elusive goal of preventing surprise.

The warning system has failed to grow beyond its threat-based origins because no one with authority has challenged the basic concept of warning, or explored its potential applications. The threat-based definitions and terminology are well established among warning professionals. The threat-oriented mission has been consistently endorsed by Presidents, members of Congress, and intelligence leaders alike. Congress' 1992 Intelligence Authorization Act declared that "the Intelligence Community's highest priority is warning of threats to U.S. interests worldwide."[114] The only other political authority which might have called for a change — the American public — has either accepted or ignored the warning system because threat-based warning does not challenge established political or cultural sensitivities. In truth, it conforms to the American democratic bias because it takes no action which is not directly provoked by a clearly perceivable threat to U.S. interests. Thus, there is political support for, and tacit social acceptance of, a warning system that is purely responsive in nature and defensive in posture.

THE VIEW FROM A NEW WINDOW

The U.S. strategic warning community needs to embrace a more balanced approach to warning. Just as the Chinese ideograph for crisis reflects aspects of both danger and opportunity, so too must warning. The effective employment of opportunity-based warning will require some fundamental changes in the way warning analysts and their customers think, communicate, and act. These changes will not be easy to initiate, as they involve long-standing analytical practices and decisionmaking processes. The scope of the change is so great that it will require the cooperative efforts of both groups to make it work. It will also require the establishment of clearly defined operating parameters to make it acceptable to the democratic sensitivities of the American public. Accomplishing these goals will dramatically expand the influence of warning intelligence, and should enable decisionmakers to proactively advance U.S. interests rather than merely defending them.

Warning professionals must somehow be taught to integrate their analytical skills with the comprehensive vision of a diplomat and the calculating perception of an investment banker if they are to be effective at producing opportunity-based warning. They must learn to recognize what Steven Mann, a career foreign service officer, has called the "ripeness" of a situation.[115] This implies having both the breadth of vision and the depth of perception to anticipate a period when the variables in a potentially profitable situation are likely to come together — a window of opportunity. Mann was specifically addressing the issue from a diplomatic perspective, but it is not difficult to see how his observations

---

[113] McCarthy, 7.

[114] U.S. Congress, House Permanent Select Committee on Intelligence, *Intelligence Authorization Act for Fiscal Year* 1992, 102d Congress, 1st session, 1991, House Report 102-165, Part I.

[115] Steven Mann, "Chaos Theory and Strategic Thought," *Parameters* 22, no. 3(Autumn 1992), 61.

could apply to warning scenarios. Warning analysts must learn to think more like diplomats, focusing on the "big picture" while retaining an appreciation for relevant nuances, in order to anticipate strategic opportunities.

Professional training programs for analysts must also promote the development of an intellectual savvy similar to that of a Wall Street investment banker, who is always seeking a profitable opportunity in the marketplace. Economic professionals use available information and projected trends to recommend capital investments to their customers. Such a recommendation will reflect a "sense" of the dynamic markets, as well as assessments which balance cost and risk with expected return. Warning professionals need to adopt this canny, calculating mentality in their pursuit of strategic opportunities.

They must treat decisionmakers like investors, with political credibility as the currency at stake and the advancement of U.S. interests as the expected return. Warning analysts must change the way they talk about warning. The negative terminology and definitions must be revised to make the overall concept of warning more impartial. One commercial provider of corporate intelligence clearly grasped this concept in its advertising by carefully counterbalancing risk management with opportunity analysis. *Strategic Forecasting's* advertisement states that its analysis "might include warnings against establishing business ties at a particular time, or arguments for entering certain markets." It certifies that its "emphasis is on opportunities as well as risks."[116] Warning analysts need to speak in a similarly balanced manner about risks and opportunities when briefing leaders about future developments.

Decisionmakers are a part of the warning community, and must also change if they are to make effective use of opportunity-based warning. Specifically, they will have to modify the way in which they make strategic decisions. Threat-based warning only requires that a decisionmaker respond to a developing situation. The leader who wishes to make profitable use of both threat- and opportunity-based warning will have to be both prescient and proactive. Decisions will correspond to a series of envisioned landmarks in a dynamic scenario rather than simple indicators in a linear chain of events.

For this reason, those making decisions will not be looking for a simple cause-and-effect progression. Instead they will be seeking "a more timely and accurate recognition of emerging trends, particularly those that are off the expected, extrapolated future...." Their goal will be to direct "a more rapid reaction to these emerging trends, whether to seize opportunities or to mitigate risk."[117] In either instance, no warning is complete until action has been taken or purposefully deferred.

The strategic warning system is not all that will have to change. It will be necessary to persuade the American people that an opportunity-based policy process is compatible

---

[116] Political Risk and Opportunity Assessment, Internet advertisement on the home page of Strategic Forecasting, URL:<www.stratfor.com/services/polirisk>, accessed 27 February 1997.

[117] Michael F. Oppeheimer, *Scenarios: Their Construction and Use*, Monograph prepared for the Defense Intelligence Agency (New York: UnterMatrix Group, September 1994), 1.

with their perceptions of basic democratic principles. This will require a clear definition of opportunity-based warning which specifies both procedural methods and objectives. It will also require a clarification of associated terminology to neutralize potentially "loaded" words or phrases. Having laid this foundation it will then be necessary to address specific concerns which arise when the government moves to take advantage of opportunity-based warning.

The Doolittle Report, submitted to President Eisenhower in 1954, demonstrated an acute appreciation of how important public perception is to proactive intelligence operations. Promoting expanded covert operations against the Soviet Union at the height of the Cold War, the committee observed:

> It is now clear that we are facing an implacable enemy [the U.S.S.R.] whose avowed objective is world domination by whatever means and at whatever cost. There are norules in such a game. Hitherto acceptable norms of human conduct do not apply. If the U.S. is to survive, long-standing American concepts of "fair play" must be reconsidered. We must develop effective espionage and counter-espionage services. We must learn to subvert, sabotage and destroy our enemies by more clear, more sophisticated and more effective methods than those used against us. It *may become necessary that the American people be made acquainted with, understand and support this fundamentally repugnant philosophy.*[118]

Even in a time when the threat was clearly defined there was an innate hesitation to engage in active measures against a dedicated opponent. In a nation where the convention of "never start a fight, but always finish one" has been a precept handed down over generations, the public has difficulty reconciling its ethics with the secrecy and duplicity of intelligence work. In a world less threatening, and yet more unstable, it is even more vital to address the American concept of "fair play" when justifying the need for proactive intelligence measures.

The definitions of threat-based warning proposed by Mary McCarthy and John McCreary (and used earlier in this paper), provide a solid framework for the definition of opportunity-based warning: *Opportunity-based warning is the process of communicating judgments about opportunities which may advance U.S. security or policy interests to decisionmakers. Such communications must be received and understood in order for leaders to take action that can encourage, enhance, or focus the opportunity for the greatest strategic advantage.* This definition states the methods and objectives associated with opportunity-based warning, highlighting both the similarities and the differences between the two warning types.

Inflammatory language was purposefully excluded from the definition. However, its proactive tone may elicit impressions — embodied in words like predatory, opportunistic,

---

[118] Loch K. Johnson, *Secret Agencies: U.S. Intelligence in a Hostile World* (New Haven, CT: Yale University Press, 1996), 138.

and manipulatory — which are negative in context. It is vital to clearly distinguish between seizing an opportunity and being opportunistic. Americans despise a predator, and are inherently suspicious of any interaction in which the strong appear to be preying on the weak. They also tend to oppose unilateral American involvement in another nation's internal affairs, unless there is a perceivable threat to U.S. interests. There is, therefore, a tendency to confuse the seizing of a strategic opportunity with "opportunism."

Advancing U.S. interests does not have to be predatory in nature, and "a policy of 'improving' the state's power is not to be confused with territorial expansion, which is the hallmark of dangerous and disruptive imperialist powers."[119] Some U.S. interests, such as those reflecting domestic issues like education, the environment, and employment, can be advanced with no impact on other nations. Others, involving broader issues like regional peace and economic stability of the Middle East, can actually benefit everyone involved to some degree.

Having said that, there is a time to be predatory in our pursuit of national interests. It is vital that a stated policy be in place to determine when this time has come. The democratic prescription against taking advantage of another nation's weaknesses is not enforced when dealing with an identified enemy. The Reagan Administration's military assistance to the Afghan Mujahedin in the early 1980s was not grounded in any love for the rebels. It was perceived to be the best way to strike at the Soviet Union, advancing our national interests against our ideological enemy and primary competitor for global superiority. It is essential that a clear distinction be drawn between opponents and enemies. With one we compete for advantage; the other we contest for dominance and survival. By acknowledging this distinction, U.S. policymakers can more accurately define whether opportunities will be pursued in a benign or predatory fashion.

OPENING WINDOWS OF OPPORTUNITY

We have no eternal allies and we have no perpetual enemies. Our interests are eternal and perpetual, and those interests it is our duty to follow.

—Lord Palmerston, 1848

Opportunity-based warning can work. It is already being demonstrated at the tactical level in the form of Intelligence Preparation of the Battlespace (IPB). IPB is an "analytical methodology employed to reduce uncertainties concerning the enemy, environment, and terrain for all types of operations."[120] Among the most important characteristics of this methodology are its emphasis on getting the decisionmaker directly involved in the intelligence process, providing a timeline of critical decision points, and clearly defining the range of action options. IPB, like warning, is designed to stimulate actions which

---

[119] Michael Roskin, National Interest: From Abstraction to Strategy, *Parameters* 24, no. 4 (Winter 1994-95): 7.

[120] Joint Chiefs of Staff, Joint Publication 2-01, *Joint Intelligence Support to Military Operations* (Washington, DC: GPO, March 21, 1996), GL-11.

eliminate a threat or exploit an opportunity. Its ability to serve both warning functions is what makes it an essential component of battlespace dominance, enabling the field commander to seize the initiative, manage the action, and retain the advantage in a conflict.

Non-Governmental Organizations (NGOs) are using a different approach to balanced warning analysis to determine where their efforts can be most productive. This is particularly useful in any region where there is, or may soon be, a serious conflict. Beyond measuring the cost of operations and threat to staff in the field, an NGO must measure the opportunities which a conflict may afford. As Hugo Slim, Director of the Complex Emergencies Program at Oxford Brookes University, observed:

> There may not be many, but the ones there are may surprise NGOs and give them a useful starting point for an emergency programme. For example, some conflicts create new levels of purpose and social cohesion in particular groups. Conflict can bring people together as well as divide them, accelerating certain social and economic activities by mobilizing society in a common cause. Such impetus can be good for relief and development programming.[121]

Such a process can be good for American interests as well. A warning system which anticipates the potentially positive elements in a conflict will make it easier for leaders to focus military and diplomatic efforts to influence that conflict. Such an effort could isolate the conflict or, at least, focus it in such a way as to eventually build a stronger society and increase long-term stability. Attempting to apply processes like IPB or the NGO model at the strategic level would be much more complex given the wider range of variables and broader field of engagement in the national policy arena. It would involve the construction of very detailed scenarios using extensive intelligence from a variety of databases. The challenge associated with this type of effort goes beyond the conceptual transition from threat-based to opportunity-based warning. It involves a fundamental change in the structure of the warning system.

The current warning system is dedicated to defending political and military interests. Even if it was already capable of producing opportunity-based warning it would only do so for a narrow field of expertise. Because there is great flexibility in the way any opportunity can be approached, there is a corresponding requirement for a broader array of specialized intelligence to support such a decision. Unfortunately, many elements of national policy (economics, the environment, and domestic interests) are not addressed by the current system.

An expanded network of warning specialists with technical expertise in areas such as trade, finance, economics, the environment, and education will have to be developed. These technical warning professionals would represent their respective agencies and departments in an expanded National Intelligence Warning System. Once in place, this

---

[121] Hugo Slim, "Planning Between Danger and Opportunity: NGO Situation Analysis in Conflict Related Emergencies," training presentations given at two NGO seminars in March and November 1995, posted on the Internet 2 May 1996, URL: <131.111.106.147/freps/fr005.htm>, accessed 27 February 1997.

comprehensive system of experts would be well positioned to produce tailored assessments which reflect both threat and opportunity. These assessments, strategic IPBs, would give decisionmakers a better appreciation of potential threats and opportunities, and enhance their ability to take appropriate actions.

BROKEN WINDOWS

There is an element of risk associated with any proactive venture, and this is true of opportunity-based warning. Some of the problems are institutional in nature and others are simply the result of a chaotic world. As Assistant Secretary of State, Toby Gaty notes:

[There is risk associated with] missed or unexploited opportunities to advance our national agenda. If we fail to recognize such opportunities, or pursue them with ill-founded and misguided strategies, we can exacerbate existing dangers or create new ones.[122]

To acknowledge these risks and problems is the first step in solving them or at least minimizing their impact on the warning process. Any system which provides warning of both opportunity and threat may find itself subject to conflicting interests. The demand for threat warning may end up competing with a personal and institutional preference for opportunity-based warning. Threat warning is subject to the "warning paradox," which states that, when successful, warning precludes the very threat it originally forecast. This means that analysts providing warning of a potential threat are likely to be blamed for being wrong (or even partially wrong), and stand very little chance of being recognized for being right. Not only is this demoralizing for the individual analyst, it prevents the warning system as a whole from building a record of success which would give it credibility. Opportunity-based warning is not subject to the warning paradox, and readily reflects the analyst's contribution to decisive action. There is a significant risk that analysts, if given a choice, will focus on the more "profitable" opportunity-based option. This would be dangerous and irresponsible. Threat warning and the protection of national interests has rightly been identified as the Intelligence Community's highest priority, and must be maintained as such.

Opportunity-based warning lends itself to abuse by those with hidden agendas. Personal ambition, economic motivation, and power politics all influence policymaking to some extent. However, strategic action resulting from warning of opportunity is particularly vulnerable to such misdirection. The number of variables and potential futures associated with any given scenario permit an unprincipled or Machiavellian manipulation of strategic policy to achieve personal objectives. Such action, even if it did not violate the letter of constitutional or federal law, would probably create a breach in the public trust and undermine the legitimacy of the associated institutions.

---

[122] U.S. Congress, House Permanent Select Committee on Intelligence, *IC21: Intelligence Community in the 21st Century*, Staff Study, 104th Congress, 1996, 246.

Opportunity-based warning is vulnerable to unanticipated consequences. This is true even when the system works properly. The Reagan Administration, engaged in what it saw as an ideological war with the Soviet Union, launched a campaign of anti-Soviet rhetoric in March 1983. Instituted at a time when the Soviets were fighting in Afghanistan and expanding their influence in Central America, the campaign was designed to demonstrate increased American commitment to democracy around the world. An already paranoid Soviet leadership misread President Reagan's denunciations, his support for development of the Strategic Defense Initiative, and his drive to deploy medium range ballistic missiles in Europe. Given their preconceptions, they read the events as indicators of an impending preemptive nuclear strike by the U.S.

When NATO forces in Europe commenced a scheduled command post exercise (code-named Able Archer) to practice nuclear release procedures in November 1983, the Soviet intelligence services and military prepared for war.[123] When the President learned how close the two countries had come to an unintended nuclear exchange he was shocked and immediately became more conciliatory in his approach toward the Soviets. A few days after the end of the exercise he wrote in his diary, I feel the Soviets are...so paranoid about being attacked that without in any way being soft on them, we ought to tell them no one here has any intention of doing anything like that."[124] A campaign of rhetoric designed to send a message had broadcast the wrong one at a bad time, and nearly led to an unintended nuclear war.

Despite the potential problems associated with opportunity-based warning, it is a concept whose time has come. Threat-based warning must remain the highest priority of the Intelligence Community, but it must not be the only form of warning which leaders receive. The strategic warning community needs to reevaluate the scope of its mission and expand its charter to include opportunity-based warning. While there are many challenges associated with such an effort, there are many compelling benefits as well. It is time to start methodically advancing our national interests rather than merely defending them.

---

[123] Christopher Andrew, *For the President's Eyes Only* (New York: HarperCollins Publishers, Inc, 1995), 471-477.

[124] Andrew, 476.

TEACHING VISION

Mark G. Marshall

(Originally Published in JMIC Occasional Paper Number Five, A Flourishing Craft: Teaching Intelligence Studies, June 1999, 57-84.)

A CHALLENGE

Looking for a teaching challenge? Try conveying the finer points of Imagery Intelligence analysis to a class of adults educated in a Western culture, most of whom work in a military hierarchy, and all of whom have been indoctrinated in intelligence production as a sequential assembly line.[125] As a basis for intelligence analysis, visual evidence is distinct from the descriptive evidence and the linear processes with which students are most familiar. The art of image visualization requires distinct training for professional interpreters, distinct education for conventional analysts who would appreciate visual evidence, and distinct mentoring for exceptionally visual students.

Before describing how image teachers can answer the challenge, the author will first illustrate the nature and magnitude of the problem by highlighting the parallel patterns[126] of diversity and domination that run through human cognition, within human culture, and between modes of intelligence evidence.

PART I
PATTERNS OF DIVERSITY AND DOMINATION

Cognitive Diversity

Could there be a more fundamental place to begin an investigation of the profession of "Intelligence" than intellect itself? Considering the similarity between the results of human intelligence and the objectives of organizational intelligence, the latter can reasonably be expected to learn much from the former.

A Pair. The human mind operates in combinations of two distinct modes of thinking. Our ability to comprehend the pictures in this article depends on the intellectual dimension that uses wholeness, simultaneity and synthesis. The other mental mode is characterized by sequence, analysis and abstraction, and dominates when one reads this line of text. This diversity of intellect is so fundamental to human thought it has a neurobiological basis and an association with the two hemispheres of the brain.[127]

---

[125] See Christopher Andrew's description of the intelligence assembly line in *For the President's Eyes Only*, 426.

[126] Pattern recognition is one of the favorite tricks in image research. See William A. Kennedy and Mark G. Marshall, "A Peek at the French Missile Complex." *Bulletin of the Atomic Scientists* 45, no. 7 (September 1989): 21-22.

Except for varying opinions among psychologists about the complexity of this asymmetry and how best to describe it,[128] the distinction between the two styles and the neurobiological basis is noncontroversial. Harvard psychologist Stephen M. Kosslyn illustrates the consensus by writing "Probably the least controversial claim in neuropsychology is that the left hemisphere is critical in language production and comprehension...[and] that the right hemisphere plays a special role in navigation."[129]

Psychologists refer to this asymmetry variously as two "modes," "styles," or "subsystems."[130] Words adequately describe subsystems associated with the left hemisphere, but aptitude associated with the right hemisphere "is not so easy to label."[131] Because words cannot adequately describe a nonverbal dimension, many authors resort to using antonyms (See Table 1 **Efforts to Label the Asymmetry**). Interestingly, the "not left" dimension of the Table represents survival aptitudes.

Left	:	Not Left
verbal	:	nonverbal
sequential	:	simultaneous
serial	:	parallel
temporal	:	spatial
digital	:	analog
logical	:	Gestalt
analytical	:	synthetic
rational	:	intuitive
local	:	global
detailed	:	holistic

Table 1. Efforts to Label the Asymmetry

Sources: David A. Kolb, Experiential Learning: Experience as The Source of Learning and Development (Englewood Cliffs, NJ: Prentice-Hall, Inc., 1984), 48-49; Restak, 216-217; Springer and Deutsch, 76, 129, 195, 272; Kosslyn, Image and Brain, 295-298; Ornstein, 37.

Domination. Psychologists also recognize that the mental style favoring sequence thoroughly dominates the synthesizing dimension. Michael S. Gazzaniga and Joseph E.

---

[127] Leonard Shlain, *The Alphabet Versus the Goddess: The Conflict Between Word and Image* (New York: Viking, 1998), 5, 17-23; Sandra Blakeslee, "New Theories of Depression Focus on Brain's Two Sides," New York Times, 19 January 1999, URL <http://nytimes.com/library/national/science/011999sci-brain.html>, accessed 1 March 1999.

[128] For several qualifiers see Richard B. Ivry and Lynn C. Robertson, *The Two Sides of Perception* (Cambridge, Massachusetts: Massachusetts Institute of Technology (MIT) Press, 1998), 2, 33, 35, 126.

[129] Stephen M. Kosslyn, *Image and Brain:The Resolution of the Imagery Debate*, 1st paper ed. (Cambridge, Massachusetts: The MIT Press, 1996), 179.

[130] Quotes from Sally P. Springer and Georg Deutsch, Left Brain, Right Brain, 4th ed. (New York: W.H. Freeman and Company, 1993), 76, 68, 274; David Galin quoted in Richard M. Restak, *The Brain: The Last Frontier* (New York: Doubleday & Co., Inc., 1979), 199; Kosslyn, *Image and Brain*, 40-42; Robert E. Ornstein, *The Psychology of Consciousness*, 2d ed. (New York: Harcourt Brace Jovanovich, Inc., 1977), 26.

[131] Springer and Deutsch, 17.

LeDoux remark that when first demonstrated, "the view that the mute [right] hemisphere was also deserving of conscious status was widely criticized and generally rejected."[132] Accordingly, psychologists Sally P. Springer and Georg Deutsch characterize the right side of the brain as the "neglected hemisphere."[133]

(Western) Culture

Culture exerts such strong influence on thinking it may be regarded as a corporate brain. Because the physiology of childbirth limits the size of a baby's skull, the human brain arrives in the world only partially formed. To name the pieces of intellect added after birth, author Leonard Shlain uses the word "culture."[134] Because thinking and learning result in a physical realignment of our neurons, Shlain's point is no exaggeration. It is a bad joke among educators that every teacher is a brain surgeon.

A Pair. In a 1959 essay, Charles Percy Snow described the characteristics of two cultures between which, he wrote, "the intellectual life of the whole of Western society is increasingly split." In Snow's characterization, a "traditional" culture lacked foresight, was slow to change, and turned its back on art while a "natural" culture was always reaching, did not hesitate to cut across mental patterns, and had a taste for color photography. Snow's description of this pair parallels the dimensions of cognitive diversity, and even Snow speculated that the basis for this diversity could include different kinds of mental activity. [135]

Domination. Paralleling the mental model, traditional Western culture thoroughly dominates natural culture. One of the most important aspects of this domination is the control conventional thinking exerts over the education systems that are rewiring the corporate brain. Mathematician Keith Devlin writes

> Western culture is dominated by an approach to knowledge that goes back to Plato, and to his teacher, Socrates. Their love of mathematics and of precise definitions led them to discount any human talent, ability, activity, or skill that could not be defined and explained and subjected to rational argument.

Devlin illustrates with the example of the German academy that "introduced the distinction between the natural sciences (Naturwissenschaften) and the humanities (Geisteswissenschaften) and gave the former higher status."[136] Shlain draws the mental parallel by describing how introducing a child into "alphabet arcana numbs her to the fact that she supplants all-at-once gestalt perception with a new, unnatural, highly abstract one-at-a-time cognition."[137]

---

[132] Michael S. Gazzaniga and Joseph E. LeDoux, *The Integrated Mind* (New York: Plenum Press, 1978), 5.

[133] Springer and Deutsch, 13.

[134] Shlain, 12-13.

[135] Charles Percy Snow, *The Two Cultures and the Scientific Revolution* (New York: Cambridge University Press, 1959), 2-8, 10, 12, 14, 15, 17, 23, 47.

[136] Keith Devlin, *Goodbye, Descartes: The End of Logic and the Search for a New Cosmology of the Mind* (New York: John Wiley & Sons, Inc., 1997), 102, 182.

The style of traditional Western education enforces an objectivism[138] that separates the student from the topic and results in a kind of cultural blindness. C.P. Snow writes that it is as though "over an immense range of intellectual experience, a whole group was tone deaf. Except that this tone-deafness doesn't come by nature, but by training, or rather the absence of training."[139] Ten years later, Berkeley Professor Rudolf Arnheim characterized the lack of art education in American education as an "educational blackout."[140] In Frames of Mind, Harvard Professor of Education Howard Gardner observes that Western schools continue to place a premium on logical-mathematical and linguistic ability while other intellectual capacities are "consigned to after-school or recreational activities, if they are taken notice of at all."[141]

This blindness extends to the present. When Professor Gregory D. Foster of the Industrial College of the Armed Forces describes education he selects terms tied almost exclusively with the left side: read, discuss, investigate (by asking), and write.[142] When the author's local government lacks the foresight to match housing construction to necessary infrastructure, some courses are to be given up to make way for more sections of preferred ones: those on the losing end come exclusively from the "not left" side of Table 1: "art, music, and physical education."[143]

Modes of Intelligence Evidence

The respective characteristics of visual and descriptive evidence parallel the diverse dimensions within both cognition and culture. Psychologist Robert Zajonc notes that "Pictorial information is organized in a synchronous and spatially parallel manner, whereas verbal information is discrete and sequential."[144] Psychologist Richard Gregory ties this diversity to the mental model when he writes that visual and verbal skills are not simply different; "they are handled by different brain processes."[145]

A Pair. Descriptive evidence may be understood or searched piecemeal, but an interpretable image must be perceived as a whole. A group of analysts cannot "read" a frame of film in unison as they can this paragraph. Because descriptive evidence is segmentable, readers may understand this sentence by reading one word at a time, sequentially, but because image perception requires simultaneity, one cannot achieve image comprehension by view-

---

[137] Shlain, 67, 122.

[138] See Parker J. Palmer, *To Know As We Are Known: A Spirituality of Education* (New York: Harper & Row, 1983), 29.

[139] C.P. Snow, 15.

[140] Rudolf Arnheim, *Visual Thinking* (Berkeley, California: University of California Press, 1969), 3.

[141] Gardner, 353.

[142] Gregory D. Foster, "Research, Writing and the Mind of the Strategist," *Joint Force Quarterly* no. 11 (Spring 1996): 111.

[143] David Nakamura, "School Budget Deal Saves Teaching Jobs," *Washington Post Loudoun News Extra*, 5 April 1998, 3.

[144] Robert Zajonc, "Feeling and Thinking," *American Psychologist*, 1980, 168, quoted by Kolb, 50.

[145] *The Artful Eye*, eds. Richard Gregory and others (New York: Oxford University Press, 1995.), vii.

ing pixels sequentially. Data are plural, but an image is singular. Chipping out a piece of film can result in a smaller, but nonetheless complete and unitary image in its own right.[146]

Descriptions are finite; visual evidence is not. A page of text can be read in its entirety, but skilled interpreters can make significant discoveries using the same frame of film, decade after decade (after decade). Descriptive evidence typically refers to one topic, but a frame of film can support research into dozens of issues. To test Loch K. Johnson's estimate that "a professional photo-interpreter may require four hours to decipher fully a single frame of satellite photography,"[147] the author totaled the time required to answer questions that could be addressed by one frame, but quit after the count climbed past 1,000 hours.[148] Arthur C. Lundahl, the first Director of the National Photographic Interpretation Center (NPIC), estimated the Intelligence Community benefited from only 15 percent of the information potential within even the small amount of satellite photography available in the 1960s.[149]

The "process" of visual research is subjective and (ironically) invisible. Remote Sensing specialist Robert A. Ryerson emphasizes that descriptions and definitions of image interpretation "do not provide an explanation of the process" itself.[150] The reports of two interpreters differ even when each studies the same image data, and while "human interpretation contains less errors than [linear analysis], it is not reproducible."[151]

Working in the "other" dimension, professional imagery analysts often "know" but cannot easily "say." Former NPIC imagery analyst Kris Stevens admitted she sometimes clearly understood an observation yet had trouble finding the words to explain it.[152] Another former NPIC Senior Analyst was exasperated by the inability to describe image research to nonpractitioners: "You don't know how you do it, you just do it."[153] To communicate what words cannot, the NPIC Update typically filled its pages with photographs.[154]

------

[146] Experimentally, image data may be reduced to a few hundred pixels and still trigger object perception in a human mind. Leon D. Harmon chased the number of pixels a person required to recognize a human face down to 16 x 16, or only 256 pixels. Leon D. Harmon, "The Recognition of Faces," *Scientific American*, November 1973, 74.

[147] Loch K. Johnson, "Making the Intelligence 'Cycle' Work," *International Journal of Intelligence and CounterIntelligence* 1, no. 4 (Winter 1986-87): 10.

[148] This statistic and the other Intelligence Community material in this paper was approved for public release by Department of Defense case 98-S-1060, 16 March 1998 in Mark G. Marshall, *Round Peg, Square Holes: The Nature of Imagery Analysis* (Washington, DC: JMIC, December 1997), 98-99; In Envisioning Information, Edward Rolf Tufte writes "Same picture, but many stories..." (Cheshire, Connecticut: Graphics Press, 1990), 108.

[149] Dino A. Brugioni, "The Art and Science of Photoreconnaissance," *Scientific American*, March 1996, 82. Massachusetts Institute of Technology Professor of Architecture and Media Arts and Sciences William J. Mitchell writes "there is an indefinite amount of information in a continuous-tone photograph. William J. Mitchell, *The Reconfigured Eye: Visual Truth in the Post-Photographic Era*, 1st paper ed. (Cambridge, Massachusetts: The MIT Press, 1994), 6.

[150] Robert A. Ryerson, "Image Interpretation Concerns for the 1990s and Lessons from the Past," *Photogrammetric Engineering and Remote Sensing* 55, no. 10 (October 1989): 1427.

[151] A. Legeley-Padovani, C. Maring, R. Guillande and D. Huaman, "Mapping of Lava Flows Through SPOT Images—An Example of the Sabancay Volcano (Peru)," *International Journal of Remote Sensing* 18, no. 15 (October 1997): 3125-3126..

[152] Kristina M. Stevens, Staff Officer, Central Imagery Office, interview by author, 6 May 1996.

Figure 10. The NPIC Update.

Source: NPIC Update, September 1996, cover.

Domination. Paralleling both cognition and culture, within the Intelligence Community, the use of linear evidence completely dominates the use of visual evidence. The ethe-

[153] David Sullivan, former National Photographic Interpretation Center (NPIC) Senior Imagery Analyst, interview by author, 2 April 1998.

[154] *NPIC Update*, September 1996.

real characteristics of image comprehension make its learning, teaching and use especially troublesome. The standard of Cartesian science is to remain on the left side of Table 1 — what cannot be explained and duplicated is not real.[155] For Westerners whose understanding of "comprehension" is restricted to the mode of verbal logic, visuospatial skill is "incomprehensible."[156] Keith Devlin complains of his students "My attempts are generally quite in vain; most of my students remain unconvinced. The ones who most steadfastly stick to the [linear] rule-based view are invariably the ones who have had a solid science education."[157]

The domination of linearity and rules in intelligence production manifests itself in the recurring demise of Imagery Intelligence. Following every major conflict, skilled image research is not merely reduced, it is practically eradicated. Between the World Wars, U.S. Imagery Intelligence became so incompetent the British had to retrain us after scrambling to revive their own capabilities.[158] The lesson unlearned, by the beginning of the Korean Conflict the craft had again returned "to its pre-World-War II status of 'military stepchild',"[159] with the few remaining practitioners scattered among the military services and barred from conducting effective research.[160] Those who are familiar with the current disarray in American Imagery Intelligence recognize this cycle repeating itself in the present era.

PART II
TEACHING THE "OTHER INTELLIGENCE"[161]

Because it represents a distinct form of evidence that faces special challenges in a Western society, visual evidence requires distinct training for professional interpreters, distinct education for conventional analysts who would appreciate visual evidence, and distinct mentoring of highly visual students. In short, visuospatiality is a performing art one learns, or learns to appreciate, by doing, and this "doing" requires shelter from segmentation.

Many authors acknowledge the need to use nonlinear techniques to teach the "other intelligence." Psychologist Robert E. Ornstein illustrates with bodily kinesthetic examples: "A written description of ski lifts, bindings, equipment, and intermediate ski techniques does not substitute for the experience of skiing down the slope."[162] Physicist Richard Feynman observes that he tells students how to do things with math,

---

[155] Lorraine Daston, "Fear and Loathing of the Imagination in Science," *DAEDALUS* 127, no. 1 (Winter 1998): 75.

[156] Arnheim, 31; Ornstein, 125. Barbara L. Forisha, "Mental Imagery and Creativity: Review and Speculations." *Journal of Mental Imagery* 2 (1978): 211; Gregory observes that some theorists continue to deny the importance of top-down (human mind) knowledge. Gregory, 13.

[157] Devlin, 181. The author feels strangely relieved to learn he is not the only teacher with this problem.

[158] Constance Babington-Smith, *Air Spy: The Story of PhotoIntelligence in World War II,* (New York: Ballantine Books, 1957), 27.

[159] Brugioni and Robert F. McCort, "Personality: Arthur C. Lundahl," *Photogrammetric Engineering & Remote Sensing* 54, no. 2 (February 1988): 270.

[160] Eliot A. Cohen, "Only Half the Battle: American Intelligence and the Chinese Intervention in Korea 1950," *Intelligence and National Security* 5, no. 1 (January 1990): 133; Andrew, 194.

[161] Gardner, xiii, xx, 177-178, 284.

but that "the drawing teacher has this problem of communicating how to draw by osmosis and not by instruction."[163] Gardner notes that apprentices learn a craft by "watching the master at work [and] forming bonds with the other apprentices and those who have already become journeymen."[164]

TRAINING PROFESSIONAL VISUALIZERS

Those who teach image research in the Intelligence Community are consistent in the view that one learns the craft by performing it. NPIC image trainer Chuck Norville questioned whether high-end imagery analysis was "teachable."[165] The author's instructor and predecessor at the Joint Military Intelligence College (JMIC), Lieutenant Commander Thomas J. McIntyre, U.S. Navy (Ret.), observed that the techniques of image research are not stored in books, but are passed down from generation to generation.[166]

Accordingly, image training employs the language of the craft guilds. The title of the U.S. Air Force interpretation course is "Imagery Analysis Apprentice."[167] For a 1996 documentary, NPIC specified that image research requires one to two years of on-the-job training (OJT) before reaching an initial apprentice level.[168] After three years experience, national imagery analysts are eligible for a course in Imagery Analysis Tradecraft.

Those who have learned to perform expert visualization acknowledge the same principles. Among NPIC Senior Analysts the most frequent response to a question of how they had learned their craft was "On-The-Job Training."[169] In response to a Central Imagery Office (CIO) survey of the entire U.S. Imagery System, when asked if they thought their training prepared them to conduct imagery analysis, practitioners responded: "This requires OJT." "OJT is the best form." "It was all OJT." "OJT was first and foremost." "OJT was the most useful tool." One used the metaphor "learning by osmosis."[170]

Blinded. In 1998 the Department of Defense closed the Defense equivalent of the National Imagery Analysis Course, the Defense Sensor Interpretation and Applications Training Program (DSIATP). The substitute for the 11-week resident program is an elec-

---

[162] "One cannot learn to ride a bicycle purely from verbal instruction." Ornstein, 33, 126.

[163] Richard P. Feynman, *"Surely You Are Joking, Mr. Feynman!"* (New York: Bantam Books, 1985), 240.

[164] Gardner, 333-334.

[165] Charles R. Norville, NPIC Training Division Instructor, interview by author, 11 July 1996. Psychiatrist Robert U. Akeret appears to agree when he writes "the best way to learn photoanalysis is through example and actual experience." Robert U. Akeret, *Photo-Analysis: How to Interpret the Hidden Psychological Meaning of Personal and Public Photographs* (New York: Peter H. Wyden, Inc., 1973), 36.

[166] Thomas J. McIntyre, Lieutenant Commander, U.S. Navy (Ret.), interview by author, 21 October 1997.

[167] 315th Training Squadron, U.S. Air Force, *Imagery Analysis Apprentice*, Training Plan X3ABR1N131 006 (Goodfellow Air Force Base, Texas, 22 January 1997).

[168] Martha Ostertag and Kurt Sayenga, prods., "Spies Above," The Discovery Channel, February 1996.

[169] NPIC, Senior Imagery Analyst Questionnaire Survey, 1 July 1992, 46 respondents, each at grade GS-14 or GS-15, tabulated results provided by Norville.

[170] "Respondents believe the most effective imagery training is on-the-job (OJT.)" Central Imagery Office (CIO), *Imagery Community Training Needs Survey*, 1995, 20 and Appendix P, "Sampling of Comments," P-1 through P-4

tronic correspondence course. Senior craftsmen are dismayed at this development.[171] After 17 months and 47 enrollments, one of the best reputed Unified Commands for image research had yet to graduate a single analyst from even one module of the new course (and knew of no other command that had succeeded). To help three students complete part of the program the Command had to exempt them from other duties and assign an image-qualified teacher to work with the students full time.[172]

Educating Nonpractitioners

The skills that define the intelligence collection disciplines are art forms beyond full explanation. Allen Dulles emphasizes this in the title of his book *The Craft of Intelligence*.[173] The Intelligence Collection Department of the JMIC represents a de facto Art Department. "At art schools, a Ph.D. is not the union card it is at universities"[174] and none of the JMIC Collection instructors is a Ph.D. Instead, each has practiced the craft he teaches. Mary McCarthy reaffirms the point when she writes that real intelligence work is distinct from academic analysis.[175] If the objective methods of Western academia were adequate to study and teach strategic intelligence, there would be no Joint Military Intelligence College.

The nondescriptive nature of visual evidence means that even within this art department, image courses represent an inner core. Colleagues can teach the other intelligence disciplines without conducting real debriefings or breaking real ciphers in class, but to understand Imagery Intelligence, students must interpret, if only at a novice level.[176] To help conventional analysts gain an appreciation for the "other intelligence," the author eases students along a spectrum from numbers and words, through symbols and drawings, to a place where they can experience image appreciation.

Pregame. The environment must suit the topic. Image classes sit in a symbolic circle, not hierarchical rows.[177] Opening the room unchains both the instructor and the class. The teacher must often relinquish the stage, and because visual evidence is so context-sensitive that the meaning of a print can change depending on the location from which it is viewed, students must also be free to move about.

---

[171] McIntyre interview.

[172] Joint Intelligence Center, Pacific message to 315 TRS, subject: "Joint Imagery Analysis Course (JIAC) Critique," 152141Z January 1999.

[173] Allen Dulles, *The Craft of Intelligence* (Westport, Connecticut: Greenwood Press, 1963).

[174] Daniel Grant, "Fine Arts and Liberal Arts," *Washington Post Education Review*, 5 April 1998, 11.

[175] Mary O. McCarthy, "The Mission to Warn: Disaster Looms," Defense Intelligence Journal 7, no. 2 (Fall 1998): 20. *Defense Intelligence Journal* articles are available at URL <www.dia.ic.gov/proj/JMIC/journal.html>.

[176] "Learning from Photographs;... Charts, Graphs, Maps, and Diagrams;... Visual Comparison and Analogy;... Film and Television." Deane W. Hutton and Jean Anne Lescohier, "Seeing to Learn: Using Mental Imagery in the Classroom," in *Mental Imagery and Learning*, eds. Malcolm L. Fleming and Deane W. Hutton (Englewood Cliffs, New Jersey: Education Technology Publications, 1983), 117.

[177] Palmer, 75.

Only the best tools can support a course about skilled image research. Most presentations require the display of 25 million bits of image data on a 10x20-foot screen, with split-second staging of any of a hundred scenes, in any order, in color, with effortless rotation and focus. The equipment must be able to store hundreds of gigabytes of data, be fully compatibility with every organization in the Intelligence Community, Y2K compliant, virtually crash-proof, and light enough to carry in one hand. To meet these seemingly impossible requirements the author uses 35mm slides[178] — when working in the other dimension, less is more.[179]

Showtime. Borrowing from professional image instruction, the author teaches non-practitioners in a style that requires internalization. His image classes are not Western-style seminars that exchange symbols, but visual demonstrations accompanied by storytelling designed to make an end-run around each student's verbal intellect.[180]

The opening lectures appear conventional on the surface but are salted with hidden lessons. At the beginning of the course, the teacher displays different representations of the Imagery Intelligence "process" graphically so students can practice "reading between the curves." To test their progress, the midterm examination asks students to speculate on the authorship of Figure 2 based on its *visual* clues:

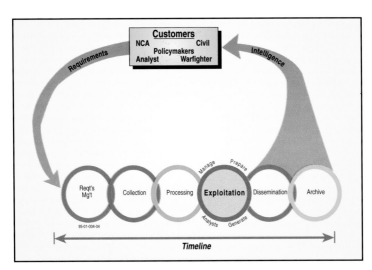

Figure 11. Imagery Production Cycle.

Source (and answer): Annette J. Krygiel, Director, Central Imagery Office, "Exploiting the Picture Through ExPReS," 1995, 6. Observe the controlling function placed on top, that the production line is disappointingly linear, the embellishment of the Exploitation

[178] See Edward Rolf Tufte, Envisioning Information (Cheshire, Connecticut: Graphics Press, 1990), 49.

[179] David Shenk, *Data Smog*, 1st paper ed. (San Francisco, CA: HarperEdge, 1998), 198.

[180] "Listening takes the burden off our eyes.... It allows us to 'picture' the events in space as they occur." Ornstein, 147.

(image visualization) function, and the up-echelon, high-resource characteristic of passing all outputs through professional exploitation.

Similarly, a lecture on the History of Imagery Intelligence contains dozens of nonverbal lessons, not all of which the teacher stops to explain.[181] Niepce's garden is the first recorded "picture," but the pewter plate also serves to demonstrate how a blurry scene can become more meaningful when the teacher takes the class on a visual tour pointing out trees and buildings. Daguerreotype "cities of the dead" are highly interpretable (to use the jargon), but the traffic missing from the streets demonstrates that images, not even those involving visible light, are never real, never "literal."[182] Neubrauner's cameras strapped onto pigeons provide comic relief but also illustrate the aspect of nonverbal intellect that "whatever works is good."[183]

Only after five weeks of surreptitiously setting the stage does the course openly turn the mental corner. At the center of the course (figuratively and literally) students comprehend Imagery Intelligence by experiencing images. The principal textbook for the central class is Robert L. Solso's *Cognition and the Visual Arts*,[184] selected because Solso, like the present author, is seeking a similar intellectual balance between seeing and science. The difference is that we are trying to move our respective classes in "opposite" directions. Solso is teaching fine arts students about the scientific dimension of visual perception; the author is teaching M.S.S.I. students about the art of seeing.

The first overt class in the art of Imagery Intelligence begins with a demonstration of the difference between data and an image. This consists of displaying increasing numbers of pixels sampled from Leon D. Harmon's famous print: 9 pixels, 50 pixels, 80 pixels... (See Figure 3.) Removed from context and viewed sequentially the image data mean nothing. Invariably, some students jump the gun and guess, Western style (hurry, hurry, rush, rush). This introduces the explanation that image comprehension is intuitive, but that contrary to Western misinterpretation, intuition is not a guess. [185]

---

[181] "Teaching stories purposely contain certain specially chosen patterns of events. The repeated reading of the story allows these patterns to become strengthened in the mind of the person reading them. The stories take the mind along unfamiliar and nonlinear paths. Thus it is not necessary to 'understand' the stories in the usual intellectual and rational mode." Ornstein, 146.

[182] Carolyn M. Bloomer, *Principles of Visual Perception*, 2d ed. (New York: Design Press, 1990), 151.

[183] Quote adopted from Philip K. Howard, *The Death of Common Sense: How Law is Suffocating America* (New York: Random House, 1994), 185-186.

[184] Robert L. Solso, *Cognition and the Visual Arts* (Cambridge, Massachusetts: The MIT Press, 1994). *The Artful Eye* is excellent, but too long for one class period.

[185] For an example, see the misrepresentation of "counterintuitive" as "not what you might guess" in Brooke A. Masters, "Domestic Violence Programs Save Men's Lives, Study Says," *The Washington Post*, 14 March 1999, C1.

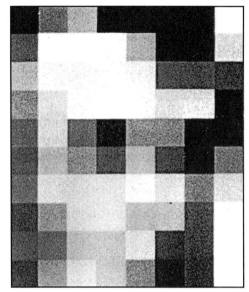

Figure 12. 80 Pixels, but not an Image.

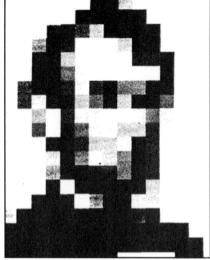

Figure 13. Harmon's Version of a Famous Face.

Source: Harmon, 74; Bloomer, 118; Ivry and Robertson, 119

As the number of pixels increases, shown enough of the display simultaneously, the viewer's intellect perceives more than the sum of the details and creates an image. Most students can make this mental leap when they view **"Harmon's Version of a Famous Face."** When someone perceives the object, they know they see it. As Solso writes "It cannot be explained, but when attained cannot be confused."[186] Harmon found that his test subjects could perceive a pixelated print even more clearly when they squinted their eyes or viewed the print from a distance — either of which accentuates the scene's whole while reducing the prominence of the details (try this with Figure 13).[187] Contrast the effectiveness of this demonstration with the futile attempt on page 65 to describe an "image" with text.

After demonstrating the nature of an "image," the course takes a step backward to employ line-drawings of optical illusions that demonstrate visual principles. It was a signals student who first suggested the author use optical illusions as an analogy for image research. Having come to the teaching job directly from imagery analysis, the author's first classes were far too visual. While line drawings appear crude to professional interpreters, they are ideal for teaching nonpractitioners, and the course now incorporates many of the classics: The Kanizsa Triangle demonstrates the subjective nature of seeing.

---

[186] Solso, 256.

[187] Harmon, 71, 76. Bloomer, 118, and Ivry and Robertson, 199, both more recently republished Harmon's print. For other examples see William J. Mitchell, 68-77.

There is no triangle; there are three chevrons and three Pac-Man symbols, but any triangle exists only in the observer's mind.

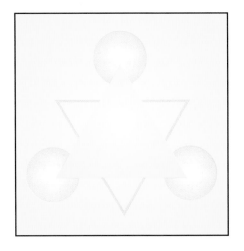

Figure 14. Kanizsa Triangle.

Source: See Gregory, 24, 42.

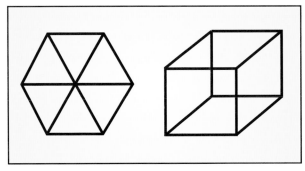

Figure 15. Necker Cube (right) and Friend.
Source: Imagery, ed. Ned Block (Cambridge, Massachusetts: The MIT Press, 1981), 71; Bruce and Green, 109.

Psychologists Vicki Bruce and Patrick Green write that visual ambiguity is uncommon in the real world,[188] but behind the veil of Imagery Intelligence, visual ambiguity is the norm. A minute spent mentally reversing a Necker Cube demonstrates visual ambiguity. Students who are better-than-average visualizers can also experience the hypnotic effect of image research by mentally manipulating the cube(s) for several minutes.[189] Students who are not strong visualizers have an opposite reaction; for them, several minutes of silence feels uncomfortable.[190]

---

[188] Vicki Bruce and Patrick Green, Visual Perception: Physiology, Psychology and Ecology, 2d ed. (London: Lawrence Erlbaum Associates, 1990), 109.

[189] Ornstein, 140-141.

[190] Palmer, 73, 81.

After explaining the lesson behind each optical illusion, the author displays prints selected from real national security research to illustrate how each principle influenced intelligence analysis. "Is this blur a bomb hit or a miss? (Hint: it is usually a miss.)" After warming up on optical illusions, it takes very few prints to illustrate why image researchers are always arguing among themselves and changing their own reports — and why the various agencies of the Intelligence Community desire control over Image Intelligence in order to specify the meanings they prefer.

Students indicate they have learned a central lesson when they hesitate to guess at challenging prints — a level of visual sophistication achieved by only a small minority of the Intelligence Community. As the students change into professional intelligence officers, they no longer believe what they see and no longer believe that untrained observers can match the effectiveness of qualified image practitioners. Doubters may attempt to refute this point by picking out the Intermediate Range Ballistic Missiles in the unannotated print below. Take your time; turning the page represents concession.

Figure 16. A Visually Noisy Frame.

Source: Systeme Probatoire d'Observation de la Terre (SPOT) 1, High Resolution Vehicle (HRV) 2, 051-261, Quadrant 3, 22 March 1986. Reprinted Courtesy of SPOT Image Corporation.

Without explaining why, the author plays his videotape of *A Bridge Too Far* during a class break.[191] As the students return, they end up watching the World War II Intelligence Chief of the British I Allied Airborne Army, Major Brian Urquhart, warn that the paratroopers preparing for Operation MARKET GARDEN are about to jump onto German armor. Urquhart's principal evidence are photographs of the German tanks, but the Corps Commander does not want to see the problem. Urquhart is relieved from duty and Operation MARKET GARDEN suffers more casualties than the Normandy invasion.[192] This is a 20th century retelling of the myth of Cassandra who was blessed with clairvoyance but cursed that no one would believe her.[193] It is also a daily experience in professional image research.

The next hour of the class is a demonstration of the enduring image "Characteristics" described in the original *Manual of Photographic Interpretation*: Size, Shape, Shadow, Tone and Color, Texture, and Pattern.[194] An example is that the solution to Figure 16 depends on recognizing the incriminating Pattern of the missile launch positions. Because of the depth of visual evidence, much of the Characteristics presentation can be demonstrated on a single print: in Figure 17 the missile pads are the right Size and the associated roads have an appropriate curved Shape. The Tone and Texture of the pads differ from the surrounding fields. Demonstrating so many points using only one scene also serves to illustrate the infinite nature of visual evidence — there is no way to fully "translate" prints into descriptions for subsequent analysis on an intelligence production assembly line.

---

[191] *A Bridge Too Far*, prods., Joseph E. Levine and Richard P. Levine, dir. Richard Attenborough, United Artists, 1977

[192] Cornelius Ryan, *A Bridge Too Far* (New York: Simon and Schuster, 1974), 131-133, 159-160, 599, 625.

[193] Shlain, 127.

[194] Ellis L. Rabben, "Fundamentals of Photo Interpretation," in *Manual of Photographic Interpretation*, ed. Robert N. Colwell (Washington, DC: American Society of Photogrammetry, 1960), 100-105.

Figure 17. Pattern.

Source: Kennedy and Marshall, 23.

The crowning point of the course is a class consisting of a series of case studies selected to help students appreciate the emotional content of visual evidence, to experience Imagery Intelligence during high-intensity war, and to join the community of Defense Intelligence. All at the same time. The nominal topic is an explanation of how the military services failed to deliver image-derived knowledge to their tactical forces during Operation DESERT STORM,[195] but the emotional lesson hinges on learning what was published, when, and that the "customers" who failed to receive these reports were fellow students and teachers. To increase the intensity of the experience, the author sets the stage by playing Gulf War newscasts of tank battles and airstrikes before class. By this point in

---

[195]A worrisome trend...emerged during the course of the war — namely, the hoarding of intelligence by [service] component command staffs who failed to pass a variety of useful intelligence reports and analyses downward to the ground units and air wings." U.S. Congress, House Committee on Armed Services, Subcommittee on Oversight and Investigations, Intelligence Successes and Failures in Operations DESERT SHIELD/STORM, 103rd Cong., 1st sess., 16 August 1993, 24.)

the course, many students begin to recognize this is a visual manipulation to carry them mentally back to 1991.

During the Gulf War, Major Michael D. Kuszewski was the intelligence officer for the 8th Regiment, 2d Marine Division. Due to a delivery disconnect, Kuszewski never learned the results of image reports that specified the Iraqi front lines had pulled back several miles. Instead, he learned of the change by accident when he saw a photomap annotated with enemy positions. The 2d Division received 60-85 copies of these elaborate products, but no staff officer could resist them, and only one copy reached Kuszewski's Regiment.[196]

After the war "Major K." graduated from the Naval Postgraduate School and served as Defense Intelligence College Faculty from 1992 to 1995. He died in a helicopter crash out of Camp Lejeune, North Carolina in 1996 and the College Award for the Outstanding Master's Thesis on Operations-Intelligence Partnership is named in his honor.

Figure 18. Major Michael Kuszewski (right).

Source: Major Michael D. Kuszewski, personal photograph, February 1991. The picture was taken during daylight but appears dark under the smoke from hundreds of burning oil wells.

---

[196] Major Michael D. Kuszewski, U.S. Marine Corps, Intelligence Officer, 8th Regiment, 2d Marine Division during Operation DESERT STORM, interview by author, 29 October 1992.

First Lieutenant Matthew S. Weingast was the executive officer of B Troop, 4th Squadron, 7th Cavalry. During Operation DESERT SHIELD Weingast's Troop received a few prints depicting enemy forces. These raised morale, but conveyed little practical information. During the 26 February 1991 tank battle, the squadron did not understand where the adversary was last seen, and even broke into a trot based on a report that the Iraqi Republican Guard was in withdrawal. The two ground troops ran smack into defending enemy forces. Out of range of supporting artillery, having outrun a U.S. tank battalion that was trailing them, and with no aircover due to the bad weather, the squadron's lightly armored vehicles were shot to pieces by Iraqi tanks.[197] Shades of *Bridge Too Far.*

Matt Weingast survived the battle and was Defense Intelligence College class of 1993. He served two years in image research before leaving active duty, and was College Adjunct Faculty from 1994 to 1998. He is now practicing law in Princeton, New Jersey.[198]

Figure 19. First Lieutenant Matt Weingast (left).

Source: Captain Matthew S. Weingast, personal photograph, 24 February 1991.

[197] Captain Matthew S. Weingast, U.S. Army, executive officer, B Troop, 4th Squadron, 7th Cavalry during Operation DESERT STORM, interview by author, 15 October 1992.

[198] Weingast, telephone interview by author, 4 February 1999

When joined with the classified details of image reporting that was available but not delivered prior to each battle, cases such as these can be so emotionally powerful they have moved some classes almost to tears. Students connect to the topic and to their colleagues. The class will forget some of the facts, but they have joined the community of military intelligence.[199]

Out of the Trance. With classes such as these, the image course strays so far from the dispassionate, objectivist style of conventional education that the author feels compelled to bring students back out of the trance. To this end, the course closes with a Western-style verbal and numeric description of the difficulties of transmitting prints (moving hundreds of millions of pixels multiplied by hundreds of shades of gray through a telephone line takes several *days*). Students who were less comfortable with the visual material in the course seem happy to be back among their old friends words and numbers.

Blinded. As Devlin cautioned, many Western students have been so thoroughly indoctrinated in segmented thinking that they do not appreciate the alternative. When the author asked one student to add material from the course to his image paper, the student did not fuse the ideas, but literally stapled his notes to the last page. Even after experiencing the Harmon/Lincoln demonstration, confronted with a choice between a data stream and a picture, some students have difficulty understanding which of these represents an "image." Some highly analytic students are unsettled by the idea of simultaneous thought as an alternative to sequential thinking. One "A" student was so uncomfortable with the new idea he felt compelled to leave the classroom. "After a lifetime of rationalizing the right brain's contributions as its own, the left brain now goes to extreme lengths to keep together the single-mind model."[200]

Mentoring Visual Talent

Serving as an art teacher, the duties of image instructor include mentoring students with exceptional visual talent.[201] This task parallels the care that must be shown members of other more "natural" cultures, but with none of the legal protections.

The association between vision and nondominant culture is downright unsettling. Sociologist Parker J. Palmer acknowledges the relationship between more natural cultures and "other ways of knowing."[202] Shlain characterizes the mental asymmetry in terms of male versus female, and spatial aptitude does vary between the sexes by a relatively small

---

[199] See Palmer, 30, 42.

[200] Inventor Thomas R. Blakeslee commenting on Gazzaniga's findings, *The Right Brain: A New Understanding of the Unconscious Mind and Its Creative Powers*, (Garden City, New York: Anchor Press/Doubleday, 1980), 17.

[201] "All too often the encouragement of visual thinking and communication has been left to the teachers of the obviously 'visual' subjects, such as art, photography, film making, and media studies." Hutton and Lescohier, 115.

[202] Palmer drew similar parallels between feminist insight, "Native American and other aboriginal ways of knowing." xii, 65-66

amount,[203] but psychologists have found much larger differences between Western and nonWestern cultures.[204] In skills associated with the "not left" side of Table 1, Hopi Indian and Black populations outperform Caucasian populations, male or female.[205] On spatial aptitude tests, Australian aborigine children consistently score three years ahead of their white Australian peers.[206] "At least 60 percent of Eskimo youngsters reach as high a score on tests of spatial ability as the top 10 percent of Caucasian children."[207] With emotional baggage like this, helping a visual student graduate with their intuition intact can feel like operating a station on the Underground Railroad.

The trick to mentoring visual students is to act as an agent working on their behalf, not a foreman trying to bring them under control. The first image-peculiar task is to reaffirm the value of visualization, which in turn reaffirms the visual student's self-worth. The second task is to shelter the student's skill from a less than accommodating environment. Finally, the author gives rounder students advice on how to survive in a straighter world, but emphasizes that regardless of the consequences, withholding their best work is not an option.

Mentoring visual talent begins with reaffirming the value of seeing. Having been ravaged by conventional education, some intuiters arrive in the College as disoriented as survivors of a mental train wreck. These students seem surprised to hear a teacher tell them that the subjective aspects of their work that other teachers and supervisors have been so consistently criticizing are actually a gift. Some are thrilled to learn that in addition to doing research *about* imagery, they are also permitted to make discoveries *with* imagery.

To make this point quickly, the author repeats an example selected by art professor Arnheim. To learn the equation $(a+b)^2 = a^2 + b^2 + 2ab$ one may either memorize the formula, Western-style, or "picture" Figure 11. If the style of seeing works for you, use it.

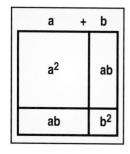

Figure 20. $(a+b)^2 = a^2 + b^2 + 2ab$.

Source: Arnheim, 221.

---

[203] Lauren Julius Harris, "Sex Differences in Spatial Ability: Possible Environmental, Genetic and Neurological Factors," in *Asymmetrical Function of the Brain*, ed. Marcel Kinsborne (Cambridge, UK: Cambridge University Press, 1978), 405; Restak, 228-231; Forisha, 224-225, 229-230; Gardner, 184; Springer and Deutsch, 201-218.

[204] Harris, 432-522; Gardner, 202.

[205] Springer and Deutsch cite Joseph E. Bogen, R. DeZare, W.D. Ten-Houten, and J.F. Marsh, "The Other Side of the Brain. IV: The A/P Ratio," *Bulletin of the Los Angeles Neurological Societies* 37 (1972): 49-61. Springer and Deutsch, 276.

[206] Restak citing Judy Kearns, 202-203.

[207] Gardner, 201-202.

A second aspect of image agency is to defend visual students from an environment that can be openly hostile to the "other" intellect. To prepare for an examination, one student *drew* his notes. His test response matched the material flawlessly, but an instructor objected that the answers were not written in Western-style lines. The author defended the technique by pointing out that this student's graphic representation was more complete than the lines written by other students. Strong visualization is not limited to the formal image career field; the student in this case was not an image practitioner, but had learned the trick as an amateur actor in order to remember long scenes.[208]

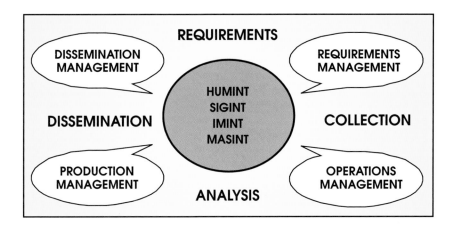

Figure 21. Study Notes.

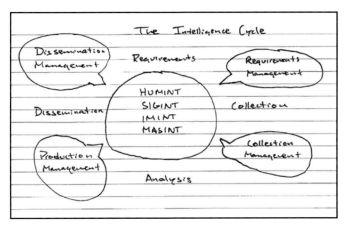

Figure 22. Test Response.

Source: JMIC, Collection 600 Final Examination, Fall 1998.

---

[208] Staff Sergeant Paul R. Wilson, U.S. Army, interview by author, 12 January 1999.

When gifted seers depart the College, the author shares an unvarnished warning about the negative aspects of their circumstances. In the modern workplace, open disparagement of age, sex, or race is rare, but diversity of intellect remains subject to all manner of abuse, and traditional thinkers will go to great lengths to defend the unnatural monopoly they have constructed for themselves. When he inconvenienced his commander's preconception with photographs, Major Urquhart was not only railroaded off the staff, the British army had him committed.

Despite this opposition, for those who work in image research, silence (ironically) is not an option — analysts who see have a duty to enlighten those who do not. The blindness resulting from conventional thinking provides something of an excuse for conventional analysts — they are not intentionally obstructing the mission; they really believe they are doing the right thing. However, for an imagery analyst who sees a threat there is no excuse for not sounding an alarm. To provide this service, image practitioners must optimize their ability to see despite the words or numbers that would obstruct them. Even in today's degraded Intelligence Community, expert image visualization remains important to our national survival.

Blinded. As a predominantly conventional institution, most of the Joint Military Intelligence College strongly favors the left side of Table 1 and typically seeks to confine student thinking to this dimension. Of 129 citation formats in the College *Style Guide*, only four pertain to visual evidence.[209] Dozens of students have completed thesis research about imagery, but in the entire history of the College, only three have demonstrated a thesis primarily with imagery. Following his graduation, Bill Brei wrote that the Joint Publication on *Intelligence Support to Operations* was "weakened because it actually promotes intuition over reason" and that intelligence customers would be better served by the fictional character Mr. Spock's Vulcan Logic than the character Yoda's intuitive "Force."[210] Shortly after his own graduation, the author wrote a paper on imaging platforms that did not include sample frames — as though images were optional in an image paper. The remarkable aspect of these two examples is that both Brei and the author had served as qualified image intuiters before the College "straightened them out."

CONCLUSION

Visual evidence is distinct from descriptive evidence. As such, it requires distinct training for image interpreters and imagery analysts, distinct education for conventional analysts who would appreciate the advantages and disadvantages of visual evidence, and special shelter for analysts with visual talent. These three tasks are especially challenging in a Western culture that prefers descriptive evidence and assembly line processes.

Two patterns of diversity and domination parallel each other within the human mind, among human cultures, and between types of intelligence evidence. In each of these three

---

[209] James S. Major, *The Style Guide*, 2d rev. ed, (Washington, DC: JMIC, August 1996), 158-240.

[210] Captain William S. Brei, U.S. Air Force, *Getting Intelligence Right: The Power of Logical Procedure*, Occasional Paper Number Two (Washington, DC: Joint Military Intelligence College, January 1996), 1.

arenas, one dimension of an asymmetry appreciates wholeness, simultaneity and synthesis while the other favors sequence, analysis and abstraction.

The problem is that in all three arenas, the sequential dimension dominates almost to the complete exclusion of the synthesizing dimension. Mentally, verbal intellect rationalizes its way into such total control that we deny intuition as a type of thinking. Culturally, the domination manifests itself in education systems that consist almost entirely of literacy and numeracy. Within intelligence analysis, the rule of sequential research leads to the cyclic demise of skilled image simultaneity.

Learning and teaching the "other intelligence" requires techniques distinct from traditional Western methods. Seeing is not something a teacher can verbally explain or something a student can learn from a book. In contrast to objectification, image comprehension requires internalization and subjective experience. People learn to see by creating images in their mind. Professional image practitioners learn their craft through years of on-the-job training, and even conventional intelligence analysts can learn more about visual evidence by conducting novice interpretation. Serving as an instructor for such an unusual topic includes the additional duties of reaffirming the value of visualization, sheltering visual talent, and advising members of the "other" intellectual culture how to survive in a square Intelligence Community.

The tone-deafness that confronts image students and teachers in our Western culture is daunting, but learning to see is worth the struggle. Within the Intelligence Community, the survival skill of expert visualization contributes to nothing less than the national survival. Furthermore, despite the challenge, it is not impossible to teach seeing, and every so often a blind student learns to draw.

SPY FICTION, SPY REALITY[211]

Jon A. Wiant

(Originally published in the Summer 2004 issue of American Intelligence Journal.)

"How long have we been sitting here?" I said. I picked up the field glasses and studied the bored young American in his glass-sided box.

"Nearly a quarter of a century," said Werner Volkmann. His arms were resting on the steering wheel and his head was slumped on them. "That GI wasn't even born when we first sat waiting for the dogs to bark."

Barking dogs, in their compound behind the remains of the Hotel Adlon, were unusually the first sign of something happening on the other side. The dogs sensed any unusual activity long before the handlers came to get them. That's why we kept the windows open; that's why we were frozen nearly to death.

"That American soldier wasn't born, the spy thriller he's reading wasn't written, and we both thought the Wall would be demolished within a few days. We were stupid kids but it was better then, wasn't it Bernie?"

"It's always better when you're young, Werner," I said.[212]

Berlin, emblematic, symbolic, the images of the city are forever fixed in our minds, the starkest reality of the Cold War. The Wall, Checkpoint Charlie, barbed-wire, guard towers, dark alleys. Berlin was the ultimate setting for the spy novel. Len Deighton captures well the atmosphere as British Secret Intelligence Service officer Bernie Samson and his German principal agent, Werner Volkmann wait for an over-due agent to come through Checkpoint Charlie. The tension, the anxious wait are integral to the experience. Here we have Alec Lemas, John Le Carre's archetypal antihero of spy fiction similarly waiting at the Wall.

"'You can't wait for ever, sir. Maybe he will come another time....How long will you wait?'" asks the young CIA case officer. "'Until he comes,'" responds Lemas. "'Agents aren't airplanes. They don't have schedule. He's blown, he's on the run, he's frightened [...] He's only got once chance. Let him choose his time.'"[213]

And there is cause for anxiety as you wait for the agent to make this narrow crossing from East to West. Karl, Lemas' agent does eventually show up and he passes through the

---

[211] The article expands on a speech by the author to the Potomac Chapter of the National Military Intelligence Association. The author holds the Department of State Chair at the Joint Military Intelligence College and is a Visiting Professor from the Department of State. The views expressed are the author's own.

[212] The opening scene from Len Deighton's *Berlin Game* (New York: Alfred A. Knopf, 1984), 3.

[213] John Le Carre, *The Spy Who Came In From The Cold* (London: Victor Gollanz Limited, 1963), 1.

East German checkpoint. Only a few yards separate him from the West. He mounts his bicycle.

Then. Totally unexpected. The searchlights went on, white and brilliant, catching Karl and holding him in their beam like a rabbit in the headlight of a car. There came the see-saw wail of a siren, the sound of orders wildly shouted. In front of Lemas the two police-men dropped to their knees, peering through the sandbagged slits, deftly flicking the rapid load on their automatic rifles.

The East German sentry fired, quite carefully, away from them, into his own sector. The first shot seemed to thrust Karl forward, the second to pull him back. Somehow he was still moving, still on the bicycle, passing the sentry, and the sentry was still shooting at him. Then he sagged, rolled to the ground, and they heard quite clearly the clatter of the bike as it fell. Lemas hoped to God he was dead.[214]

We see those images, whether from spy novels or films of the era in black and white for those are the colors of the Cold War, philosophically as well as geographically. The scenes of fiction fuse in our mind with Cold War images from nightly TV news and together they shaped our reality of a Cold War from the end of World War II until Novem-ber 1989 when the Wall came crashing down. And it is no longer clear which was fiction and which was reality for Le Carre and Deighton, undisputed masters of the genre of spy literature became also instructors in our spy reality.

SPY FICTION, SPY REALITY

Shortly after joining the faculty of the Joint Military Intelligence College, I proposed teaching a seminar on spy fiction. "Bunkum!" said my colleagues. "It is not a fit subject for serious study let alone professional education of the contemporary military intelli-gence officer." I suspect many of you would agree.

Let me argue that this fictional milieu has, in a very real and pervasive way, shaped the reality of intelligence officers in a variety of circumstances. To begin with, has it not shaped your very identity? For example, who among you have not had a parent or a friend describe your work as "James Bond" like? Ian Fleming's swashbuckling James Bond has become a more or less accepted synonym for our work, a shorthand way of saying every-thing about the secret life without saying anything? The name is a perfect symbol, con-veying, without explaining, a sense of the intelligence professional. I think for all of us the James Bond image has more facility to symbolize positively our sense of self than many other spy fiction characters. Certainly better known that Alec Lemas or George Smiley, the James Bond image is also more embraceable with his dashing infallibility and worldly knowledgeability. Admittedly, within the profession the James Bond label can be apply derisively to an officer too caught up in the Bondian role but even in this use it is the spy fiction that informs our reality.

---

[214] Le Carre, 8-9.

Examples of this practice are fairly legion, manifested in ideas from how to dress to the implications of mastery in everything from foreign languages and exotic weapons to wines and culinary delights. Even in the hard world of operations, a particularly challenging operation may well be characterized as a "Mission Impossible."

Fiction intercedes in other ways. Take for instance the term "mole." *Spy Book: The Encyclopedia of Espionage*[215] authoritatively states that a mole is:

> A high-level AGENT who is hidden within an enemy's government or military organization in the expectation that he will provide extremely valuable information. The most important Soviet moles were the members of the CAMBRIDGE SPY RING, who penetrated the British government, and ALDRICH H. AMES, in the US CIA.[216]

At one time we called such penetrations "agents in place." Today, however, "mole" has become the term of choice for a long- term penetration of an intelligence service. William Hood titled his masterful study of the recruitment and running of Pytor Popov, CIA's first recruitment of a Russian intelligence office, Mole.[217] Yet the word "mole" itself is a fictional creation of John Le Carre introduced in *Tinker, Tailor, Soldier, Spy*, perhaps the greatest of spy novels and a work of literature in its own right. This fact, William Hood somewhat sheepishly notes, is problematic:

> One last confession. The title [Mole] may be misleading. However descriptive of a penetration it may be, the word mole was not in the intelligence lexicon in my day. John Le Carre found it — Marx had used it, but in a political sense — and popularized it. Mole is, however, so apt an expression that, for all I know, it may now be part of the professional vocabulary.[218]

While Le Carre attributes the term to the Soviets intelligence services, the Russian translator of his novels told me that she had puzzled over the term mole since she could find no comparable term in Russian. But William Hood had a prescient sense when he made his observation about the term more than twenty years ago and speculated that it might become part of the professional vocabulary. In fact, a Google search of the word "mole" and the word "espionage" will give you 6,000 or so hits, mostly stories of Aldrich Ames and Robert Hanssen and a dozen other American traitors who have filled out headlines for the last 15 years.

Our reality then is deeply embedded in the fictional world of spies for both good and bad.

---

[215] *Spy Book: The Encyclopedia of Espionage.* (Updated and Revised Edition. Norman Polmar and Thomas B. Allen. (New York: Random House, 1998).

[216] Spy Book, 374.

[217] William Hood, *Mole* (New York: William Norton and Company, 1982).

[218] Hood, 16.

WHY STUDY SPY FICTION

As I argued with my querulous colleagues over whether there was a place for a course in spy fiction within our curriculum, I suggested there were at least four compelling reasons for reading spy fiction:.

First, and I need to get this out of the way right up front, I am evangelistic about reading spy fiction because it can be good, entertaining reading. At its finest — Graham Greene's *The Human Factor, Le Carre's Tinker, Tailor, Soldier, Spy* — is great literature, ranking among the best of novels in the English language. These works transcend the genre dealing with themes of love, alienation, and betrayal — essential themes of our age.

Eric Ambler, Charles McCarry, W. T. Tyler. John Gardner, Alan Furst, Clive Egleton, Brian Freemantle to name among the best will all give you a great spy story with writing both crisp and compelling along with a reasonable grounding in tradecraft.

And, if you must, add a little Tom Clancy, Robert Ludlum, and what have you. There are worst ways to waste your time on a long flight but neither Clancy nor Ludlum enjoy a significant place in my canon of spy literature.

A second, and I think more persuasive professional reason for giving some serious attention to the spy novels and films is that they are also artifacts of our understanding of the social history of the era in which they are written. In this sense, spy novels are the stuff of history. Through the spy novel you can see and understand a number of factors that have shaped the contemporary world of intelligence.

The transition of the intelligence officer from the amateur of pre-World War II period to the trained, professional of contemporary times is well developed in the literature. Somerset Maugham's post-World I spy novel Ashenden and Alfred Hitchcock's subsequent film of the book, re-titled *Secret Agent*, portray some of Maugham's real life adventures as an intelligence officer during World War I. One is struck by the simplicity of the intelligence organization then and on governments' reliance on gifted amateurs for intelligence activities. Lt. Ashenden is simply asked by a colonel of intelligence to take on an important mission and with little more than his natural guile and his ascribed qualities as a British officer he ventures forth into the world of espionage. John Fisher's recent study, *Gentleman Spies: Intelligence Agents in the British Empire and Beyond* [219] makes clear that Ashenden's preparation, or lack thereof, was fairly common for those early 20th Century intelligence officers, a far cry from the highly specialized officer in both reality and fiction at the end of the 20th Century. Contrast their recruitment with the arduous examination and investigation of current recruits for intelligence employment.

While historians have produced a rich literature of intelligence in World War II, there are fewer noteworthy spy novels that give us an authentic portrayal of the wartime intelli-

---

[219] John Fisher, Gentleman Spies: Intelligence Agents in the British Empire and Beyond. (Gloucestershire, UK: Sutton Publishing, 2002).

gence officer. W. E. B. Griffins multi-volume *Honor Bound,*[220] a fictional work tracing the story of several characters in the Office of Strategic Services (OSS), does give a fairly accurate picture of the recruitment, training, and deployment of the officers that became the embryo of the post-War Central Intelligence Agency but it is the fiction of the Cold War that gives the student the best insight in the transformation of the profession.

Along with the professionalization of the intelligence officer, we can also see the transformation of the intelligence organization from a simple activity, often largely concerned with information of tactical importance, to the complex bureaucracies of the contemporary national intelligence organization where the focus is primarily strategic. With this shift, or expansion, of focus has come the extraordinary specialization along the lines of collection disciplines. Accompanying that specialization there has been a concomitant growth in the complexity of intelligence organizations. Ashenden's Intelligence Department would be dwarfed today by even the staff of a combatant commander's intelligence section and there is no historical parallel to the large intelligence agencies that form our contemporary intelligence community.

What spy literature affords us, however, is not simply an appreciation of the complexity that accompanies the modern transformation. Rather, at its best the literature gives us a window into the organizational pathologies that complicate the lives of the modern intelligence officer.

John Le Carre instructs us with his *Smiley's People*[221] that the great conflict of the 20th Century was not between communism and democracy, but rather more fundamentally between profession and bureaucracy. His "Circus," the fictionalized Secret Intelligence Service, is recognizable to us all with his well drawn bureaucrats shaping operations for political expediency or budget prerogatives, generally at the expense of the professional. Le Carre suggests with this novel that our intelligence organizations have become so bureaucratized that only those who retired from an earlier, simpler service, and by this I think Le Carre is arguing that the earlier service was more professionally grounded, have the capability to conduct successful operations. This is a harsh indictment of the modern organization but numerous presidential commissions and congressional inquiries have suggested similar bureaucratic conditions percolate through our organizations.

In this regard, it strikes me that a critical failing of the techno-thriller popularized by Tom Clancy and the like is its neglect of these bureaucratic realities. Clancy's Jack Ryan is never hassled over his travel vouchers nor do we find him arguing with headquarters over whether he has provisional operating authority to move forward on a recruitment. For my mind, the instructive spy novels deal centrally with the bureaucratic condition not because they celebrate a cynicism but precisely because they capture the reality of today's

---

[220] So far there are three volumes in the series, Honor Bound and Blood and Honor published by the Putnam Group in 1994 and 1997; Secret Honor was published in 1999 by Severn House Publishing Limited. All three volumes are also available in mass-market paperback.

[221] John Le Carre, Smiley's People (New York: Alfred A. Knopf, 1980).

intelligence world. Contrast Jack Ryan's derring-do with Tom Rogers in *Agents of Inno-cence*.[222] David Ignatius wrote this as a *roman a clef* about CIA officer Robert Ames's operations against the Palestinian Liberation Organization. Ignatius brilliantly draws out the tension between headquarters and the field officer over whether Rogers' relationship with a PLO official must be forced into a recruitment. The exchange of cables carries the sting of headquarters that many have felt. Similarly, in *Rouge's March*,[223] W. T. Tyler's novel set in an American Embassy in central Africa, we can get a real feel for the prob-lems of politicization of intelligence as the acting Chief of Station battles with the deputy chief of mission over the release of station cables reporting situations at variance with the country team's assessment.

A third reason we might consider for studying spy literature is how it helps us to under stand the growing centrality of technology in intelligence. Admittedly, my ignorance of how much of contemporary technical collection works verges on the encyclopedic. That said, fictional treatment of code breaking in works like *Enigma* [224] provides the layman with an easily digestible tutorial on how ciphers are deciphered and how the product of this exploitation contributes to war fighting. With their technological fascinations, Tom Clancy's novels have introduced the public to a wide range of technical collection capa-bilities across the numerous INTs. While his books, and those of others with like minded points of view, may educate students in the wizardry of intelligence and how collection systems have enhanced our capabilities, they have also fed our expectations about what intelligence can accomplish and fed the paranoia among those threatened by the implica-tions of collection. I will discuss some of the more untoward effects of this later.

Finally, a careful study of the evolution of spy literature will show how these novels and films reflect, and often anticipate the world around them. At their best, these novels explore not just the changing capabilities of intelligence but also the motivations of the intelligence officer and educate us in their tradecraft.

For instance, spying in the novels of the 1930's are preoccupied with the underside of a decaying and transforming Europe. Writers like John Buchan, Geoffrey Household, and early Eric Ambler paint for us a political landscape preoccupied with the intrigues of pass-ing monarchs and exiled princes, of a moral bankruptcy of the post-World I period. They set the stage for our understanding of the emerging totalitarians of communism and fascism.

The onset of World War II gives us the Germans and Japanese as enemies and rich films about the Gestapo, our own emerging counterintelligence organizations catching Nazi spies, etc. There are many films made during or shortly after the war that popularize spying, counterspying and, at the time, the new focus on support to resistance movements. Many of these were made to celebrate the Allied effort and like war films of the time reflect our propaganda themes. Watch a young Gene Kelly in *Cross of Lorraine*[225] and

---

[222] David Ignatius *Agent of Innocence* (New York: W. W. Norton and Company, 1987).

[223] W. T. Tyler Rogue's March (New York: Harper Collins, 1982).

[224] Robert Harris, Enigma (Random House, 1997).

[225] Cross of Lorraine, [movie]1943.

you feel the appeal of the Resistance, albeit a Resistance neither plagued by collaboration nor deep political division. Two films of the period stand out in their instructional value for in them we can find the roots of the modern intelligence organization — Alan Ladd in OSS[226] and James Cagney in *13 Rue Madeline*.[227] Both were made with the assistance of the Office of Strategic Services, and both seek to make the compelling case for the continuation of a national intelligence organization. Incidentally, the Cagney character reminds the viewer dramatically that our world has changed and that we must jettison our [read pre-war American] cultural dislike of intelligence. Addressing new OSS recruits about the realities of the secret war, Cagney chides them:

> Now, you're going to have a lot to remember, and a couple of things to forget. The average American is a good sport, plays by the rules. But this war is no game, and no secret agent is a good sport — no living agent. You're going to be taught to kill, to cheat, to rob, to lie, and everything you learn is moving you to one objective — just one, that's all — the success of your mission.
>
> Fair play! That's out! Years of decent and honest living? Forget all about them — because the enemy can forget — and has! [228]

Several novels based on World War II have become best sellers, Ken Follett's *Eye of the Needle* [229] comes to mind, but I have generally found that the fine histories of intelligence operations in World War II are more satisfying and instructive than the fictional accounts. One exception is Jack Hunter's The Expendable Spy.[230] Hunter, a veteran of the Army's Counterintelligence Corps, gives us a picture of Army intelligence in the last days of World War II that is better than many of the official histories.

Let us turn now to the Cold War. The spy and counterspy are the archetypal warriors of the Cold War. The global conflict between the USA and its allies, primarily the UK in this context, and the Soviet Union produced a rich literature that continues to shape our understanding of that conflict today. Surprisingly, this literature is less about spying than it is about counterspying — the threat of the avenger who stole upon the citadel and destroyed it from within.

The case of Kim Philby and his Cambridge University confederates dominates the Cold War spy novel. Lest I be accused of an undue fascination with British espionage and counterespionage, Philby's treachery had extraordinary costs for American intelligence operations because of our close, daresay seamless, collaboration with the Brits against the Soviets. John Le Carre's *Tinker, Tailor, Soldier Spy*[231] explores the ideological rot at the center of the British service and the difficulty of understanding the motivations of a close colleague to betray his own service, and his own class. W. T. Tyler examines the impact of

---

[226] Paramount Pictures, 1946

[227] Twentieth Century Fox, 1947.

[228] Quoted in G.D.A. O'Toole, *Honorable Treachery: A History of U.S. Intelligence, Espionage, and Covert Action from the American Revolution to the CIA* (New York: The Atlantic Monthly Press, 1991), 422.

[229] Ken Follett, *Eye of the Needle* (New York: G. K. Hall and Company, 1976).

[230] Jack D. Hunter, *The Expendable Spy* (New York: E. P. Dutton, 1965).

[231] New York: Pocket Books, 2002.

this treachery and that of George Blake, another significant British spy, on American intelligence operations in Berlin in *The Man Who Lost the War.* [232] Charles McCarry concludes his Paul Christopher tetrology with *The Last Supper*,[233] the story of an American officer who is recruited by the Soviets in World War II and advances to head an operational component of CIA during the Cold War. The symbolism of the title reflects the depth of betrayal. All of these novels explore the sociology of treachery but they also illustrate the craft of counterintelligence and the role it played in the first line of defense during the Cold War.

Le Carre wrote *Tinker, Tailor, Soldier, Spy* as a methodical examination of rooting out a spy from within the ranks of the British secret service and he uses George Smiley as our guide through the complicated investigation. Surveillance and penetration are important tools, but for Le Carre the tedious exploitation of records, of access lists to sensitive reporting, of background investigations and other archival sources are key to identifying the traitor. The clues to treachery are more likely found in the files of central registry than in dark alleys. In *The Secret Pilgrim*, Le Carre offers a test-book example of counterintelligence interviewing as Smiley's protégé, Ned, systematically and sympathetically leads cipher clerk Cyril Frewin into a confession of his long-time spying for the Soviets.[234] This deserves a place in any counterintelligence curriculum. In an aside here, let me note that I am not alone in arguing for the value of spy novels in our training. In 1991 I had a conversation in Moscow with recently retired KGB General Oleg Kalugin who told me that every KGB officer assigned to the United States was required to read Victor Marchetti's *The Rope Dancer.*[235] Kalugin felt this was an excellent tutorial in American counterintelligence activities.

Two other novels of the Cold War should also command space on the counterintelligence officer's book shelf for their philosophical plumbing of the essential nature of espionage and betrayal: Le Carre's A Perfect Spy,[236] considered by many intelligence officers to be Le Carre's most authentic work, and W. T. Tyler's *Last Train from Berlin.*[237] Perhaps the spying of Ames, Hanssen, Howard and others will inspire spy literature though the baseness of their motivations and the simple greed that drove them somehow seems to lack the powerful themes of love, alienation, and betrayal that informed Le Carre and Tyler.

The Cold War also produced our archetypal intelligence officers — James Bond and George Smiley. In James Bond we find the maven of espionage style. As I noted earlier, Ian Fleming's elegant and expedient character has colonized the image of the intelligence officer. Le Carre's podgy and rumpled George Smiley stands in starkest contrast, one of the grey men of the profession, known not for their sartorial splendor bur rather for its absence:

---

[232] W. T. Tyler, *The Man Who Lost the War* (New York: The Dial Press, 1980).

[233] Charles McCarry, *The Last Supper* (New York: E. P. Dutton, Inc., 1983).

[234] John Le Carre, *The Secret Pilgrim* (New York: Alfred A. Knopf, 1991), 259-319.

[235] Victor Marchetti, *The Rope Dancer* (New York: Grosset and Dunlap, 1971).

[236] John Le Carre, *A Perfect Spy* (New York: Alfred A. Knopf, 1986).

[237] W. T. Tyler, *Last Train from Berlin* (New York: Henry Holt and Company, 1994).

Short, fat and of a quiet disposition, he appeared to spend a lot of money on real bad clothes, which hung about his squat frame like a skin on a shrunken toad. Sawley, in fact, declared at the wedding [Smiley married the aristocratic Anne Sercomb] that "Sercomb was mated to a bullfrog in a sou'wester." And Smiley, unaware of that description, had waddled down the aisle in search of a kiss that would turn him into a prince.[238]

The James Bond figure did dominate the popular thriller but many Cold War writers did try to recreate more realistic characters along the lines of Smiley and set them in circumstances more grounded in Cold War realities. Even John Gardner, hired by Ian Fleming's estate to continue the James Bond series, jettisons this Cold War superman, in his own spy novels. His *The Garden of Weapons,*[239] which introduces case officer Herbie Kruger, a man whose one concession to style is a love of Gustav Mahler, is both a crackerjack spy story and a careful exposition on agent handling. Len Deighton's *Funeral in Berlin*[240] gave us Harry Palmer, an anti-hero in the fashion Of Le Carre's Alec Lemas, though the Bond influence of the time once again inserts itself with Palmer's culinary fussiness in the kitchen. Deighton subsequently developed Bernard Samson as the protagonist for his multi-volume[241] unmasking of a traitor within the leadership of British Secret Intelligence Service. Samson, like Brian Freemantle's Charlie Muffin in *A Dangerous Game*[242] is kind of a working class officer trying to do his job in a service still suffering from class-consciousness. All of these have been made into films, each of which is commended to the viewer. Alec Guinness's portrayal of George Smiley and Ian Holm's interpretation of Bernard Samson forever etch the image of case officer in the collective memory of the Cold War.

While many pondered what role the Intelligence Community might play in the post-Cold War period, others speculated whether the end of the Cold War presaged the end of the spy novel. John Le Carre, who undoubtedly profited from his Cold War spy novels, tries to deal with this changing world in *The Secret Pilgrim*. He has the now retired George Smiley reflect on how the world has changed and to belie the critics who have sensed a nostalgia for the Cold War among those confronting the new world. Speaking to the first post-Cold War graduates from British operations officer training, Smiley gives both elegy to an earlier age and a warning about that which has replaced it:

> "There are some people," Smiley declared comfortably (...) "who, when their past is threatened, get frightened of losing everything they thought they had, and perhaps everything they thought they were as well, No, I don't feel that

---

[238] John Le Carre, *Call for the Dead* (Boston: Hill and Company Publishers, 1961), 1.

[239] John Gardner, *The Garden of Weapons* (New York: The Mysterious Press, 1981).

[240] Len Deighton, *Funeral in Berlin* (New York: G. P. Putnam and Sons, 1965).

[241] Len Deighton's series runs ten volumes, daresay an espionage epic. Of the ten, *Berlin Game, Mexico Set,* and *London Match* (all published by Alfred A. Knopf) are the first three and most rewarding. The tenth volume, *Winter* (New York: Alfred A. Knopf, 1987) looks back on Samson's roots in Berlin and the German families who shaped his circumstance.

[242] Brian Freemantle, *Charlie Muffin* (New York: Doubleday Press, 1977). BBC Productions made a sparkly film of this in 1979 called *A Dangerous Game*.

one bit. The purpose of my life was to end the time I lived in. So if my past were still around today, you could say I failed. But it's not around. We won. Not that victory matters a damn. Perhaps they just lost. Or perhaps, without the bonds of ideological conflict to restrain us any more, our troubles are just beginning. Never mind. What matters is that a long war is over. What matters is the hope."[243]

Smiley, of course was right. Our troubles were just beginning and terrorism, narcotics trafficking, transnational crime and the full range of possibilities of their combinations recast our national security concerns. The spy literature prefigured this, producing a new spy story capable of conjuring up the worst fears but hardly worse than those brought on us on September 11. Le Carre thrust the British Service into new situations from the Arab-Israeli conflict in *The Little Drummer Girl*[244] to war in Chechnya and Ingushetia as the old Soviet Union breaks up in *Our Game*.[245] Tom Clancy's Jack Ryan takes on Irish terrorists[246] and moves on to fight narcoterrorists in Colombia.[247] In the world of post-September 11, we can expect themes of counterterrorism to predominate in the spy fiction genre as writers explore ways both to fashion new villains and to weave together plots of our increasing vulnerability in a post-Cold War world of disorder.

SPY FICTION THAT SHAPES THE WORLD IN WHICH WE WORK

Let me conclude with some observations on how the popular fascination with spy novels and spy films has complicated the world of the intelligence professional. In a perverse way, spy fiction and spy reality have turned on each other in a kind of double helix where our fictional world begins to shape our reality and it becomes increasingly difficult to separate out in the popular mind the distinctions between the two.

The problem is not new. President John F. Kennedy was a great fan of Ian Fleming's James Bond novels; in fact, Kennedy's comment at a news conference about his love of Fleming's thrillers did much to move the Bond novels to the top of bestseller lists. Kennedy invited Fleming for a stay at the White House and during the course of the visit, Kennedy turned to his preoccupation with getting rid of Fidel Castro. Kennedy reportedly asked Fleming how Bond might eliminate Castro. Fleming suggested the way to get at Castro was to attack his manliness and proposed having an agent slip some chemical into Castro's drink that would make his beard fall out. Alternatively, Fleming suggested that you might be able to kill Castro by booby-trapping a conch shell that would be conveniently placed where Castro might discover it while skin-diving.[248] Many years later during the Congressional inquiry into alleged CIA wrong doing conducted by Senator Church, a CIA witness testified about a number of attempts to

---

[243] The Secret Pilgrim, p. 12.

[244] John Le Carre, *The Little Drummer Girl* (New York: Alfred A. Knopf, 1983).

[245] John Le Carre, *Our Game* (New York: Alfred A. Knopf, 1995).

[246] Tom Clancy, *Patriot Games* (New York: Putnam Publishing Group, 1987).

[247] Tom Clancy, *Clear and Present Danger* (New York: Putnam Publishing Group, 1989).

[248] Ron Kurtus, "The Relationship Between John F. Kennedy and James Bond 007, 15 September 2001, accessed 8 November 2002 at www.school-for-champions/history/jfk007.

assassinate Castro; the list included both an attempt to destroy Castro's beard and a plot to blow him up with an explosive ladened conch shell while Castro was skin-diving.[249]

Fleming's influence on Kennedy also shaped his ideas about the kind of leadership he wanted at CIA. He touted Bill Harvey, CIA's chief of Western Division and manager of the anti-Castro program as an "American James Bond." This swashbuckling view of intelligence operations under Harvey is loosely fictionalized in *The Company*, Robert Little's recent addition to spy literature.[250]

An even more insidious influence of the James Bond genre was the acceptance that intelligence officers had a "license to kill," the defining attribute of Bond's designation as 007. In the argot of the 1960's intelligence officer this became known as "termination with extreme prejudice." One of the young intelligence officers implicated in the killing of a double agent in Vietnam offered in his defense that he believed he had "a license to kill." The way in which this sentiment of expedient demise had been reinforced by popular spy culture can be seen in some of the writing discussing the 1969 killing of a suspected North Vietnamese double agent in what became known as "The Green Beret Murder Trial."[251]While the specifics of that case have long faded from memory, popular culture retains the idea of "termination with extreme prejudice." Despite Presidential Executive Orders explicitly forbidding any intelligence officer to engage in assassination, the public continues to hold fast to the notion that killing is an essential part of the intelligence profession and many seem dismayed with arguments to the contrary. The current war against terrorism seems to cloud the distinction further.

If intelligence life occasionally apes art, then this life has also increasingly come to expect art. It is a sad fact for most intelligence professionals that most of the people for whom we work draw their understanding of our business from this popular culture of spy novel and spy film. It does curious things to all of us. Remember our challenge as intelligence officers: Understand capabilities, understand intentions! Popular literature and films have fundamentally distorted our profession by exaggerating what we can do and often confounding the reasons for what we do. Consider for example, what our theater commanders and national security managers expect us to produce if they have accepted as gospel the satellite technology in 1987 that permitted Jack Ryan in *Patriot Games*[252] to watch a live feed of infrared imagery of less than one meter resolution of a terrorist camp. How could we compete with that? Is it an intelligence failure if our earnest efforts fail to live up to these expectations?

If *Patriot Games* overstated our collection capabilities then, how can we possibly meet the insatiable appetite for information stimulated by *Enemy of the State*[253] with its infi-

---

[249] John Ranelagh, *The Agency: The Rise and Decline of the CIA* (New York: Simon and Shuster, Inc. 1987), 357. Ranelagh notes a variety of exotic assassination plots against Castro, any one of which could find a fictional equivalent. Ranelagh comments, "All of these attempts were conducted during the Kennedy's presidency and ended when he died."

[250] Robert Little, *The Company* (New York: The Overlook Press, 2002).

[251] The best discussion of this case is in Jeff Stein, *A Murder In Wartime* (New York: St. Martin's Press, 1992).

[252] Paramount Studios, 1992.

nitely targetable imaging and intercepting satellite systems? With this extraordinary capacity for information collection and management, how could the terrorists of September 11th have slipped by us? It is no wonder that the public questions the intelligence community's performance when played out against these expectations.

At the same time, however, the popular spy culture has also fed America's paranoia about its intelligence agencies. It is hard to remember a time when America publicly looked at its intelligence organizations as part of the arsenal of democracy. Certainly, the 1970s Age of Inquiry, ushered in with the Ervin Committee hearing on domestic spying in 1971 and continuing through the Church and Pike inquiries, raised serious questions about the conduct of intelligence organizations. The Iran-Contra investigation in the mid-1980s brought further concern about whether activities done in the name of the state had not now become threats to the state. Regardless of the seriousness of the allegations, popular literature and films built on them and played to a growing paranoia. *Three Days of the Condor*,[254] the first film to come out of the inquiries, warned us that there was a deadly conspiracy within CIA's Directorate of Operations and that senior DO officers would kill to keep it secret. Steven Segal's *Above the Law*[255] has CIA officers moving from the Green Beret murder case in Vietnam to running death squads in El Salvador and bringing their deadly war home against Catholic priests who protested against them. In *Clear and Present Danger*,[256] Jack Ryan must contend with a corrupt Deputy Director of Operations who conspires with the President of the United States to eliminate a Colombian drug trafficker in direct violation of the President's own Executive Order. The list goes on. With *Enemy of the State*[257] no vestige of privacy is left in the face of the National Security Agency's awesome capabilities. CIA might commend its cooperation in the filming of *The Recruit* but who could take comfort in an agency that had given the Al Pacino character responsibility for the recruitment and training of its next generation of officers.

Perhaps there are elements of the Intelligence Community that have escaped the paranoiac pen of the spy novelist or filmmaker. NIMA, for the present, seems immune but few others do. Even the Joint Military Intelligence College has not escaped the dark side. Illustrative of this problem, let me close with a brief citation from *Under the Cover of Law*,[258] a police procedural novel set in Santa Fe, New Mexico in the late 1980. The police chief is conducting a murder investigation of the estranged wife of a U.S. ambassador. His inquiries point to a covert intelligence operation with ties to death squads in Central America and the police chief suspects unscrupulous government agents are acting illegally under the cover of law. A priest has also been murdered and after his death the police discover he had conducted interviews with the U.S. Army School of Americas, DEA, NSA, all somehow connected with the Central American death squads. A detective notes:

---

[253] Touchstone Films, 1998.

[254] Paramount Studios, 1975. The film is based on James Grady's Six Days of the Condor but the film's plotting was impatient.

[255] Warner Studios, 1988.

[256] Paramount Studios, 1994.

[257] Touchstone Films, 1998.

[258] Michael McGarrity, Under the Cover of Law (New York: Dutton, Penguin Press, 2001).

A number of interviews touched on a government institution he'd never heard of before, a Joint Military Intelligence College that offered undergraduate and graduate spy-craft degrees to carefully selected military and civilian intelligence personnel.[259]

Later he finds a videotape of an interview with a former DEA agent who (...) "revealed that the Joint Military Intelligence College had developed a field-intelligence and drug interdiction curriculum for the Ecuadorian army.[260]

So we have come full circle. I began this with my argument for teaching spy fiction at the JMIC and end with the reality that JMIC has become part of the fiction — or vice versa.

---

[259] McGarrity, 137.
[260] McGarrity, 141.

PART I. DISCOVERY — PROOF — CHOICE

By Frank T. Hughes

(Originally disseminated as class notes for his JMIC class on The Art and Science of the Process of Intelligence Analysis.)

> *Information and expertise are a necessary but not sufficient means of making intelligence analysis the special product that it needs to be. A comparable effort has to be devoted to the science of analysis.*

—Douglas MacEachin
Former DDI, CIA

This course concerns the marshaling of intelligence evidence and the construction of defensible and persuasive arguments based on this evidence. Both of these tasks are crucial in effective intelligence analysis and form the very foundation for later decisions based on intelligence analyses. It has been recognized for years that we are far better at collecting, transmitting, storing, and retrieving intelligence information than we have been at drawing defensible and persuasive conclusions from it.[261] This gap between collection and analytic methods has been brought into particularly sharp focus by the tragic events that took place on September 11, 2001 involving the terrorist attacks on the World Trade Center and the Pentagon. Intelligence analysts face extremely complex inferential tasks involving the generation and analysis of true masses of evidence of every conceivable kind. In short, intelligence analysts face the task of trying to make sense out of masses of evidence that, on the surface at least, may not appear to make any sense.

> *The NSA along with its counterparts in Canada, UK, Australia, and New Zealand uses a worldwide network to intercept messages. How much raw data these intercept facilities haul in every day is classified. But some observers speculate it is comparable to all the information in all the books in the Library of Congress!*

Glenn Borpette, Senior Editor
IEEE Spectrum Online, Jan 02
www.spectrum.lieee.org

Everyone agrees that the collection of relevant and credible intelligence evidence of a variety of sorts is vitally necessary. But collection by itself, however necessary, is not sufficient; we must become more adept at drawing imaginative, defensible and persuasive conclusions from it. It would not be stretching the point to say that our future may depend upon your ability to productively generate imaginative and plausible hypotheses and then to be able to defend hypotheses you believe are most likely based on coherent

---

[261] See: Schum, D., (University Press of America, Lanham, MD, 1987), Vol I, pages 4 and 470-471.

and persuasive arguments you construct from the evidence at hand. These are the core activities of intelligence analysis — the "science of analysis," if you will — **discovery, proof, and choice.**

As we all know, failures of intelligence analysis are often widely advertised while successes are not made public, and often cannot be. The truth is that analysts are routinely asked to perform tasks for which they have received little if any tutoring. Conventional courses in logic, probability, and statistics do not prepare a person for the task of drawing conclusions based on masses of evidence whose items suggest many, often complex and interrelated, lines of arguments on hypotheses of interest. The evidence of interest to intelligence analysts usually concerns events that are unique, singular, or one-of-a-kind and are thus not replicable or repeatable. This means that there are rarely any useful or relevant statistical records available to draw upon in making inferences about the capabilities and intentions of potential or real adversaries. We had no existing statistical records regarding the intentions of foreigners who showed up in our civilian flying schools wishing only to learn how to steer multiengine aircraft and not how to perform takeoffs or landings. Lacking existing statistical records to draw upon, we must generate new information by inquiry, the asking of questions. Skill in asking productive questions is as vitally necessary in intelligence analysis as it is in any other situation in which discovery and investigation are necessary. Effective intelligence analysis rests upon mixtures of both imaginative and critical reasoning. Intelligence analysts whose work has been exemplary have almost certainly acquired their skill through years of experience and, perhaps, through often-painful trial and error experiences. Given the need for accurate and timely intelligence analyses, whose urgency is evident in light of current events, we cannot afford to have intelligence analysis learned just on the basis of many trial and error experiences.

But where are the skills of marshaling evidence, analyzing evidence, and the construction of persuasive arguments in support of intelligence estimates taught? Do we assume that such analysis is something that can be done instinctively? Or do we think that collecting and cataloging evidence is more specialized than analyzing evidence? I start from the premise that such assumptions are false. Basic skills in marshaling and analyzing evidence are important and teachable skills that are largely neglected in our intelligence analysis education.

Just as you cannot do very much carpentry with your bare hands, there is not much thinking you can do with your bare brain.

Bo Dahlbom and Lars-Erik Janlert
As cited by Dennitt in "Kinds of Minds," 1996

Fortunately, there are methods for marshaling masses of evidence and for constructing complex arguments that are very useful and that may at least reduce the number of trial and error experiences that so often accompany learning the business of accurate and timely intelligence analyses. Some of these methods have been in existence for decades, but have not been given the attention they deserve. The exception is in the field of law where courses concerning these methods have been offered for over a decade in several prominent law schools. The present course draws upon the experience gained in these attempts to provide persons with better methods for making sense out of masses of evidence. Our view is that these methods represent one very important step in attempts to close the collection-analysis methods gap mentioned above. These analytic methods cannot be learned effectively just by listening to lectures about them. Nor can they be learned by just listening to first-hand accounts of successful analyses or by post-mortem accounts of analytic failures. They can only be learned by hands-on experience with collections of evidence whose meaning must be established by imaginative and critical thought. The major part of this course will involve your performing three assignments involving collections of various kinds of intelligence data whose meaning is to be established. The major purpose of these assignments is to help you acquire habits of imaginative and critical thought that will serve you well when it becomes your turn to try to make sense out of a mass of evidence in some situation vital to our nation's defense. Here is a brief review of our course objectives as they concern the tasks of evidence marshaling and argument construction.

A. Objectives Concerning the Marshaling of Thoughts and Evidence

On some rare occasions we may be lucky to have what are termed "nuggets"— those single items of credible evidence that immediately suggest important specific possibilities or hypotheses to which we ought to attend carefully. If we had been in possession of such nuggets in advance of September 11, 2001, we might have been able to prevent the disaster that occurred. In most cases, however, lacking such nuggets, we must mine and process enormous amounts of "lower grade evidential ore." In such instances, new possibilities or hypotheses are generated, discovered or suggested only by examining *combinations* of information. Two or more items of information, considered together, often suggest hypotheses that are not apparent when the items of information are considered separately. The necessity for considering combinations of information in order to generate new hypotheses exposes an extraordinarily difficult problem. The number of possible combinations of two or more items of information increases exponentially with the number of items we have. Even if we could examine all possible combinations of our items of evidence, it would not make any sense to do so. This would be the act of trying to look through *everything* in the hope of finding *something*.[262] Here is precisely where useful methods for marshaling, organizing and combining our thoughts and evidence become so important.

Intelligence information rarely, if ever, comes to us already organized or marshaled in ways that immediately suggest new hypotheses or possibilities. Experienced intelligence analysts adopt a variety of methods for organizing the information they receive or request. Developing strategies for marshaling our thoughts and evidence that are useful

---

[262] The number of combinations C of two or more items of information, when we have n items of information, is the number $C = 2n - (n+1)$. When n is just 10, C = 1013; for n = 50, $C \approx 1.3(10)15$; for n = 100, $C \approx 1.26(10)30$.

and necessary in any discovery-related situation has been an object of study for nearly fifteen years. One of our objectives in this course is to bring to your attention the results of these studies. *How well we marshal our existing thoughts and evidence greatly influences how well we are able to generate new potential evidence and new hypotheses that we do not have, but would be wise to consider.* No single method for marshaling thoughts and evidence is adequate. As an episode of intelligence analysis unfolds, we need to bring our thoughts and evidence together in different ways, each of which is crucial in any kind of discovery or investigative activity, such as intelligence analysis. In Part III of these notes we will describe some alternative ways for marshaling or combining your thoughts and evidence that have proven useful in a variety of contexts. In the three exercises you will perform your first task will be to marshal or organize the evidence we provide.

B. Objectives Concerning the Construction of Defensible and Persuasive Arguments Based on Evidence.

> *Logic is concerned with the soundness of the claims we make — with the solidity of the grounds we produce to support them, the firmness of the bcking we can provide for them — or, to change the metaphor, with the sort of CASE we can present in defense of our claims. The legal analogy implied in this last way of putting the point can be of real help ... logic (we may say) is generalised jurisprudence.*

> *Stephen Toulmin*
> *The Uses of Argument*

Intelligence evidence, like any other, has three major credentials: relevance, credibility, and *inferential force or weight*. Relevance answers the question: So What? How is the evidence related to hypotheses whose likeliness is at issue? Credibility answers the question: Can we believe what the evidence says? Inferential force or weight concerns the question: How strong does the evidence favor or disfavor hypotheses at issue? The trouble of course is that no evidence comes to us with these three credentials already established; they must be established by effective arguments. As we will later discuss in detail, arguments in defense of these credentials can be astonishingly complex. They can be quite complex even for single items of evidence. But when we have a mass of evidence whose meaning we are trying to establish, they can be extremely complex when they are considered carefully. To use a modern term, these complex arguments can be considered as inference networks represented as chains of reasoning, often long and interrelated, that link our evidence to hypotheses whose likeliness is at issue.

> *Because of the consequences attendant to the decisions they render, doctors and lawyers are held to a higher standard of reasoning than any other profession. Intelligence Analysis should be held to the same standards.*

> *—F.J. Hughes*

From experience we learn that some defensible arguments can fail to be persuasive; we also learn that some people are persuaded by arguments that are not, in fact, defensible. Concern about the validity of arguments from evidence dates from antiquity and, in logic courses, we learn how to avoid various well-known fallacies in argument. However, courses we may have taken on this subject do not prepare us for the array of difficulties encountered when our arguments rest on masses of evidence that can be linked to hypotheses by often-long chains of reasoning having several important ingredients. As you will see in Part IV, concern about methods for constructing complex defensible arguments based on masses of evidence dates from the year 1913 in the work of an American legal scholar named John Henry Wigmore [1863-1943]. He was the very first person to systematically study what we today refer to as inference networks. The methods he advocated have not, until recently, been given the attention they deserve. Wigmore was far ahead of his time in his concern about how we might make sense out of masses of evidence that may not seem to make any sense. One reason why Wigmore's methods for argument construction were not taken seriously in the past is that his original methods were not, in modern terms, "user-friendly." But recent research on Wigmore's methods, coupled with the availability of computer systems, have made his methods far easier to implement. No one ever questioned the logic residing behind Wigmore's methods. Indeed, as we will note, later scholars employed the same reasoning as Wigmore but in total innocence of Wigmore's much earlier work.

The fact that Wigmore was a legal scholar and not an intelligence analyst[263] should not detract from the applicability of his work to modern intelligence analysis. In each of the three exercises you will perform in this course, we will ask you to use a modern-day version of Wigmore's methods for constructing arguments from collections of intelligence evidence having various characteristics. As you will see, these methods provide you far more than just strategies for charting complex arguments. These methods have very important heuristic merit; they will allow you to generate new questions and new potential evidence you might not have thought about if you had not employed these methods. Perhaps even more important, learning about Wigmore's methods will put you in a frame of mind that will stand you in good stead regardless of the analytic problems you face in the future. Employment of his methods rests upon imaginative as well as critical reasoning, two attributes that are so vitally necessary in intelligence analysis.

We begin this course on structured intelligence analysis with a consideration of some important properties and uses of evidence. Careful study of these matters pays big dividends in our later work on evidence marshaling and argument construction. Before commencing, the student should review the Appendix: Definitions and Terms of Reference.

---

[263] However, Wigmore did serve in World War I as a colonel in the U. S. Army.

... it is rather more difficult for me to describe what they do with this enormous quantity of material once they get it. Tapping into even a single fibre for a few minutes would produce a quanity of data that could not be reasonably stored aboard a submarine.

John Pike, Dir. Global Security
Think Tank on National Security in Alexandria, VA
(Commenting on NSA's ability to tap undersea
fibre-optic cables by specially built submarines. Jan 02)

FAILURES OF IMAGINATION: THOUGHTS ON THE 9/11 COMMISSION REPORT

Thomas Dowling

(Originally published as the keynote speech at the Third Annual Homecoming of the Joint Military Intelligence College Alumni Association at the United States Naval Academy in October 2004.)

Thank you for the opportunity to speak with you today. When Tom Van Wagner first approached me about speaking, I was a bit hesitant. A talk like this could easily become a back-stage-at-the-9/11 Commission monologue, long on details and short on insight of real use to intelligence professionals.

I also have first-hand knowledge of only one portion of what was an enormously complex operation spread over two cities — Washington and New York. In fact, the Washington operation was itself split between two locations. Focused on the origins of Al Qaeda and, in particular, on the role of Iraq, Iran, and Pakistan in Al Qaeda's rise and evolution, I was a bystander to the critical debates on intelligence reform that lie at the heart of the Commissions reform proposals.

However, on reflection, I decided to share my thoughts on another of the Commission's key findings that is of direct relevance to everyone in this room — the profound failure of vision in the Intelligence Community (IC).

Let me begin by including myself solidly in the ranks of those who failed. Most of my 30 years in the Foreign Service were spent in, or working on, the problems of the Middle East or South Asia. In 1996, after graduation from the Joint Military Intelligence College (JMIC), I became the deputy director and acting director of the Office of Near East and South Asian analysis in the U.S. Department of State, Bureau of Intelligence Research (INR). I remained in INR until I retired in 2002. Thus, I was in a responsible and informed position on regional issues for the key years that saw the rise of the Taliban and Al Qaeda.

And about the rise of Al Qaeda, let me also say that I believe that no part of the IC got it right. A few analysts scattered across the IC understood the threat; elements of the community saw pieces of the problem, but, as agencies and as a community, we did not get it. And, what was "it?" — that we were facing a new, lethal, and pervasive threat in an entirely new form.

What follows are my views on what we missed, on how our vision failed. They are strictly personal opinions, not those of the 9/11 Commission, the U.S. Department of State, or the JMIC.

I emphasize that I am speaking about the analytical side of the IC. The operational side also failed in many ways, but that discussion is unsuited for this unclassified forum.

I will, however, note one crucial problem that became apparent during the Commission's work: compartmentalization and access controls served to keep from analysts the very information that would have profoundly altered their understanding of the threat.

To have information that cannot be shared with analysts in the acquiring organization, let alone elsewhere in the community, is — to put it kindly — profoundly self-defeating. We must have a system that gives at least two senior analysts in every agency access to all relevant information on their issue areas no matter where the information is developed.

On the national level, policymaker assumptions in more than one administration played crucial roles in our collective inability to understand Al Qaeda and its base of tolerance, if not open support.

One key element was our focus on the Cold War. This focus led the United States to see the Afghan war for national liberation as strictly a means to damage the Soviet Union. Although individual American analysts and operatives early on recognized the complex stew of regional, tribal, and factional rivalries at play in Afghanistan, as a nation we did not. This lack of recognition led us to support individuals and groups whose long-term ambitions were directly hostile to our own.

More critically, this mind-set led us to walk away once the Soviets were beaten, allowing a thousand poisonous flowers to bloom in the chaos that followed the Soviet withdrawal. We understood Afghanistan as simply a battlefield against the Soviets; our erstwhile friends saw the ouster of the Soviets as simply the precondition for attaining their own strategic goals.

A second, crucial failure was our failure to understand the fundamental problems of the Middle East. We focused on the handful of mostly tiny, but vastly enriched Gulf oil states and the intractable Arab-Israeli dispute. In the Gulf, our concerns were originally economic but came to be almost exclusively focused on supporting our ever-growing military presence directed at Iraq and Iran. The Arab-Israeli dispute is essentially a set of interlocking, bilateral issues. Both sets of problems are basically traditional diplomatic issues posed in terms long familiar.

To the extent that policymakers watched internal-stability issues, their focus was on the effects of these issues on our military presence or on the latest moves in the Arab-Israeli dispute, not the impact of social forces within those societies. A near-total lack of policymaker interest in internal issues in some areas, such as North Africa, helped ensure that these policymakers had little grasp of the forces that fed, and still feed, Al Qaeda and its clones.

The widespread image, shaped by the many excesses of the Gulf oil states in their boom years, of the Middle East is a region swept up by a whirlwind of unsettling modernization. For a handful of Gulf societies, this is true. For most, the situation is exactly the opposite.

Most of the Middle East and North Africa are stagnant societies. Their great ideologies of the 1950s and 1960s are dead; their economies are shackled by outdated economic policies, corruption, and dictatorships sometimes legitimated by ritual elections. Far from being wracked by globalization, most of these societies are drifting along untouched by change. Seeing little chance of any improvement in their lifetimes, their citizens are frustrated by the incompetence, selfishness, and unwillingness of their leaders to adapt. Almost all these societies face an even more unmanageable threat — a vast surge of young people into economies with no prospect of offering them any job at all.

To these circumstances add an intense, near universal anger at U.S. support of Israel and our sanctions on Iraq. Let us be clear here. A handful of our enemies, believers in a twisted, arrogant, and profoundly ignorant distortion of the Islamic faith, hate our society for its values. However, the vast majority of the Middle East does not hate us for our freedom or openness, for that is exactly what they seek for their own societies. Many, especially among the surprisingly large and diverse educated classes, are products of our schools and respecters of our values. What they detest are our policies, which for them contradict the America they envy and admire. This deeply held revulsion at our actions drives so many, who have no desire to live in a future built to Bin Laden's model, to abstain from actively opposing Al Qaeda and its clones.

In the Gulf oil states, especially Saudi Arabia, these governments' seemingly endless expenditures on American military equipment and the growing U.S. defense presence provided additional grievances.

A third and, in my view, critical failure was within the IC as a whole. Over the years, a relentless emphasis on current intelligence has shifted our focus from the long term to the issue of the moment. Reviewing the available material produced before 9/11, I was struck by how small a portion of our product on Al Qaeda and its clones was long-term analysis. I recognize that policymakers must want to read our products and that they often much prefer the latest tidbit to what they view as simply speculation. However, at the same time, we in the IC have an obligation to press them to understand what they might not have the experience or inclination to consider.

Annotating the latest report is an important task, but it is not the only one or often the best one. To the extent that the drive to meet the question of the moment blocks analysts from developing longer-term analysis, we shortchange our readers, ourselves, and, most importantly, the nation.

That said, the balance of my comments address the problems of analysis.

As a whole, the IC recognized the regional problems as background factors and not as key drivers. In the Afghan case, for example, the analytical community failed to understand the participants' vision of the future. With limited resources and the background of Pakistan-India nuclear weapons and the Pakistani invasion at Kargil, Afghanistan seemed a side show of little importance.

What we in the analytical community absolutely failed to recognize was the attraction of politicized religion as the next big "ism." Here we reflected a common assumption drawn from Western history that societies tend over time to move from pervasive religious feeling toward secularism in a one-way evolution. This assumption made us unready to understand the attractive power of politicized faith to societies where highly secular ideologies had failed.

To be sure, we recognized the power of traditional Islam and the deep religiosity of Middle Eastern societies. We also understood the influential role of traditional Muslim clerics. But political Islam, especially as embraced by those regarded as middle class and professional — what we thought of as the most Westernized elements in society — was seen as a marginal force. In truth, for most of the past century, political Islam had failed to gain broad traction anywhere outside Iran. We failed to see that the ground was shifting.

Part of the reason for that failure of vision was the region's history of violent extremists. The most recent violence was political, aimed primarily at Israel or its friends. For decades, the Palestinian groups committed most of the big attacks, drew most of the headlines. And, those groups were resolutely secular and relatively narrowly focused. Even the rise of Hizballah and Hamas did not really change the perception. Although claiming religious motives, both were, and are, nationalist movements operating in specific environments.

We had simply no experience with regional groups aspiring to reshape the world. As a result, the known threats were seen as serious. They drew the main attention, not the rabid fringe-religious groups.

The experience with the region's two most powerful Islamist threats — in Algeria and Egypt — reinforced that tendency. In Algeria, the issue was seen as a straightforward civil war in which religion motivated one side in a nationalist struggle focused within a single country. In Egypt, too, the Islamist threat appeared to have no international ambitions. The self-destruction of Islamist popular support through the Luxor massacre reinforced the idea of limited Islamist staying power. These experiences reinforced a tendency to assume that local regimes could contain an Islamist threat.

The one Islamist group to which the United States did devote extraordinary attention was Hizballah. Although a vicious and successful enemy in the 1980s, Hizballah had become — for the United States — a major potential foe in the 1990s. Focused on ousting Israel from Lebanon, Hizballah worked hard to build its capacity for mischief, but it waged active war only on the Israelis, not the United States. To be sure, Hizballah sought the ability to harm us and was actively engaged in criminal activities in the United States to fund itself. But it was not killing Americans, Al Qaeda was.

Yet, to the extent that U.S. efforts concentrated on an Islamist terrorist threat, the attention was overwhelmingly on Hizballah, not on those directly involved now in killing our citizens and attacking our forces. This overfocus on Hizballah remains today marked by repeated high-level claims, after 9/11, that Hizballah is the "A-Team" among our foes. No, it is not.

Hizballah is a dangerous threat to be watched and thwarted. It may become the main threat again, as it was in the 1980s, but for over the past decade it has been only a potential threat. Unlike Al Qaeda, Hizballah has not chosen to attack us at home.

The main enemy — to use a term beloved by the Soviets — is Al Qaeda. Nothing must make us lose sight of that core truth.

A further analytic problem was rhetoric. The Middle East has a fondness for hyperbole unmatched by deeds. Bin Laden's first proclamations seemed to be more of the same empty rhetoric. Starkly put, until the African embassy bombings, he seemed to be the region's latest bit player with wild claims and little achievement. Only later did we recognize how wrong we were. Even when the attack on the USS COLE (DDG 67) made clear that Bin Laden was a man of his word, that he was at war with us, policymakers hesitated to wage war on him.

A final problem was that experience and history had taught us what seemed eternally true — that Sunni and Shia Muslims divided by centuries of rivalry, war, and martyrdom would never make common cause against an enemy. Until Bin Laden bridged that gap, there was no reason to assume such an alliance ever would occur. A mass of historical experience argued it would not. As a result, hints of cooperation were dismissed without real examination.

There also was no reason to assume that Arabs would make common cause with Malay or Indonesian extremists, no reason to think that such links were emerging. Long experience had taught us that Arab Muslims were often disdainful (or worse) of their coreligionists from outside the Middle East. Organized regionally, the IC had little ability to match events in one region with those in another and then to recognize what was emerging.

We all proved to be prisoners of a received wisdom that was, unknown to us, out of date. Our failure here was in not considering that perhaps times had changed. I know of no one in the IC who took the time to ponder that possibility.

The factors I have just outlined are general ones that shaped our collective misperception of Bin Laden's threat. This background is critical for understanding a fundamental failure of vision. Collectively, as we learned during the Commissions work, more than enough information was available to the IC to shape a correct understanding of Bin Laden's menace.

I would like to turn now to two specific examples: the Afghan training camps and the destruction of the Bamiyan Buddhas — of how we had the information, but we drew the wrong conclusions.

First, the Afghan training camps.

We now know that, for several key years, the Taliban allowed Al Qaeda and its allies to operate substantial training camps in Afghanistan. We knew their location, size, and many other details. From that information, it was possible to estimate the number of those being trained. Admittedly, we did not know enough about the courses and schedules to develop precise numbers. But, plainly, a substantial number of people were passing through those facilities. And, the IC made efforts to estimate those numbers.

This information should have led to an obvious analytical issue. Where were the graduates going? Neither the Taliban nor the Kashmiri militants were taking substantial casualties, so that the replacement of their losses would not absorb numerous recruits. Nor were the Taliban or Kashmiri militant forces expanding markedly. If so, then the camps' graduates were going elsewhere. Why? In retrospect, an obvious question, but, at the time, it went unasked. Or, if asked, it went unaddressed. Either way, it was a failure of vision.

The destruction of the Bamiyan Buddhas in the spring of 2001 is an even clearer example, albeit in hindsight, of our failure of vision. Despite enormous international pressure, including efforts made by a number of major Islamic nations, to emphasize that these massive rock carvings were a global treasure, the Taliban regime destroyed them in a world-class act of cultural vandalism. At the time, we judged that it was yet another ignorant act of the Taliban, reflecting simply their primitive hostility to anything outside their narrow worldview. In a word, the vandalism seemed to serve no purpose. What we did not stop to consider is that the destruction actually served a very clear purpose for Bin Laden.

Since arriving in Afghanistan from Sudan, Bin Laden used his close ties to Mullah Omar, the Taliban ruler, to gradually develop a state within a state. Al Qaeda personnel not only enjoyed free rein within Afghanistan, they gradually moved to assert increasing control over security and general Taliban policy. We now know that other Taliban leaders were becoming increasingly wary of the influence of Bin Laden's ambition. They also were becoming worried by their regime's growing international isolation.

These leaders were by no means agreed on the destruction of the Buddhas, a decision that seems to have been Omar's alone. For Omar, the destruction appears to have been driven by his skewed vision of Islam. Other Taliban leaders worried that the destruction would further weaken their ties to such key supporters as Saudi Arabia and Pakistan, both of whom opposed the act, and other Muslim states. The destruction produced exactly that result.

The originator and energizer of the destruction was Bin Laden. While his religious convictions played a role, the true purpose of the destruction was indeed to further isolate the Taliban regime internationally. Such isolation was helpful, if not essential, to his gaining de facto control of the Taliban state.

Our failure of vision settled on assuming that this destruction was an act of spectacular ignorant vandalism. No one in the IC stopped to ponder whether there were other motives, that is, another, more rational logic for this act. Had we done so, we might have had a much better sense of Bin Laden's ambition and his strategic skill.

As we are all now well aware of Al Qaeda's actions and our efforts to destroy it, I will conclude my remarks here with a few final observations.

Some may object that the failures outlined above are of concern only to those who work political or terrorism issues, that such problems have little relevance to those working on issues of technology, weaponry, force structure, or other fields. Admittedly, the details of what went wrong are specialized. But my work on the Commission, especially the constant discussions with colleagues with a broad range of experience from aviation security to covert operations, impel me to warn all of you to consider the broader lessons.

The mistaken judgments we made were not based on stupidity, inexperience, or the willful actions of a few analysts. Consider, for example, Israel's failure to anticipate the 1973 attack, a topic studied carefully by JMIC students. There are similarities to our problem, but our failure is broader. In the Israeli case, a number of analysts did see the truth, but their superiors refused to agree. In our case, the overwhelming majority of analysts did not understand the threat.

This failure to understand was rooted in a massive body of experience that had proved correct for decades. The evidence against reconsideration, certainly before the African embassy bombing and even up to the Cole attack, was substantial. I cannot help but fear that lurking out there, in the world of technical and military-operational intelligence, are equal bodies of evidence that something cannot be done or must be done in a certain way. I cannot help but think that in those fields, too, there are lines of inquiry closed off, because of a failure of vision, of clues ignored because "everyone knows that this can't work" or "no sensible person would do it that way."

The only antidote is to institutionalize a process of identifying and then challenging our past assumptions. Having attempted and largely failed at such an effort in the National Intelligence Estimate (NIE) process, I have no illusions that this will be anything but nightmarishly difficult. There is no worse professional sin than asking analysts to rate the validity of their past predictions.

But unless we try, there is another different but equally disastrous 9/11 surprise waiting for us. In the interim, I would ask that all of you think hard about what might be the certainty that could be built on sand in your own professional world. For there surely is one out there lurking undetected.

The views expressed in this paper are those of the author and do not reflect the official position of the U.S. Government, to include the 9/11 Commission, the U.S. Department of State, or the Joint Military Intelligence College.

HOMELAND SECURITY AND INTELLIGENCE: CAN OIL MIX WITH WATER IN AN OPEN SOCIETY?

William C. Spracher, COL, USA (Ret)

(Originally published in Low Intensity Conflict & Law Enforcement, 11, No.1 (Spring 2002): 29-54.)

INTRODUCTION

The world is a dangerous place to live, not because of the people who are evil, but because of the people who don't do anything about it.[264]

—*Albert Einstein*

Stealing the headlines in the United States since the tragic events of September 11, 2001, has been the federal government's almost single-minded focus on homeland security. This is not at all hard to understand given the national and international trauma which that series of terrorist atrocities produced and the approximately 3,000 lives lost in a matter of only a couple of hours. An assessment often heard in the painful days and weeks following the al Qaeda attacks, almost to the point of becoming trite, was that the world had changed forever that day, and the sense of calm assurance historically felt by most U.S. citizens that they were safe from harm by terrorists inside the country's borders would never return. Some international pundits glibly observed that it was about time for the U.S. to wake up from its false complacency and experience what most of the rest of the world had been suffering for years. A few of the more cruel and sadistic observers even celebrated the attacks in the streets and claimed the U.S. deserved what happened or, in something of a stretch, had actually provoked the attacks.

The fact that Washington and New York City were seemingly caught totally by surprise immediately brought the nation's intelligence community into the spotlight, producing consternation that it had failed to predict the attacks and protect the innocent victims, who represented not only the U.S. but scores of other countries. It was truly a terrorist onslaught directed against the U.S., but one having spillover effects on the entire civilized world. High-level government officials and friends and relatives of the victims alike were left asking how such a horrible day could have happened without someone detecting the warning signs. In the nearly two years since "9/11," a series of inquiries and investigations has been conducted to try to determine what went wrong and how. Some structural changes have already been made to enhance coordination among U.S. government agencies; others will surely follow. The newest and most talked about Cabinet member in the U.S. government is the recently created Department of Homeland Security (DHS), headed up by former Pennsylvania Governor Tom Ridge. One of the most controversial

---

[264] Albert Einstein, quoted in *Combating Terrorism in a Globalized World*, Report by the National War College Student Task Force on Combating Terrorism, May 2002, vii.

aspects in the process of developing this entity, and refining the concept of homeland security overall, is the role of intelligence in gathering information on the increasing terrorist threat and analyzing it for key decision makers.

This article will examine the intelligence challenges for homeland security. In doing so, it will explore the problems of merging disparate cultures — law enforcement vice intelligence, civil actors vice military, federal efforts vice those at the state and local levels, and the domestic focus vice the international perspective. It will also briefly look at control and oversight mechanisms to ascertain if the new department is performing its mission adequately and sustaining the public trust. It was only a few weeks after the dust at "Ground Zero" had settled and the embers at the Pentagon had cooled that critics began pointing fingers at the Bush Administration for going too far too fast in trying to catch the perpetrators and prevent another 9/11-type event from occurring in the future. At play here is the traditional tradeoff between the rights to privacy of ordinary citizens and the national security imperatives of the country at large, a delicate balancing act that has taxed the patience and sensitivities of the American people.

The civil rights versus national security conundrum is faced not only by the U.S. but by all freedom-loving peoples of the world. Given the nature of the globalized, asymmetric threat now confronted by all nations, and especially those sharing democratic ideals, the need for more and better intelligence sharing is obvious, both internal to each government and external with counterpart elements in allied countries. As we all now recognize, terrorists and other international criminals do not respect territorial integrity and national sovereignty. In fact, they exploit these somewhat outmoded ideas and national boundaries in an effort to prevent effective and timely countermeasures. Even though homeland security is receiving more coverage in the U.S. than anywhere else, increasingly other countries are starting to pay more attention to their internal security procedures. Internal security has long been a salient topic in most corners of the Western Hemisphere, but for reasons other than the threat of international terrorism. It was not until this threat penetrated the protective barrier that the U.S. assumed it had around it that Washington began paying so much attention to internal security, and several other capitals are following suit.

This paper will discuss primarily those challenges faced by the U.S. government as it tries to shore up protection for its own people, systems, and critical infrastructure. Nevertheless, all the nations of the hemisphere are in this new game together, and a threat to one spills over and becomes a threat to all. Only with a concerted effort among them — in part military, in part diplomatic, and in part economic — can the terrorist threat ultimately be neutralized. Of course, this demands that robust multinational collaboration and interagency coordination be practiced. Lessons learned by scholars studying these problems in the U.S. must be shared with those of other nations that may soon be facing, if they are not already, these same pernicious threats. Some of the lessons learned will be about the nature and sources of the threat itself, some will be about the application of enhanced technology, while some will be about the internal bureaucratic politics of trying to organize a set of structures that will complement, rather than detract from, the overall defensive posture of the society at large.

Finally, we must ask how all this can be done in such a way that the cherished freedoms the effort is designed to protect are not themselves destroyed in the process. As time passes, memories fade, and the "shock and awe" of 9/11 dims while other national concerns, such as the economy, take center stage, criticism of the government's efforts grows. And as more details are revealed about what certain officials knew, and when they knew it, scrutiny of the intelligence agencies' roles intensifies. In an attempt to "connect the dots," to use another cliché of recent vintage, fingers are being pointed at certain players. The sense of unity that bound the executive and legislative branches of the U.S. government after 9/11, and the feeling that all citizens are in this together and must support the President's efforts loyally and without question, has dissipated. Now that the patriotic euphoria has subsided and citizens have been able to reflect not only on the events of 9/11, but also on the domestic measures taken in the wake of that disastrous day and the international linkages used to justify the war in Iraq, more pointed questions are being raised. This paper will examine some of those issues and assess whether intelligence can enhance security without destroying the civil liberties U.S. citizens have been accustomed to enjoying for over two centuries.

SETTING THE SCENE

Internal threats are not new to the United States, though many of today's citizens may not realize it. During the Civil War, a clampdown on domestic terrorist acts was ordered by that great advocate of civil freedoms, Abraham Lincoln. Always the master pragmatist, the President knew that in order to maintain the Union and restore domestic order he had to take tough measures for tough times. This included the suspension of the writ of *habeas corpus* (the right to challenge in court one's detention by the government), the arrests of thousands of suspected disloyal civilians, the trials of civilians before military commissions (to include Lincoln's own assassination conspirators), and the denial of certain press freedoms.[265] As Supreme Court Chief Justice William H. Rehnquist told a group of law students in 1996, five years before 9/11: "Lincoln felt that the great task of his administration was to preserve the Union. If he could do it by following the Constitution, he would quite willingly choose the former course. . . If may be that during wartime emergencies it is in the nature of the presidency to focus on accomplishing political and strategic ends without too much regard for any resulting breaches in the shield which the Constitution gives to civil liberties."[266] In hindsight, this observation seems highly prophetic.

Nevertheless, there are some differences between what the U.S. faced during the early 1860s and what it faces today. President Bush reminds us that we are "at war" in the fight against global terrorism. "But how the country prosecutes that war is vital to maintaining the fabric of our open society. A crackdown that is highly targeted is justified. In all likelihood, foreign agents — some of whom may be U.S. citizens or are in line for achieving that status — are continuing to work in this country to abet Islamic extremists. But they need to be found and identified through careful, selective intelligence, not racial profiling.

---

[265] Warren Getler, "Civil Rules for the Terror War," *The Washington Post*, 25 May 2003, B4.
[266] Getler, B4.

These issues will likely be taken up eventually by the Supreme Court, particularly those concerning lengthy detentions without charge of noncitizens, government secrecy in such cases and the use of military tribunals when civil courts are available in peacetime."[267]

The issue of how best to warn citizens of an impending threat also can be traced back at least as far as the Civil War. In November 1864, Southern agents devised a plan to use arson to spread panic throughout Northern cities. Like the situation of today, the Lincoln Administration knew that these terrorists were planning attacks but did not have specifics. Consequently, Secretary of State William Seward (famous for being the namesake of "Seward's Folly" when Alaska was purchased by the U.S. from Russia in 1867) issued an official warning to the nation in the form of a letter to the mayor of Buffalo, New York, which was released to the press. Curiously, although *The New York Times* printed Seward's warning the next day, the Washington papers did not. All five major newspapers remained mute on the arson threat, although one of them did report on a fire drill that day at the Washington Navy Yard. For whatever reason — blind luck or Washington's already adequate security — the expected attacks occurred elsewhere. The big assault was in New York three weeks later, when Southern arsonists tried to burn down several hotels and a museum. Damage was minor, and no one was hurt. Naturally, when word of the arson spread, security in the capital city was tightened considerably. Soldiers patrolled Washington's streets, and more guards were added at government offices and installations.[268] Sadly, however, less than four months later when Lincoln was assassinated at Ford's Theatre by John Wilkes Booth, an itinerant actor and Southern sympathizer, the President settled for only one police guard, who left his post, and Seward's residence had no guards at all. The Secretary of State nearly perished too from an attack by one of Booth's gang.

Unlike in many other nations of this hemisphere, U.S. society has always reflected a deep aversion to internal security and countersubversion. The country traditionally has trusted its own citizens and rationalized that any serious threats would be of an external nature. Despite a brief period of insecurity after Pearl Harbor due to fears of Japanese air attacks on the West Coast and German submarine shenanigans on the East Coast, the U.S. has enjoyed a sense of relative security due to friendly neighbors to the north and south (except for occasional lapses with Mexico that ended in violence) and broad expanses of ocean to the east and west. Whenever threats from within have manifested themselves, such as the 1995 bombing in Oklahoma City or the much smaller 1996 bombing incident during the Olympics in Atlanta, they have generally been written off as perpetrated by crackpots or devious criminals, and not viewed as legitimate threats to the government or society at large.

Similarly, until about six decades ago intelligence, just like the armed forces, was deemed a wartime-only commodity that could be built up temporarily for a national emergency and then dismantled as soon as things returned to normal. The Vietnam War and its

---

[267] Getler, B4.

[268] John Lockwood, "We Had Terrorists Even in the Time of Lincoln," *The Washington Post,* 16 February 2003, B8.

turbulent aftermath produced a lot of fallout on this score too. Domestic intelligence agencies were ordered by their superiors to collect information on U.S. citizens considered to be disloyal or sympathetic to foreign interests. By the mid-1970s, as the war ended and tumult on college campuses (spurred not only by antiwar sentiment but also by civil rights for minorities and women, student empowerment, and other issues) began to diminish, Senate and House special committees were convened to determine if intelligence entities had overstepped their legal bounds. The result was the plethora of control and oversight mechanisms put in place to watch the National Intelligence Community, to include select committees on intelligence in both houses of Congress, the President's Foreign Intelligence Advisory Board and the Intelligence Oversight Board in the executive branch, enhanced coordination powers given to the Director of Central Intelligence, an intelligence oversight office set up at the Pentagon, and other corrective measures.

This may be a convenient juncture to highlight the term *foreign* intelligence. Nearly all the control and oversight fixes of the 1970s emphasized the distinction between collecting information on foreign elements operating from *outside* the U.S. and on U.S. citizens or so-called "U.S. persons" living and working *inside* the country. The restrictions on intelligence-gathering activities against the latter are extremely tight compared to those against the former, and many laws are in place to protect the rights of those inside the U.S. Of course, 9/11 changed the nature of the game completely, and the distinction between internal and external threats has blurred considerably. In essence, homeland security tries to deal with threats perpetrated by outsiders but operating from inside the country's borders. Most experts agree that some of the restrictions on the intelligence community which made eminent sense in the 1970s are overly limiting in the changed international environment of the 21st century. Intelligence agency officials, backed by supporters in the Congress and academia, argue that their hands were tied behind their backs and the result was a lack of sufficient capacity to foresee 9/11 and react swiftly. As a result, the legal framework for intelligence activities in the U.S. is being revised to a degree, alongside the creation of a parallel homeland security community. How complementary these efforts are, or should be, will be addressed later. Suffice it to say for now, however, that both homeland security and intelligence functions are under a microscopic lens, in large part because of the impact they have had on traditional civil liberties and freedoms, and to a lesser degree because some feel the intelligence agencies are not being forced to collaborate closely enough with homeland security entities to make the threat data produced truly effective.

Aside from the historical backdrop so far discussed, there are also sociological, political, and economic aspects to what the U.S. is going through post-9/11. Many historians and disciples of the Founding Fathers thirst for democracy and individual liberty at all costs. They do not see the threat from al Qaeda as dangerous enough to change the laws regarding how much government intrusiveness should be permitted. These critics of the Bush Administration's strong-arm tactics celebrate the country's fluid borders and open immigration. They continue to champion the public's right to know and denigrate any moves by the government to keep things from them in the interest of national security. They believe in openness and total transparency in dealings with the government. They feel excessive secrecy is nothing more than a tactic to cover up mistakes by the intelligence community or blunders by executive officials in properly using the intelligence provided. Bureaucratic wrangling has long been a political tradition in the U.S., but some critics point to what is going on now with all the inquiries and investigations as nothing more than one agency trying to "cover its behind" and deflect blame to another or, more pointedly, to the overseers and decision makers who bound its hands in the first place or reduced its budget to levels where it could not do its job to the expectations of the American people.

Concomitantly, certain economic characteristics of the U.S. have played a part in the current morass. The deficit spending currently plaguing not only the federal government but also nearly all state governments and many municipalities is not making the homeland security effort any easier. The short budget cycle practiced in the U.S. is a further complicating factor, as are the tendencies to bury questionable expenditures in other program lines and to practice post-crisis planning. The "brinksmanship" attributed to Secretary of State John Foster Dulles in the 1950s may have worked during the slower, more predictable Cold War epoch, but it is ill-advised in the uncertain times brought on by the so-called "Global War on Terrorism." Speaking of the word "global," the whole concept of *globalization* is very contentious, whether it be globalization of the economy or globalization of the threat. To affluent citizens of Western Europe, East Asia, or the U.S., globalization may be a blessing, but to those in the Third World ravaged by poverty, disease, ethnic or religious conflict, and lack of freedom of expression it may be nothing more than the latest external enemy with which they are powerless to contend.

A FEW BASIC DEFINITIONS

Before proceeding further, it might be helpful to define some terms, given that this paper is written from a U.S. perspective but for a diverse, international audience. "Intelligence" is defined officially by the U.S. Department of Defense (DOD) as "(1) the product resulting from the collection, processing, integration, analysis, evaluation, and interpretation of available information concerning foreign countries or areas; and (2) information and knowledge about an adversary obtained through observation, investigation, analysis, or understanding."[269] In a more general sense, Webster's Dictionary defines "intelligence" as, among other things, "the ability to learn or understand from experience; the ability to acquire and retain knowledge; the ability to respond quickly and successfully to a new situation; the use of the faculty of reason in solving problems; news or information; gathering of secret information, as for military or police purposes; and the persons or agency employed at this."

Of course, the distinction between intelligence and information is somewhat arbitrary. Virtually all practitioners would agree that certain elements of government have the function of taking raw information and processing and analyzing it into finished intelligence. The precise point in the so-called "Intelligence Cycle" at which this transformation

---

[269] U.S. Department of Defense Joint Electronic Library, "Dictionary of Military Terms," accessed through the Defense Technical Information Service website on 16 January 2002.

occurs is in the eyes of the beholder. If one assumes that the essential phases of the cycle include collection, processing, analysis/production, and dissemination, with planning and direction by superiors ongoing throughout, most U.S. experts would agree that raw data or information collected becomes intelligence somewhere between the processing and production steps in the cycle. The specific point can vary depending on the type of information collected, the technology or discipline employed, and the policies and procedures of the agency doing the processing. Moreover, the doctrine of the particular country being looked at may stipulate this point. Generally speaking, however, once the information is packaged in a form in which it can be understood by decision makers, backed up by a degree of reasoned judgment and careful analysis, and properly classified to protect sensitive sources and methods, it can be considered to be finished intelligence.

The above involves looking at intelligence as a *product* that results from a *process*. Intelligence can also refer to the *organization* that produces this material, as when a government employee states that he or she "works for U.S. intelligence" or is part of the "National Intelligence Community." Then again, intelligence can be viewed as a *function* within the state.[270] All states rely on information to survive and all governments require some sort of intelligence or national security mechanism to produce data used by their leaders to make foreign policy decisions. A government that claims it does not need accurate intelligence is operating in the blind and opening itself up to attacks by adversaries from outside the state and also from within. In the last three decades or so, most states have had to deal with international terrorism as one of the most dangerous threats to their stability and safety. The U.S. has experienced terrorist attacks of differing types and intensity around the globe, which is to be expected for a global power that is the world's remaining superpower and whose intense international activities, though well-meaning, invariably spark passions and tensions. U.S. intelligence has been increasingly active in recent years in the counterterrorism arena, but more often than not it has been outside the country's borders and managed separately from the law enforcement effort inside the country.

In the wake of 9/11, U.S. officials began to realize that the functional separation traditionally maintained between *foreign* intelligence and *domestic* law enforcement, both cognitively and legally, was not at all useful for the effort to protect the security of the homeland. The two would have to be coordinated more tightly and respective agencies responsible for these functions would have to collaborate more closely, perhaps calling for entirely new structures and ways of thinking about how to link them together. Thus the Office of Homeland Security in the White House was born only a month after 9/11, and finally after a lot of executive posturing and legislative chest-beating the Department of Homeland Security (DHS) was formally established in March 2003. The issues surrounding these developments will be discussed later.

For now, suffice it to say the term "homeland security" rapidly jumped into the U.S. national consciousness, even though the concept had been bouncing around the Washing-

---

[270] Andres Saenz and William C. Spracher, master lecture on "Intelligence," presented to Fellows of the Center for Hemispheric Defense Studies Defense Planning and Resource Management course, 7 April 2003.

ton community — particularly within DOD, some defense contractor firms, a few think tanks, and academia — for several years beginning in the 1990s. Prior to that, when experts discussed such ideas, they tended to use such terms as operational security, domestic counterintelligence, countersabotage, counterespionage, or counterterrorism. Probably due to the aforementioned aversion to talking about such perfidious concepts as subversion and internal security, which connote dastardly deeds by disloyal U.S. citizens or legal residents, the term "homeland security" seemed more politically acceptable, suggesting threats to the homeland from outside terrorists operating either externally or internally to the borders of the U.S. Homeland security in the U.S. is focused almost exclusively on terrorism, whereas the previous terms cover broader threats to the stability of the government and the values shoring up American society.

A QUESTION OF CULTURE

Given that the thrust of homeland security required bringing together agencies that were not accustomed to working closely with each other in the past, some cultural clashes were inevitable. During the maturation process of the new (or at least revised) homeland security community, organizations have been obligated to subordinate their individual interests and cultural identities to the greater national interest, and this has not been easy. First, there has been a need to accept the blurring of lines between *foreign* and *domestic* activities. Traditionally, the Central Intelligence Agency (CIA) has been responsible for the production of foreign intelligence since its founding in 1947 under the provisions of the National Security Act. Its charter also makes the Agency accountable for counterintelligence *outside* the borders of the U.S., while the Federal Bureau of Investigation (FBI) has been responsible since the 1920s for counterintelligence *inside* the U.S., and more importantly, at least until recently, for investigations of organized crime and other criminal activity warranting federal involvement above the level of crimes prosecuted at the state and local levels. The *foreign* distinction is key here. The CIA and FBI have always jealously guarded their respective turfs, which were backed up by a legal framework and reinforced after the previously discussed intelligence abuses of the 1960s and early 1970s. What many critics fail to realize or acknowledge is that at least some portion of the lack of coordination between the two agencies was levied by law, which means that the outdated statutes must be changed by Congress.

Another cultural division is between the roles of *intelligence* and *law enforcement* in general. This author discovered during the late 1980s when counternarcotics support became an official mission of DOD that there was a huge gap in the way military people look at the drug threat and the way law enforcement agencies such as the Drug Enforcement Administration (DEA) view the problem. The latter see narcotraffickers as common criminals who need to be brought down and prosecuted as soon as possible. The former agree that drug producers and dealers are despicable criminals, but prefer to use them to gather information that will best enable the U.S. government to reduce the overall threat. When DOD was tasked by the President in a September 1989 National Security Decision Directive to assist the federal law enforcement community with intelligence and other technical support, and to help train DEA agents in how to do intelligence, it was evident that the cultural mentalities were quite different. DEA's goals were all about making arrests, while DOD's goals were to use intelligence gathered on drug criminals to do long-term pattern analysis, to help track down other criminals, and to diminish the overall threat to government stability. DOD intelligence officers knew a lot about intelligence collection, analysis, and production of reports on drug activity, but little about legal requirements, rules of evidence, chain of custody, and other such concepts, not to mention the international hurdles that must be dealt with like extradition procedures, maritime agreements, and law of the sea protocols. Much progress has been made overseas in drug detection and interdiction, but cooperation among intelligence and law enforcement agencies has not always been smooth. Incidentally, Asa Hutchinson, up until recently the DEA Director and prior to that a member of the House Permanent Select Committee on Intelligence, is now the DHS Undersecretary for Border and Transportation Security.[271] If anyone understands how to integrate law enforcement with intelligence, it should be Mr. Hutchinson.

As the homeland security effort continues, agencies focusing on terrorism are similarly discovering that it is not always easy to mesh their cultural proclivities with those of other elements. The FBI has been forced to focus more on terrorism and less on other targets such as narcotics, white-collar and violent crimes, and smuggling.[272] Some observers have argued the FBI does not possess the proper mentality for counterterrorism and a separate national-level agency needs to be created for this purpose, reporting neither to the FBI nor the CIA.[273] Since 1986 the Director of Central Intelligence (DCI), in his role as overall coordinator of the intelligence community and not merely as Director of the CIA, has overseen an entity known as the DCI Counterrorist Center (CTC).[274] As a result of 9/11, however, and much clamoring for a more centralized structure at a higher level, President Bush in his January 2003 State of the Union Address announced his decision to create a new threat assessment center that could dramatically revise the way the U.S. government analyzes and responds to terrorist threats. The result was the Terrorist Threat Integration Center (TTIC), which is overseen by the DCI, George Tenet. The Center was initially housed at the CIA compound in Langley, Virginia, but later will move elsewhere (just like DHS was housed temporarily at an old Navy compound in the northwest part of the District of Columbia but is expected to get a new headquarters whenever the budget will permit). This move was greeted with mixed reaction at the FBI, where Director Robert Mueller has been struggling against internal resistance and technological obstacles to transform his Bureau into an agency focused on detecting and thwarting terrorism. The TTIC is charged with providing analyzed intelligence gathered by the CIA, FBI, DOD, and DHS, and is staffed by top coun-

---

[271] Jason Peckenpaugh, "Under One Roof: It Hasn't Been Easy to Combine Disparate Border Agencies in the New Homeland Security Department," *Government Executive*, April 2003, 28.

[272] Kevin Johnson, "FBI to Focus 520 More Agents on Terrorism," *USA Today*, 29 May 2002, 3A.

[273] No author, "Senator Edwards Calls FBI 'Wrong Agency' to Track Terrorists," *FEDmanager Weekly E-mail Newsletter*, 4 March 2003. See also Laurence Arnold, "Panel Ponders New Intelligence Agency," Associated Press release, 13 October 2003, accessed on *Yahoo!News*. The independent, bipartisan commission set up to study the 9/11 attacks discussed the possibility of recommending the creation of a domestic intelligence agency modeled after the United Kingdom's MI5 and designating an independent Director of National Intelligence.

[274] No author, "The War on Terrorism: DCI Counterrorist Center," accessed through CIA website on 9 March 2003.

terterrorism officials from each of those entities. The proposal for the Center came under immediate attack from some lawmakers and civil libertarian groups which argued either that the plan did not go far enough or that it went too far in removing the historic distinctions between foreign and domestic intelligence.[275] Additionally, some critics insist that no new structures should be allowed to report solely to the DCI or to the FBI Director, whom they blame for the security troubles the country is experiencing.

Another cultural divide can be found between the *federal* level and *state* and *local* levels. Law enforcement has long been executed well by the different levels, and cooperation between them on domestic criminal activities has generally been excellent. Nevertheless, the introduction of international terrorism into the equation has taxed the state and local levels. In most cases, with the exception of certain "SWAT" teams and disaster recovery elements existing in some of the more well-financed jurisdictions (e.g., Fairfax County, Virginia, which has responded to earthquakes and other disasters around the globe), these units are not trained or equipped to deal with terrorist incidents. Perhaps more troubling is the area of intelligence sharing. Most of the police departments at these lower levels are not configured to receive or process classified information, and even those that are often are not accustomed to interpreting national-level intelligence reports and applying them to local situations.

Nevertheless, serious attempts are being made to close the gap and better integrate the various levels. For example, last spring President Bush selected New York City's counterterrorism chief, Frank Libutti, a retired Marine lieutenant general, for the top intelligence-related post at DHS, Undersecretary for Information Analysis and Infrastructure Protection (IAIP).[276] Interestingly, a high-profile DOD intelligence official had earlier turned down the job after sending out signals he was interested. Retired Air Force Lieutenant General James Clapper, former Director of the Defense Intelligence Agency (DIA) and current Director of the National Imagery and Mapping Agency (NIMA), decided to stay on at his post at NIMA, where he had been for only about a year.[277] There was some speculation that Clapper's decision not to join DHS reflected a broader feeling in DOD, CIA, and elsewhere in national security circles that the new department was not the place to ensure continuation of an outstanding intelligence career, though Bush was later successful in naming some CIA executives to significant homeland security billets. The Agency's Deputy Executive Director, John Brennan, was named to head the interagency TTIC effective 1 May 2003.[278] In addition, a former Agency counterintelligence official who helped catch CIA spy Aldrich Ames in 1994 was designated DHS Assistant Secretary for Information Analysis, the division in charge of sifting through databases and other electronic information to find signs of terrorist activity.[279] On the oversight side, John Gannon, former Deputy Director for Intelligence at the CIA and subsequently Chairman of the National Intelligence Council, where he supervised all analysts and the preparation of

---

[275] Dan Eggen and John Mintz, "Agency to Concentrate Intelligence Analysis," *The Washington Post*, 30 January 2003, A9.

[276] Judi Hasson, "NYC Official Heads to DHS," *Federal Computer Week*, 24 March 2003.

[277] Brian Krebs, "Bush Choice for Security Job Decides Not to Accept It," *The Washington Post*, 15 January 2003, E5.

[278] Sara Michael, "CIA Veteran Named Threat Center Chief," *Federal Computer Week*, 11 March 2003.

[279] Judi Hasson, "Bush Names Top Homeland Execs," *Federal Computer Week*, 14 March 2003.

national intelligence estimates, respectively, was named majority staff director for the House Homeland Security Committee.[280]

The process of merging the best intelligence thinkers with the homeland security structure has not been easy, however. As of when the new department was formally established on 1 March 2003, the President had still been unsuccessful in filling the three top intelligence-related posts. Some observers were not surprised, claiming that Bush Administration actions were casting doubts about the DHS intelligence mission. For instance, Bush's decision to create the TTIC and place it under the DCI signaled that the DHS role in intelligence assessment would be limited. An unnamed former Bush Administration official insisted that doing intelligence at DHS was "the ultimate thankless job, where the people in charge will be raked over the coals by Congress the next time things go wrong." Likewise, a former deputy national security advisor for the Clinton Administration called the DHS recruiting problems unsurprising, adding that the creation of the TTIC under CIA leadership leaves the DHS Undersecretary for IAIP with a great deal of accountability but little authority on intelligence matters.[281]

These personnel hang-ups relate back to the cultural mindset of the intelligence business, where prospective officials understandably want to have influence on policy making but do not aspire to be the scapegoat the next time a terrorist attack against the U.S. is not foreseen in advance. When discussions were ongoing in 2002 over the proposed makeup of DHS, some observers were critical that the CIA and FBI were not included in the new department, since those are the two most involved agencies in exercising vigilance against terrorists. The decision was made, correctly in this author's opinion, to leave them out of the mix because they have numerous other missions than counterterrorism. After all, the CIA, along with DIA, is responsible for all human source intelligence (HUMINT) at the national level, and its boss, the DCI, is statutorily the senior intelligence advisor to the National Command Authority (President and Secretary of Defense) through the National Security Council (NSC). To place Mr. Tenet under the supervision of Mr. Ridge would make no sense at all. The same is true of the FBI. As the key investigative component of the Department of Justice, responsible not only for counterterrorism but also for counterintelligence and law enforcement inside the U.S., it would be foolish to have Mr. Mueller reporting to Mr. Ridge instead of to the nation's senior law enforcement officer, Attorney General John Ashcroft. True, most of the headlines regarding the CIA and FBI over the last two years have dealt with their successes, and even more so their failures, related to homeland security. Yet, these two agencies perform a host of other functions vital to U.S. national security, some well known by the public and some more invisible. If they were totally subordinated to the homeland security community, which now has its own security council by executive order and subsequent legislative action (the Homeland Security Act of 2002), their performance in other areas could be jeopardized. The CIA and FBI must broadly support all Cabinet departments, not just DHS.

---

[280] U.S. House of Representatives news release, "Intelligence Experts to Head Homeland Security Committee Staff," 18 March 2003.

[281] Brian Krebs, "White House Finds Homeland Security Jobs a Tough Sell, *The Washington Post,* 27 February 2003, A1. See also Shana Harris, "Homeland Security Cedes Intelligence Role," *GovExec.com Daily Briefing,* 26 February 2003.

Finally, culture has a lot to do with power and influence. All senior government officials want to be influential and as close to the ear of the President as possible. They do not want to be buried in the bureaucracy where there are multiple layers of oversight between them and the key decision makers. They also want to have authority over the budget and unfettered access to adequate resources to get the job done. Governor Ridge is thus in a much better situation now as a full Cabinet member and Secretary of DHS than he was as merely a Presidential advisor heading up the Office of Homeland Security. He is able to interact on a level playing field with other key Cabinet members like Ashcroft, Secretary of Defense Donald Rumsfeld, and Secretary of State Colin Powell. Even though he cannot demand priority intelligence support for homeland security, as a Cabinet member he can expect it and make waves if he does not receive it. Conversely, he must respond to Congressional oversight committees, but can more easily mobilize legislative support for his activities than when he was merely a White House advisor not subject to Senate confirmation and not having his own budget. In fact, a few months ago a bill was introduced in Congress to move the DHS Secretary up in the line of succession to the Presidency, on the grounds that, even though he is the newest and most junior Cabinet member, the nature of his responsibilities dictates that he be nearer to the inner circle of critical officials protected in the event of a national catastrophe.[282] Given that such disasters are DHS's *raison d'etre,* the feeling is that the head of this department merits being in the upper echelon of critical national security officialdom.

OTHER PROBLEMS IN GETTING GOOD INTELLIGENCE INTO THE MIX

In addition to the disparate cultures challenge, which probably is the thorniest of them all, there are other problems in integrating homeland security and intelligence. Although some would consider it a cultural challenge, getting *civilian* and *military* elements that are not accustomed to doing so working together has proven difficult. Outside the U.S., the role of the armed forces, and their military intelligence arms, is clear. Inside the U.S., the armed forces are obliged to follow the concept of *"posse comitatus,"* which limits the role of the military in police-type functions, though a few observers believe the military uses this justification to resist some law enforcement support roles it legally could perform. The Posse Comitatus Act, passed by Congress in 1878 in the wake of Civil War Reconstruction and which means in Latin "power of the country," does not apply to the Coast Guard or the National Guard when called up by state governors and not federally activated by the President. The Coast Guard, which is officially one of the U.S. armed services but has a law enforcement role, is the only service not part of DOD (except in time of declared war when it is under the operational control of the Navy). When DHS was established in March 2003, the Coast Guard was transferred to that department from the Transportation Department.[283]

---

[282] Jim Abrams, "Bill Would Change President Succession," *FederalNewsRadio.com*, 11 July 2003.

[283] No author, "Military Resists Domestic Role," *Government Executive,* November 2001, in special issue entitled "Intelligence Crisis: What Must Be Done," and "Homeland Security: The Bureaucratic Obstacles." See also Katherine McIntire Peters, "Troops on the Beat: The Military's Role in Homeland Security Is Growing," in another special issue entitled "On Guard: Homeland Security," April 2003, 56-61.

The military is in a support role only when it comes to counterterrorism, and it has been very effective in supporting the State Department, which runs overseas embassies, the CIA, the FBI (in those countries where there are legal attaches posted), and other government agencies in combating the terrorist threat. The difficulties emerge when military units are expected to perform roles they are not trained for, or to substitute for more appropriate civilian agencies, and this is what is happening in Iraq today. The U.S. military, and the token units of allied armed forces there, are doing a commendable job in trying to win the peace as effectively as they won the war. However, they are trained mainly as warfighters, not as peacekeepers, and their rogue adversaries take advantage of that. Intelligence is having success in gradually ferreting them out, but overnight success cannot be expected.

Not all observers agree with this author that the war in Iraq was a necessary part of the overall global war on terrorism. Some consider it a distracter from continuing priority support to places like Afghanistan, where Osama bin Laden and al Qaeda are still active, not to mention a huge drain on the U.S. economy. In fact, the resignation in March 2003 of the NSC's senior director for counterterrorism, Rand Beers, a former State Department Assistant Secretary for International Narcotics and Law Enforcement Matters under the Clinton Administration, has been attributed to his alleged concern that war with Iraq would hurt the fight against terrorism.[284] This follows up a warning by the CIA to Congress in 2002 that an invasion might lead to a rise in terrorism. Some critics are now saying that events since the President declared an end to major combat on 1 May prove the point, as U.S. casualties continue to mount on almost a daily basis.

The intricate involvement of intelligence estimates in the decision to go to war, and the attempts to locate weapons of mass destruction ever since, reflect the dangers of the politicization of intelligence.[285] Nevertheless, despite being intriguing and pertinent topics, these controversial subjects are beyond the scope of this paper and will not be further discussed, other than to say that the role of intelligence in homeland security and counterterrorism will be viewed in part through the prism of how it has been used, or abused, by the Bush Administration in mobilizing support for the President's decisions regarding Iraq, Afghanistan, and elsewhere. Bush has been accused of fabricating intelligence, or perhaps merely of embellishing the limited intelligence available to justify policy decisions (what those of us in academic circles might refer to as "selective footnoting"), while his supporters respond that critics are trying to turn this into a partisan issue as election year approaches. Whatever the case, it is sure to fan the flames over whether the U.S., while coping with the aftermath of 9/11 and the war in Iraq, has experienced "intelligence failures" or, perhaps worse, "policy failures."

---

[284] P. Mitchell Prothero, Washington Politics and Policy Desk, United Press International, "Top White House Anti-Terror Boss Resigns," 19 March 2003.

[285] Steven Murfson, "Forget WMD. What's an NIE?" *The Washington Post*, 20 July 2003, B3. See also Walter Pincus, "CIA Director George J. Tenet Discusses the National Intelligence Estimate," *The Washington Post*, 10 August 2003, A10-A11.

Another problem related to overcoming culture clashes is how to tinker with the government bureaucracy so as to streamline solutions rather than just create additional unintended consequences. Any bureaucratic restructuring takes time and cautious planning. That the Department of Homeland Security was approved and established in less than a year after President Bush finally went along with the idea is a minor miracle. In fact, the DHS was formally stood up only 17 months after the initial "Executive Order Establishing the Office of Homeland Security and the Homeland Security Council" on 8 October 2001.[286] The new department brought together 22 separate agencies from several other Cabinet departments, requiring the transfer of upwards of 170,000 government employees and the rectifying of diverse personnel systems. This represented the largest, most complex federal government reorganization since the National Security Act of 1947 had created the National Military Establishment (later designated as DOD), the Air Force (as an armed service separate from the Army), the CIA, and the NSC. That it happened so quickly is truly remarkable, though of course the maturation of DHS will be ongoing for a long time. It is testament to the dogged determination of the executive branch, close cooperation by the legislative branch, and recognition by a wary public that something had to be done to prevent another 9/11-type of event.

Still, there was a lot of pulling and hauling among involved players and attempts either to gain turf or to protect turf already held. There were interminable arguments over centralization versus decentralization, open hearings versus closed hearings, and carefully controlled budgets versus more flexible ones. As is always the case when discussing intelligence reform, there were disputes over how much redundancy in collection, analysis, and reporting is needed and whether intelligence support to homeland security should be done in a dedicated fashion or by treating DHS as merely another large consumer. Just because DHS has been set up does not mean the discussion on reforming intelligence has ended. The ongoing situation with Saddam Hussein's thugs in Iraq and al Qaeda's activities in Afghanistan and elsewhere will only fuel that discussion further, as will demands for U.S. intervention in other hot spots such as Liberia, Colombia, and the Philippines. The most comprehensive recent assessment of what needs to be done to strengthen the National Intelligence Community and integrate it with homeland security is found in a 2003 book by a former Director of the National Security Agency (NSA) and Army Deputy Chief of Staff for Intelligence, retired Lieutenant General William Odom, who is now a professor at Yale University.[287] Congress will no doubt play an important role in any reform, as it already has demonstrated in its joint inquiry into the intelligence failures related to 9/11 and its investigation into the application of intelligence to weapons of mass destruction in Iraq. Even before these issues captured the limelight, the Senate was deep into the effort to maximize intelligence support to homeland security. A 119-page unclassified report by the

---

[286] George W. Bush, "Executive Order Establishing the Office of Homeland Security and the Homeland Security Council," The White House, 8 October 2001.

[287] William E. Odom, *Fixing Intelligence: For a More Secure America* (New Haven, CT: Yale University Press, 2003), 185-193. See also an excellent review of this book by Lorraine Adams in "Book World," *The Washington Post*, 6 April 2003, 5, which also examines another relevant book by Thomas Powers entitled *Intelligence Wars: American Secret History from Hitler to Al-Qaeda* (New York: New York Review, 2003).

Committee on Governmental Affairs in June 2002, which is accessible electronically, is entitled "A Review of the Relationship Between a Department of Homeland Security and the Intelligence Community."[288] That committee is chaired by one of the Democratic Presidential contenders for 2004, Joseph Lieberman of Connecticut.

Yet another problem, which certainly helped spur the rapid organizational actions just discussed, is the immediacy of the threat facing the U.S. and the rest of the world today, a threat which is increasingly globalized and "asymmetric," to use the popular buzzword indicating that the two sides are radically different in resources, technology, and attentiveness to the norms of international law. Gone are the days of the Cold War when intelligence agencies talked about indications and warning time in terms of weeks or days, but that was principally a conventional threat that was fairly predictable. Now we must deal with a threat that follows no rules or expected timelines and has no respect for the sanctity of innocent life. Democracy is truly under siege, and the actions taken to counter the potential adversaries have already sparked a perceived erosion of the civil liberties of those innocent human beings who have no way of fighting back. It is very difficult to distinguish the "good guys" from the "bad" these days. Several of the 9/11 attackers entered the U.S. legally and were living apparently normal lives, as most immigrants do while pursuing the American dream.

There is also a great deal of complexity in information sharing, which is imperative if the threat is to be identified before it strikes again. Secretary Ridge and Attorney General Ashcroft have been wrestling with how best to render adequate warning of a potential threat to the public without causing undue alarm. This must be done without compromising sources and methods and without tipping off the potential attackers, who may very well be part of that attentive public. The on-again, off-again "Code Orange" alerts have caused consternation among those who wonder if the federal government knows what it is doing and whether it realizes how much personnel and budgetary turmoil the alerts cause. On the other hand, the government must show a degree of healthy paranoia so as not to be accused of "falling asleep at the switch" as it allegedly did before 9/11. How to do this consistently without succumbing to the "cry wolf" syndrome is indeed a challenge.

Some progress has been made in pushing intelligence from the top down to state and local levels. In the winter of 2003 the Senate introduced a bill that calls for the CIA Director to provide classified information to state and local governments, including law enforcement, rescue, fire, health, and other so-called "first responder" personnel. Those receiving the information would require security clearances and be trained in handling classified material. The legislation, cosponsored by another Democratic Presidential contender, John Edwards of North Carolina, and Charles Schumer of New York, is called the "Antiterrorism Intelligence Distribution Act of 2003."[289]

---

[288] Hearings before the Committee on Governmental Affairs, U.S. Senate, "A Review of the Relationship Between a Department of Homeland Security and the Intelligence Community," 107th Congress, 2nd Session, 26-27 June 2002.

[289] No author, "CIA Would Provide More Terrorism Info to State, Local Officials Under New Bill," *FEDmanager Weekly E-mail Newsletter*, 18 February 2003.

Since the public responses to alerts most often have to be managed at the lower levels of government, this complicates the effort to pass threat information upward, downward, and laterally among law enforcement elements that in a federal system such as the U.S. differ substantially in mission, makeup, funding, equipment, communications capability, and capacity to respond. One of the biggest criticisms of late has been a lack of priority to first responders. A recent television magazine examined the nationwide lack of preparation and funding for these personnel. The program revealed a paucity of modern gas masks, chemical protective suits, and compatible radios. The federal government had promised more money to cities for homeland security. Representative Christopher Cox, Chairman of the House Committee on Homeland Security, was quoted as saying the focus has been on intelligence for homeland security rather than equipment, since intelligence is cheaper and more cost-effective.[290] Along the same lines, a week later another television news program featured an interview with former Senator Warren Rudman, head of the NSC's Task Force on Emergency Response, who revealed many of the same vulnerabilities.[291] When the homeland security budget was proposed by the White House in the summer of 2003, New York and California received by far the biggest shares of the $3 billion allocated. On a per capita basis, however, twelve states did better than New York, mainly because the federal government divided significant portions of the money into equal pieces for distribution to all the states. This rankles lawmakers from urban areas, who insist the government should be less interested in keeping all states happy and instead emphasize targeting money to cities and states most at risk of terrorist attack.[292]

A final problem in the homeland security debate from time to time has been the relationship between government and the media. Of course, in a democracy a critical aspect of government oversight is scrutiny by the media. The media have championed the public's "right to know" versus the government's justifiable emphasis on "need to know" and the need to protect its "sources and methods." The fact that the threat is now at home as much as it is overseas has heightened press scrutiny, as has the perceived erosion of civil liberties. The contentious war in Iraq, and complaints about the role of intelligence, has only intensified the spotlight even more. A recent court case points out the delicacy of this issue. In late June 2003 a federal appeals court ruled that the U.S. government could continue to keep secret the names of hundreds of people arrested and detained after the 9/11 attacks. The decision dealt a setback to more than 20 civil libertarian groups that had invoked the Freedom of Information Act to challenge the secret arrests. The groups also argued that First Amendment freedom of speech guarantees dictated release of the information, a position rejected by the court.[293] Such disputes between the government trying to suppress information and interest groups and the media trying to reveal it will undoubtedly continue as long as the war on terrorism continues. Though challenging for the secretive Bush Administration, this is what open democracy is all about and the President embraces the challenge.

---

[290] ABC television news program "20/20," 20 June 2003.

[291] NBC television news program "Meet the Press," 29 June 2003.

[292] No author, "Homeland Security Funds Divvied Up," *Herald Tribune,* 1 July 2003.

[293] James Vicini, "Court Rules Sept. 11 Arrest Names Can Be Secret," *The Washington Post,* 17 June 2003.

LEGAL FRAMEWORK AND POLITICAL/MILITARY DEVELOPMENTS

Several of the topics listed below have already been addressed in detail, and therefore will not be discussed further. One in particular, the so-called USA PATRIOT Act, has not been addressed yet, but will be covered in the next section on "controversies." The basic judicial framework within which the concept of homeland security was designed and the organizational structure arranged can be summed up by these developments, listed chronologically:[294]

- Fourth Amendment (prevents intrusive searches and seizures, 1791) and Fourteenth Amendment (guarantees due process and equal protection under the law, 1868) to the Constitution
- Alien and Sedition Act (1798)
- Posse Comitatus Act (1878)
- Espionage Act (1917)
- U.S. Sedition Act (1918)
- National Security Act (1947)
- Freedom of Information Act (1967)
- Privacy Act (1974)
- Foreign Intelligence Surveillance Act (1978)
- Various Executive Orders still in effect such as EO 12333 (1981)
- Electronic Communications Privacy Act (1986)
- Office of Homeland Security created (2001)
- USA PATRIOT Act (2001)
- Increased Congressional oversight of both intelligence and homeland security (2001-present)
- Homeland Security Act (2002)
- U.S. Northern Command (NORTHCOM) established for homeland defense (2003) (there is also now an Assistant Secretary of Defense for Homeland Defense)
- Department of Homeland Security established (2003)

Of the 22 agencies brought under the DHS umbrella, the largest and most significant in terms of interest to the defense establishment were the Coast Guard, the Transportation Security Administration, the Border Patrol, the Customs Service, the Immigration and Naturalization Service, the Federal Emergency Management Agency, and the Secret Service.[295] Most of these entities have now been subsumed under DHS' Bureau of Customs and Border Protection or its Bureau of Immigration and Customs Enforcement.

---

[294] No author, "Several Laws Restrict Agency Access To and Use of Information," *Government Computer News*, 21 April 2003, 2.

[295] John Mintz, "Ridge's Rise from Adviser to 'Mr. Secretary': As Some Questioned His Power, He Quietly Shaped Future of Homeland Security," *The Washington Post*, 2 March 2002, A5.

CONTROVERSIES

Since 9/11, probably the single most controversial development has been the passage of the USA PATRIOT Act (which is actually a clever but unwieldy acronym for "Uniting and Strengthening America by Providing Appropriate Tools Required to Intercept and Obstruct Terrorism"). This legislation was ramrodded through Congress quickly within a month of the attacks, and signed by President Bush on 26 October 2001, at a time when the executive and legislative branches were united in a flush of patriotism and an unprecedented spirit of collaboration. The Act is really nothing more than a 342-page patchwork of many previous bills granting the federal government expanded powers to gather information on potential terrorist suspects.[296] There have been numerous complaints that in normal times such a long, clumsy, poorly prepared piece of legislation would never have passed. Civil rights groups have decried such provisions as detentions of personnel for indefinite periods without due process, profiling of U.S. residents of Muslim or Arab descent, expanded wiretapping powers, interception of e-mails, a clampdown on visas for visitors from certain countries, and increased government intrusion on college campuses. The Justice Department inspector general is required to monitor and issue regular reports on allegation of civil rights and civil liberties violations as part of the PATRIOT Act, which broadened government powers of surveillance and investigative methods.[297] Attorney General Ashcroft previously wanted to push through essentially a "PATRIOT Act II" in 2003 that would expand executive powers even more, but the Bush Administration began to realize it may be difficult enough just to fend off critics who want to repeal the first Act. In August 2003 it was announced by the White House that Ashcroft would soon be conducting visits across the country explaining why the Act is critical to protect citizens and prevent another 9/11, while reassuring the public that there are adequate safeguards in place to protect their civil liberties.

Related to the PATRIOT Act has been the recent implementation of the Student and Exchange Visitor Information System (SEVIS), which requires colleges and universities to maintain detailed databases on international students and share information with the federal government.[298] The idea is to prevent potential terrorists from entering the U.S. on the grounds of being students and later being discovered never to have enrolled or attended classes. College administrators are uneasy about the potential chilling effect on academic freedom and the possibility that some legitimate prospective candidates from foreign countries will be intimidated into not applying. They also are opposed to students being tracked down on campus and questioned by federal investigators without probable

---

[296] Katherine McIntire Peters, "Protecting America: The War on Terrorism Is Profoundly Reshaping the Role of the Federal Government," *Government Executive*, April 2003, 8-10.

[297] Curt Anderson, "Patriot Act Abuse Complaints Documented," *FederalNewsRadio.com*, 21 July 2003. For a more critical account of the perceived negative aspects of this statute, see Pat M. Holt, "Driving Dangerously with the Patriot Act," *Christian Science Monitor*, 2 October 2003, p. 9.

[298] William C. Spracher, "The Impact of September 11 on International Students," 22 July 2002, unpublished paper for George Washington University course on Current Issues in Higher Education. See also his "Implementation of the Student and Exchange Visitor Information System," 9 April 2003, unpublished paper for George Washington University course on Federal Policy in Higher Education.

cause and to their computer and library records being subjected to surveillance. Foreign students are a tremendous financial boon to institutions hurting from federal and state budget cuts for higher education, since most of them request little or no tuition assistance. By and large, these students are supported by their families and/or home governments. Moreover, they add a degree of diversity to the student population and an ancillary benefit for U.S. international relations and academic prestige that the federal government has found highly desirable in the past. SEVIS is now part of a broader effort known as the U.S. Visitor and Immigrant Status Indication Technology system (U.S. VISIT).[299]

A final topic that generated a firestorm of controversy a few months ago but now seems to be dead is DOD's proposed Total Information Awareness (TIA) program. This was essentially a terrorism "database mining" effort designed by the Defense Advanced Research Projects Agency (DARPA), which would allow analysts to sift through vast amounts of banking, medical, credit card, travel, and other personal information to look for patterns suggesting terrorist activity. Although Pentagon officials tried to reassure critics that the program would be tightly controlled and that safeguards would protect the privacy rights of U.S. citizens, opposition continued to grow and finally the Senate voted unanimously to cut off funding for the program.[300] This was after a feeble effort by DOD supporters to soften the public image of TIA by renaming it the Terrorism Information Awareness program. The Senate's vote was hailed by civil rights groups, which condemn the TIA concept as an invasion of privacy. Interestingly, the same individual who was pushing TIA, retired Navy Vice Admiral John Poindexter, also created the highly outrageous scheme known as Policy Analysis Market (PAM), which was intended to help military authorities predict terrorist action by carefully scrutinizing investor information and analyses.[301] Harsh reaction was immediate from all sides, with critics expressing disbelief that a White House professing ethical values would condone what essentially would be a futures market that encouraged gambling on people's lives. Poindexter, infamous as President Reagan's national security advisor during the Iran-Contra scandal of the late 1980s, has since resigned his DOD post and it is assumed that neither PAM nor TIA will ever see the light of day.

In the minds of the harshest critics, the fact that these questionable programs were even suggested casts doubts about the wisdom of Bush Administration officials and contributes to the public relations problems of a White House considered by many as too intrusive and prone to secrecy. Such programs also give a bad name to legitimate intelligence activities that are invaluable for protecting the homeland from the threat of terrorism. TIA certainly had potentially serious civil liberties problems. Nevertheless, though this author had doubts about the

---

[299] Doug Sample, "Homeland Security: Better Prepared than Ever Before," *Pentagram*, 1 August 2003, 5. For a more detailed description of the entire U.S. VISIT program, to include a list of civilian firms vying for the lucrative government contract, see Anitha Reddy, "U.S. Readies Program to Track Visas," *The Washington Post*, 29 September 2003, E1-E2.

[300] No author, "Senate Blocks Funding for Terrorism Information Awareness Program," *FEDmanager Weekly E-mail Newsletter*, 29 July 2003. See also Michael J. Sniffen, "Senate to Kill Pentagon Surveillance Bill," *The Washington Post*, 15 July 2003, and Shana Harris, "The Big Brother Complex," *Government Executive*, January 2003, 58-59.

[301] Eric Schmitt, "Poindexter to Resign Following Terrorist Futures Debacle," *The New York Times*, 31 July 2003. See also Dennis Ryan, "Devious DARPA Design Daft," *Pentagram*, 8 August 2003, 4.

utility of PAM, the shrill hue and cry over such DARPA efforts is unfounded. Indeed, these are precisely the kinds of unorthodox experimental programs that DARPA was created to conceive in the first place. DARPA is supposed to "think outside the box." Perhaps PAM was too far outside the box, since it produced a public relations disaster for the Pentagon.

CONCLUSIONS AND RECOMMENDATIONS

As highlighted earlier, a balance needs to be struck between protecting the national security and safeguarding the rights of U.S. citizens and legal residents. This is not an easy task, and it is impossible to achieve a national consensus on just where the fulcrum should be. The Bush Administration has asked the American people (not to mention allies around the world) to trust its judgments and support its actions to reduce the terrorist threat. Generally, the public has agreed to do that, despite attempts by some elements of the media to show that support is deteriorating. The question is how much patience and trust society will continue to demonstrate, and what level of vulnerability people are willing to accept while endeavoring to retain the civil liberties they have long cherished. This author surmises the general public is nowhere near its breaking point, though some media portrayals would suggest otherwise. As the two-year anniversary of 9/11 was commemorated, and citizens were again reminded of the devastation of that fateful day, their fortitude and commitment to see the war on terrorism through to the end (assuming it will ever end) was likely renewed.

To answer the question posed in the title, this author concludes that not only can homeland security and intelligence mix, they *must* work closely together. Intelligence support to homeland security is not a serious threat to democracy, with the condition that the intelligence is managed with care and the control and oversight procedures in place are appropriately applied. Securing the homeland without quality intelligence would not only be futile; it is unthinkable. To gather the type of information needed will require some loosening up of previous proscriptions, such as the permissible degree of ill repute of foreign agents recruited, the language capabilities such recruitment demands, the frequency and intensity of covert operations, and perhaps even rethinking the feasibility of government-sponsored assassination of notorious foreign actors.

Many recommendations have already been made by Congressional and private commissions charged with exploring the alleged intelligence failures surrounding 9/11 and the war on terrorism. Senator Bob Graham of Florida, former Chairman of the Senate Select Committee on Intelligence and a former Democratic Presidential hopeful, was co-chairman of the House-Senate Joint Inquiry and in testimony in May 2003 made five recommendations regarding improved Congressional oversight of the National Intelligence Community:[302]

---

[302] Senator Bob Graham (D-FL), "Prepared Testimony for the National Commission on Terrorist Attacks Upon the United States," 22 May 2003.

(1) Make membership of the House and Senate Intelligence Committees permanent.

(2) Create within the Congressional appropriations process a separate sub-committee for intelligence, such has been created for the new Department of Homeland Security.

(3) Establish a closer linkage between the financial reporting of the intelligence agencies and the oversight committees.

(4) Adopt what has come to be known as the Eleanor Hill approach to over-sight, which means that — much as was done during the Joint Inquiry hearings (for which Hill was staff director) — staff should be given more authority to conduct detailed reviews under the direction of the chairman and vice chairman of the committee.

(5) Make it a practice to seek testimony from witnesses outside the adminis-tration. There are a range of experts from the academic community, think tanks, and other sources whose views can provide an alternative to the official administration perspective.

Along with Graham's common-sense suggestions, none of which is entirely new or earth-shattering, let us look at a list of more general recommendations for enhancing intelligence support to homeland security:

■ More openness and transparency in government, while maintaining protection of sensitive sources and methods

■ Reasonable legislative control and oversight ("reasonable" meaning that some closed sessions of key committees must continue; not everything can be open to the public)

■ Revitalization of the intelligence community's HUMINT capability

■ Expanded role for the National Guard

■ Broader sharing of intelligence among federal, state, and local agencies

■ Increased budgetary support pushed downward to first responders

■ Expanded authority for the Secretary of Homeland Security in procuring intelli-gence, with inclusion of DHS as a formal member of the National Intelligence Community as a necessary first step (there are currently 14 members)

■ More academic attention to the subjects of national security, homeland security, and intelligence

■ Better programs for enhancing public understanding and awareness

Regarding the point on academic focus, fortunately the number of courses on intelli-gence offered by civilian colleges and universities is increasing, and 9/11 has likely inten-sified interest in this area. No longer is intelligence viewed as some sort of esoteric tradecraft taught only in government-sponsored training programs in classified form. The National Military Intelligence Association conducted its annual National Intelligence Symposium in March 2003 at DIA, with the theme "Homeland Security: Intelligence, Law Enforcement and the American Public."[303] DIA's annual summer conference in 1999 dealt with intelligence education in colleges and universities. The National Defense University (NDU) is also beginning to focus on the topic of homeland security, having established in 2002 a special committee with representatives from its subordinate components to determine how best to incorporate this subject into the various NDU curricula. The so-called University Committee on Homeland Security (UCHS) even has its own webpage to keep students and faculty posted on current activities.

Moving to the last point on public awareness, Attorney General Ashcroft's visits across the country to explain government actions related to the USA PATRIOT and President Bush's continual pronouncements to the nation hopefully helped reassure Americans that they can be safe and free at the same time. Keeping the public informed is critical. The White House periodically releases fact sheets to the public relating what counterterrorism measures are being enacted and how they can be of benefit to public safety. For example, a fact sheet on "Operation Liberty Shield" was released in March 2003 that described the operation as "a comprehensive national plan designed to increase protections for America's citizens and infrastructure while maintaining the free flow of goods and people across our border with minimal disruption to our economy and way of life" . . . The operation is "a multi-department, multi-agency, national team effort," which includes:[304]

— Increased security at borders

— Stronger transportation protections

— Ongoing measures to disrupt threats against our nation

— Greater protections for critical infrastructure and key assets

— Increased public health preparedness

— Federal response resources positioned and ready

All the above actions require accurate and timely intelligence. In addition, they involve what is known as "actionable" threat information, i.e., data which can be acted upon immediately. This does not require DHS to produce its own intelligence and duplicate what is already being done elsewhere. It has experts on its staff with vast experience in the National Intelligence Community, and that should be capitalized upon. As the noted political pundit George Will astutely observed, "Intelligence is cheaper than cleaning up the damage from attacks. The federal government's intelligence apparatus is a $40 billion asset. The Homeland Security Department's job is not to have its own intelligence operation but to analyze and distribute intelligence so that immigration, customs and border officials have a better idea of what they should be looking for."[305] All this can be done without destroying the democratic ideals upon

---

[303] National Military Intelligence Association brochure, National Intelligence Symposium 2003, "Homeland Security: Intelligence, Law Enforcement and the American Public," 12-13 March 2003.

[304] The White House, "Fact Sheet: Operation Liberty Shield," 17 March 2003.

[305] George F. Will, "Homeland Worriers," *The Washington Post*, 6 April 2003, B7.

which the nation was founded, such as personal privacy, openness to immigrants wishing to join American society, and transparency in government. And democracy is the bottom line—only with homeland security and intelligence working hand in hand will the U.S., and all freedom-loving nations, be able to defeat terrorism and, to end with one last cliché, "make the world safe for democracy."

THE HISTORY OF INTELLIGENCE

THE SAN CRISTOBAL TRAPEZOID

By A. Denis Clift and John T. Hughes(c)

(Originally published in Clift Notes, 2nd ed. (Washington, DC: Joint Military Intelligence College, 2002).)

Following the author's move from The White House staff to defense intelligence in 1981, he was named DIA's Assistant Deputy Director for External Affairs, serving with then-Deputy Director John T. Hughes. Following Hughes' retirement in 1984, Clift replaced him as Deputy Director. He urged Hughes to document his extraordinary role in the Cuban Missile Crisis and volunteered to do both the additional research required and the writing. The result is "The San Cristobal Trapezoid," co-authored with Hughes and published in the first unclassified edition of *Studies in Intelligence* shortly after Hughes' death in 1992. The work would receive the Director of Central Intelligence's Sherman Kent Award for that year's best contribution to the literature of intelligence. Written in the first-person of Hughes, it recounts the role of intelligence prior to, during, and after the crisis. Reading like a novel, it is an enormously instructive insight into the inner workings of the Intelligence Community during national crisis, the intelligence-policy interface, and the importance of both strategic warning — which had failed — and all-source tactical intelligence. The essay climaxes with Hughes' nationally televised briefing on 6 February 1963.

Aerial photos give crisp hard information, like the dawn after long darkness.

— Arthur Lundahl
Director of the National Photographic Interpretation Center

A courier stepped forward to meet me as I reached the Pentagon's River Entrance. I remember the moment: 7:30 a.m., 8 February 1963, a wintry morning brightness just emerging. "Mr. John Hughes?" "Yes," I said. "I've been asked to deliver this to you." He handed me a manila envelope, then departed. The return address, in block letters, read "The White House."

My office was nearby inside the Pentagon in the Joint Staff spaces next to the National Military Command Center, almost directly beneath the Office of the Secretary of Defense. I opened the letter. It was from the President.

Dear Mr. Hughes:

I thought you did an excellent job on television in explaining our surveillance in Cuba. I understand it was done on short notice. I want you to know how much I appreciate your efforts. With best wishes.

Sincerely,
John Kennedy

Cuba. For the past seven months, the U.S. Intelligence Community had riveted its attention on that island nation. Its topography, road network, cities, military garrisons, storage depots, deployed ground-force units, airports and airbases, seaports, merchant shipping, and naval units had been photographed, categorized, and studied. U.S. reconnaissance also zeroed in on Soviet merchant ships, fighter aircraft, surface-to-air-missile (SAM) units, missile patrol boats, and rocket forces.

As photointerpreters, my colleagues and I could recall the key features of the intermediate-range and medium-range ballistic missile (IRBM and MRBM) sites the Soviets had been rushing to complete in October 1962: the missile-servicing buildings, the nuclear warhead storage bunkers, the oxidizer vehicles, propellant vehicles, missile shelter tents, and the missiles. San Julian, Holguin, Neuvitas, Mariel, Sagua La Grande, Remedios, and San Cristobal were names that took on a special meaning after the discovery of the missiles and bombers, the peaking of the crisis, Soviet withdrawal, and my briefing to the nation on network TV on 6 February 1963, two days before the President's letter arrived.

As Special Assistant to Lieutenant General Joseph F. Carroll, Director of the Defense Intelligence Agency (DIA), I was responsible for providing reconnaissance intelligence support during the crisis to Secretary of Defense Robert McNamara, Deputy Secretary Roswell Gilpatric, Chairman of the Joint Chiefs of Staff (JCS) General Maxwell Taylor, and the Joint Chiefs. There had been intensive coordination with Arthur Lundahl, Director of the National Photographic Interpretation Center (NPIC). In his capacity, he was responsible for providing critical national intelligence support to the President, Director of Central Intelligence (DCI) John McCone, and the Executive Committee of the National Security Council.

Building on the CIA's initial U-2 reconnaissance flights in the summer and early autumn of 1962, the Department of Defense would eventually fly more than 400 military reconnaissance missions over Cuba during the crisis. Targeting information for each photo mission had to be developed for the JCS Joint Reconnaissance Center (JRC) to coordinate the operations and allow for policy review by the Secretary, the Deputy Secretary, and the White House, and then be delivered to the reconnaissance units that would fly the missions. The highest priority was to move that film from the returning aircraft through the photo labs, through analysis, to the policy level of government — a 24-hour-a-day operation, with intense time pressures and a crucial need for accuracy.

In his introduction to Robert F. Kennedy's memoir of the Cuban missile crisis, *Thirteen Days*, McNamara wrote:

> The performance of the U.S. Government during that critical period was more effective than at any other time during my seven years' service as Secretary of Defense. The agencies of government — the State   Department, the civilian and military leaders of the Defense Department, the CIA, the White House Staff, and the UN Mission — worked together smoothly and harmoniously.[306]

---

[306] Robert F. Kennedy, *Thirteen Days* (New York: W.W. Norton & Company, Inc., 1969), 14.

The entire intelligence-operations team for U.S. reconnaissance against Cuba demonstrated a sense of urgency and national mission that epitomized this effort.

TACTICAL DATA

Intelligence did not perform flawlessly during the crisis. The Intelligence Community had not provided clear warning of the Soviet Union's intention to place offensive nuclear weapons in Cuba. Indeed, the debate over Khrushchev's motives and the USSR's strategic intentions continues. The community did, however, provide tactical intelligence on the USSR's rapid deployment of missile and bomber forces in Cuba. As the crisis mounted, tactical warning and targeting data were developed and steadily updated in support of strike options being developed by the JCS and the NSC Executive Committee. Targets included the MRBM and IRBM missile installations, the IL-28/BEAGLE bombers, the 24 SA-2 SAM sites, the MiG-21 fighters, and other ground, air, and naval targets.

The intelligence flowing from the reconnaissance missions provided the irrefutable evidence the U.S. required to document to the world the basis for its response, as well as the targeting data that would have been needed if the crisis touched off an armed conflict. It tracked the surge of Soviet military personnel to some 22,000 by the end of October 1962, and then the ebb in those numbers to some 17,000 as the troops manning the offensive weapons departed.

STRATEGIC WARNING

Strategic warning is the most important component of effective intelligence. Perhaps the greatest barrier to developing effective strategic indications and warning for decision-making is the tendency of the human mind to assume that the status quo will continue. The Cuban missile crisis and many other conflicts of the postwar era, including the Arab-Israeli Yom Kippur war and the Falklands conflict, confirm that nations generally do not credit their potential opponents with the will to take unexpected acts. We did not believe the Soviets would do so in 1962.

I was part of a team assisting General Carroll in his responsibilities as a member of the U.S. Intelligence Board (USIB), the top policy forum of the Intelligence Community, whose membership included the DCI and the Deputy Director of Central Intelligence, the Director of DIA, the Department of State's Director of Intelligence and Research, the Director of Naval Intelligence, the Army and Air Force Assistant Chiefs of Staff for Intelligence, the Director of the National Security Agency, the Assistant General Manager for Administration of the Atomic Energy Commission, and the Assistant to the Director of the FBI. Each person brought the intelligence strengths of his respective organization to the table. It was the Board's primary duty to produce the formal National Intelligence Estimates (NIEs) and Special National Intelligence Estimates (SNIEs) on key international issues and events for consideration by the NSC. With the memory of the Bay of Pigs disaster still fresh, and with the politically charged U.S. concern over Fidel Castro's consolidation of communist power in Cuba and the growing Soviet military presence there, the USIB focused on Cuba in its estimates. At the same time, the Intelligence Community tracked and recorded the entry of Soviet weapons by type and capability.

TWO NIES

NIE 85-2-62, *The Situation and Prospects in Cuba*, was issued by the Board on 1 August 1962. It underlined Castro's political primacy, the loyalty of the Cuban armed forces to Castro and his brother Raul, the provision of Soviet Bloc military equipment and training to Cuban forces, and the deepening commitment of the Soviet Union to preserve and strengthen the Castro regime.[307]

As of 1 July 1962, the monitoring of Soviet military deliveries indicated that there were 160 tanks, 770 field artillery and antitank guns, 560 antiaircraft guns, 35 jet fighters, 24 helicopters, and 3,800 military vehicles of various types in Cuba.[308] On 27 July, Castro announced that Cuba would soon have new defenses against the United States. On 29 August, as the weaponry continued to roll off Soviet ships in Cuban ports, a CIA U-2 photographed the first SA-2 SAMs. Human intelligence sources in Cuba were reporting the sighting of rockets on the island. We concluded that the rockets were not MRBMs/IRBMs.

On 19 September 1962, in NIE 85-3-62, The Military Buildup in Cuba, the Intelligence Community reiterated its belief that the USSR would not introduce offensive strategic weapons into Cuba. Its key conclusion stated:

> The USSR could derive considerable military advantage from the establishment of Soviet MRBMs and IRBMs in Cuba, or from the establishment of a submarine base there. As between these two, the establishment of a submarine base would be the more likely. Either development, however, would be incompatible with Soviet practice to date and with Soviet policy as we presently estimate it. It would indicate a far greater willingness to increase the level of risk in U.S.-Soviet relations than the USSR has displayed thus far, and consequently to other areas and other problems in East-West relations.[309]

DCI McCone personally was not persuaded that the Soviet buildup was essentially defensive. Fate, however, would have him in Europe on an extended honeymoon when the crisis began. His messages to the President from Europe in mid-September advising that the evidence pointed to Soviet preparations for introducing offensive weapons into Cuba could not compete with the contrary judgment of the formal NIEs that the missiles would be for defensive purposes.

Following the discovery of the defensive SAMs in late August, the President warned Khrushchev that the U.S. would not permit the introduction of offensive weapons. The

---

[307] National Intelligence Estimate (NIE) 85-2-62, *The Situation and Prospects in Cuba*, 1 August 1962.
[308] CIA Fact Sheet, *Soviet Forces in Cuba*, 5 February 1963.
[309] NIE 85-3-62, *The Military Buildup in Cuba*, 19 September 1962.

Soviet leader's responses through several channels from Moscow to Washington repeated the official Soviet position that only defensive weapons were being introduced into Cuba. In his news conference on 13 September 1962, the President delivered a clear statement of the U.S. position on Cuba and on the possibility of Soviet offensive weapons being deployed there.

SOVIET BUILDUP

The Intelligence Community continued to monitor the rapid buildup and assess its implications. From July to 1 November 1962, the number of tanks would grow from 160 to 345; the field artillery and antitank guns from 770 to 1,320; the antiaircraft guns from 560 to 710; the jet fighters from 35 to 101; the helicopters from 24 to 70 or more; the military vehicles from 3,800 to between 7,500 and 10,000. And through late August, September, and early October we continued to identify new categories of weaponry: the construction of 24 SAM sites with 500 missiles by 1 November; the introduction of some 24 to 32 Free Rocket Over Ground (FROG) rockets; the installation of four cruise missile sites and 160 air defense radars; and the arrival of 12 Soviet KOMAR-class cruise-missile patrol boats at Cuban ports.[310]

U-2 MISSIONS

From 1956 on, I had participated in the Intelligence Community's tasking of the U-2 by contributing the Army's and DIA's intelligence collection requirements to the flight planners of the operational missions. I had helped analyze the photographic intelligence from the U-2 flights over the Soviet Union from 1956 to 1960. Its advanced photographic gear complemented the extraordinary capabilities of the U-2 as an aircraft. The U-2 carried the HR-73B camera system, a big, high-technology camera with a 36-inch focal-length lens able to capture considerable detail from altitudes of 14 miles. The camera load was two 6,500-foot rolls of 9-1/2-inch film. Each mission could produce more than 4,000 frames of film, with vertical, single-frame ground coverage of 5.7 x 5.7 nautical miles.

Following the flight of 29 August 1962, CIA launched additional U-2 missions on 5, 17, 26, and 29 September and on 5 and 7 October. Working through an interagency committee, collection requirements were formulated that would shape the flight profile of each mission. The work of reading the film from each mission took place in NPIC in an atmosphere of intense analytical debate throughout September and early October. These U-2 missions established an excellent baseline for judging the nature and pace of the Soviet military buildup.

The success of our efforts owed much to the brilliant leadership of Art Lundahl, who was internationally recognized for his contributions to photographic interpretation and photogrammetric engineering. His dedication to improving the nation's reconnaissance

---

[310] CIA Fact Sheet.

capabilities and his professional standards shaped the work of all who were a part of his crisis team.

SA-2 CONTROVERSY

One issue for the photointerpreters was the intended role of the Soviet SA-2 GUIDELINE SAM, which had been operational with Soviet air defense forces since the late 1950s. The 30-foot-long SA-2 had a solid-propellant booster and a kerosene-based second-stage sustainer, and it could sprint to Mach 3 carrying a 280-pound high-explosive warhead with a proximity fuse to a range of 30 miles. Radio guidance from ground-based target acquisition radar fed steering commands to the missile's control fins. We assessed it as reliable and accurate.

The U-2 missions through 5 September revealed a disproportionate buildup of SA-2 launch sites in western Cuba. One school of thought contended that this deployment pattern was not particularly worrisome, given that Havana and the larger part of the Cuban population were in that region. Further, most of the sites were along Cuba's periphery, where one might expect such missiles arrayed in a national air-defense network.

Another line of analysis held that the disproportionate concentration of SA-2s in the west meant that the Soviets and the Cubans had important military equipment there requiring greater protection. The photointerpreters pushed on with their analysis, somewhat hampered by a policy-level decision following the 5 October mission to avoid the western sector on future U-2 missions because of administration concerns that an SA-2 might shoot down a U-2, thereby escalating the crisis.

Analysis was not based exclusively on photo interpretation. One of my DIA colleagues, Colonel John Wright, directed the work of a center in DIA that collated intelligence from all sources. The center evaluated the photography together with other sources, including reports from refugees and agents in Cuba. These reports continued to warn of large rockets, possibly missiles, arriving in Cuba and of suspicious military activity in western Cuba.

FOCUS ON SAN CRISTOBAL

Colonel Wright and his staff became increasingly interested in the SA-2 sites near San Cristobal, in the western part of the island. Most important, the U-2 photography indicated that these sites formed the outline of a trapezoid. This suggested that the sites were forming a "point defense" to protect some extremely important weapons emplacements or installations. This deployment pattern was similar to those identified near ballistic-missile launch sites in the Soviet homeland. The stationing of these SA-2s, together with human-source reporting of the missiles in western Cuba, strongly suggested that there were offensive Soviet ballistic missiles to be found within the San Cristobal trapezoid.

SHIFT IN RESPONSIBILITY

The President's advisers largely agreed that the new evidence warranted resuming U-2 missions over western Cuba. New requirements were issued for photographic reconnaissance of the San Cristobal area. Because of continuing concern over the international repercussions should one of the U-2s be shot down, it was decided that future U-2 missions should be flown by the Air Force. If any questions about the flights should arise, they would be acknowledged as military reconnaissance missions.

The 4080th Strategic Wing of the Strategic Air Command, based at Laughlin Air Force Base in Del Rio, Texas, was given the assignment. The next flight was set for 14 October, with major Rudolph Anderson, USAF, as the pilot. The mission went flawlessly, and copies of the photography were sent by courier to NPIC, Navy analysts, the Strategic Air Command (SAC), and other key commands.

EVIDENCE OF MRBMS

Photointerpreters at NPIC called me at the Pentagon on 15 October. MRBMs had been found and confirmed. I called General Carroll to tell him what I had just heard and that I was on my way to NPIC. He asked me to give him another call as soon as I had personally reviewed the evidence.

After a quick look at three or four of the frames, I called General Carroll back and told him that the film showed ballistic-missile carriers, associated equipment, and support trucks. The U-2 camera had caught an MRBM convoy just as it was preparing to pull into the cover of a wooded area.

That evening General Carroll, my colleague John McLauchlin, and I reported directly to Deputy Secretary Gilpatric. He asked me the same question that the President would ask Art Lundahl the following morning. It was the same question that would be asked by each of the select senior U.S. officials being informed of the discovery as they looked at the tiny objects and patterns on our photographs of the Cuban countryside: "Are you sure that these are Soviet MRBMs?" I answered, "I am convinced they are." The next morning, Lundahl told the President he was "as sure of this as a photointerpreter can be sure of anything."

STRATEGIC INTELLIGENCE

The urgent work of the Executive Committee would begin on the morning of 16 October. While the world remained ignorant of the mounting crisis, those supporting the President and the Executive Committee were aware of the responsibility and trust that had been given us. The President needed absolute confirmation of the presence and numbers of MRBMs and any other offensive weapons that the Soviets had in place in Cuba. He needed time to marshal U.S. ground, sea, and air forces and to consider the options for their use should military action be required. He also needed time to decide how best to confront Khrushchev with the evidence, and he had to plan how to implement the U.S. response. Secrecy was essential. More documentary evidence was required.

U-2s from SAC were moved to Florida. Between 15 and 22 October, they flew 20 missions over Cuba to search the entire island. These reconnaissance flights helped us to understand what the Soviets were up to and what stage of weapons deployment they had reached. This information enabled the Intelligence Community to give the President and his advisers its best judgment as to whether the missiles were operational and, if not, when they would most likely become operational.

As a result of highly classified and urgent work, the community would determine that the first of the MRBMs would become operational on 28 October. While U.S. intelligence had not provided strategic warning that the Soviets would introduce such weapons, intelligence had discovered the weapons before they became operational, giving the President an advantage in planning his response.

Analysis of U-2 photography went on around the clock, with few, even in the Intelligence Community, given access to the intelligence. As new photography became available, General Carroll and I would brief the Secretary and then take the same findings to the Chairman and the Joint Chiefs to prepare the Defense representatives for the continuing deliberations of the Executive Committee. Our photointerpreters pored over earlier U-2 photography of the geographic locations where we were now discovering the offensive weapons. These comparisons enabled us to determine when the Soviets had begun construction, a process which confirmed the clandestine and time-urgent design of the Soviet operation.

SEABORNE SHIPMENTS

With the deployment of the missiles in Cuba now established, we began to reexamine earlier photointelligence to determine how they had arrived. From September to mid-October, the navy had photographed several Soviet merchant ships en route to Cuba, including the *Poltava* and the *Omsk*, riding high in the water and with unusually long cargo hatches. It was apparent that these merchant vessels must have been transporting a high-volume cargo that was not particularly heavy. We then realized that they had, in fact, been delivering missiles that were to be offloaded at night.

SS-4s AND SS-5s

The photography of the 17 October U-2 mission revealed a major new development: the construction of a fixed IRBM site at Guanajay, just west of Havana. While the mobile MRBM posed a serious threat, its range was limited to targets in the southern United States.

We had studied the SS-4 MRBM since before its first appearance on parade in Moscow the year before. It had an overall length of just over 73 feet with warhead attached. It had a support crew of 24 men, and it was serviced by a dozen vehicles. The SS-4 had sufficient fuel and thrust to deliver a 1-megaton nuclear warhead on short notice up to 1,000 miles, a range that threatened the southeastern U.S. in an arc extending from Savannah, Georgia, to New Orleans, Louisiana.

The SS-5 IRBM, by contrast, had a range of over 2,200 miles, and it could hit any target in the continental U.S. except Seattle, Spokane, and other cities in Washington state. It was clear that we were not facing a temporary expeditionary force in Cuba. The SS-5 required complex permanent launch sites, with troop quarters, missile shelters, warhead bunkers, and a large logistic train.

We had monitored the development and testing of the SS-5 SKEAN since the late 1950s. Operational in 1961, the SS-5 was the newest of the Soviet Union's IRBMs and the product of its intensive strategic rocket program. The SS-5's warhead yield also was estimated at 1 megaton, but it had better inertial guidance than the SS-4.

FOUR KEY SITES

Continuing intelligence analysis provided irrefutable evidence that the Soviets were pushing ahead simultaneously with the installation of ballistic missiles at four separate locations: MRBMs at San Cristobal and Sagua La Grande, and IRBMs at Guanajay and Remedios. Soviet construction was progressing at a breakneck pace; photointelligence from successive U-2 missions indicated that sites were rapidly approaching operational status. Their construction workers were experiencing some difficulties as was evident from earth scarring and deep tire ruts produced by heavy transporters in the soft soil of the semitropical countryside.

The Soviets and Cubans were working almost continuously to set up 24 MRBM launchers plus 18 reserves for a total of 42 SS-4 MRBM nuclear missiles, as well as three fixed IRBM launch sites, each with four launchers. If these sites were completed, their missiles would significantly affect the strategic balance.

CRATOLOGY

The U-2 mission of 15 October discovered a third dimension to the impending nuclear threat. In late September, U.S. maritime surveillance had spotted a merchant ship bound for Cuba carrying a number of large crates on its deck. To deduce their content, U.S. photointerpreters had to resort to the fledgling "science" of cratology.

Unique dimensions, shapes, volumes, and other features of the apparently innocuous-looking crates allowed analysts to determine with some precision by mid-October that the crates contained disassembled IL-28/BEAGLE bomber aircraft. The U-2 photographed 21 of these crates, one with the top open and the BEAGLE fuselage exposed, at San Julian Airfield on 15 October. This was our first sighting of part of the total force of 42 bombers the Soviet Union was delivering to the San Julian and Holuin Airfields.

MEETING WITH GROMYKO

At the White House, the Executive Committee weighed the new evidence in its deliberations on the best course of action to recommend to the President. On 18 October, the President proceeded with an office call by Soviet Foreign Minister Gromyko, an appointment that had been made many weeks before. Without tipping his hand about the U.S. discovery of the Soviet MRBMs, IRBMs, and bombers in Cuba, President Kennedy underscored to Gromyko the unacceptability of Soviet offensive nuclear weapons on the island. Gromyko responded with assurances that the weapons being introduced were strictly defensive.

SNIE's JUDGMENTS

The Executive Committee soon narrowed the options to airstrikes against the missile sites and bomber bases versus a naval blockade of the island. On 20 October, the Intelligence Community published its views on the implications of the committee's options in SNIE-11-19-62, *Major Consequences of Certain U.S. Courses of Action on Cuba.*

SNIE 11-19-62 was cautious about the likely results of either a selective or a total blockade of Cuba. It argued that nuclear warheads could be delivered covertly aboard aircraft or submarines evading the blockade, that the Soviet missiles already in Cuba would still be poised to strike, that it would not weaken Castro's regime, and that either a selective or total blockade would give the Soviet Union time to mobilize world pressure against the United States. The SNIE judged that neither type of blockade would necessarily escalate to war, either in Cuba or elsewhere, and that the Soviets would not be driven to immediate military retaliation.

The estimate also judged that, whatever the nature of any U.S. military action against Cuba, it would not be likely to provoke Khrushchev and his colleagues into launching all-out nuclear war. The authors wrote:

> We believe that there would probably be a difference between Soviet reaction to all-out invasion and Soviet reaction to more limited U.S. use of force against selective objectives in Cuba. We believe that the Soviets would be somewhat less likely to retaliate with military force in areas outside of Cuba in response to speedy, effective invasion than in response to more limited forms of military action against Cuba. We recognize that such an estimate cannot be made with very great assurance and do not rule out the possibility of Soviet retaliation outside of Cuba in case of invasion. But we believe that a rapid occupation of Cuba would be more likely to make the Soviets pause in opening new theaters of conflict than limited action or action which drags out.[311]

THE PRESIDENT'S DECISION

Proponents of the alternate options of U.S. response continued to argue with the Executive Committee until the President had chosen a course which he had judged would not push Khrushchev beyond the brink. It would demonstrate U.S. resolve, and it would pro-

---

[311] SNIE 11-19-62, *Major Consequences of Certain U.S. Courses of Action on Cuba*, 20 October 1962.

vide the President and his advisers the time and the leverage they required in their communications with Khrushchev to demand that the USSR withdraw its missiles and bombers from Cuba.

President Kennedy's report to the American people on the Soviet missile and bomber buildup in Cuba was delivered from the White House Oval Office at 7:00 p.m., 22 October, one week after the discovery of the MRBMs at San Cristobal. I was with Navy photointerpreters in Suitland, Maryland. We listened to the President's somber, electrifying words. As stated in the second of his announced actions, the President had ordered low-level surveillance photo missions by Navy and Air Force tactical reconnaissance squadrons to begin the following morning.

Given the array of MiG-21 fighters, antiaircraft guns, and SAM defenses that would confront our reconnaissance planes, tactical intelligence support was vital to their success. In turn, their success would be essential to the President's strategy. As we worked to prepare for the following day's briefing, there was a profound sense of urgency.

LOW-LEVEL MISSIONS

Shortly after dawn on 23 October, Navy pilots of Light Photographic Squadron 62 and Air Force pilots of the 363 rd Tactical Reconnaissance Wing took off on the first low-level photo missions over Cuba. Later that day, the President issued Proclamation 3504: *Interdiction of the Delivery of Offensive Weapons to Cuba*. It stated that as of 2:00 p.m., 24 October, forces under his command had instructions to intercept any vessel or craft proceeding toward Cuba and to interdict the delivery of surface-to-surface missiles, bombers, bombs, air-to-surface rockets and guided missiles, warheads, mechanical and electrical equipment for such weapons, and any other materials subsequently designated by the Secretary of Defense.

Our aerial reconnaissance of Cuba took a quantum leap both in volume and in precision of detail with the low-level missions. The Navy and Marine Corps pilots assigned to Light Photographic Squadron 62 (VP-62) were flying the single-engine reconnaissance RF-8A version of the F-8 Crusader fighter. It carried five cameras. The Air Force pilots of the 363 rd Tactical Reconnaissance Wing were flying the RF-101 reconnaissance version of the F-101 Voodoo fighter.

The RF-101's reconnaissance eyes were the KA-53 aerial reconnaissance cameras with black-and-white and color emulsion 5-inch aerial roll film loaded in 250-foot film cassettes, cameras with shutter speeds up to 1/3,000th of a second. The combination of planes and cameras in these Navy and Air Force tactical units was as remarkable in its sophistication as was the technology aboard the U-2s.

The RF-8As and RF-101s covered their targets 500 feet off the ground at speeds of 600 mph. With this speed and altitude, the Soviets and Cubans had no warning, only the sonic roar as the reconnaissance planes flew by on flight profiles that brought them in low over the Gulf of Mexico with a pop-up over the target. At the successful conclusion of each mission, the VP-62 pilots would paint another dead chicken on the fuselages of their Crusaders to symbolize Castro's chickens coming home to roost.[312]

The reconnaissance photography these pilots were delivering was spectacular. It was clear, large-scale documentation. It permitted us to gain full understanding of the MRBMs that would be operational by the 28th and to track the continuing intensive construction of the IRBM sites. The photography provided our combat-mission planners with the precise detail they required in the event the President were to order a strike against the island.

As soon as each low-level mission delivered its film to the squadron and wing photo labs, it was developed and flown to Washington and to other photographic analysis centers.

THE JRC

The nerve center for the U.S. reconnaissance effort was the Joint Reconnaissance Center (JRC) in the Pentagon, under the direction of then-Colonel Ralph D. Steakley, USAF. The JRC had been created to provide the JCS, the Office of the Secretary of Defense, the Department of State, and the White House with a focal point for policy decisions on the U.S. reconnaissance missions being undertaken worldwide long before the Cuban missile crisis. The Intelligence Community, the Unified and Specified Commands, and others would identify reconnaissance requirements. The JRC would clear mission plans through the appropriate policy level of the government, and, with approval received, authorize the reconnaissance missions.

We fed our reconnaissance targeting requirements to Steakley. He had assigned liaison officers from the Center to the Tactical Air Command and SAC. The JRC and the operational planners of the Air Force and Navy drew up detailed flight plans to fulfill the latest intelligence requirements. The work proceeded around the clock. Steakley had a cot in his office, where he lived throughout the crisis. He was under relentless operational pressure. He had received a telephone call from President Kennedy's secretary with the message, "The President has directed that you not be away from your phone for more than three rings." Secretary McNamara had made it clear that he personally wanted to be certain that each mission flown was in accordance with a determined plan and a predetermined approval cycle. Steakley was regularly summoned to the White House to brief the President on the planned flights.

The President and the Executive Committee were seeing explicit details of the Soviet nuclear offensive buildup. They were following the advances of the MRBMs and IRBMs toward operational status with each day's low-level reconnaissance take. The missions, as the President knew, were dangerous and might escalate the crisis beyond the control of either side.

---

[312] Newsletter, *Light Photographic Squadron Sixty-Two* (VPF-62), February 1963.

A BAD DAY

On 27 October, an Air Force RB-47 flying maritime surveillance missions against Soviet shipping crashed on takeoff from Bermuda with the loss of all four crew members. That same day a Soviet SA-2 GUIDELINE missile brought down a U-2 over Cuba flown by Major Rudolf Anderson, the pilot of the U-2 flight on 14 October that had filmed the discovery of the Soviet MRBMs. Anderson was killed, and the pressure to retaliate intensified.

AN EFFECTIVE CYCLE

We felt this pressure in our support to Secretary McNamara and the JCS. The work cycle began with the delivery of hundreds of feet of new photography in Washington, usually each evening, which had to be analyzed around the clock. I would arrive at either the Pentagon or NPIC early each morning to review the findings and to prepare to brief McNamara and the JCS, usually before the start of the morning Executive Committee sessions at the White House. Current intelligence for targeting of SAM sites was fed to the military planners for inclusion in the target folders. There was a growing consensus that the U.S. would have to act.

The gravity of the situation was confirmed by the results of the low-level reconnaissance missions. The JRC worked with Air Force and Navy planners in drawing up the final flight plans. The pilots agreed that flight tracks for each mission were flyable, and that they were the best tracks to achieve coverage of the requested targets. This success was matched by the cycle we had developed of film processing, readout, and feedback to both the national level and the operators. The results of each day's reconnaissance were available to feed into the following day's planning and execution.

WHITE HOUSE STATEMENT

On 26 October, the President approved the release of a statement updating the American people on the status of the Soviet missile sites. It reported that development of the IRBM sites was continuing, with bulldozers and cranes observed clearing new areas within the sites. It noted that MRBMs had been observed, with cabling running from missile-ready tents to nearby power generators. And it concluded that the Soviets were trying to camouflage their efforts at the sites.

The USSR's measured response to the quarantine was of critical importance to the President's restrained approach to the crisis. No ships with prohibited or even questionable cargoes had tried to run the blockade. The shootdown of Major Anderson had brought the U.S. to the brink of a retaliatory strike against military targets in Cuba, but the President remained determined to force Soviet compliance with U.S. demands on terms short of war. Intelligence had given him the information he needed to catch Khrushchev red-handed. There could be no question of the validity of the U.S. charges. But the President knew he was running out of time: The MRBMs would become operational on 28 October.

MESSAGES FROM KHRUSHCHEV

On 26 October, Khrushchev sent President Kennedy first one message, then another. The first couched the Soviet Union's conditions for the withdrawal of its missiles and bombers from Cuba in terms of a requirement for an end to the U.S. blockade and for a promise from the U.S. that it would not invade Cuba. The second Khrushchev letter added another, far more difficult demand:

> You are worried over Cuba. You say that it worries you because it lies at a distance of 90 miles across the sea from the shores of the United States. However, Turkey lies next to us. Our sentinels are pacing up and down watching each other. Do you believe that you have the right to demand security for your country and the removal of such weapons that you qualify as offensive, while not recognizing this right for us?
>
> This is why I make this proposal: We agree to remove those weapons from Cuba which you regard as offensive weapons. We agree to do this and to state this commitment in the United Nations. Our representatives will make a statement to the effect that the United States, on its part, bearing in mind the anxiety and concern of the Soviet state, will evacuate its analogous weapons from Turkey. Let us reach an understanding on what time you and we need to put this into effect.[313]

THE U.S. REPLIES

While the U.S. missiles would eventually be withdrawn from Turkey, at the peak of the Cuban missile crisis the President rejected including them or any mention of them in the terms that would be set for the withdrawal of the Soviet missiles from Cuba. In the midst of the Executive Committee meeting on 27 October on the next step to be taken by the U.S., Attorney General Robert Kennedy proposed that the U.S. reply to Khrushchev's first letter and not to the second. He actually drafted the reply, stating the terms we were willing to accept, plucking them from several often-disparate Soviet messages. They were the terms on which the settlement ultimately was based.[314]

The President's reply of 27 October opened on a positive note, welcoming Khrushchev's "desire to seek a prompt solution to the problem." The President then stressed that if there were to be a solution, work had to cease on the missile bases, and the offensive weapons in Cuba had to be rendered inoperable and removed, with supervision of the removal under appropriate UN arrangements. The U.S. in turn would lift the quarantine and would assure the Soviet Union that it would not invade Cuba. The President then hinted at future U.S. willingness to consider the missiles in Turkey, without explicitly so stating: "The effect of such a settlement," he wrote, "on easing world tensions would enable us to work toward a more general arrangement regarding 'other armaments,' as

---

[313] Kennedy, 198-199.
[314] Kennedy, 15-16.

proposed in your second letter which you made public." The President closed his reply by again stressing the imperative of an immediate Soviet halt to work on the MRBMs and IRBMs and rendering the weapons inoperable.[315]

Attorney General Kennedy handed over a copy of the President's reply to Soviet Ambassador Dobrynin, stressing the President's belief that the substance of the Soviet response to this message would dictate swiftly whether the two superpowers would resolve the crisis or escalate to war.

On 28 October 1962, Khrushchev agreed to President Kennedy's terms: Work would stop on the missile sites, and the weapons would be dismantled and withdrawn. The word arrived quickly as we continued to support preparations for U.S. military action. There was tremendous exhilaration. The Intelligence Community and the military shifted gears, moving to the responsibility of monitoring Soviet dismantlement and withdrawal.

MONITORING THE WITHDRAWAL

New orders from Moscow to the Soviet missile and bomber forces in Cuba were dispatched immediately. As early as 29 October, low-level reconnaissance flights brought back evidence that the MRBM missile erectors were no longer in their missile-ready firing positions. We would monitor every step of the Soviet withdrawal through photography, reports from human sources, ship-to-ship inspections, air-to-ship surveillance, and other sources and methods. Weather permitting, the Navy RF-8As and Air Force RF-101s flew across Cuba on daily missions collecting thousands of frames of up-to-the-minute evidence for examination by the photointerpreters, analysts, and the senior levels of government.

Early on, the Soviets started to break up the IRBM sites — sites which would never meet their planned 15 December operational date, chosen to coincide with Khrushchev's planned address to the United Nations. Bulldozers tore up the missiles' concrete launch pads and smashed through missile-support facilities. Each of the sites was systematically monitored. The status of the support equipment, propellant trailers, nuclear weapons-handling vans, and communications vans was also an intelligence indicator. We tracked their withdrawal from the missile sites to the ports and onto a succession of Soviet merchant ships. The reconnaissance cameras documented Soviet personnel boarding ships for the voyage back across the Atlantic.

The Navy quarantine remained in effect, examining any inbound ships and, in a new phase, inspecting outbound ships to determine their cargoes. The Soviets complied with orders to strip away canvas covering each of the missiles in their canisters, with each clearly in the open, riding as deck cargo. They also complied with orders to break open the wooden crates containing the IL-28 bomber wings and fuselages, permitting us to count each and to confirm their departure.

---

[315] Kennedy, 203.

Quarantine commander Admiral Ward reported that while the business was deadly serious and while the U.S. forces insisted on full, precise compliance with all demands, there was no sign of Soviet hostility.

STATUS REPORTS

On 2 November, President Kennedy provided his first formal status report on the dismantling of the Soviet missile bases in Cuba in an address to the nation. He reported that careful examination of aerial photography and other information was confirming the destruction of the missile bases and preparation of the missiles for return to the USSR. He said that U.S. surveillance would continue to track the withdrawal closely and that this unilateral inspection and monitoring would continue until the U.S. arranged for international inspection of the cargoes and overall withdrawal.

By the time of his news conference on 20 November, the President had received sufficient intelligence to be able to report that the missile sites had all been dismantled, that the missiles and associated equipment had departed Cuba aboard Soviet ships, that U.S. inspection at sea had confirmed that the numbers departing included all known missiles, and that Khrushchev had informed him earlier that day that the IL-28 bombers would all be withdrawn from Cuba within 30 days. Following this Soviet compliance with U.S. demands, the President announced that he had ordered the lifting of the quarantine. He went on to stress that close surveillance of Cuba would continue, bearing in mind that Castro had still not agreed to allow UN inspectors to verify the removal of all offensive weapons or to set safeguards in place to prevent their reintroduction.

In his news conference of 12 December, the President had to repeat his position of 20 November, stating that, while the U.S. continued to press for on-site inspection, he would take every step necessary through continuing close daily surveillance to ensure that no missiles or offensive weapons were reintroduced.

PAYING TRIBUTE

With the quarantine lifted, the President flew to Florida on 26 November to pay tribute to the reconnaissance wings and squadrons. At Homestead Air Force Base, the President presented Outstanding Unit Awards to the 4080*th* Strategic Reconnaissance Wing and the 363*rd* Tactical Reconnaissance Wing. He saluted the work of the pilots and their ground crews:

> I may say, gentleman, that you take excellent pictures, and I've seen a good many of them. And beginning with the photographs which were taken on the weekend in the middle of October, which first gave us conclusive proof of the buildup of offensive weapons in Cuba, through the days that have followed to the present time, the work of these two units has contributed as

much to the security of the U.S. as any units in our history, and any group of men in our history.[316]

He then flew to Key West, to Boca Chica Naval Air Station, to present Unit Citations to Navy Light Photographic Squadron 62 and Marine Light Photographic Squadron VMC-J2.

On 28 November, SAC Commander in Chief General Thomas Power awarded the Distinguished Flying Cross to 10 U-2 pilots of the 4080*th*. Admiral Robert Dennison, USN, presented the same decoration to 25 pilots of the Navy, Marine Corps, and Air Force tactical reconnaissance units. The next day the planes' cameras were again in action over Cuba.

MONITORING CONTINUES

The reconnaissance missions of November enabled us to monitor the disassembly and crating of the IL-28 bombers at San Julian and Holguin Airfields and the departure of the crates from Cuba, just as we had earlier monitored the destruction of the IRBM sites at Guanajay and Remedios and the departure of the MRBM missiles from San Cristobal and Sagua La Grande. The first missions of 1963 also enabled us to continue to monitor the status of the Soviets' considerable remaining defensive installations, weaponry, and personnel, ostensibly in place to protect against the threat of invasion.

The number of Soviet troops had swollen between 22,000 and 23,000 on Cuba at the peak of the crisis. With the departure of the missile and bomber forces, we could now identify some 17,000 troops still on the island. Our order of battle in early 1963 showed that Soviet military equipment in Cuba included 24 SAM sites with 500 missiles; 104 MiG fighters, including 24 of the new MiG-21 jets capable of Mach 2 performance; 200 air defense radars; 12 KOMAR-class missile patrol boats; upwards of 100 helicopters; four cruise-missile sites with 150 cruise missiles; more than 700 antiaircraft guns; 24 to 32 FROG rockets; 7,500 to 10,000 military support vehicles; more than 1,300 pieces of field artillery and antitank guns; and some 400 tanks.[317]

Taken together, this weaponry would have given the Soviets a layered set of ground, sea, and air defenses for their missile sites and bomber bases. And there could be little doubt that the remaining weapons were defensive in character. While the Intelligence Community assessed the MiG-21 as being capable of carrying a nuclear weapon, we knew that was not the fighter's intended mission. With a nuclear weapon aboard, the MiG-21 would have a combat radius of little more than 200 miles restricted to clear weather, daytime missions. Of prime importance, our analysis of each new batch of reconnaissance photography showed absolutely no evidence of the types of security facilities that one

---

[316] *Public Papers of the Presidents of the United States: John F. Kennedy,* 1962 (Washington, DC: U.S. Government Printing Office, 1963), 832-833.

[317] CIA Fact Sheet.

could expect with confidence that the Soviets would have in place if there were still any nuclear weapons stored on the island.

We were confident of the complete withdrawal based on the comprehensive character of our reconnaissance and monitoring in late 1962 and early 1963.

REFUTING RUMORS

When the U.S. Congress reconvened in late January 1963, our hard evidence on the defensive nature of the Soviet forces in Cuba remained largely classified. The public debate was feeding rumors that Soviet nuclear offensive capabilities remained in Cuba, that missiles were hidden in caves, and that the MiG-21s and KOMAR patrol boats could deliver nuclear weapons. Such rumors were pouring in from anti-Castro Cuban refugees, and they were fueled by those still angry that the President had not invaded the island and done away with the communist regime.

Following his Congressional testimony on 5 February, DCI McCone issued a formal unclassified statement in the name of the USIB reviewing the entire Soviet buildup and the departure of the missiles: "We are convinced beyond reasonable doubt, as has been stated by the Department of Defense, that all offensive missiles and bombers known to be in Cuba were withdrawn soon thereafter... Reconnaissance has not detected the presence of offensive missiles or bombers in Cuba since that time." Referring to the alleged storage of missiles in caves, McCone said, "All statements alleging the presence of offensive weapons are meticulously checked. So far the findings have been negative. Absolute assurance on these matters, however, could only come from continuing penetrating on-site inspection."[318] The statement still did not defuse the issue.

In my appearance with Secretary McNamara before the House Subcommittee on Defense Appropriations on 6 February, the Secretary reviewed each phase of the Soviet buildup since the spring of 1962. To set the stage for my classified presentation to the sub-committee of the most important photography, the Secretary described the role of recon-naissance in some detail. Immediately after my presentation, the President decided that the photographic evidence had to be declassified and shared with the American people.

BRIEFING THE NATION

Shortly before noon, Secretary McNamara informed me that I was to present the brief-ing to the nation that evening on national television from 5:00 to 7:00 p.m. I was to make the presentation in the State Department Auditorium to an audience of journalists and photographers assigned to the White House, State Department, and Defense Department. The briefing requested by the President included photos, charts, and tables that would document clearly the discovery of the Soviet ballistic missiles, their assembly and opera-tional readiness, and their dismantlement and removal from the island. The photos were

---

[318] Statement on Cuba by the DCI, 6 February 1963.

selected from among the best available and reflected the superb quality of the photography regularly provided by our reconnaissance jets.

Secretary McNamara told me that he would introduce the presentation and take the follow-on questions. He asked to see the text of my briefing and was surprised when I told him that there was no written text because I had committed the briefing to memory, and that the sequence of the photography and charts would shape and pace the presentation. The Secretary directed his military assistant, Colonel George Brown, USAF, who would go on to become Chairman of the Joint Chiefs of Staff, to take me under his charge for the remainder of the day and ensure that I was at the State Department by 4:00 p.m.

By 3:30 p.m., we were ready. The graphics had been checked and rechecked, classifications removed or covered, and some descriptive annotations added. Colonel Brown and I arrived at the State Department at 4:00 p.m. The auditorium was larger than I had expected, and the viewing screen — at least 12 feet by 8 feet — towered above the stage. This screen would enhance and display the photography to maximum advantage. To tell the story effectively, however, I had to be able to point to photographic details that would be well beyond reach. I contacted my special assistant, Captain Billy R. Cooper, USAF, at the Pentagon about the problem, and he was more than equal to the challenge. He grabbed a roll of tape, securely joined two long fishing poles, and rushed to his car. I had this tailor-made pointer in hand and was set and ready to go at 5:00 p.m.

The air was charged in the auditorium. The press was out in full force and McNamara was to the point:

Good afternoon, ladies and gentlemen. In recent days questions have been raised in the press and elsewhere regarding the presence of offensive weapons systems in Cuba. I believe beyond any reasonable doubt that all such weapons systems have been removed from the island and none have been reintroduced. It is our purpose to show you this afternoon the evidence on which we base that conclusion.

Since 1 July, over 400 reconnaissance flights have been flown over the island of Cuba by U.S. military aircraft. These reconnaissance flights provided the essential basis for the national decisions taken with respect to Cuba in October. They provided the basis for the military preparations necessary to support those decisions. They provided the evidence we were able to present to the world to document the basis and the rationale of our action.

The reconnaissance flights recorded the removal of the offensive weapon systems from Cuba, and they continued to provide the foundation for our conclusion that such weapons systems have not been reintroduced into the island.

Mr. John Hughes, the Special Assistant to General Carroll, the Director of DIA, will present to you a detailed photographic review of the introduction of Soviet military personnel and equipment into Cuba, with particular emphasis on the introduction and removal of the offensive weapons systems.

After Mr. Hughes completes his review, I will summarize very briefly our current estimates of the Soviet military strength in Cuba.

Mr. Hughes.

I began my briefing.

EDITOR'S NOTE

At the time of the Cuban Missile Crisis, I was a 20-year-old college senior anticipating my future as an Army officer, fully expecting that the immediate future might include a tour of duty in Cuba. I would watch John Hughes' briefing that night on national television, and would marvel at the photographic evidence being revealed to the nation. Twenty years later, I would be assigned to the Pentagon office of John T. Hughes, then the Deputy Director for External Affairs of the Defense Intelligence Agency, as Hughes' Executive Officer, responsible for overseeing the myriad operational and administrative details swirling about this man and his office.

Eight months into my tour, President Ronald Reagan chose John Hughes to give another special presentation to the nation — this time on another hot-spot: Nicaragua. With déjà vu apparent, the site for the briefing was to be the State Department Auditorium with the giant screen, and again, Hughes would need a long pointer to reach every part of the enormous projected images. This time it was his Deputy, Colonel Al Jones, who pulled from his desk a sectional bamboo fishing pole, which Hughes assembled on-site for the briefing. If one looks closely at the pictures of John Hughes that appeared on the front pages of the *New York Times* and the *Washington Post* that Wednesday, 10 March 1982, one can make out the ridges separating the sections of the bamboo fishing pointer.

EXPANDING THE HORIZON:
THE ORIGINS OF ISRAEL'S
RECONNAISSANCE SATELLITE PROGRAM

E. L. Zorn

(Originally published in Studies in Intelligence, the Unclassified Edition No. 10 (Winter-Spring 2001): 33-38.)

Israel's successful orbiting of its *Ofeq*-3 satellite in April 1995 was the realization of a longstanding desire: an independent space reconnaissance capability. For more than 20 years before they began receiving imagery from the satellite, Israeli defense officials had recognized that spacecraft offered unique capabilities to intensify information gathering in adjacent countries while extending their intelligence reach to more distant lands. After the nation was almost overwhelmed in the October 1973 Yom Kippur War, Israeli intelligence officers focused their efforts on preventing future surprise attacks. Satellite photography was seen as a vital tool, able to provide unprecedented warning about the movement of enemy troops and equipment in preparation for war, as well as the movement of enemy forces once hostilities were underway.

SATELLITE IMAGERY AND THE OCTOBER 1973 YOM KIPPUR WAR

The value of satellite imagery was not unknown to the Israelis prior to the Yom Kippur War. Faced with invading armies on two fronts in October 1973, Israeli military attachés in Washington urgently requested satellite information about the disposition of the Egyptian and Syrian forces from the United States. According to former IDF Chief of Staff General Mordecai Gur, who had been one of those attachés, United States authorities responded that the information was unavailable due to "damage" to the satellite.[319] An unnamed CIA analyst subsequently recalled that the United States had acquired "wonderful coverage, but...didn't get the pictures until the war was over."[320] Even those photos showed the positions of invading forces only during the earliest part of the war.[321] The findings of the House Select Committee on Intelligence (the "Pike Committee") in its *Recommendations of the Final Report* in 1976 also indicate that the United States was unable to obtain adequate imagery and other information about the conflict while it was underway. As part of its criticism of United States intelligence activities, the committee

---

[319] Interview in *Ha'aretz* (Tel Aviv), 3 September 1992, quoted in Dan Raviv and Yossi Melman, *Friends in Deed: The U.S.-Israel Alliance* (New York: Hyperion, 1994), 161.

[320] Quoted in Representative George E. Brown, Jr. (D-CA), "'The Spies in Space' (By Jeffrey T. Richelson) (Extension of Remarks-November 26, 1991)," *Congressional Record* (26 November 1991): E4120. URL: <http://www.fas.org/irp/congress/1991_cr/h9111126- richelson.htm>, accessed 14 February 1999.

[321] Jeffrey T. Richelson, *America's Secret Eyes in Space: The U.S. Keyhole Spy Satellite Program* (New York: Harper & Row, 1990), 117.

concluded that the United States had gone "to the brink of war" with the Soviet Union during the 1973 war because it lacked timely intelligence.[322]

If the United States was unable to obtain the satellite photography necessary to satisfy its own intelligence needs during the conflict, then it logically follows that it was likewise unable to provide any information derived from satellite intelligence to Israel. Faced with the possibility of imminent military defeat at the hands of enemies whose avowed purpose in past conflicts had been the total annihilation of the so-called "Zionist entity," however, the Israelis were distrustful of United States statements that it was unable to respond with desperately needed intelligence assistance. As Gur noted in 1992, "How could I know if [the satellite] was really damaged? The bottom line was that we didn't get the information."[323] The general had expressed himself far less ambiguously as Israeli technicians were completing the final preparations for the launch of Israel's first experimental satellite, Ofeq-1, in September 1988: "The United States did not give us enough information [during the October 1973 war].[324] When I say not enough, I mean less [than] what we got before the war."[325]Exactly how long "before the war" Gur meant is unclear, since he is also said to have asserted that the United States had actually withheld satellite data from Israel immediately prior to the war.[326]

Presumably, the information which Gur believes had been held back by the United States would have revealed the true scope of Egyptian and Syrian preparations for war, thus providing adequate warning for the Israelis properly to prepare for the Arab attack. Instead, the Israelis found themselves in such a desperate situation that they deployed long-range missiles capable of delivering nuclear warheads on Cairo and Damascus after then-Minister of Defense Moshe Dayan warned that the nation might be on the verge of destruction at the hands of the Egyptians and Syrians.[327]

Gur's statements have been dismissed by some as "specious" and "probably made to help justify the Israeli space venture."[328] In fact, Gur's sentiments merit far more serious consideration. Just as the war itself marked a defining moment for Israelis, so too did Gur's experiences in trying to obtain satellite intelligence from the United States clearly leave a deep and lasting impression on him. From Gur's perspective, the United States had kept critical satellite warning data from the Israelis before the two-front attack. Shortly thereafter, when the nation and people of Israel were threatened with imminent annihilation by the invading Arab armies, the United States had demonstrated to the Israe-

---

[322] Brown, Jr. (D-CA),"'The Spies in Space' — (by Jeffrey T. Richelson) (Extension of Remarks — 26 November 1991)."

[323] Quoted in Raviv and Melman, 161.

[324] John Kifner, "Israel Launches Space Program and a Satellite," *New York Times*, 20 September 1988, Late Ed., A1.

[325] Kifner, A12.

[326] "Israeli Satellite Is 'Threat' Say Arabs," *Jane's Defense Weekly* 10, no. 13 (1 October 1988): 753.

[327] Danny Gur-arieh, "Israel Deployed Nuke-Capable Missiles in 1973 War," Reuters, 26 October 1998.

[328] Michael Russell Rip and Joseph F. Fontanella, "A Window on the Arab-Israeli 'Yom Kippur' War of October 1973: Military Photo-Reconnaissance from High Altitude and Space," *Intelligence and National Security* 6, no. 1 (January 1991): 76.

lis that it could not be relied upon to provide information vital to Israel's survival. Given Gur's assignment at that time and his later positions of influence, there seems little question that he would have been able to share his views with other Israeli security officials and decisionmakers.

For the Israelis, the lesson was immediate and unmistakable: they would have to acquire an independent space reconnaissance capability. Details about the earliest Israeli investigations into an indigenous satellite program are extremely limited, but the little information which is available unambiguously indicates that it was at this time that Israeli scientists and engineers first seriously explored the possibility of launching a satellite. In little-noticed remarks following the launch of *Ofeq-1* in 1988, Israel Space Agency (ISA) chairman Yuval Ne'eman disclosed that Israel had been working on the satellite since the early 1970s.[329] Even more telling, as part of a legal action against a former employee, Israel Aircraft Industries (IAI), the manufacturer of the *Ofeq* satellites and their *Shavit* ("Comet") launch vehicles, revealed in March 1995 that it had in 1973 examined its capability to launch an *Ofeq*-style satellite using a *Shavit*-type launcher, and that it had determined that such a project was feasible.[330] Unfortunately for the Israelis, however, desire and theoretical capability were not in and of themselves sufficient basis for a space program. The large scale and expense of the project kept a reconnaissance spacecraft beyond their reach as they continued to rely upon the United States for their satellite intelligence needs.

THE POST-WAR YEARS

Israel began seeking greater access to United States satellite intelligence to augment its early warning capabilities immediately after the 1973 war. Their efforts proved more successful than they had during the conflict, although perhaps only marginally so in the view of Israeli officials. Ne'eman, then Israel's chief defense scientist, included a request for intelligence satellite "services" in Israeli demands to be presented to the United States following the negotiation of the interim agreement at the conclusion of the 1973 war.[331] According to late Prime Minister Yitzhak Rabin, then-Minister of defense Shimon Peres formally presented the United States with the Israeli request for a $1-billion satellite system in December 1975. Some months later, while testifying before Members of Congress who were concerned that such a measure would hurt prospects for peace in the Middle East, Rabin indicated that Israel really did not require the satellite, after all.[332]

United States policy with regard to providing satellite intelligence to Israel was uneven throughout the remainder of the 1970s, and seemed to the Israelis to vary with each Director of Central Intelligence (DCI). George Bush was said to have approved providing

---

[329] Juan O. Tamayo, "Israel Launches Satellite with Military Potential," *Miami Herald*, 20 September 1988, Final Ed., 14A.

[330] Sharon Sade, "IAI Confirms Having Satellite-Launching Capability in 1973," TA1603171095 in Tel Aviv Ha'aretz (16 March 1995), A6. FBIS Tel Aviv IS, 161710Z March 1995.

[331] Yuval Ne'eman, "New Horizons-A Personal View," *Jerusalem Post*, 23 September 1988, 5.

[332] Joshua Brilliant, "A Peek Under the Shroud of Secrecy," *Jerusalem Post*, 23 September 1988, 4.

actual satellite photographs to Israel while he was the DCI in 1976 and 1977.[333] When Stansfield Turner replaced Bush in 1977, he allowed the Israelis to receive only interpretive analysis, that is information based on satellite imagery, but not the images themselves.[334] The Israelis were to grow increasingly concerned over these and other inconsistencies in United States policy.

The arrival of William Casey as the DCI in 1981 proved a positive experience for the Israelis, at least initially. Casey permitted them to requisition actual satellite photography once again. However, the imagery to be provided was to be limited to that depicting potential direct threats to Israel's security.[335] Having regained entrée to the imagery, Israel then asked the United States in early April 1981 for direct access to a U.S. reconnaissance satellite. Israeli officials justified the request as "compensation" for the planned sale by the United States of airborne warning and control system (AWACS) surveillance aircraft to Saudi Arabia. Israel also voiced its increased need for real-time intelligence data and improved surveillance and warning capabilities due to its scheduled withdrawal from the Sinai Peninsula in April 1982.[336]

The precise details of the Israeli requirement are not clear. A contemporary account, citing unnamed United States and Israeli sources, notes that the Israelis had indicated that they would be satisfied with either a new satellite and ground station to be provided by the United States for Israel's exclusive use, or with "full and equal access" to an existing U.S. satellite.[337] A later report asserts that Israel had "demanded" exclusive access to a United States satellite already on orbit as the alternative to receiving its own new satellite.[338] In either case, United States officials considered the Israeli request seriously. However, the Israelis soon damaged their own cause.

In early June 1981, Israeli Air Force aircraft successfully bombed an Iraqi nuclear facility near Baghdad. Curious about how the Israelis had obtained the necessary targeting information to carry out the dramatic long-range strike, Deputy Director of Central Intelligence (D/DCI) Bobby Inman asked for a review of imagery and other materials that had been provided to Israeli intelligence officials. As previously noted, policies in effect at the time called for limiting Israeli access to satellite imagery to those photos showing potential direct threats to Israel. Inman quickly found that the Israeli and United States concepts of what constituted such threats differed substantially. During their nearly six months of renewed access to United States satellite imagery, the Israelis had obtained "a

---

[333] Bob Woodward, "CIA Sought 3rd-Country Contra Aid," *The Washington Post*, 19 May 1984, Final Ed., A13.

[334] Woodward, "CIA Sought 3rd-Country Contra Aid," A13.

[335] "Transcript of the Statement by Inman on His Decision to Withdraw," *New York Times*, 19 January 1994, Final Ed., A14.

[336] Bernard Gwertzman, "Israel Asks U.S. for Gift of Jets, Citing Saudi Sale," *New York Times*, 4 April 1981, Late City Ed., 2.

[337] Bernard Gwertzman, "Israel Asks U.S. for Gift of Jets, Citing Saudi Sale", 2.

[338] (No title), UPI, International Section, 26 November 1982 (LEXIS-NEXIS, n.d.).

lot" of information not only about Iraq, but also about Libya, Pakistan, and other countries lying at considerable distances from Israel.[339] The D/DCI immediately restricted future distribution of satellite photography. The Israelis were to be allowed to receive imagery only of areas within 250 miles of Israel's borders. They could, however, make specific requests for any other coverage desired, to be approved or denied by the DCI on a case-by-case basis.[340]

According to Inman, Israel's then-Minister of Defense Ariel Sharon was "furious," and immediately protested the decision directly to United States Secretary of Defense Caspar Weinberger.[341] The Secretary backed the D/DCI. DCI Casey, who had been traveling abroad, disagreed with his deputy's decision, but did not reverse it on his return. Instead, he effectively ignored it. Retired Israeli Major General Yehoshua Saguy, who served as the head of Israeli military intelligence from 1979 to 1983, confirmed that "Casey [said] 'yes' all the time" to Israeli requests for satellite photography of areas lying farther than 250 miles from Israel's borders."[342] An unnamed Israeli official has been quoted as saying that the level of support in furnishing satellite intelligence provided by DCI Casey was considered extremely valuable by the Israelis, and that they referred to it among themselves as "Casey's gift."[343]

The Israeli attack on the Iraqi nuclear facility became a significant factor in the continuing debate among United States officials over whether to grant Israel's earlier request for a reconnaissance satellite. Advocates on both sides of the argument cited the raid to justify their positions. Proponents argued that satisfying the desire would reduce the likelihood of future preemptive strikes by helping to soothe Israel's insecurities about its ability to detect Arab preparations for a surprise attack. Opponents noted that Israeli officials might use unhampered access to satellite intelligence to plan and execute even more attacks throughout the region. They also raised the matters of expense and the transfer of sensitive technologies. Finally, they pointed out that Arab concerns about the advantages that a satellite afforded Israel might prompt the Soviet Union to provide similar capabilities for Syria, Libya, or other nations in the region.[344]

Israel and the United States were expected to discuss the Israeli request and other facets of satellite intelligence during talks in September 1981 aimed at strengthening strategic ties between the two countries.[345] The sessions reportedly included discussions about

---

[339] "Transcript of the Statement by Inman on His Decision to Withdraw," A14.

[340] "Transcript of the Statement by Inman on His Decision to Withdraw," A14.

[341] "Transcript of the Statement by Inman on His Decision to Withdraw," A14.

[342] Woodward, "CIA Sought 3rd-Country Contra Aid," A13.

[343] Bob Woodward, "Probes of Iran Deals Extend to Roles of CIA, Director," *The Washington Post*, 28 November 1986, Final Ed., A33.

[344] Bill Roeder, "A U.S. Spy Satellite for Israel?" *Newsweek*, 7 September 1981, 17.

[345] Bernard Gwertzman, "U.S.-Israeli Talks on Military Links Are Reported Set," New York Times, 6 September 1981, Late City Ed., 1.

sharing intelligence as part of a broader joint effort to counter Soviet expansion and influence in the Middle East.[346] However, according to United States defense officials, there was no specific mention of satellites during the conference.[347] As a result, the Israelis did not receive their own reconnaissance satellite system from the United States, nor were they given direct access to a United States spacecraft already in orbit. However, Weinberger and Sharon signed a memorandum of understanding for "strategic cooperation" between the two countries in November.

The agreement proved extremely short-lived. President Ronald Reagan ordered it suspended after the Israelis formally annexed the Golan Heights in December 1981. Israel's invasion of Lebanon in mid-1982 even further provoked the ire of United States officials. It would be November 1983 before the United States, trying to make headway with its Middle East peace initiatives, offered to renew "strategic cooperation" with Israel.[348]

Israeli officials grew increasingly impatient with the manner in which the United States responded to their needs for satellite intelligence. When the Israelis took actions that they considered to be in the best interests of maintaining their own security and protecting the Israeli people, the United States replied by further restricting access to the information or by abrogating existing agreements. Apparently, the Israelis perceived themselves as victims of the vagaries of United States policy. They could not depend on the United States to provide satellite intelligence. Indeed some Israeli officials, most notably Sharon, concluded that the United States was not a reliable ally, period.[349]

Even in the best of times, the Israelis had found fault with the arrangements for their access to United States satellite intelligence. They complained that their requests for information based on satellite photography were often delayed or denied outright, or that the information that they did receive was frequently incomplete or dated.[350] They objected that when actual satellite photos were provided to them, the image quality was intentionally degraded, sometimes rendering them useless for the purposes desired.[351] Finally, they protested that United States intelligence authorities frequently refused their requests for specific collection against targets of special interest to the Israelis.[352]

Immediately after the launch of *Ofeq*-1, Saguy compared Israel's limited access to United States satellite information to the relationship between "a patron and his depen-

---

[346] John Brecher, with Milan J. Kubic and John Walcott, "Begin Wins Round One," Newsweek, 21 September 1981, 61.

[347] John M. Goshko, "Reagan, Begin Hold 'Warm' Meeting; No Decisions Reached on Closer Ties," *The Washington Post*, 10 September 1981, Final Ed., A13.

[348] Bernard Gwertzman, "Reagan Turns to Israel, *New York Times Magazine*, 27 November 1983, 84.

[349] Seymour M. Hersh, *The Samson Option: Israel's Nuclear Arsenal and American Foreign Policy* (New York: Random House, 1991), 16.

[350] "Israeli Spy Satellite Suspected," 46.

[351] Gerald M. Steinberg, "Middle East Space Race Gathers Pace," *International Defense Review* 28, no. 7 (October 1995): 20.

[352] "Military Eye-in-the-Sky Over Syria, Iraq, Iran, and Libya," *Mideast Mirror*, 6 April 1995 (NEXIS, 7 April 1995).

dent."[353] On the same occasion, another former head of military intelligence — who had also served as the head of Mossad, the Israeli secret service — described the situation in even less flattering terms: Meir Amit told Israeli radio that "if you are fed from the crumbs of others according to their whim, this is very inconvenient and very difficult. If you have your own independent capability you climb one level higher."[354]

Clearly, Israeli authorities would have preferred to have bypassed these difficulties altogether with an independent space intelligence capability. Twice, in 1975 and again in 1981, they had tried to obtain from the United States either a complete photoreconnaissance satellite system of their own or unfettered access to an existing system. In both instances, their requests were refused. Intelligence officials continued to press for an indigenous Israeli photoreconnaissance satellite. Then-Chief of the Israeli Military Intelligence Branch Shlomo Gazit in 1979 included a "spy satellite" on a list of military intelligence needs for the following decade. Gazit later noted that his request had been met by "a mixture of astonishment and scorn" by other Israeli officials.[355] There could have been no other reaction. The Israelis had made little substantive progress toward developing a satellite, a launcher, or any of the infrastructure necessary to support a space program in the years following IAI's 1973 study. Alon Ganei, a senior Israeli researcher in rocket propulsion, indicated in 1998 that even "in the [early] 1980s there was still considerable debate over whether to enter the aerospace field at all."[356]

Those favoring an Israeli space capability finally triumphed in 1982. Ne'eman, then Israeli Minister of Science and Technology, announced in November that Israel was establishing a space agency to build and launch satellites, including reconnaissance satellites.[357] Later statements by ISA officials, including ISA Chairman Ne'eman, emphasized the commercial and scientific nature of the Israeli space program, denying outright that Israel intended to field a "spy" satellite.[358] There was little question, however, that Israeli officials had reached their own conclusions about how best to satisfy Israel's satellite intelligence needs.

CONCLUSION

A recent ISA description of the *Ofeq* satellite program indicates that the project began in 1982, with "parallel efforts [in] research and development, construction of the neces-

[353] Yehoshua Saguy in *Hadashot* (Tel Aviv), n.d., quoted in Masha Hamilton, "Israel Launches Test Satellite," Associate Press, International Section, 19 September 1988 (LEXIS-NEXIS, n.d.).

[354] Glenn Frankel, "Israel Puts Its First Satellite Into Orbit," *The Washington Post*, 20 September 1988, A16.

[355] Shlomo Gazit, "Gaps in Satellite Intelligence Collection," 95P50108B in Tel Aviv *Yedi'ot Aharonot* (10 April 1995), 5. FBIS Reston VA, 260345Z April 1995.

[356] Amnon Barzilai, "Outer Space-Clean Up Your Act," *Ha'aretz* (Tel Aviv), 28 July 1998, B3. URL: <http://www.fas.org/irp/news/1998/07/980728-space.htm>, accessed 11 August 1998.

[357] (No title), UPI, International Section, 26 November 1982.

[358] "Israel: A Communications Satellite" (text), ME/W1230/B1 Israel Home Service, 1500 GMT (22 March 1983). BBC Summary of World Broadcasts: The Middle East, Africa, and Latin America, 5 April 1983 (LEXIS-NEXIS, n.d.); and Dan Fisher, "Israeli Space Program Sets Lofty Goals; Security, Industrial Development Are Prime Concerns," *Los Angeles Times*, 10 June 1985, Home Ed., Section 4, 1 (LEXIS-NEXIS, n.d.).

sary infrastructure, training [of] hundreds of engineers and technicians, and then design-ing, building, testing, and finally launching the satellites."[359] It goes on to describe very briefly the characteristics of each of the satellites successfully orbited so far, and accom-panying materials provide an informative overview of the Israeli space program and the sophisticated products and technologies supporting it.

None of the ISA information, however, addresses the single overriding factor that drove the Israelis to initiate such a complex and expensive undertaking: their need for uninterrupted, independent access to satellite imagery for intelligence and early warning. For Israel, which not only faces hostile neighbors on its borders but is also increasingly at risk from long-range missile threats from more distant countries, intelligence and early warning equate directly to the preservation of the state and the survival of the Jewish peo-ple. From the very earliest days of satellite reconnaissance, the Israelis understood and appreciated its value, and they came to depend on the United States to include informa-tion from overhead imagery in the intelligence data that it provided to Israel.

Immediately prior to and during the October 1973 Yom Kippur War, however, the United States was incapable of providing the information that Israel considered essential to its very survival. Just when Israel needed it most desperately, the United States had demonstrated that it was an unreliable source of satellite intelligence. As a direct result of that experience, Israeli officials took their first tentative steps toward an indigenous space program, investigating and confirming their theoretical capability to develop and deploy their own satellite. However, they balked when confronted with scope and economic real-ities of such a venture. The Israelis again turned to the United States for satellite imagery to satisfy their intelligence requirements.

If the United States had shown that it was unable to provide satellite intelligence infor-mation to the Israelis during the 1973 war, it then proved unwilling to provide all of the information requested by the Israelis in subsequent years. United States officials consid-ered some of the data requested by the Israelis to extend beyond the scope of valid warn-ing requirements. Fearing that the Israelis might use satellite photographs to obtain targeting information about facilities in Arab nations, the United States limited Israeli access to the imagery. Whenever the Israelis took actions viewed by the United States as inimical to stability in the Middle East or to other United States interests, further restric-tions were imposed.

To the Israelis, United States practices with regard to providing satellite intelligence were at best erratic, appearing to change with each new administration and every fluctua-tion in United States policy. The sole constant seemed to be that the situation was never satisfactory to the Israelis. The information provided by the United States was never enough, and its continued flow was never assured. The Israelis knew that the only solution lay in acquiring a satellite reconnaissance capability of their own. Still, they sought the answer from the United States: a complete system of satellites and a ground station exclu-

---

[359] Israel Space Agency, "The *Ofeq* Satellites Program," 16 March 1999. URL: <http://www.most.gov. il/isa/OFEK.html>, accessed 18 March 1999.

sively for Israel's use was preferred, but independent Israeli access to an existing system would be acceptable. The United States declined the Israeli request, lest granting it prove more harmful than beneficial to regional stability.

From a distance, Israel's expectations for United States satellite intelligence support may seem excessive, even preposterous. For the Israelis, however, the enhanced warning capabilities provided by satellites meant survival. Where the preservation of the state and the people were concerned, there could be no compromise. Unfortunately, the United States could not be trusted to furnish all of the satellite intelligence that Israel needed to meet its security requirements. In November 1982, Israeli officials committed to the development of a space program and a reconnaissance satellite.

The Israeli decision came nine years after Egyptian and Syrian forces attacked on separate fronts while Israeli citizens observed their most holy day. Not quite another six years later, Israel launched its first satellite. That the launch of *Ofeq*-1 occurred just two days before Yom Kippur was almost certainly no coincidence.

EXPERIENCES TO GO: TEACHING WITH INTELLIGENCE CASE STUDIES

Thomas W. Shreeve

(Originally published in JMIC Discussion Paper Number Twelve, Experiences to Go: Teaching with Intelligence Case Studies, September 2004.)

LEARNING BY THE CASE METHOD

The cases and case studies that make up the Intelligence Community Case Method Program are fundamentally accurate descriptions of real historical events or dilemmas. While the names of the people involved and sometimes a few other details have been changed in some of the cases — mostly out of respect for personal privacy or concerns about security — the descriptions are basically true. (At the bottom of the first page of a case, in what is called the "users' note," the case writer outlines where he or she may have departed from the literal truth.) Most of the cases involve an individual or a small group that must try to analyze a problem and propose a workable solution, or "plan of action" as it is called in case method teaching. The case writer has included in summary form the same basic information available to the person or group that had to make the decision.

The Educational Purpose of Cases

In the low-risk environment of a classroom, students get opportunities using this method to practice analyzing tough problems and proposing realistic solutions. Cases help students sharpen their analytic skills when they confront the need to identify the problems facing the characters in the case and their decision-making skills when they propose solutions to resolve the problems they have identified. The process is highly interactive and demanding, since students using this technique are challenged by the instructor and their peers to use evidence from the case — together with their own experience and common sense — to defend their arguments and recommendations. Effects on students include a heightened ability to think and reason rigorously, skills that are highly valued wherever decisions must be made under ambiguous or uncertain conditions. Many students using the case method also find that they have improved their ability to express their analyses and recommendations articulately, and to defend them against constructive criticism.

How to Prepare a Case

Use of the case method requires that students read the case carefully and think critically about the problems it presents, as well as to be prepared to propose solutions. After preparing a case, students meet in class under the guidance of a trained instructor to discuss it and to test their analyses and recommended action plans against those of their peers, who have different backgrounds and experience and may have arrived at quite different conclusions regarding the same material. Before meeting in class, many students also find it helpful to gather in small groups to exchange their views on one or more cases.

Although there is no "best" way to prepare a case, experience with this technique suggests that students should first scan the case quickly, getting a general sense of what it is about before reading it very carefully and noting basic facts and observations. It is also important to consider what information is lacking in the description of the situation or dilemma; as in real life, the characters in a case often must act in the absence of complete information. While cases vary in their levels of difficulty for different students, a general trend is for students to devote about an hour or so to each case, including an analysis of the problem and a proposed plan of action to resolve it. In many cases and case studies, material that illustrates or amplifies the text is included in various exhibits at the end of the document.

The Instructor's Role

The instructor's role in the case method is much different than it is when using conventional techniques. Normally, the case method instructor will not express an opinion about the nature of the problem under consideration, or about what the central characters in the case should or should not do. Instead of telling students what they should think about the problems described, the instructor asks questions that guide the discussion toward the teaching objectives. The instructor's primary responsibility is to use the key case method skills of questioning, listening, and responding to draw the teaching objectives from the students. Thus, the case method instructor does not "teach" in the conventional sense of telling the students what or how to think, but instead is focused on creating the conditions under which the students teach themselves, and each other.

The instructor may at the end of the discussion summarize the teaching objectives for the group, but it is important to understand that this summary is not "the answer" to the problem under discussion. The case method of learning does not provide "the answer" or "the school solution." Instead, several viable analyses and solutions will be developed, questioned, and supported by participants in the discussion. The instructor may tell the class "what happened," but the important point is not "what happened" so much as it is the group's analysis of the problem and the solutions that students propose.

The Bottom Line

Learning by the case method is not easy or passive. Students grasp the teaching objectives with this technique through rigorous analysis and controversy, and internalize those objectives more effectively for having been required to think for themselves. Each member of the class accepts a responsibility for coming to class prepared to discuss the case in detail, and for contributing ideas to the group's examination of the problem and proposed solutions. Case-based discussions are far more engaging than conventional classroom experiences and are often spirited and full of conflict. The reward for these responsibilities can be an exciting and dynamic educational experience that results not only in greater factual knowledge but in an improved ability to make decisions about tough problems.

NOTE ON CASE RESEARCH AND CASE WRITING

Teaching by the case method requires a supply of relevant, well-crafted cases and case studies. These are a unique literary form: part history, part drama, part research paper. In this Note, I will pass on some useful hints I've picked up while researching and writing cases for a major university's business school and throughout the Intelligence Community.

Fitting the Case into a Course

The first requirement for a successful case is to understand how it will fit into a specific course. The instructor and the case writer (these may be the same person and for the purposes of this Note, I will assume they are) must know what teaching points are to be communicated to the students through their exploration of the case. In courses in which several cases will be used, instructors need to examine carefully how the concepts that students will derive from each one will fit together, so that the students can apply what they have learned to new and increasingly difficult material.

Finding the Right Context

Once an instructor/case writer has a clear idea of the teaching points, he or she needs to find a situation that will serve as an appropriate context for the case. Fortunately, the diverse and often intrinsically exciting operations of the Intelligence Community make this part of the task fairly easy. Sources for good leads include colleagues in various parts of the Community, former students, and sometimes components with specific functions. For example, the Office of General Counsel or an IG Staff are logical places to look for cases involving legal or ethical conflict. An Office of Personnel is a place to look for cases dealing with "problem employees."

Sources

Sources fall into two categories: documents and people. In the first category, you may consider as appropriate research material any document that helps you tell the story in a clear and concise manner. This includes published material, of course, such as books, journal or newspaper articles, "after-action" reports, or finished intelligence. (The latter is often very well written, so it is a good source.) Whenever you rely heavily on published material, I think it is appropriate to credit your sources in the "users' note" at the bottom of the first page of your case. Other documentary sources include notes, diaries, cables from the field to headquarters, or anything else that is in a written form. While exploring around for your documentary sources, be on the lookout for graphics, such as maps or photographs, which might be useful as a way to enliven your case for the reader.

Human sources require special handling. Once on the trail of a potential case, the case writer needs to contact the people who were involved in it and persuade them to cooperate. This is not always easy, especially in cases in which people have made mistakes — something we all do but which we don't necessarily want untold numbers of future students to examine in exhaustive detail! The sources — particularly the main characters in the drama — must trust the case writers, or they will not be candid. Earning that trust requires absolute fidelity, in my experience, to a few simple rules:

- Never reveal to anyone else what a source has told you without the source's permission. Moreover, you must be sure that the more substantial sources of your case have an opportunity to review your notes, and to change material that is inaccurate, offensive, or gratuitously embarrassing. This does not mean that the sources get to edit the case, but they should at least have the chance to review it. You will find that a reputation for accuracy and fairness will be extremely valuable to you as a case writer.

- Don't quote one source to another. Frequently, sources in a case will not entirely agree about events and their meaning. This is normal, because we often tend to see things differently, but encouraging conflict among sources by highlighting disagreement diminishes your chances of using your case successfully in a classroom.

- Listen carefully to what is said, and to what is not said. It is OK to challenge sources to provoke them to be more specific or forthcoming, but do it with courtesy and respect. You are not trying to prove anything with your case — you are just telling a story from which people can learn to make better decisions.

Research

With regard to documentary sources, case research is just like any other form of research: You work carefully — and usually slowly — through the material and take notes. As you do so, you will find that you develop an increasingly accurate sense of the story you are trying to tell, and you will be able to expand your outline into greater detail.

For cases that are particularly difficult or which present students with challenging quantitative data, it may be necessary to include a good deal of background material to orient your readers to the dilemma or event under consideration. This is particularly true of case studies, which are typically richer in historical detail than cases. When it is appropriate, you may place quantitative or sometimes other types of material in "exhibits" at the end of your basic document.

With regard to human sources, my advice at the initial meeting with a prospective source is to begin by explaining your purpose clearly. I have found it helpful to spend the first 20 minutes or so in non-substantive conversation, to allow the source to become comfortable talking with you. You might ask, for example, for a source to describe for you what they did before they entered on duty with the Agency, or some other aspect of their lives that has nothing to do with the subject of the case. In general, people like to talk about themselves, and your interest in them will communicate courtesy and respect. Once you have developed some rapport, you may then steer the discussion toward the substantive issues of your research. In those cases that are about successful outcomes, it is usually easy to get people to talk: everybody likes to talk about success. But if your story involves failure or bad judgment, as many of our cases do, be especially alert to the need for sensitive listening. It is helpful, of course, to have in mind the main questions you are going to ask before you begin. Others will come up during the conversation.

I have never used a tape recorder, although I know some case writers who do. In my experience, as soon as the subject of the interview sees the recorder, he or she slips immediately into a form of "legalese." I just take notes, writing as fast as I can, and then hurry back to my computer to transcribe my notes into a readable form. If a source is a major contributor to your story, it may be appropriate to send your transcribed notes of the discussion back to that individual to check for errors or misunderstandings.

Writing and Editing the Case

Good cases require room for disagreement among equally well informed and intelligent readers as to what the main characters should do in the dilemma you have described. Indeed, constructive conflict is the engine that drives this method of teaching, so be sure that your case encourages the discussion process by allowing room for dispute. The reader should have all the basic data that the protagonist had when the need for decision or action arose, but if it is obvious what the protagonist should or should not do, the discussion is not likely to be very interesting.

Write in the past tense, just as if you were telling a story (which you are). I have found also that students can more readily identify with the characters in the case if the characters have personal names and some descriptive data — if they can be accepted as real people. Further, I think that students can identify better with the main decision-maker in the case if they have something in common with that characters, such as age, experience, type of assignment, and so on. This isn't absolutely necessary, and sometimes it doesn't matter at all, but it's something to keep in mind, especially if you are dealing with a readership that is very narrowly focused.

Cases should be clear and concise. This does NOT mean that the dilemma described in the case should be unambiguous (indeed, requiring students to untangle ambiguity is part of the point to the case method), but that the reader should have no difficulty understanding what was ambiguous, and why. It is very difficult to edit one's own material, so if you do not have access to a professional editor, it is helpful to have other people, including colleagues or supervisors review your case before you use it in the classroom. Also, most case writers like to "pilot" a new case with a group of colleagues before roll-out; this is a good way to identify gaps and errors, and to get an idea of the classroom dynamics that the case is likely to create.

Getting the Case Released

Except for cases that are entirely historical, I have always tried to follow a policy of getting cases formally "released" by the sponsoring organization before using them in class. This is especially true of cases that describe sensitive issues in the life of an organization. Usually, though not always, I have tried to do this in writing, with a note or an e-mail from a responsible officer in the sponsoring organization that explicitly allows the use of the case. Sometimes, getting a case released may require that it be moderated or "watered down" in some way. This is unfortunate, but it is better than not using the case at all. Infrequently, the sponsoring organization will get cold feet after the case is completed, and will insist that it be diluted past the point of usefulness. This may test your powers of persuasion, or your patience, or both. I don't have any answer for this problem, but you will find that an investment up front in getting the sponsor on your side — or at least neutral — will pay off at the end if there are controversial issues in your case that cause anxiety in the sponsoring organization.

It is almost always possible to disguise the characters in your drama with pseudonyms, and you can if appropriate even make up fictitious locations or organizational components in order to get a case released for use in class. The sources and the releasing organization must, of course, be comfortable with any disguises you use. In the "users' note," tell the reader what you have done; you may notice that many of our cases have this feature. When characters are so prominent that they cannot possible be disguised (Rick Ames or Robert Hanssen, for example), there is no reason not to use true names. I have generally used pseudonyms, however, even for people who have retired or resigned, simply out of respect for their privacy.

Credibility

I am aware of cases that have been made up — technically known as "scenarios" in case method jargon — and I know that some have been used successfully. However, I don't like hypothetical cases and prefer not to use them. It seems to me that one of the strongest features of the case method is that it is grounded in reality. I believe cases have much greater credibility with students if the students understand that what they are discussing actually happened, and that something very similar could happen to them personally, and soon. I realize that cases can be created which appear as real as those that are really real, but I would be uncomfortable using hypothetical cases unless students were aware of the fiction. Anyway, good cases are so plentiful in the Intelligence Community that finding them is easy.

A Final Word

Cases are not meant to illustrate either the effective or the ineffective handling of administrative, operational, logistic, ethical, or other problems, and the characters in your cases should not be portrayed either as paragons of virtue or as archvillains. The case writer must be careful not to tell students what to think; they are not empty vessels waiting to be filled with your wisdom. With this method of teaching, a major share of the responsibility for thinking critically about the issues under discussion is shifted to the students, where it belongs.

Attached to this Note is a one-page "case writer's template" that includes questions I believe case writers will find helpful as a point of departure when writing an Intelligence Community case or case study. Case writers don't necessarily need to answer all of the questions on the template, but by at least considering each one, case writers will be more likely to get headed in the right direction from the beginning of the case writing process.

A CASE WRITER'S TEMPLATE

Who is the client for this case? What does the client need?

In one sentence, what is the overall purpose of this case?

What are the teaching objectives? (List no more than four, each expressed in not more than one or two sentences.)

What is the subject-matter knowledge level of the students who will use this case? (The answer to this question will influence the amount of background material you include in the case and its level of conceptual difficulty.)

Where does the action in the case occur? Do you have the permission of a senior manager in this component to proceed with your research and writing?

To what written records will you require access? Who has custody of these records?

Who will you need to interview? How will you contact them? Where are they located?

How much time do you estimate will be required to complete the research and writing phases of this case?

What graphics do you anticipate using? (Getting these identified and reproduced early can save time; these tasks can occur in parallel with your research.)

Have you provided those individuals or components who have a substantial stake in the case with an opportunity to review the material you have written that is based on their cooperation or in which they are prominently mentioned? Have you secured their permission for quotes attributed to them?

Who will release the case? Does he or she understand its purpose?

HOW TO WRITE AN EFFECTIVE TEACHING NOTE

A teaching note is the map for the intellectual journey that a case-based discussion represents. A strong teaching note significantly increases the probability that an instructor will arrive successfully and on time at the pedagogical objectives of a case or case study.

This is particularly true when the instructor is using material that he or she did not personally research and write. Effective teaching notes tend to evolve as instructors acquire experience with a case or case study, and instructors should be prepared to revise their teaching notes substantially in the early stages of the normal lifespan of a case.

Effective teaching notes include a brief summary of the story; the teaching objectives; a suggested teaching plan that includes discussion questions that will move the discussion from one block of analysis to the next; and some guidance concerning the timing of these questions. If appropriate, a teaching note may also include a suggested "board plan," which is an outline of what the board should look like in order to lend emphasis and structure to the instructor's summary at the end of the discussion.

A teaching note should begin with a brief summary of the case in one or two paragraphs, highlighting the central issues of the case. A description of the intended classroom context may also be included, with reference to the professional discipline of the audience and the level of experience or skill that may be required before students are able to benefit fully from a detailed discussion of the material. In academic use, teaching notes may also include a reference to the research techniques that the case writer employed, and to the details of coordination, if appropriate.

A teaching plan — the most important part of the teaching note — begins with the identification of the objectives. These should be stated in one or two sentences each, and should be few in number — I suggest no more than four. Instructors should keep these in mind; they are the "destination" of the journey. The objectives are simply those concepts that instructors want students to internalize — the central lessons of the discussion. It is important that the objectives be stated simply, and instructors should not be concerned with getting students to "parrot" the objectives as written in the teaching note. The exact words that students use are much less important than the concepts that the words represent.

The teaching plan should then suggest a lead-off question, designed to get students headed in the right direction. I strongly recommend as a lead-off question one that is fairly easy to answer and requires little analysis. In my experience, it is helpful to establish the norm of student participation early in the discussion, and a difficult questions or one that requires extensive analysis is unlikely to accomplish this goal. A teaching plan should include reference to the range of probable responses that the lead-off question is likely to provoke, so that instructors are well prepared to keep the discussion on track in its early stages.

The teaching plan should clearly identify the "blocks of analysis" that represent the milestones on the journey. These are the main ideas or concepts that students should visit on their progress toward the objectives. AT each milestone, instructors should be prepared with "probing questions," designed to push students to inquire into the issue of the case in greater depth or with increased sophistication as they wrestle with each block. "Bridging questions" are those that are designed to move from one block of analysis to the next as the discussion evolves. I have found it helpful to include a rough sense of timing, so that instructors have a sense of how much time should be spent in discussion of each block of analysis. (This timing should not be regarded as rigid, only as general guidance.)

A useful teaching note may also include a board plan, and experience suggests that the best board plans are very general. (A board plan that is too specific will result in a discussion that is stilted and dull.) To the extent possible, instructors should use the board as a general structure for their summary at the end of the discussion, highlighting the objectives of the discussion as they have emerged from student contributions. Ideally, instructors will refer to individual contributions that moved the discussion in a productive direction to it ultimate intellectual destination. (For example, pointing to a student contribution on the board, an instructor might say, "As John observed at the beginning of our discussion, the incentive system in the Directorate of Operations puts a high premium on recruitments at the expense of counterintelligence concerns.")

If the case or case study is part of an overall plan to reinforce theoretical concepts provided to students through other pedagogical techniques, a teaching note should suggest ways in which instructors can link the discussion to knowledge, skills, or principles that the students have acquired. A strong teaching note reinforces the central idea of case-based teaching: that the instructor's job is to guide the group toward the objectives through the use of questions rather than declarative statements, so that the students discover the objectives through their own efforts and express them in their own words. This is the paramount art of case-based teaching.

EVACUATING THE AMERICANS FROM RWANDA

On Wednesday, 6 April 1994, second-tour Foreign Service Officer Pamela Smith was the State Department Duty Officer for the US Embassy in Kigali, Rwanda. Then 26 years old, Pamela had sought the assignment to Kigali because she hoped that in a small Embassy she would acquire experience at a wider range of Department functions and have greater autonomy than as a member of a larger staff. Pamela and her husband Jack arrived in Rwanda in August 1993.

The Embassy staff in Kigali consisted of seven other officers, including the Ambassador, the Deputy Chief of Mission (DCM), an administrative officer, a General Services Officer (GSO), two communicators, and a secretary. Ambassador David Rawson had been raised in a missionary family in Rwanda and spoke the local language fluently. Pamela was the consular officer and also served as the econ/commercial officer and military security assistance officer. The Embassy community also included 10 personnel from the Agency for International Development (AID) and a public affairs specialist from the U.S. Information Service (USIS). There was no Marine Security Guard detachment. The Regional Security Officer (RSO) was based in Bujumbura, Burundi, and visited the post in Kigali periodically. The defense attaché — U.S. Army Lt. Col. Mike Kalinowski — visited Kigali three times annually from his post in Yaounde, Cameroon. After his arrival in Kigali, Jack Smith was hired on a local contract as the assistant GSO.

At this time there were 258 Americans in Rwanda, most of them members of missionary groups. There were also some personnel from nongovernmental organizations that did not have a religious affiliation, and a few representatives of private firms. Some 60 American children attended the Kigali International School. In April 1994, the admin officer was on leave, and the AID director had recently departed the post. Colonel Kalinowski had just arrived for a one-week visit.

Pamela and the other Americans had grown accustomed to the occasional gunfire that marked the longstanding conflict between Rwanda's two major ethnic groups, the Hutus and the Tutsis. In October 1993, UN forces under the command of a Canadian general officer had arrived to enforce a fragile peace agreement, according to which the Tutsi-dominated Rwandan Patriotic Front (RPF) was allowed to position a 600-man battalion on the grounds of the Rwandan Parliament building. Uprisings had continued in February 1994, with some 200 killed in ethnic violence, prompting Ambassador Rawson's order to revise and expand the Embassy's emergency action plan (EAP). As the junior member of the Emergency Action Committee, which was headed by DCM Joyce Leader, Pamela was deeply involved in the details of this planning.

As part of her planning, Pamela made a point of personally meeting every one of the Americans residing in Rwanda, even those in the outlying areas. She set up a schedule of regular meetings with all of them, 15 or 20 at a time. She collected information about each individual and kept it in two identical files, one at the Embassy and one in her home. In addition to the name of each person, the files included date and place of birth, passport number and issue date, next-of-kin in the United States, telephone number or radio call-sign, and a list of dependents, if any. In cases of those located outside Kigali, the file also included a photograph of each individual.

On that Wednesday evening, Pamela and Jack Smith were joined in their home by Colonel Kalinowski. Other Americans also were present. At around 2100 hours, Pamela and the others heard a muffled explosion from the direction of the airport, some 12 kilometers away. Jack Smith, who was a former U.S. Marine, looked at Colonel Kalinowski. "Colonel," Jack said, "that didn't sound like a grenade. It was something much bigger."

Colonel Kalinowski nodded his agreement. "Let's see what we can find out," he said. Pamela began to call a number of contacts she had developed in the Rwandan military and among UN forces.

The Americans did not yet know it, but the sound they heard was made by the fiery crash of a French-built aircraft carrying Presidents Juvenal Habyarimana of Rwanda and Cyprien Ntaryamira of neighboring Burundi and eight others returning from Dar es Salaam, Tanzania, where they and other African leaders had met in an attempt to end the ethnic warfare that plagued Rwanda and Burundi. All aboard the aircraft were killed. In a variety of statements soon issued in Kigali and at UN headquarters in New York, Rwandan Government officials claimed the aircraft had been brought down by gunfire or a missile of some kind on its approach to the airport.

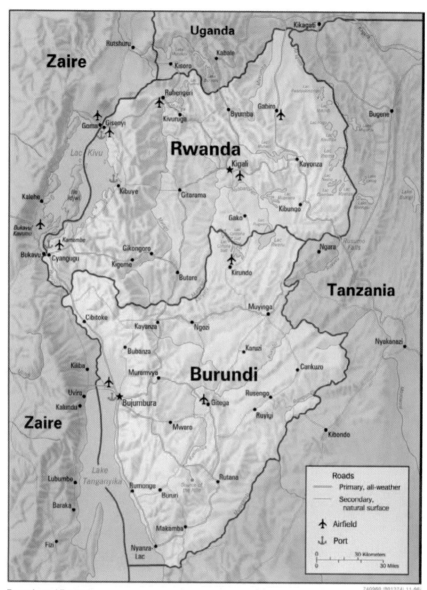

Rwanda and Burundi.

The crash of the Presidents' aircraft triggered a nightmare of ethnic violence that resulted in the deaths of hundreds of thousands of Rwandans, most of them Tutsis and moderate Hutus. Over the next several days, Pamela's duty would be to coordinate the evacuation of the American citizens — most of them members of missionary groups or commercial contractors — residing in Rwanda who now faced grave danger. The Emergency Action Committee's planning would now be tested.

A Tradition of Tribal Violence

Conflict between Rwanda's two major ethnic groups, which spoke the same language and shared similar religions, had a long history, dating back to the 15th Century when the nomadic Tutsi moved south from Ethiopia to dominate the agricultural Hutu, a Bantu people. The area that eventually became the nations of Rwanda and Burundi was populated by about 85 percent Hutus and about 14 percent Tutsis. European colonial powers — at first Germany and later Belgium — allied themselves mainly with the dominant Tutsi. Shortly before granting independence to their former colony in Rwanda in 1962, the Belgians turned political, economic, and military power over mainly to the Tutsis. The majority Hutus objected violently and lashed out in a 1959 uprising in which many thousands of Tutsis were killed and another 200,000 fled into neighboring Burundi and Uganda. The two groups had fought each other savagely since then in a cycle of bloody reprisals.

In October 1990, a group of about 2,000 Rwandan exiles belonging to the RPF invaded northeastern Rwanda from their bases in Uganda, threatening President Habyarimana's regime and raising the specter of renewed ethnic violence. This group — mainly but not exclusively Tutsi — soon was joined by other Tutsis and disaffected Hutus, bringing the exiles' strength to around 20,000. An RPF-led rebellion dragged on for the next several years. After nearly a year of negotiations, the Hutu-dominated Rwandan Government and the Tutsi-dominated RPF reached a fragile agreement in August 1993, with both sides agreeing to the deployment of UN troops to help ensure peace.

Efforts to form a transitional government acceptable to both groups quickly stalled in an atmosphere of mutual distrust. The two slain presidents had agreed to meet in Dar es Salaam to continue the talks, hoping to avert full-scale civil war in Rwanda. These hopes were dashed by the attack on the returning aircraft as extremists on both sides sought revenge or political advantage. Within a few hours of the crash, members of Habyarimana's Presidential Guard — joined by bands of Hutu extremists known as the Interhamwae ("those who stand together" in the local language) — a ragtag militia armed mainly with clubs and machetes and with a well-earned reputation for viciousness — went on a rampage, killing dozens and perhaps hundreds of their opponents, chiefly Tutsis and moderate Hutus.

The Warden System

Within about an hour of the attack on the presidents' aircraft, US Ambassador Rawson telephoned DCM Joyce Leader to relay the news of the fatal crash. Leader heard similar reports soon after on a Rwandan radio station. Together, Rawson and Leader composed a message to relay to the US community through the so-called "warden system," a network of 15 selected members of the American community, known as wardens, who volunteered to maintain communications between the Embassy and other US citizens during a crisis. The wardens also served as observers, reporting critical information back to the Embassy. Each warden had a specific list of individuals for whom he or she was responsible. As news was passed to the warden, he or she would send it on by telephone, by radio, or in

A Rwandan Army Armored Personnel Carrier (APC) was permanently posted outside the US Embassy during the first few days of fighting between Rwandan factions.

person. If an evacuation were to become necessary, the Ambassador planned to use this system to convey the Embassy's instructions and assemble personnel.

The DCM immediately contacted Pamela Smith, who relayed the Ambassador's message by radio and telephone, telling the members of the American community to hold fast and wait for further word at 0700 the next morning.

Colonel Kalinowski returned to his nearby hotel. Throughout the night, Pamela and Jack could hear the sound of mortars and both light and heavy machinegun fire. A number of wardens called in, reporting that the road to the airport, which ran past the Parliament building where the RPF battalion was headquartered, was under heavy fire.

Thursday, 7 April

In his 0700 hours radio message, Ambassador Rawson confirmed the Presidents' deaths and instructed all the Americans to remain inside their homes. Pamela and Jack spent most of Thursday on the telephone, reassuring the Americans — many of them now on the edge of panic — who called in. At around 1045 hours, while on the phone with the DCM, Pamela could hear Rwandan soldiers break into her residence and loudly accuse her of hiding Rwanda's interim Prime Minister Agathe Uwilingiyimana, who lived next to Leader and had developed a friendship with her. (Leader had a personal friend staying with her at this time as a houseguest. The friend was an African-American woman whom the soldiers mistook for the interim Prime Minister. Using their passports, credit cards, and other documents, the two American women eventually were able to convince the soldiers that the houseguest was not the person for whom they were searching.) Unable to escape into the DCM's compound, Uwilingiyimana sought refuge in the nearby UN Development Program complex, but was quickly discovered there by Rwandan soldiers and shot to death. Other members of the Rwandan Cabinet and their families also were killed. Also on Thursday morning, a group of 10 Belgian soldiers — members of the UN peacekeeping force — were disarmed and brutally murdered by the rampaging gangs as the city gave way to anarchy.

From her home, Pamela began to call contacts she had developed among Rwandan officials and members of other embassies. Earlier, whenever she had reason to deal with Rwandans on either side of the ethnic conflict, Pamela had made a point of assuring them of her neutrality in the fight between the Tutsi-dominated RPF and the Hutu-dominated Rwandan Government. Now that neutrality began to pay off, as Rwandan military officials stated that the mainly Hutu Rwandan Army would not fire on Americans. They could not, they added, speak for the RPF.

Pamela relayed news of her contacts to the Ambassador, but on Thursday night, the telephone lines to the Ambassador's neighborhood were cut. Further, the Ambassador lived in an area that was directly between the centers of the two warring factions, and there was heavy fighting around his home, with a few artillery and mortar rounds landing inside the walls of his villa. It was clear that Rawson was not going to be able to get to the Embassy any time soon. The high-frequency radio he kept at his residence enabled the Ambassador to stay in contact with Nairobi, however, and through that route he could communicate with senior State Department officials in Washington.

Friday, 8 April

Hoping soon to be able to move to the Embassy where they could better carry out the evacuation, Jack had packed camping gear and personal firearms for himself and Pamela. (As a former Marine Security Guard, Jack was skilled in the use of firearms and had encouraged Pamela to practice shooting. They owned two 9 mm pistols, a 12-gauge shotgun, and a hunting rifle.) On Friday morning, Colonel Kalinowski called from his hotel.

Several Embassy homes were ransacked by Rwandan looters.

"I'll be there in five minutes," he said. "Be ready to get in your car immediately and we'll get to the Embassy."

Right on schedule, Kalinowski showed up with a Rwandan Army escort accompanied by Peace Corps volunteer Andrew O'Dwyer, who happened to be staying in the same hotel. Pamela, Jack, O'Dwyer, and Kalinowski entered the Embassy without incident around 1100 hours on Friday.

Using their contacts among Rwandan Government officials and in the RPF, Colonel Kalinowski and Pamela began negotiating the details of an evacuation of the trapped Americans, should the Ambassador decide on that course of action. In their negotiations, they relied on occasion on a battalion of Rwandan gendarmes led by an able commander who had evidently decided not to allow his unit to get caught up in the tribal violence. The gendarmes assisted the Americans by providing escorts for movement around the city.

The emergency evacuation plan called for a departure either from the airport or overland by road to Burundi. Pamela telephoned the US Embassy in Burundi and spoke to the RSO there. He volunteered to drive north toward the border to check on conditions outside Kigali. Meanwhile, Pamela established an open line with the State Department and Colonel Kalinowski did the same with US military officials at the US European Command (USEUCOM) in Stuttgart, Germany. They also discussed evacuation plans with members of other Western embassies. Jack destroyed the cryptographic equipment and assembled the radios that the Americans would need. Andrew O'Dwyer, who had no security clearance of any kind, went to work destroying classified files. Anticipating the possibility of an overland escape, Jack and Andrew also filled the Embassy vehicles with gasoline as best they could.

Both Colonel Kalinowski and Pamela were able to leave the Embassy and meet with Rwandan Government officials on Friday, seeking assurances that U.S. citizens would not be fired on. At one point they met also with Canadian General Dallaire, the senior UN officer in Kigali, who offered his assistance in the evacuation. Pamela reported these developments to the Ambassador by radio.

In their discussions with Colonel Kalinowski, USEUCOM officials offered to send a reinforced company of U.S. Marines to help get the Americans out of Kigali by way of the airport, assuming that it remained open. The Marines also could provide helicopter gunship cover for an overland route, EUCOM officials added, though they cautioned that it would take time to plan and implement either of these options. A third option was to leave overland without a US military escort. The four Americans reviewed the options for the Ambassador in a Friday afternoon radio call.

Interim Study questions:

1. What is your assessment of the ways in which Pamela Smith has prepared for the possibility of an emergency evacuation? What insights does this provide into her character?

2. What is your assessment of the various options you see as available under the circumstances that prevailed in this case? Which option should the Ambassador select? Be prepared to defend your choice.

"Sir," Colonel Kalinowski told Ambassador Rawson, "I think trying to get to the airport is a bad idea. Even though it's a short distance, we'd have to pass through some of the worst fighting and there is no way to guarantee that our convoys will not be fired on." Kalinowski pointed out also that the Marines were not familiar with Kigali; it was very unlikely that any spoke the local dialect and few if any were likely to be fluent in French. If either of the warring factions mistook their attempts to evacuate the Americans for assistance to one side or the other, the situation might become worse. Further, if either faction fired on a US helicopter, the Marines would almost certainly return fire, with deadly results for the Rwandans who had provoked the violence. So far at least, Kalinowski observed, the Americans had not been targeted, except for the looting of unoccupied homes and apartments; it would have been easy for the Interhamwe or other groups to have done so. This suggested, Kalinowski believed, either that the rampaging gangs did not want to target Americans, or were afraid of retaliation, or both. Finally, the Bujumbura RSO's reconnaissance revealed no signs of unrest between the Burundi border and the southern outskirts of Kigali.

"We'll go overland," the Ambassador replied. "Thank EUCOM for their offer, but tell them we don't need the Marines to come into Kigali. We'll link up with them in Bujumbura."

The overland option in the evacuation plan called for the Americans in and around Kigali to gather at previously designated assembly points — depending on where they lived — and leave in three convoys, heading west out of Kigali and turning south to Burundi. Those located outside the Kigali area would take overland routes to Burundi, Zaire, or Tanzania.

The Ambassador reached his decision around 1500 hours on Friday, too late for an assembly and departure that day. He told Colonel Kalinowski and Pamela to implement the evacuation plan beginning on Saturday morning. By this point, Americans were calling into the Embassy from locations all over the city, seeking help and advice. Pamela passed the word through the warden system. She learned that one of the women in a missionary group was now in labor and began searching for a qualified physician to help.

Saturday, 9 April

On Saturday morning, Americans from different parts of the city began to assemble at their assigned areas. Lew Giordano, a State Department communicator who had been able to join the others at the Embassy, drove an Embassy van into parts of the city marked by heavy fighting to help bring Americans to safety. At times, Rwandan gendarmes were available to escort Giordano; at other times, he went alone. General Dallaire used his contacts to get RPF assurance that U.S. convoys would not be attacked.

Pamela and Colonel Kalinowski passed the word for the Americans to place a US flag or a white flag on their vehicles as a sign of neutrality. They wanted to avoid having the three convoys bunch up at the roadblocks, which now dotted all of the routes out of Kigali, so they timed the departure of each one to phase the evacuation. The first convoy left its assembly point at 1230 hours on Saturday. Citizens from several other Western nations, including Canada, Germany, and Switzerland, joined the Americans and swelled the size of the convoys. Once out of Kigali, the Americans saw no sign of the carnage that marked the fighting inside the city. As they crossed the border with Burundi, US officials were able to check off their names using Pamela's list of U.S. personnel.

Hoping to avoid hostile fire, Embassy personnel attached white flags to the vehicles in their evacuation convoy as a sign of their neutrality. The convoy was not fired on.

The last convoy, led by Ambassador Rawson and the DCM, left Kigali around 1300 hours on Saturday. This convoy consisted of 108 vehicles carrying more than 600 people, only nine of them Americans. All 258 Americans residing in Rwanda either left on one of the convoys or were accounted for, a few choosing to remain behind and leave with the Belgian and French evacuations later.

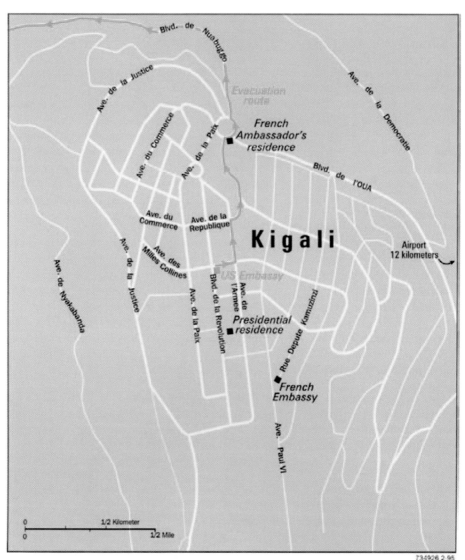

Site of US Embassy, Kigali. The Embassy compound consists of a two-story concrete Chancery building and a USIA cultural center adjoining it.

TEACHING NOTE FOR USE WITH THIS CASE

A Summary of the Case

"Evacuating the Americans from Rwanda" describes efforts by U.S. Embassy staff officers to respond to the dramatic collapse of civil order in Kigali, Rwanda in April 1994. The small U.S. Embassy faced the task of evacuating or otherwise accounting for some 258 U.S. citizens at a time when extremist Hutu gunmen and soldiers were indulging in a murderous slaughter of Tutsis and moderate Hutus. The main protagonist in the case — a young female foreign service officer given the name "Pamela Smith"— is introduced in the first paragraph, followed by a brief description of the Embassy staff that included a Defense Attaché (a U.S. Army lieutenant colonel, here named "Mike Kalinowski"). These two officers-supported by several others-later proved instrumental in carrying out the evacuation.

The opening paragraphs describe how Smith carried out her assignment to revise and expand the Embassy's emergency action plan and sets up the early stages of the civil collapse that followed the apparent destruction of an aircraft carrying the presidents of Rwanda and Burundi, along with other African political leaders, returning from a conference held to find a solution to the tribal violence plaguing Rwandan society. This is followed by a brief historical overview of the conflict between the Hutus and the Tutsis. The early paragraphs also include a description of the Embassy's "warden system," designed to maintain communications between the Embassy and the widespread community of Americans, most them missionaries, throughout the country.

The rest of the case is a day-by-day description of the evolving crisis and of how Smith, Kalinowski, and others responded to the extreme danger posed for the U.S. community, resulting within a few days in a successful evacuation without any U.S. losses. Photographs taken by Smith are sprinkled through the case, lending a sense of drama.

The research for "Rwanda" consisted almost entirely of interviews of State Department personnel who were directly involved in the actual situation. Several of these individuals are referred to by pseudonyms; others, such as Ambassador Rawson, are described in true name. Finished intelligence from the CIA's Directorate of Intelligence provided the background for the historical parts of the case study. The case was coordinated within the Foreign Service Institute (FSI) and with Ambassador Rawson, who offered several useful suggestions.

Intended Context

Rwanda was written for a State Department FSI course "The Security Overseas Seminar," and is intended to support a 60-minute discussion. The purpose of this case is to capture the value of the Rwandan experience, describing the preparations that Smith and others took before the crisis exploded, and how they responded once the rampaging mobs took control of Kigali. Instructors using this case at FSI have experienced no difficulty focusing students' attention on these issues, particularly in view of the unusually dramatic nature of the events described. In addition to the "nuts-and-bolts" details of Smith's preparations, the case may also be used to draw students' attention to broader issues, including the leadership characteristics that Smith demonstrated during the crisis, including foresight, personal courage, and acceptance of responsibility for the safety of those in her care.

Teaching Objectives

Students who discuss this case study should be able to:

- Describe in detail specific steps that State Department personnel should take in anticipation of the possibility that an emergency evacuation may be required. This description should include noting the importance of planning, coordination, and system testing; an awareness of where all of the prospective evacuees are located and how to contact them; how to coordinate with prospective sources of assistance, such as U.S. military forces; and how to keep State Department headquarters personnel informed.

- Describe in detail how to respond effectively to the outbreak of civil violence once it begins. An effective response to crisis would include the establishment of a communications center; keeping an accurate record of events as they occur; liaison with local or other authority; the destruction of classified material; and others as determined by the instructor.

- Identify those elements of leadership that comprise an effective response to a physically dangerous crisis.

This case is based on open sources and on interviews with State Department officers who were directly involved in the events described. The case was written in February 1995 by Thomas W. Shreeve with assistance from Foreign Service Institute instructor DanaDee Carragher. "Pamela Smith," "Jack Smith," "Mike Kalinowski," "Andrew O'Dwyer," and "Lew Giordano" are pseudonyms. The photographs were taken by Pamela Smith. For further information, please call Thomas W. Shreeve & Associates, LLC at 703-848-9003. He is also available at tomshreeve@aol.com.

THE CREATION OF THE NATIONAL IMAGERY AND MAPPING AGENCY: CONGRESS'S ROLE AS OVERSEER

Anne Daugherty Miles

(Originally published as part of JMIC Occasional Paper Number Nine, April 2002.)

PREFACE

In October 2000, the National Imagery and Mapping Agency (NIMA) celebrated its fourth anniversary. That occasion marked a significant milestone for the newest member of the Intelligence Community. In the previous four years the leaders and people of NIMA had established an identity and culture for the agency and had defined and refined its vision and strategy. That is not to say that there are no more challenges for this organization. Like all government agencies, NIMA faces issues of downsizing and outsourcing, modernization, transformation and integration. However, in view of the agency's customer-sensitive plans for meeting these challenges, at the Agency's fourth annual customer conference General Henry H. Shelton, Chairman, Joint Chiefs of Staff, remarked, "NIMA has established itself as a key component in arming decisionmakers and operators with superior information and knowledge... NIMA's customer focus is the big reason that you've been such a success story in the four short years of your existence as a separate agency."

During the spring and summer of 1995, I served as executive secretary of what was then known as the NIA (National Imagery Agency) Steering Group, as well as coordinator of various NIA Working Groups. I was in a unique position to observe the processes and politics that led to the decision to establish NIMA. Thereafter, I led the Integration Team during the implementation period from December 1995 until NIMA stand-up in October 1996. NIMA was formed from eight different agencies from throughout the Department of Defense and the Intelligence Community. At the outset, NIMA leadership decided that above all else, the quality and timeliness of service to customers would not fail during transition. This meant "protecting" imagery intelligence and mapping production processes from the bureaucratic blizzard of new policies and procedures that come with establishing a new organization (literally hundreds of policies had to be reviewed and either disestablished or modified, and the streamlining process still goes on today). But perhaps the most daunting task was to begin the process of creating a NIMA culture and identity.

In December 2000, the congressionally-mandated independent NIMA Commission found that "NIMA is an essential component of U.S. national security and a key to information dominance." This agency has come a long way in a short time. But in December 1995, the future of this agency was dependent on the approval of the U.S. Congress. *The Creation of NIMA: Congress's Role as Overseer* provides an accurate and detailed look at the "behind the scenes" roles played by NIMA leaders, other members of the executive branch, and most interestingly, the role of the U.S. Congress and its various oversight committees. This paper provides government leaders and students of government with a primer on "how things get done" so that they may have a greater appreciation for the complex relationships within and between the executive and legislative branches.

David A. Broadhurst
Director, National Imagery and Mapping College

FOREWORD

Although several articles have been written on the creation of the National Imagery and Mapping Agency (NIMA) from the executive branch's perspective, none have chronicled the attendant debate on Capitol Hill. "Creating the National Imagery and Mapping Agency: A Studies Roundtable," is the most comprehensive of those articles, being based on a discussion in November 1997 between the editorial board of *Studies in Intelligence* and key participants of the NIMA implementation team.[360] That article provided a starting point for the present case study of congressional decisionmaking in the intelligence arena, which focuses on the struggle in Congress, rather than in the executive branch. The present monograph may be characterized as a case study of congress's role as over-seer of the U.S. Intelligence Community. A case study can follow an intelligence issue in Congress on a day-to-day basis, offering a perspective that goes beyond textbook descriptions of procedure to illustrate the human dynamics of the decisionmaking process. Thus, a case study offers the advantage of depth and detail, but only one case does not provide a basis for generalization. Works that do offer a more theoretical overview based on many cases provide a context within which to judge whether elements of a particular case are usual or unusual. Thus, it is has become the norm in academic treatments to pair the general with the specific. Eric Redman's, *The Dance of Legislation*, is a classic example. [361] Redman's story focuses on the creation of the National Health Service Corps in the early 1970s and has been used to augment textbooks about Congress in countless classrooms across the country since its publication in 1973. Similarly, Birnbaum and Murray's more recent *Showdown at Gucci Gulch* details the passage of the Tax Reform Act of 1986 and has also become a common textbook supplement in courses on the Congress.[362] Unfortunately, in-depth case studies of congressional decisionmaking on intelligence issues are too few to have resulted in a comprehensive textbook offering a theoretical context for this decisionmaking.

The case study presented here illustrates the combination of personality and process that resulted in the establishment of NIMA in 1996. It has been written specifically for those who are studying Congress and the U.S. Intelligence Community. It

---

[360] "Creating the National Imagery and Mapping Agency: A Studies Roundtable," in *Studies in Intelligence* 42, 1 (1998): 39-49.

[361] Eric Redman, *Dance of Legislation* (NY: Simon and Schuster, 1973).

[362] Jeffrey H. Birnbaum and Alan S. Murray, *Showdown at Gucci Gulch* (NY: Vintage Books, 1987).

highlights the role of the House and Senate Intelligence Committees and how those committees interact with other committees-most specifically the Armed Services Committees. It augments the few good sources that exist on this very narrow subject-the most important being Frank Smist's *Congress Oversees the U.S. Intelligence Community*,[363] Loch Johnson's *A Season of Inquiry*[364] and Britt Snider's *Sharing Secrets with Lawmakers*.[365] This case should be read with that context in mind, and any generalizations based on this one case should be made with extreme care.

Although oversight is often associated with confrontational investigation into suspected wrongdoing, the reality is that most oversight is routine and occurs within the normal authorization and appropriation process.[366] Legislative oversight is designed to ensure that Congress has the information it needs to develop legislation, monitor the implementation of public policy and disclose to the public how its government is performing. Oversight objectives vary. "The focus may be on promoting administrative efficiency and economy in government, protecting and supporting favored policies and programs, airing an administration's failures or wrongdoing, or its achievements, publicizing a particular member's or committee's goals, reasserting congressional authority vis-à-vis the executive branch, or assuaging the interests of pressure groups."[367] Oversight continues after a law is passed. According to Senator Phil Gramm (R-TX) "Congress's duty didn't end in passing this law. We have to make sure the law works."[368] In the NIMA case, Congress adopted its role as overseer in first determining whether the concept of NIMA was a good one, and it has continued to exercise its oversight responsibilities in the years since its establishment to ensure that the agency evolved in the way envisioned by its creators.

Beyond the personality and politics evident in this case, it is important to recognize the fact that congressional members and staffers take their oversight responsibilities very seriously. The creation of NIMA was an executive branch proposal that was scrutinized from every angle on the Hill. The concerns of a myriad of interested parties — to include federal workers, NIMA customers, NIMA components, constituents, the White House Chief of Staff — were all funneled into 13 different congressional committees — to be resolved primarily by the Intelligence and Armed Services committees. The beauty of Congress is its ability to weigh the merits of a host of special interests in a way that satisfies a majority of its members and hopefully results in good public policy. In its role as overseer it must be skeptical, demanding justification for each and every proposal. To continue its role as

---

[363] Frank Smist, *Congress Oversees the U.S. Intelligence Community*: 1947-1994, Second Edition (Knoxville: University of Tennessee, 1994).

[364] Loch Johnson, *A Season of Inquiry: The Senate Intelligence Investigation* (Lexington: University of Kentucky Press, 1985).

[365] L. Britt Snider, *Sharing Secrets with Lawmakers* (Washington D.C.: Center for the Study of Intelligence, 1997).

[366] See Walter Oleszek, *Congressional Procedures and the Policy Process* (Washington D.C.: CQ Press, 1989), 266-272 for a comprehensive list of oversight techniques.

[367] Oleszek, 266.

[368] Roger Davidson and W. Oleszek, *Congress and Its Members* (Washington D.C.: CQ Press, 2000), 324.

overseer, to stay a part of the process, "to have a seat at the table," congressional committees must have jurisdiction over an executive branch agency or program. As may be seen in this case, jurisdictional concerns were paramount largely because Members sincerely wanted to play a part in guiding NIMA's evolution over time.

THE CREATION OF NIMA:
CONGRESS'S ROLE AS OVERSEER

Mr. Chairman and Members of the Committee... we can no longer afford redundant capabilities in several different agencies... I will move immediately to consolidate the management of all imagery collection, analysis, and distribution. In my judgment both effectiveness and economy can be improved by managing imagery in a manner similar to the National Security Agency's organization for signals intelligence.[369]

—*Director of Central Intelligence (DCI) Candidate John Deutch*

WHY NIMA?

The consolidation of imagery promised by John Deutch during his testimony to the SSCI, in his confirmation hearings for the position of Director of Central Intelligence, was a direct reference to the concept of a National Imagery and Mapping Agency. Deutch agreed with those who wanted to assemble all or part of as many as eight agencies or programs into a single, focused imagery agency. The pieces to be assembled would include:

Defense Mapping Agency (DMA),
Central Intelligence Agency's National Photographic Interpretation
    Center (NPIC),
Central Imagery Office (CIO),
National Reconnaissance Office (NRO) Imagery Processing, .
Defense Airborne Reconnaissance Office (DARO),
Defense Intelligence Agency's Photographic Interpretation
    Section (DIA/PGX),
Defense Dissemination Program Office (DDPO) and
Central Intelligence Agency's imagery-related elements/programs.

According to Leo Hazlewood, then CIA Deputy Director for Science and Technology, Deutch's announcement "came as a complete surprise to the bureaucracy at Langley" (CIA headquarters).[370] Senior leadership there thought the NIMA idea had died in the early 1990s, due to Chairman, Joint Chiefs of Staff (CJCS) General Colin Powell's opposition. Deutch brought the idea back to life in April 1995.

---

[369] U.S. Congress, Senate, Select Committee on Intelligence, Confirmation Hearings of John Deutch, 94th Congress, 1st sess., 26 April 1995, 1, 8 and 9.

[370] Leo Hazlewood, Deputy Director, NIMA Implementation Team, interview by the author, 6 October 2000

The idea for such an agency seems to have been first put into writing as a conclusion in the Burnett Panel Report.[371] The panel, established in 1992 by DCI Gates, was charged with examining the structure guiding the Intelligence Community's imagery assets and one of its recommendations was to integrate imagery and mapping.[372] Reorganization of the entire defense establishment was a popular idea in the early 1990s, following the fall of the Berlin Wall in 1989.[373] At about the same time, reorganization of the Intelligence Community was popular in the aftermath of DESERT STORM. Leo Hazlewood attributes the attractiveness of a NIMA concept to three particular problems encountered during that operation: jurisdictional disputes over the dissemination of imagery, competing tasking authorities, and confusion over who owned NPIC (CIA or DIA).[374] The Burnett Panel sought solutions to these problems and many others. Its recommendation for an agency like NIMA was based on a conceptual seed planted by Keith Hall, the person Leo Hazlewood calls the "intellectual father" of the NIMA concept. As Deputy Assistant Secretary of Defense for Intelligence and Security at the time the Panel was deliberating, Hall sold his idea to several panel members. In fact, the FY 1992 Intelligence Authorization Bill recommended establishing a National Imagery Agency (NIA) in line with the Burnett Panel recommendation. The timing was not right, however, in either the executive or legislative branches, for reasons discussed later in this article. It would take another four years and the notoriety of problems associated with the Central Imagery Office (CIO) to "make NIMA happen."

NIMA was created near the end of the l04th Congress-a Congress in which there were numerous proposals to reorganize the U.S. Intelligence Community (IC). An intensive review undertaken by the House Permanent Select Committee on Intelligence. (HPSCI) culminated in a lengthy document titled *IC21: Intelligence Community in the 21st Century* and legislation called the *Intelligence Community Act* (H.R. 3237), reported to the floor of the House on 13 June 1996. Also in 1996, the Senate Select Committee on Intelligence (SSCI) was engaged in its own hearings, building upon an extensive set of interviews carried out in the early 1990s. The Commission on the Roles and Capabilities of the U.S. Intelligence Community, known as the Aspin-Brown Commission, was also winding up a year-long investigation along these same lines. The Aspin-Brown Commission presented its report to the SSCI in formal testimony on 6 March 1996;[375] the SSCI Chairman

---

[371] The Burnett Panel was made up of active or retired senior military officers according to Greg Jay, Contractor with Booz, Allen and Hamilton, in "Creating the National Imagery and Mapping Agency: A Studies Roundtable," in *Studies in Intelligence* 42, no. 1 (1998): 42. According to Hazlewood, DCI Gates handpicked its members. It was one of 15-17 task forces created by Gates when he first became DCI. Hazlewood interview.

[372] According to Leo Hazlewood in "Creating the National Imagery and Mapping Agency: A Studies Roundtable," in *Studies in Intelligence* 42, no. 1 (1998): 42. Article cited hereafter as "Creation of NIMA."

[373] The "peace dividend" was widely viewed as an opportunity to cut defense spending and increase spending on domestic issues such as education. Thus, a variety of terms such as *downsizing, restructuring, streamlining, consolidation of assets*, and so on, came to be associated with budget cutting. These ideas fit nicely with Vice President Gore's *Reinventing Government* initiatives. Many reorganization studies, undertaken in the name of greater efficiency, also had budget cutting goals as a high priority.

[374] Hazlewood interview.

[375] Harold Brown, Warren Rudman, and Les Aspin, *Preparing for the 21st Century: An Appraisal of U.S. Intelligence* (Washington, DC: GPO, 6 March 1996). The report is widely known as "Aspin-Brown."

and Vice Chairman, Senators Specter and Kerrey, introduced the report to the Senate as S. 1593 on the same day.

In all of these reviews, one theme predominated: "the extent to which the Nation's various intelligence agencies should be managed more *corporately*. DCIs have had coordinative mechanisms... but they have not created a corporate body with more tightly controlled budget execution, missions, procedures, products and methods of dissemination."[376] The reports recommended, to varying degrees, expanded authority for the DCI to allocate, allot, obligate or spend IC funds to better manage his domain. These expanded authorities came at the expense of the Secretary of Defense's authorities — creating immediate opposition by the Armed Services committees. There was a feeling that intelligence agencies had evolved in different ways without any plan — creating redundancies and such organizational chaos that no DCI could manage it well. Part of the need for an increased corporate structure was to increase efficiency, and in the process, also increase the *quality and timeliness* of customer support. Thus, the NIMA was part of a larger plan to group similar kinds of intelligence activities together in an effort to improve management of the IC, eliminate redundancies, improve efficiency, and improve customer support. Disagreement within the Congress centered on whether a NIMA would, in fact, accomplish those goals. In order to understand the larger context in which NIMA was created, we begin with the activities of the intelligence committees in the early 1990s.

EARLY 1990s — POWELL OBJECTS

The early 1990s found the intelligence committees concerned with how best to reorganize the community — but not equally so. The two committees have much in common, yet act autonomously much of the time. The priorities and attributes of these committees change over time and have much to do with the leadership provided by the Chairman and Staff Director. Senator Boren (D-OK) was nearing the end of his tenure as Chairman of the SSCI and clearly saw this reorganization effort as his legacy to the committee and the IC. Senator Boren was also a good friend of DCI Bob Gates and the two undoubtedly worked closely throughout this period.[377] A staffer remembers that the SSCI interviewed approximately 185 people, all "off the record," and for "nonattribution." [378]

The House Permanent Select Committee on Intelligence (HPSCI) was also concerned with reorganization of the Community but not to the same extent as the SSCI. Chaired by Representative David McCurdy, the HPSCI tackled reorganization once it discovered how

---

[376] Richard A. Best, Jr., "Intelligence Reorganization in the 104th Congress: Prospects for A More Corporate Community," *CRS Report for Congress* 96-681F (Washington DC: Congressional Research Service, 13 Sep 96), 1.

[377] According to Gates, "Apart from the President, my most important ally and friend was Senator David Boren... Boren and I had developed a strong mutual trust and friendship (along with Vice Chairman, Senator Bill Cohen) in the aftermath of Iran-Contra when, as Acting Director, I worked with him to build a new relationship between the CIA and Congress. He had confidence that I was a true believer in congressional oversight and that I played straight and honest." Robert Gates, *From the Shadows* (NY: Simon and Schuster, 1996), 545.

[378] A source, SSCI Professional Staffer in 1996, who wishes to remain anonymous, interview by the author, 14 July 2000.

deeply the SSCI was immersed in it. Despite the fact that the two intelligence committee chairmen were both from Oklahoma, they did not get along and did not work in concert with one another. The extensive recommendations proposed by the SSCI (Senate Resolution 2198) caught the HPSCI off guard, but the HPSCI struggled to regain lost ground and emerged with recommendations of its own. In a show of unity that belied the true relationship between the two committees, the package of reorganization details was offered jointly by Boren and McCurdy — the bulk of which made it into the FY 1992 Authorization Bill.[379] The legislation recommended establishing a National Image Agency (NIA)[380] in line with the Burnett Panel recommendation.

Some of the recommendations in the intelligence authorization bill were not well received by either the executive branch or the Armed Services committees. The details were considered "too far reaching."[381] DCI Gates, in a statement to the Congress on change in the Intelligence Community, warned of "deep reservations" held by CIA, DMA and the Military Services about a proposed NIA that would include NPIC and DMA and Military Imagery. He said that he, Secretary of Defense (SecDef) Cheney and CJCS Powell had agreed to approach the problem "a step at a time including at a minimum, defense making changes to strengthen the coordination and management of tactical imagery programs and my creation of a small organization that will become part of this new defense structure." [382]

According to Leo Hazlewood, Gates recognized the fact that imagery problems had to be solved and was willing to place national imagery assets within the DoD if that would fix the problems associated with DESERT STORM. He remembered that the real stumbling block to a NIMA in 1992 was CJCS Colin Powell.[383] Secretary of Defense Cheney was supportive, telling a staffer, "We need a strong DCI, and we need to support these DCI initiatives."[384] General Powell was briefed on the Burnett Panel recommendations but, convinced that DMA was "not broken," could not be persuaded to include DMA in the NIMA plan. According to Hazlewood, once Powell "killed NIA," Gates got all the players together to see what could be done "to fix imagery" within the Intelligence Community. From that meeting, the Central Imagery Office (CIO) was born. [385]

The CIA was deemed acceptable by all parties in the executive branch and Congress. Leo Hazlewood stressed that CIA was an executive branch compromise that the Congress

---

[379] SSCI Professional Staffer interview. The HPSCI and SSCI offered separate bills but the reorganization effort was offered jointly.

[380] Though referred to as NIA from 1992-1995, NIA stood for the IC imagery community plus DMA to some, minus DMA to others. DMA was opposed to joining an NIA throughout this period, arguing that it was an imagery user, not producer, and that inclusion into an intelligence agency could jeopardize international mapping agreements. "NIMA Decision Brief," October 1995, JCS "Tank" Presentation, Slide 8.

[381] SSCI Professional Staffer interview.

[382] DCI Gates' "Statement on Change in the IC, U.S. Congress, Joint Committee Hearings, 1 April 1992," *American Intelligence Journal* (Winter/Spring 1992): 10.

[383] Hazlewood interview.

[384] Rich Haver, Special Assistant to SecDef Cheney in a conversation with Hazlewood, Hazlewood Interview

accepted as a first-step solution.[386]   The CIA alternative had limited functions and authorities. As noted in the Aspin-Brown report, "most imagery elements of the Intelligence Community, including the largest imagery exploitation organization (NPIC), remained outside the new office, which had limited policy authority and no resource authority over outside elements. CIO did retain control of the tasking of imagery collectors, however, and made strides in setting standards and policy to govern exploitation and dissemination.[387]   In sum, "Politics," after all, "is the art of the possible. [388]

CIO — "A SPONGE HAMMER"

In January 1993, Senator Dennis DeConcini (D-AZ) took over the SSCI as Chairman with Senator John Warner (R-VA) as the Vice Chairman, while Congressman Dan Glickman (D-KS) took over the HPSCI with Congressman Larry Combest (R-TX) as Ranking Minority Member. During this period, a growing number of people in Congress and the executive branch became convinced that CIO was "not the answer."[389]

Its Director, Dr. Annette Krygiel, described CIO as a "sponge hammer,"[390] lacking any real clout because of its lack of budget authority and lack of ability to enforce policy. CIO's problems stemmed from the fact that DMA, NPIC, CIA Imagery and DIA Imagery were all outside its authority! It had real control over only DIA collection assets and the DCI's tasking committee (the Committee on Imagery Requirements and Exploitation). Despite these organizational difficulties, its responsibilities were large.

By the time the 1994 elections ushered in a new Republican Congress, some said that the climate had shifted and there was "more of a grassroots interest in a national imagery agency."[391]   Leo Hazlewood recalls, however, that if there was support in 1994/early 1995 for an NIA, it was only in DIA/PGX (Imagery) and CIO. DMA, CIA and NPIC were still opposed.[392] In fact, many organizations were vocal in their opposition, lobbying Congress against an NIA (despite Deutch being in favor), and refusing to accept the inevitability of the situation, all the way up to its actual establishment.[393]   Sharon Basso was at CIO before being brought onto the NIMA Implementation Team as its Director of Communications and Congressional Liaison. She recalls that the Team was surprised by "the inten-

---

[385] Hazlewood interview. Despite Powell's opposition, Powell and Gates were close friends. The two went back many years, both having been deputies to Weinberger and Casey, respectively, at the same time. As such, they met, with their bosses, every week at the "Friday Breakfasts." Both had also been on the National Security Council, though not at the same time, and had many Washington experiences in common.

[386] Hazlewood interview.

[387] *Preparing for the 21st Century*, 23. Former SecDef Les Aspin died three months after commission work began. Aspin was replaced by former SecDef Harold Brown as Chair and the final report was signed by Brown and Vice-Chairman and former Senator Warren Rudman.

[388] SSCI Professional Staffer interview.

[389] Bobbi Lenczowski, Leader of Implementation Working Group on Organization, "Creation of NIMA,"

[390] Greg Jay, Contractor from Booz, Allen and Hamilton who supported the Implementation Team, "Creation of NIMA," 42.

[391] Lenczowski, "Creation of NIMA," 42.

[392] Hazlewood interview.

sity of the guerilla warfare aimed at us, The Implementation Team was often in the middle of some tough bureaucratic fights between CIA and DoD, and we were 'the enemy.'" [394]

January 1995 ushered in the first session of the l04th Congress.[395] Congressman Larry Combest (R-TX) took over the House Intelligence Committee with Congressman Norm Dicks (D-WA) as Ranking Minority Member. Senator Arlen Specter (R-PA) took over the Senate Intelligence Committee as Chairman[396] with Senator Bob Kerrey (D-NE) as the Vice Chairman. [397]

Senator Specter's opportunity to Chair the SSCI came somewhat as a surprise.[398] Senator Specter left the committee in 1990, even though he had served only six years of his eight-year term, having made an agreement (in writing) with Senate Minority Leader Dole to return in January 1993, with his seniority intact, and serve as the committee's Vice Chairman. However, by 1993, Senator John Warner, who was co-equal to Specter in committee seniority and had lost his ranking member position on the SASC, also wanted the Vice Chairmanship position. After heated discussions among Dole, Specter and Warner in January 1993, and more assurances from Senator Dole, Senator Specter agreed to delay his return until January 1995. By waiting the extra two years, Senator Specter became SSCI's Chairman when the Republicans gained control of the Senate in the November 1994 election.

Also in January 1995, DCI Woolsey's resignation was accepted by President Clinton, General Michael Carnes (USAF, Ret) was nominated[399] to take his place, and John Deutch was still Deputy Secretary of Defense. In his role as DepSecDef, Deutch was briefed by Keith Hall (in his role as Deputy Assistant Secretary for Intelligence and Security) on problems in the Intelligence Community along with Hall's solutions — one of which was an NIA.

The idea was apparently well received because when John Deutch was nominated to be the new DCI, Hall's idea emerged in Deutch's testimony, and the creation of NIMA became just a matter of time and determination. The agenda laid out by Deutch in his tes-

---

[393] David Broadhurst, Director, NIMA College, Interview with the author, 27 November 2000. That helps to explain why many lower level employees in the organizations that eventually made up NIMA were unaware of what was happening at the top or in Congress. Top managers were aware, but many probably believed that NIMA was not going to happen and thus did not feel compelled to spread the word.

[394] Sharon Basso, email interview by the author, 1 January 2001.

[395] Each Congress is numbered, lasts two years, and has two regular sessions. The first session begins after an election, with the start of the terms of all representatives and one-third of the senators. The second session begins in January of even numbered years. Thus, January 1995 was the 104th Congress, first session.

[396] Charlie Battaglia, Staff Director for SSCI in 1996, interview by the author, 24 August 2000.

[397] See Appendix A and B for a list of key players on the SSCI and HPSCI respectively. Editor's note: Please see the original publication for Appendixes.

[398] The details of Senator Specter's rise to chairmanship are included to illustrate the complexity and politics of the committee assignment process.

[399] General Carnes subsequently withdrew his nomination due to allegations that he may have violated immigration and labor laws when he brought a Filipino to the U.S. in 1987 to live in his home. See Douglas Waller, "Undesignated Director," *Time* (20 March 1995): 37.

timony became known as "the symphony," and Admiral Dennis Blair was placed in charge of implementing it. To achieve the NIMA objective, Admiral Blair established the NIA Steering Group. [400]

In mid-June, the Steering Group approved a Terms of Reference (TOR) which chartered an NIA Task Force. The Task Force, chaired by Evan Hineman,[401] developed options for the NIA that took the current CIA with a few additional authorities as one extreme (the so-called "CIA on steroids" solution) and a highly centralized NIA with full budgetary and management authority as the other extreme with nine incremental choices in-between. Over the summer, the options were narrowed down from 11 to 3 to finally 1.[402] DIA, the Service Intelligence Chiefs and the J2s of the United Commands agreed to some "Abiding Principles," one of which was that NIA should be a Combat Support Agency. [403]

MID 1990s — THE EXECUTIVE BRANCH PRESENTS A UNITED FRONT

The mid 1990s found the entire Congress fully engaged in reorganization issues. The Aspin-Brown Commission, chartered by the Congress in 1994, had conducted its hearings throughout 1995 and reported in March 1996 that its conclusions concerning imagery coincided with the DCI's.[404] Despite early promises that Aspin-Brown would "put everything on the table,"[405] the final report made only modest, incremental suggestions for change.[406] The SSCI began building on its previous research and the modest Aspin-Brown recommendations, with many staffers still present who had conducted the original SSCI interviews. Because the changes the committee ended up with tended to have come from IC members themselves, they were largely evolutionary in nature and were accept-

---

[400] See Appendix C for a brief list of executive branch players.

[401] Evan Hineman had been a member of the Burnett Panel and had argued for an NIA in the Panel's final recommendations. A 30-year veteran of CIA, he spent the last seven as its Deputy Director for Science and Technology. He was reputedly "brilliant," and a "straight shooter." Hazlewood interview.

[402] According to Mark Lowenthal, staffers felt that these options were "false choices, that the options reflected a broad range of alternatives but only a few really had any chance of happening." Lowenthal remembers saying as much to Keith Hall, suggesting that they had "rendered the verdict before the trial." Interview with the author, 24 August 2000. Dave Broadhurst, one of those on loan from CIO who drafted the eleven original options, confirmed this perception, saying that the NIMA Deutch wanted was a forgone conclusion." Broadhurst interview.

[403] DCI Plans a National Imagery Agency," *DIA Communique* 7, no. 8 (Aug 1995): 1. The combat support agency designation became a big issue between the SSCI and SASC. Senator Kerrey's position is detailed later in this article in the section titled "Legislative Strategy."

[404] Aspin-Brown, 124. According to Leo Hazlewood, the NIMA Implementation Team had many meetings with members of the Aspin-Brown Commission justifying the concept of NIMA. Hazlewood interview.

[405] L. Britt Snider, Staff Director, Aspin-Brown Commission and General Counsel, SSCI, quoted by John Fialka in "Congress Set to Approve Big Review of Costly U.S. Intelligence Community," *Wall Street Journal*, 26 Sep 94, 6.

[406] David Wise, "I Spy a Makeover," *The Washington Post*, 24 Mar 96, C2. "The panel labored mightily and came up with a mouse."

able, for the most part, to both the executive branch and other committees such as Armed Services. [407]

The HPSCI elected to break new ground, not having previous testimony to rely on, and took a different path under Chairman Larry Combest, resulting in the lengthy *IC21: Intelligence Community in the 21st Century*, published by the HPSCI in April 1996. Chairman Combest hired Mark Lowenthal, a man with many years of experience within academia and the executive branch and noted for his numerous publications on the IC, specifically because he could conduct the broad type of inquiry Combest wanted to see. Lowenthal and Combest agreed on a manner of approach.[408] The report summarized its approach by saying, "Everything is on the table. There are no sacred cows in terms of organizations, missions or functions."[409] The changes proposed in IC-21 were revolutionary, far reaching, I and largely unacceptable to both the executive branch and other committees such as Armed Services (at least at first, for reasons mainly due to turf).[410]

A major theme in IC-21 was the elimination of "stovepipes,"[411] within the IC. The House Intelligence committee suggested more "synergy" and "corporateness" as a way to break down barriers created by too many stovepipes and warned that "the current trend within the IC seems to be one that would reinforce the stovepipe approach, further compounding problems for little or no perceived gain. [412] Thus, the HPSCI's response to the executive branch proposal for an NIA was "Why do you want another stovepipe?[413] (In fact, the SSCI thought that the HPSCI's reorganization of the IC would create new and different stovepipes by inserting another layer of authority over all the organizations.)[414] Leo Hazlewood remembers responding that NIMA would be a "porous stovepipe" designed to improve access to imagery-derived information. [415]

The HPSCI was also opposed to NIMA because it thought that "tactical support would win, strategic support would lose.[416] As Mark Lowenthal recalls, "We thought that NIMA would 'suck up' imagery to the military with nothing left over for State, etc. It would be

---

[407] The SSCI was more invested in Aspin-Brown recommendations than the HPSCI, because Aspin-Brown had come largely at the initiative of Senator Warner and was thus more a Senate creation than a House one." Lowenthal interview.

[408] Lowenthal interview.

[409] Lowenthal interview.

[410] For example, IC-21 recommended increased budgetary authority for the DCI; the creation of an independent Clandestine Service made up of the Defense HUMINT Service and CIA's DO; and regrouping of IC agencies so that management of all technical collection assets would be consolidated together, all acquisition assets consolidated, and so on.

[411] Stovepipes refer to any narrow hierarchy of assets. For example collection stovepipes are defined in IC-21 as "types of collection that are managed so as to be largely distinct from one another" resulting in too much competition for resources and too little central control of overall collection needs. IC-21, 22.

[412] IC-21, 22.

[413] Hazlewood, "Creation of NIMA," 41.

[414] 55 SSCI Professional Staffer interview.

[415] Hazlewood interview.

[416] Lowenthal interview. Lowenthal was defining "strategic" as support to the national policymakers, particularly the White House and State Department, and "tactical" support as that to military commanders. Lowenthal had worked at State's Bureau of Intelligence and Research (INR) prior to his position on the HPSCI.

too hard for non DoD to get the assets they needed when they needed them. We didn't believe that an "organizational fix" like NIMA was the right way to tackle distribution problems associated with the Gulf War And, we also saw too many cultural differences between cartographers and imagery analysts for the agency to overcome.[417]

It is important to note, however, that the *House Intelligence Committee members were not united in their opposition to the NIMA concept*. While Chairman Combest, Staff Director Lowenthal and most of the Republican members or staffers opposed it as "another stovepipe," the Democratic members and staffers either supported it, or remained undecided. The Democrats were more inclined to support the Administration's position than the Committee Chairman's.

UNDERSTANDING TURF

In Turf Wars: How Congressional Committees Claim Jurisdiction, David King explains that committee jurisdictions are like property rights "and few things in Washington are more closely guarded or as fervently pursued.[418] Turf "battles are about power and influence in their rawest forms. They are about property rights over public policies.... Within legislatures, jurisdictions distinguish one committee from another. They are, in almost every sense, a lawmaker's legislative power base." [419]

The two intelligence committees are not equal in their jurisdictions. Within the Intelligence Community, resources have traditionally been categorized for budgetary purposes as national intelligence assets in the National Foreign Intelligence Program (NFIP) falling , under the supervision of the DCI, or tactical intelligence assets in the Tactical Intelligence and Related Activities (TIARA) Program, belonging to the Secretary of Defense. At their creation in the 1970s, *the HPSCI was given jurisdiction over both NFIP and TIARA Programs, while the SSCI was given jurisdiction over only the NFIP.*[420] In 1994, a third category, the Joint Military Intelligence Program (JMIP), was added to encompass joint or defense-wide intelligence assets.[421] This development caused a number of turf disputes until a Memorandum of Understanding was signed between the SSCI and SASC conceding that the SSCI had no formal jurisdiction over either the JMIP or TIARA.[422] The SSCI can and does make recommendations to the SASC concerning JMIP and TIARA authorizations, and those recommendations are usually accepted. (see Appendix D).

---

[417] Lowenthal interview.

[418] David King, *Turf Wars: How Congressional Committees Claim Jurisdiction* (Chicago: University of Chicago Press, 1997) 11.

[419] King, 11-12.

[420] *Rules of the House of Representatives*, 106th Congress, Rule 10, Section D, i-iii. *Senate Resolution 400*, 94th Congress, Section 3 (a) (4) A-G and Section 14, (a) (4).

[421] JMIP assets serve multiple defense consumers outside a single service, such as the Defense Cryptologic Program. See Dan Elkins, *An Intelligence Resource Manager's Guide* (Washington D.C.: DIA, 1997), 17 and Ch 6.

[422] Senate Res 400 from the 94th Congress and *Memorandum of Agreement, 26 April 1996, between the SASC and SSCI, Relating to the JMIP and TIARA*. See Appendix F for a copy of this MOA.

Within the NFIP, the situation for the two intelligence committees is the same. The SSCI and HPSCI have sole jurisdiction over the *non-defense* National Foreign Intelligence Program (NFIP).[423] Armed Services has the authority to review these programs on sequential referral, but they cannot claim shared or sole jurisdiction over any of these programs.[424] The SSCI and HPSCI share jurisdiction with Armed Services over the *defense* portions of the NFIP. [425]

Thus, in 1995, since the House National Security Committee[426] shared jurisdiction with the HPSCI for all defense intelligence programs, it was important that the NIMA concept be supported by both the Intelligence and Armed Services committees. Since the Pentagon (the JCS and the Office of the Secretary of Defense) supported an NIA, the HNSC had little reason not to. According to Mark Lowenthal, "The HNSC saw it as increasing its turf."[427] Since *members of the HNSC were united in their support of NIMA, the HPSCI Republicans ultimately stood alone in their opposition to NIMA.* [428]

The SSCI's concerns about NIMA were jurisdictional in nature. The committee wondered "whether all the money associated with imagery was going to go into the Joint Military Intelligence Program"[429] and thus remain under the purview of the SASC.[430] The SSCI's jurisdictional concerns reflected its deeply felt commitment to keeping NIMA's strategic focus intact. Senator Kerrey[431] in particular, was worried that if NIMA was designated a combat support agency that fell entirely under the Secretary of Defense, NIMA would focus all or most of its energy on military support to the exclusion of national-level policymakers at the National Security Council, State Department, and the like. Without jurisdiction, the SSCI would lose important influence in shaping the way in which NIMA was conceived and implemented. [432] The NIMA Implementation Team saw NIMA as falling within the NFIP and briefed it that way. [433]

---

[423] Non-defense NFIP programs fund civilian intelligence activities: Central Intelligence Agency Program (CIAP); Dept of State, Bureau of Intelligence and Research (INR); Dept of Justice, FBI Foreign Counterintelligence Program; Dept of Treasury, Office of Intelligence Support Program; Dept of Energy, Foreign Intelligence Program; and CIA Retirement and Disability System (CIARDS). Dan Elkins, 44-45.

[424] Sequential referral is explained, in detail, later in this article.

[425] Defense NFIP Programs include: General Defense Intelligence Program (GDIP), Consolidated Cryptologic Program (CCP), DoD Foreign Counterintelligence Programs (FCIP), NIMA Program (NIMAP), National Reconnaissance Program (NRP), and the Specialized DoD Reconnaissance Activities. Elkins, 44-45.

[426] The House Armed Services Committee became the House National Security Committee in 1994, and was changed back to the House Armed Services Committee in 1999.

[427] Lowenthal interview. He believes that Intelink is helping to solve dissemination problems much better than creation of NIMA did, and that time has proved him right about the insurmountability of cultural differences.

[428] SSCI Professional Staffer interview; confirmed in Lowenthal interview.

[429] Hazlewood, "Creation of NIMA," 41.

[430] To be considered a national-level intelligence agency under DCI and SSCI jurisdiction, NIMA needed to fall under an amended Title 50 of the United States Code. If NIMA fell under Title 10, it would belong to the Secretary of Defense and be outside the SSCI's budgetary jurisdiction and thus outside its oversight and control.

[431] Senator Kerrey was Vice Chairman of the SSCI and handled most of the organizational issues. Chairman Specter preferred to take the lead on the more contentious oversight issues such as evidence of IC wrongdoing. SSCI Professional Staffer interview.

Like its House counterpart, the Senate Armed Services Committee was receptive to the idea of NIMA. Unlike the Senate Intelligence Committee, the SASC had no jurisdictional issues because the new agency would fall either completely within SASC jurisdiction or be shared with the SSCI. The DoD wanted NIMA designated a "Combat Support Agency" and as such, to fall under an amended Title 10 of the National Security Act—the result of which would place it within SecDef and SASC jurisdiction but outside SSCI jurisdiction.

DMA BROUGHT INTO THE FOLD

Sometime between September and November 1995, it was decided, over DMA's objections, that DMA would be included in the envisioned agency. Records reveal that DMA continued to have reservations about joining throughout 1995; however, DCI Deutch's remarks throughout 1995 indicate that he always included DMA in the new organization.[434] From a strategic point of view, Deutch would have recognized that DMA's 7,000 people added great clout to the proposed organization in terms of both budget and jurisdiction. In addition, as William Allder recalls, "When John Deutch looked at the potential for shared and complementary technologies that would be driving both the imagery and mapping businesses in the future, he saw a set of technological opportunities that could be pursued most effectively through a single set of plans and programs.[435] The target date for stand-up of the new agency was set for 1 October 1996.

On 27 November 1995, a joint letter of agreement on the "concept" to establish the agency, to be known as NIMA, was sent to House Speaker Newt Gingrich, Senator Majority Leader Robert Dole and "appropriate Congressional Committees."[436] Signed by Secretary of Defense Perry, DCI Deutch, and General Shalikashvili, CJCS, the letter began,

> We believe that the consolidation of imagery resources and management in a single agency within the Department of Defense will improve the overall effectiveness and efficiency of imagery and mapping support *to both national and military customers*. Accordingly, we have agreed in concept to create a National Imagery and Mapping Agency that would have responsibility for imagery and mapping similar to what the National Security Agency has for signals intelligence.

---

[432] SSCI Professional Staffer interview, and a source, SASC Professional Staffer in 1996, who wishes to remain anonymous, Interview by the author, 26 September 2000.

[433] See Appendix I for a diagram of the Intelligence Budget. The NIMA budget (or "NIMAP") falls entirely within the NFIP on this briefing slide.

[434] According to a "NIMA Decision Brief," Oct 95, slide presentation (Slide 8) prepared for the Pentagon's "Tank," proponents of DMA's joining NIMA included the Senior Steering Group, agencies and services, and some unified commands. Opponents included DMA, EUCOM, PACOM and SOCOM.

[435] William Allder, "Creation of NIMA," 41.

[436] William J. Perry, John Deutch and John M. Shalikashvili, Letter to the Honorable Newt Gingrich, 27 Nov 95. Provided as attachment to "Memo to Under Secretary of Defense (Acquisition and Technology) et al. Subj: Background Information for 16 Jan 96 Meeting," by RADM J.J. Dantone. See Appendix E for copy of letter.

At this point, a NIMA Director-Designate was appointed to lead an Implementation Team drawn from the intelligence and mapping communities. On 28 November 1995, RADM Joseph ("Jack") Dantone, Jr., USN, was announced as the Director-Designate. His three deputies were Dr. Annette Krygiel from CIO, Leo Hazlewood from CIA and W. Douglas Smith from DMA. Sharon Basso moved over from CIO to take charge of Communications and Congressional Liaison and was responsible for developing a "legislative strategy" to push NIMA through Congress quickly. The team had a package ready for Congress by 15 April 1996.[437] Leo Hazlewood was told by staffers on the Intelligence Committees, "If it ain't here by 15 April, it ain't."[438]

THE LEGISLATIVE STRATEGY

Thus, by the time the Implementation Team was assembled, it had about four months to craft a package acceptable to both the executive branch and Congress. The pressure from Deutch was constant. He ordered them to be on the Hill in December to determine the interests and concerns of relevant committees, members and staffers. Sharon Basso was the team's "eyes and ears" on the Hill. She remembers the extraordinary support the team received from CIA's Congressional Affairs Office.[439] Team members arranged meetings with anyone who would agree to hear them out. According to Hazlewood, members rarely had the time and most considered it "a staffer issue." He found House Republican Members the hardest group to schedule time with and remembers rescheduling an appointment four times with one Congressman before finally giving up.[440] It was an election year, and setting up a new agency was not high on their list of priorities. [441]

Leo Hazlewood remembers that the team had to worry about thirteen different committees — Intelligence, Armed Services, Appropriations, Foreign Relations, Judiciary (on Freedom of Information matters), Government Operations (on personnel authorities) (six each in the House and Senate) — plus the Joint Committee on Printing (for a GPO exemption, since in-house capability was needed for printing classified information). Most of its time, however, was spent with the Intelligence Committee staffers. Questions usually focused on committee jurisdictional concerns (protecting DCI or Secretary of Defense interests), how to balance national and combat commander support, the nature of NIMA's leadership structure, cost and programmatics (NFIP or JMIP), personnel concerns such as the DMA union membership issue, and constituent interests. He recalled being asked, "Are you going to take jobs out of my district?" This became a big concern of Minority Leader Dick Gephardt (DMA in St Louis, MO) and Senator Arlen Specter (DMA in Philadelphia, PA).[442]

---

[437] "Creation of NIMA," 45. See Appendix G for a copy of a briefing summarizing NIMA's purpose, Implementation Team members, and team schedule, working groups, and other background material. See Appendix H for a diagram of the NIMA decision process. See Appendices J and K for what agencies or programs were included in or excluded from the NIMA concept.

[438] SASC Professional Staffer interview. See Appendix F for a copy of the MOA.

[439] Hazlewood interview.

[440] Basso interview.

[441] Hazlewood interview.

In both January and February 1996, the team held "NIMA Days" at its offices in Reston, inviting staffers from all relevant committees out for briefings to explain "Why NIMA and Why Now?" About nineteen staffers came to the first, representing Appropriations, Armed Services and the Intelligence Committees. Staff members from the Aspin-Brown Commission were present as well. Sharon Basso remembers it was at the first session that Eric Thoemmes, a Senate Armed Services Committee staffer, became convinced that "we knew what we were doing. He had been skeptical prior to that point. From that day on, he was the staffer who successfully eliminated many obstacles on the Hill.[443] The February event drew other staffers from the same committees plus DoD representatives.[444] The team also went to the Hill to hold meetings with all the appropriate committee Staff Directors in February.

Edward Obloy, the team's legal counsel and Chairman of the Legal Working Group, described three most contentious issues the legislative strategy had to take into account: (1) personnel issues to include how to keep employee unions in DMA and whether to transfer CIA personnel into NIMA, (2) how to ensure both a strategic and tactical focus for the agency, and (3) who (the DCI or SecDef) should be responsible for collection and tasking. Compromise characterized the final solution to all three concerns.

The union issue was particularly sensitive because it was an election year, and the White House had no intention of alienating a key constituency. The Intelligence Community has always prohibited unions based on national security concerns, but clearly an exception had to be made for DMA union members or the NIMA concept was not going to make it out of the executive branch. Leo Hazlewood remembers that Harold Ickes, White House Deputy Chief of Staff, became personally involved in resolving the issue. Union members were eventually accepted into NIMA with resolution of the issue deferred until after NIMA was established.

The strategic and tactical focus was resolved through language placed in *both Title 10 and Title 50*. The CJCS was placed in charge of reviewing NIMA's ability to provide combat support and the DCI was tasked to review its ability to provide support to its national-level customers. Likewise, collection and tasking responsibilities were placed in both Title 10 and 50. Thus NIMA officially, by statute, serves two masters — the DCI and Sec-Def-and two congressional overseers — Armed Services and Intelligence.

On the floor of the Senate, Senator Kerrey explained his position concerning NIMA's status as a combat support agency, which would distance NIMA from the four defense agencies officially designated by Congress as combat support agencies. He reminded the Senate that the term was first used in the Goldwater-Nichols Defense Reorganization Act of 1986 to describe DoD agencies that have wartime support func-

---

[442] Basso interview.

[443] "IMA News," Internal DIA Report, Feb 1996.

[444] Senator Bob Kerrey (D-NE), *Congressional Record* (26 June 1996), vol 142, no. 96, S7012-13. The four combat support agencies specified in Goldwater-Nichols are the Defense Communications Agency, Defense Intelligence Agency, Defense Logistics Agency, and the Defense Mapping Agency.

tions and a requirement for periodic review by the CJCS to ensure combat readiness.[445] Using that logic, Congress did not designate the National Security Agency (NSA) as a combat support agency because NSA serves customers outside the DoD. Congress subjected NSA to periodic review by the CJCS only so far as its combat duties were concerned. Senator Kerrey argued that NIMA should have been treated like NSA. However, he agreed that since DMA would make up the largest portion of NIMA, the SSCI would go along with the combat support agency designation under Title 10 "for the purposes of JCS review" (but only with respect to its combat support functions)-so long as the same sentence also included a reference to the NIMA's "significant national missions." According to Senator Kerrey, "We would not object to this formulation because it emphasizes that NIMA has two equally important functions: combat support and support for national missions." [446]

The team was willing to do whatever it took to get NIMA approved. According to Sharon Basso, "We did have some tension with SSCI, which felt we had put a knife in its back by moving toward larger control for Defense, but that aside, HPSCI was our only serious problem.[447] By March, Hill staffers had a pretty good idea of what the agency would look like. Obloy's legal team wrote the statute, legislative history and legislative findings, acting as a "drafting service" for the Hill.[448] This saved considerable time for the legislative branch.

In putting the legislative package together so thoroughly, the team was also ensuring that all the "stakeholders"[449] in the executive branch (including the Office of Management and Budget) knew what was going on. Regular meetings were held with all the players and all the working groups were drawn from throughout the relevant agencies. For example, the NIMA team briefed all the CINCs at a CINC Conference being held in Washington, DC in February 1996. At that meeting, General Shalikashvili reiterated his support for establishing NIMA.[450] February 1996 was also when the first meeting of the Customer Advisory Board (CAB) was held. That group comprised national and military organizations brought together to provide a customer perspective to the Implementation Team. The CAB was co-chaired by the National Intelligence Council and Joint Staff representatives.

Ultimately, the most important executive branch player was the Office of Management and Budget (OMB). A "clearinghouse" for all executive branch legislative proposals, OMB had to bless NIMA by 15 April. Fortunately, by mid-April, the legislative package had been extensively coordinated within DoD, was in OMB at the time, and had the blessing of two cabinet officials and their general counsels. The final signature was pro forma

---

[445] Kerrey, S7013

[446] Sharon Basso, "Creation of NIMA," 46. "Serious" added to quote in email interview.

[447] Edward Obloy, NIMA General Counsel, Interview by the author, 4 October 2000.

[448] Stakeholders referred to leadership of the organizations contributing resources to NIMA.

[449] "IMA News," Internal DIA Report, February 1996.

[450] Obloy interview.

at that point. Ed Obloy remembers having to take the package to the Hill on 15 April, without OMB's final blessing, although it did get cleared by the 23rd. He knew the Hill staffers were firm on the 15 April deadline, that missing the deadline would kill all chances of passage during that legislative session, and he was sure enough of OMB support to take the chance. He credits Judith Miller, DoD General Counsel, for helping NIMA through its last executive branch hurdle.[451]

"INSIDE BASEBALL" — DAVID VERSUS GOLIATH

The jurisdictional disputes between the SASC and SSCI came to a head in the Spring of 1996 when the committee bills were ready for markup. Committees and subcommittees often revise bills in a process called a "markup session" in which the bill is reviewed line by line. According to congressional rules, a bill with overlapping jurisdictions (meaning that two or more committees have. formal budgetary authority over some part of that one bill) are referred sequentially so that each concerned committee has an opportunity to markup the bill before it goes to the floor for a vote. This is not uncommon because any broad subject typically overlaps numerous committees. Sequential referral allows the gaining committee 30 legislative days to consider the bill's provisions. In practice, this can amount to two months. [452]

The Senate Intelligence Committee Authorization bill is always sequentially referred to the Senate Armed Services Committee, just as the House Intelligence Authorization bill is always sequentially referred to House Armed Services Committee (or House National Security as it was known then) in large measure because most of the intelligence budget is hidden in the defense budget. Because so many bills involve several committees, sequential referral is a necessary evil but one that can play havoc on bill timing "strategies." Some staffers like to refer to sequential referral as "inside baseball." [453]

In terms of member priorities-reelection, influence within the chamber, and policy-the intelligence and armed services committees are not equal. The four top member choices include: Appropriations, Armed Services, Commerce and Finance.[454] Since defense spending is the single largest controllable segment of the yearly federal budget, membership on the Armed Services Committee has always been popular. With jurisdiction over the entire defense establishment, the immense size of the annual Armed Services Committee authorization bill makes these committees the "thousand pound

---

[451] See Senate Resolution 400 establishing the SSCI for sequential referral provisions. Senate Resolution 400 is available on-line at <wwwintelligence.senate.gov>

[452] SSCI Professional Staffer interview.

[453] Davidson and Oleszek, 208. In comparison, the intelligence committees are prestigious from the perspective that membership indicates a congressman's trustworthiness and access to the nation's top secrets, but its members get little in terms of publicity or pork.

[454] SASC Professional Staffer interview

gorilla" on Capitol Hill. The Armed Services committees are used to being deferred to. As one staffer reminds us, members and other committees are always trying to get a piece of that pie.[455] Because human dynamics and interpersonal relationships are so important on the Hill, it is unusual for any member to do anything to upset cordial relations with any committee-especially Armed Services!

In 1996, this baseball game (the sequential referral process) suddenly got more interesting than usual. The Senate Armed Services Committee took the Senate Intelligence Committee's authorization bill (numbered S. 1718) on sequential referral. In other words, the SASC took the SSCI's bill in order to have a chance to change it — to mark it up. This was as usual, and in accordance with Senate rules, precedent, and normal routine. During its referral period, the SASC took exception to many of the SSCI's reorganization proposals, and *crossed out all SSCI references to NIMA* (placed by the SSCI under Title 50) during its "mark." Still supportive of the NIMA concept, the SASC transferred all language establishing NIMA into the SASC bill under Title 10 and eliminated other SSCI proposals completely, particularly those that appeared to increase the power and authority of the DCI at the expense of the Secretary of Defense. [456]

The SASC's actions so infuriated the SSCI that *Senator Specter personally directed the SSCI's taking the SASC's National Defense bill (numbered S. 1745) on sequential referral — a highly unusual move!* In other words, it was not unusual for Goliath to take David's bill on sequential referral, but very unusual for David to take Goliath's bill.

In the committee report issued by the SASC to accompany the SSCI's Intelligence Authorization Bill, SASC Chairman Senator Thurmond voiced his displeasure with the SSCI over the issue of sequential referral. [457]

> The SSCI nonetheless included many of the controversial provisions in S. 1718, thereby creating a significant disagreement between the SASC and the SSCI. Once S. 1718 had been referred to the SASC on sequential referral (as

---

[455] In the normal course of events, the HPSCI/SSCI always try to pass their respective bills before the Armed Services committees pass theirs. Armed Services then takes the Intelligence bill on sequential referral after the Intelligence Committee reports it out. Once Armed Services reports the Intelligence Bill to the floor (after the sequential referral), the Intelligence Committee can take it back or let it go to the floor. If the Intelligence Committee takes it back to reassert its jurisdictional rights, there probably will not be sufficient time to finish another round on the bill before the end of that Congressional session! Thus, as an alternative, the Intelligence Committee can begin negotiating changes to the Armed Services report — of the Intelligence bill — and can offer the results of the negotiations as floor amendments. The Intelligence Committee can also disregard the Armed Services report of the Intelligence Authorization Bill and try to get a better outcome during the HPSCI-SSCI conference of the bill. Because a conference report cannot be amended and is not available to be taken on sequential referral, Armed Services must accept the outcome of the conference — they either have to accept all of it or lobby other Senators to have it defeated on the floor. As always, the selection of what to do will largely depend on the issues and the personalities involved. SSCI Professional Staffer interview.

[456] U.S. Congress, Senate, Armed Services Committee, *Report 104-277*, 104th Congress, 2d Session, 1. (See Appendix D-1 for a complete copy of this report.)

[457] SASC Professional Staffer interview. See Appendix F for a copy of the MOA.

the Intelligence Authorization Bill is every year), the SASC Chairman and Ranking Minority Member agreed to enter into negotiations with the SSCI to attempt to resolve these differences. Notwithstanding this effort to work out a consensus in good faith, the Chairman and Vice Chairman of the SSCI took the unprecedented step of requesting sequential referral of the Defense Authorization Bill.

The SASC Chairman's anger was also apparent in other paragraphs of the same report. His comments concerning a "Department of Intelligence" are in reference to other proposals in the SSCI bill which would have expanded the DCI's authority at the expense of the SecDef's. (Italics added by author.)

S. 1718, as reported by the SSCI, contains a number of controversial provisions, which the SASC opposes and the executive branch does not support. On April 15, 1996 the Chairman and Ranking Minority Member of the SASC wrote to the Chairman and Vice Chairman of the SSCI to express concern regarding these issues and to urge the SSCI not to include such provisions in the Intelligence Authorization Bill for Fiscal Year 1997.

In general, these provisions seek to shift a significant degree of authority from the Secretary of Defense to the Director of Central Intelligence (DCI), especially in the area of budget formulation and execution. *The bill also contains a number of provisions that, taken together, lay the foundation for the creation of what amounts to a 'Department of Intelligence.'*

The SASC supports a strong DCI yet maintains that the DCI's function is not to act as a quasi-departmental head, but to coordinate the intelligence activities of various departments and to act as the principal intelligence advisor to the President and the National Security Council. Providing the DCI the type of authority recommended by the SSCI would seriously undermine the Secretary of Defense's ability to manage the Department of Defense. The committee notes that the Secretary of Defense strongly opposes such a shift of power and the DCI has not sought such authorities. If S. 1718 were passed in its current form, it would almost certainly be vetoed....

Title VIII of S. 1718, as reported by the SSCI, establishes the National Imagery and Mapping Agency (NIMA) in Title 50, V.S.C., not as a Combat Support Agency. The executive branch had requested that NIMA be established in Title 10, V.S.C., and be designated in law as a Combat Support Agency. The SASC-reported Defense Authorization Bill contains a comprehensive legislative charter for NIMA, which, with a few minor exceptions, is consistent with the executive branch proposal.

As one staffer notes, the SASC is "used to assaults from all sides," and viewed this as just another assault to be warded off. In fact, he remembered that tensions between the SASC and SSCI were high at that particular time. The two committees had only recently resolved the issue of jurisdiction over JMIP funds, with the SSCI finally signing a Memorandum of Agreement in April 1996 relinquishing to the SASC any claim to jurisdiction.[458] According to both Leo Hazlewood and Ed Obloy, Eric Thoemmes (a staffer on the SASC) was NIMA's guardian angel. Convinced at the January "NIMA Day" (held at Reston) that NIMA was "the right thing to do," and persuaded by the letter to the Hill that both the SecDef and CJCS approved, Thoemmes helped to shepherd the legislative package through the committee. He helped team members talk to the right people at the right time and calm the waters stirred up by the sequential referral uproar.[459]

SASC members may have been unaware of how deep the SSCI commitment was to NIMA under Title 50 — thinking it to be a "Staffer issue" as opposed to a "Member issue."[460] In fact, the SSCI felt so strongly about keeping NIMA within the DCI's jurisdiction that members decided as a committee to fight the SASC by requesting the SASC authorization bill on sequential referral-a request never made by the SSCI before or since. This led to a confrontation between the two committee chairmen — Strom Thurmond and Arlen Specter.[461]

A SASC staffer remembers that confrontation and the many meetings it led to at the staff level. Ultimately, it came down to a meeting between "the Big Four"[462] to hammer out the most contentious issues. At one point, these Members met with DCI Deutch, DepSecDef White and Vice-Chairman, JCS Ralston to decide whether the DCI could live with NIMA as a Combat Support Agency under the DoD.

One big issue between the SASC and SSCI had to do with whether NIMA's Director would be military; if military, whether it would be a two- or three-star billet; and if a three-star billet, whether the services would get an additional three-star ("plus one") or would have to take it "out of hide" (meaning the total number already authorized and divided among the services). A three-star billet was agreed to so that the NIMA Director would be equal in rank to the Director of DIA, NSA, NRO and so on. However, the SASC wanted no increase in three-star billets. According to Hazlewood, DCI Deutch did not lobby hard enough for an additional three-star billet with the SASC and thus, although NIMA did end up with the option of either a senior civilian or a three-star, the three-star

---

[458] Hazlewood Interview.

[459] Some programs or initiatives are considered "staffer issues," others "Member issues." Not surprisingly, Members tend to pay greater attention to, and be less ready to fight "Member issues." When the SSCI and HPSCI were created, each committee was designated one or two "crossover members" from the Judiciary, Foreign Relations, Armed Services, and Appropriations committees. One of the purposes for this arrangement was to facilitate information sharing between all these committees since their oversight responsibilities regarding the Intelligence Community overlapped. In 1996, there were six members on the SSCI who also were members of the SASC. Thus the apparent lack of communication between the two committees was all the more surprising. The SSCI and HPSCI lists at Appendix A and B indicate crossover members.

[460] SSCI Professional Staffer interview.

[461] SASC Chair Thurmond, SASC Ranking Member Nunn, SSCI Chair Specter, and SSCI Vice-Chair Kerrey.

[462] U.S. Congress, Senate, Select Intelligence Committee, Report 104-278, 104th Congress, 2d Session, 1. (See Appendix D-2 for complete copy.)

billet has to be "borrowed" from the service that nominates the NIMA Director. Thus, RADM Dantone had to be called Acting Director after 1 October 1996 because he had two stars, not three.

Having taken the SASC bill, and earned the wrath of Senator Thurmond and others such as Senator Stevens, the SSCI released it ahead of schedule. Senator Specter, in the SSCI committee report accompanying the SASC Defense Authorization Bill (S. 1745) is conciliatory, although he makes some pointed references to Senator Thurmond's committee report. Senator Specter makes a point of justifying the SSCI's taking of the SASC bill and the speediness of its review.[463]

After careful review, including extensive discussions and negotiations at the staff and member level with the Armed Services Committee and with the Director of Central Intelligence, the Deputy Secretary of Defense, and the Vice Chairman of the Joint Chiefs of Staff, *the Committee voted to report the bill with amendments on June 11 — well before the expiration of the thirty days of session allotted in Senate Resolution 400 for consideration upon referral.*

The SSCI report also discussed points of contention with the SASC such as Senator Thurmond's remark about a "Department of Intelligence." Senator Specter used the report to highlight the SSCI's success in protecting NIMA's national mission and to downplay its losses over expanded DCI authorities.

According to Senator Specter, the Committee believes the consensus reached by the two Committees preserves significant elements of the reform effort and significantly enhances the ability of the DCI to manage intelligence activities. In addition, the Committee is more comfortable that, with the changes agreed upon, the DCI will have the ability to ensure that a new National Imagery and Mapping Agency will be responsive to the needs of all national customers. [464]

NIMA IN CONFERENCE — HNSC AND SASC

Typically, once the HPSCI and SSCI have resolved their differences with Armed Services, and any other committee with overlapping concerns, such as Foreign Relations or Judiciary, each bill is "reported from committee" and subject to a vote by the entire chamber. Here is where the reputation of the Intelligence committee and its chairman is most critical. In the words of one HPSCI staffer, the chairman has to present the bill to the entire chamber and ask fellow members to "trust him, and trust the committee" to have made the right decisions because the majority of the bill's contents are classified. Members can come to the committee's work spaces and review the classified annex to the bill but few do. Most trust the committee and its staffers to have "done the right thing." He calls the committee's role "the lubricant" between the wheels of the executive and legisla-

---

[463] Report 104-278, 5.

[464] A source, HPSCI Professional Staffer, who wishes to remain anonymous, interview by the author, 5 May 2000.

tive branches, allowing a secret part of the government to function smoothly in an open society that inherently distrusts any operation that operates in secret.[465]

Before bills can be sent to the president, however, they must be passed by both the House and Senate in identical form. House and Senate differences are reconciled "in conference." In the usual course of things, conferees include all members from the committees that sponsored the legislation, but can sometimes include members from committees with important overlapping jurisdiction. [466]

NIMA would normally have been "conferenced" by the HPSCI and SSCI — a process in which HPSCI committee members sit across the table from SSCI committee members to "iron out" any differences.[467] Had that happened, the SSCI would probably have tried to take advantage of the "divided House," using the isolated position of House Republicans on the NIMA issue to win its passage.[468] NIMA, however, was not in the SSCI bill (since the SSCI had, in fact, eliminated NIMA language in its FY 97 Intelligence Authorization Bill in order to gain Senate passage of the bill) and *there was now nothing in the HPSCI or SSCI bills pertaining to NIMA. NIMA was in the SASC bill, so it was up to the HNSC to conference directly with the SASC.* Thus, with the SASC and HNSC in favor of NIMA, HPSCI objections stood little chance of carrying the day.

A THREE-RING CIRCUS

Newspaper articles discussing committee differences referred to the dispute as a three-ring "turf battle par excellence." *Washington Post* staff writer and intelligence specialist Walter Pincus named the ring leaders as DCI John Deutch, DepSecDef John White (representing SecDef Perry) and Senator Specter. "Waiting just outside the center ring," wrote Pincus, "is Senator Ted Stevens (R-Alaska), Chairman of the Appropriations Defense Subcommittee and booster of the Pentagon and Senate Armed Services Committee. As Chairman of the Senate Governmental Affairs subcommittee handling civil service matters, he has gotten sequential referral on Specter's bill and is holding it hostage." [469]

Senator Stevens' actions came as a great surprise to the SSCI members and staff. According to Charlie Battaglia, Senator Stevens' staff never provided him with a reason for why the committee was taking a sequential referral on the SSCI's authorization bill in spite of his several offers to negotiate changes or provide clarification. Mr. Battaglia judged that Senator Stevens was using the procedure as a tool to show support for Senator Thurmond and reprimand the SSCI for "overstepping its bounds. [470]

---

[465] Davidson and Oleszek, 253.

[466] "In conference anything is tradeable. It's like a 'congressional swap meet.'" Lowenthal interview.

[467] SSCI Professional Staffer interview.

[468] HPSCI Intelligence Authorization Bill, HR 3237, contained no reference to NIMA. HNSC Defense Authorization Bill, HR 3259, amended the HPSCI Bill and added NIMA language comparable to the SASC language as amended by the SSCI.

[469] Walter Pincus, "Intelligence Battleground: Reform Bill," *The Washington Post*, 30 May 1996, A 29.

[470] Battaglia interview. See S *Report 104-337.* (The complete report can be found in Appendix D-3.)

THE APPROPRIATORS

The committees discussed thus far (Intelligence, Armed Services, Foreign Relations, and so on) are authorizing committees and through their bills programs are permitted to exist. Authorization committees review the merit of existing or proposed programs and decide whether to authorize money for them in the corning fiscal year. The basic issue for authorizers is whether programs have merit, and how to prioritize a variety of good ideas.

There is only one Appropriations Committee in each house. The federal budget is divided up among its 13 subcommittees. Each agency in the federal government depends upon one of those thirteen appropriations bills for its budget dollars. In theory, every program is both authorized by an authorizing committee, such as Armed Services, and appropriated funds by an appropriating subcommittee such as the Appropriation Committee's Subcommittee on Military Construction.

Authorizers set ceilings for how much money should be spent on a program, and often outline conditions to control how the money is spent. Appropriators, on the other hand, must decide exactly how much money an authorized program can receive, working within budgetary spending level constraints. Broadly speaking, they are more concerned with a program's cost than with its merit. In theory, if authorized, it must have merit. In practice, authorizers and appropriators try to work closely together.

Ordinarily, the House and Senate Appropriations Committees (HAC and SAC) would have little reason to fight a concept like NIMA, if authorized by both the Intelligence and Armed Services Committees, since its authorization required little, if any, additional funds. NIMA constituted a "policy issue" and as such, would normally be left to the authorizers. In addition, Sharon Basso recalled that Senator Stevens, Chairman of the Defense Appropriations Subcommittee, had wanted a NIA/NIMA organization for some time. "He was unhappy with CIA and his staffer kept whacking at CIA's budget to force it to pay attention." She also remembered that "House appropriators were only concerned that information 'got to the guy in the foxhole' and thought that NIMA would be better able to do that."[471]

Not surprisingly, appropriators focused in on DCI Deutch's promises of greater efficiency and cost savings as a result of the consolidation of imagery assets and tried to discover ways in which the new agency could save money. The money issues were already resolved, however, and the implementation team considered the Appropriators to be little cause for concern.[472]

A LETTER FROM THE SPEAKER

Despite their isolated position, Leo Hazlewood remembers that HPSCI Republicans tried to mobilize other House Republicans to "Just Say No" to NIMA in the HNSC/

---

[471] Basso Interview.
[472] Obloy Interview.

SASC conference committee over the DoD Authorization Bill. Furthermore, Chairman Combest and the HPSCI staff briefed Speaker Gingrich on the issue and convinced him that it was a bad idea. In response, the Speaker wrote a letter of objection.[473] Lowenthal points out that the Speaker is, after all, an *ex officio* member of the HPSCI and is therefore, perfectly within his rights to express his opinion on the subject within the House and Senate.[474] The letter was rumored to have been circulated among key Republican members throughout the House and Senate as a signal to the conference committee members not to support the creation of NIMA.

The fact that the Speaker's letter had so little effect illustrates not only the autonomy of the Senate, but also the momentum that the NIMA concept had gained. It had too much support from both key players in the executive branch and Congress to be brought to a halt at this late stage. Leo Hazlewood recalled that the NIMA team "discovered during this period the importance of reaching out to people who could contact influential people on the Hill."[475] One such person was Senator Trent Lott.[476] Sharon Basso explained that "NIMA was particularly lucky because Senator Lott was the subcommittee chairman who sponsored the NIMA legislation." As its sponsor, he had a "personal vested interest in the legislation," and as Majority Leader was in a good position to aid its passage.[477]

CREATED "ON SCHEDULE"

Sharon Basso kept a board in her office from January to October 1996 that registered the "NIMA heartbeat." Depending on where the center of gravity seemed to be on any given day, the heartbeat grew stronger or weaker. Team members discovered interesting correlations, like the fact that the more the HPSCI disliked NIMA, the greater the SSCI support! They also learned that proposed legislation can falter at any moment, as the potentially disastrous Gingrich letter demonstrated at the very end of the process. [478]

Having survived the scrutiny of these many committees as a concept for streamlining the management of imagery intelligence, and having faced huge opposition within the executive branch, NIMA was legislated into existence in the FY97 DoD Authorization Bill.[479] The bill passed on 30 September 1996 — meeting the 1 October 1996 timeline set by DCI Deutch in November 1995 — an incredibly short time from a congressional perspective. This retrospective case study highlights just how remarkable its survival was. How can we explain its success despite all the odds against its passage?

---

[473] Interview data conflicts over exactly whom the letter was addressed to. It may have been to Republicans on the SSCI or it may have been to the Chairman of the HNSC, Mr. Spense.

[474] Lowenthal Interview.

[475] Hazlewood, "Creation of NIMA," 46.

[476] Basso, "Creation of NIMA," 46.

[477] Basso Interview.

[478] Hazlewood Interview.

[479] See Appendix L for the *DoD Directive 5105.60*, 11 Oct 96, establishing NIMA.

The importance of the combined support of the Secretary of Defense, Chairman of the Joint Chiefs of Staff and Director of Central Intelligence cannot be overstated.[480] Had they not been united, the "fast track" approach would not have been possible. Their unity overcame the tremendous opposition within the executive branch, as organizations clashed over such fundamentally contentious issues as budget, turf, employee rights and benefits, and organizational cultures. Despite all that, the "big three" had decided the timing was right, and so it happened. As David Broadhurst concludes, the creation of NIMA was the biggest change in the Intelligence Community since the National Security Act of 1947.[481] Such revolutionary change probably had to happen quickly to minimize the weight of the opposition.

In conclusion, it appears that policymakers in the executive branch sometimes find that Congress is an ally, sometimes a foe. In the case of NIMA it was primarily an ally and advocate. According to Helen Sullivan, Office of the Deputy General Counsel, DoD and a primary drafter of the NIMA legislation,

> [i]t has been said that it can be easier to get legislation through Congress than through the executive branch. NIMA may be proof of that. If we had tried to seek an administration solution to the problem, having the DCI and Secretary of Defense sign some kind of charter, that would have played into the hands of the bureaucracies, and we would probably still be waiting for approval. Bureaucracies can take a look at senior leadership, recognize the amount of turnover at that level and wait them out. [482]

RECOMMENDATION FOR FURTHER RESEARCH

This case concentrates solely on NIMA's creation, but Congress's role in its evolution after October 1996 continues. As overseer of the Intelligence Community, the congressional intelligence committees have a variety of responsibilities-one of which is to exercise "continuous watchfulness" over the agencies within their jurisdiction because the "administration of a statute is, properly speaking, an extension of the legislative process.[483]Congress gave the NIMA several years to overcome the initial hurdles inherent in starting a new agency and then sought an independent assessment of whether the concerns of the various committees were well-founded and what changes might be needed to support national policymakers more fully. Using the Classified Annex to the FY 2000 DoD Appropriations Conference Bill, Congress established a commission to review the NIMA and directed the DCI and SecDef to appoint its members. The Commission, chaired by Peter Marino, conducted its study throughout 2000 and released its report in January 2001. The Commission concludes that "while NIMA's transformation is still incomplete, and progress against some goals is mixed, the Commission observes progress in virtually

---

[480] Obloy, "Creation of NIMA," 41.

[481] Broadhurst Interview.

[482] Helen Sullivan, "Creation of NIMA," 45.

[483] Oleszek, 263-264. Oleszek is quoting from the *Legislative Reorganization Act of 1946.*

every area.[484] The commission's report offers a useful snapshot of progress as of the year 2000. Researchers might consider using this report as a baseline from which to measure progress at some future date.

[484] Independent Commission on the National Imagery and Mapping Agency, "Introduction," *Report of the Independent Commission on the National Imagery and Mapping Agency* (Washington D.C.: GPO, 2001), Section 1.5, URL: <*http://www.nimacommission.com*>, accessed 21 Jan 01.

THE APPLICATIONS OF INTELLIGENCE

HEALTH AND NATIONAL SECURITY

George C. Fidas

(Originally Published in the book Divided Diplomacy and the Next Administration: Conservative and Liberal Alternatives, edited by Henry R. Nau and David Shambaugh, Washington, DC: The Elliott School of International Affairs, The George Washington University, 2004.)

INTRODUCTION

Health is a transnational issue because microbes know no borders. Health is a development issue because studies increasingly demonstrate that good health can contribute to economic growth while bad health can constrain it. Health also is a national and global security issue because it can contribute to insecurity at the personal, communal, national, and international levels. For the most part, health security also has become a bipartisan issue as both American liberals and conservatives have come to realize that attenuating the growing health divide between rich and poor in the world is an important component of the broader effort to deal with failing states, the roots of terrorism, and other 21st-century threats.

THE GROWING INFECTIOUS DISEASE THREAT

Despite earlier optimism in the health community, infectious diseases remain a leading cause of death, accounting for a quarter to a third of worldwide annual deaths and two-thirds of childhood deaths. The renewed threat from diseases owes to environmental degradation and global warming that are spreading diseases; changes in human demographics and behavior, such as accelerated urbanization and unsafe sex and drug injection practices; and high-tech medical procedures that also carry a higher risk of infection. It also results from changing land and water use patterns that increase contact with disease vectors; growing international travel and commerce that can spread microbes as fast as the speed of aircraft; and the inappropriate use of antibiotics that fosters microbial resistance and makes them increasingly useless.

Although smallpox has been eliminated, 20 other well-known diseases such as tuberculosis and malaria have re-emerged or spread geographically over the past three decades, often in more virulent and drug-resistant forms. More ominously, 35 new diseases have been identified, including HIV, Ebola, hepatitis C, and, most recently, SARS, for which no cures are yet available.

- Some 60 million people have been infected with HIV over the past two decades, and 38 million are living with the virus. The disease has killed more than 20 million people, and by 2020, at least another 68 million are projected to die of AIDS, 55 million of them in Sub-Saharan Africa.

- The threat from TB, especially drug-resistant TB, continues to grow, fueled by poverty, the AIDS pandemic, and immigration. Nearly 9 million develop TB annually, 2 million die each year, and some 35 million will die by 2020.
- Malaria is making a deadly comeback, killing over 1 million people annually, afflicting another 300 to 500 million worldwide, and stunting productivity and economic growth.
- Hepatitis C, acute respiratory infections, and diarrheal diseases appear to have peaked at high levels and will continue to take a heavy toll among young and old.
- And epidemiologists continue to believe that it is only a matter of time before another killer flu or related disease emerges on the scale of the catastrophic flu pandemic of 1918, which took over 20 million lives.
- Even diseases that are not particularly contagious or deadly, such as SARS, are capable of bringing commerce to a near halt owing to the globalization of fear itself as an unwelcome facet of broader globalization trends.

AIDS and related diseases are likely to aggravate and may even provoke social fragmentation, economic decay, and political instability in the hardest-hit countries in Sub-Saharan Africa and elsewhere. AIDS is slashing life expectancy by up to 30 years and producing a huge orphan cohort of up to 25 million young people by decade's end that will be subject to exploitation and radicalization. It is making major inroads into the professional classes of teachers, civil servants, and health workers, who are dying as fast as replacements can be trained. It is taking an increasingly heavy economic toll, reducing GDP growth by 2 percent or more annually, eroding profits, and constraining foreign investment. Its infiltration into the ruling political and military elites is likely to slow democratic development as it intensifies the struggle to control scarce state resources, reduces the capacity of governments to provide needed services, and thereby reduces their legitimacy. And AIDS also will hamper national and international security and peacekeeping efforts as military and police forces are ravaged by the disease. When combined with the growing threat from non-communicable diseases such as heart disease and cancer in developing countries — the probability of dying from a non-infectious disease already is higher in Sub-Saharan Africa and India than in developed countries — the stage is set for a further erosion of state capacity and stability.

Competing or Converging Paradigms?

Four years ago, a U.S. National Intelligence Estimate on the global infectious disease threat opened the debate about a link between disease and security by warning that "New and emerging infectious diseases will pose a rising global health threat and will complicate U.S. and global security over the next 20 years. These diseases will endanger U.S. citizens at home and abroad, threaten U.S. armed forces deployed overseas, and exacerbate social and political instability in key countries and regions in which the United States has significant interests."

The NIE contributed to a broader debate between those emphasizing the importance of state security entailing protection of a state's government, territory, and population from recognizable external military threats and a growing body of scholars and some in government who emphasize personal security.

The state-centric or conservative model focuses on protection of a state's territory and population from external military, economic, and ideological threats emanating from another recognizable sovereign state or alliance. Its responses call for strong defense budgets, military counter-alliances, and the projection of diplomatic, economic, and military power.

The human security-centric or liberal model argues that states cannot be stable or secure if the individuals that they comprise feel insecure and threatened by pestilence, crime, poverty, environmental degradation, and unresponsive or repressive governments. Human security also assumes that many of these threats — such as disease — do not emanate from recognizable or intentional threateners or enemies and thus call for global cooperation.

Since publication of the NIE, several studies have elaborated on its points and given them more empirical content. Convincing the world's political leaders that infectious diseases such as AIDS pose a national and global security threat has been a more daunting task because there is rarely if ever a smoking gun that can tie diseases directly to national and global security and mobilize the world's countries to deal with them. Instead, to paraphrase Thomas Hobbes, diseases will make life even more nasty, brutish, and short. It is the cumulative effects of this Hobbesian process that will erode national and global security as mass killers such as AIDS, TB, and malaria undermine social and economic growth and development, stymie political development, and intensify the struggle for scarce resources and thereby destabilize already troubled polities.

Clinton Administration Links Disease to National Security

Responding in part to the 2000 National Intelligence Estimate, the Clinton administration declared AIDS to be a national security threat and launched a major effort in Congress, the U.N., and with U.S. allies and lending institutions to secure more funding for it and related diseases. The upshot was a tripling of U.S. funds to over $1 billion annually and a similar surge in global spending. Both former Secretary of State Madeline Albright and National Security Adviser Samuel R. Berger subsequently highlighted the Clinton administration's elevation of the fight against infectious diseases to that of a "national security priority" as one of its chief accomplishments.

A Conservative Bush Administration Follows Suit and Ups Ante

After some hesitancy, including elimination of the senior international health adviser position on the National Security Council established during President Clinton's tenure, the Bush administration raised the health and security nexus to an even higher level of importance. It also added a more visible moral imperative championed by its evangelical political base. "I know of no enemy in war," declared Secretary of State Powell at the U.N. Special General Assembly Session on HIV/AIDS, "more insidious than AIDS, an enemy that poses a clear and present danger to the world." The administration's 2002 National Security Strategy included a U.S. commitment to "lead the world in efforts to reduce the terrible toll of HIV/AIDS and other infectious diseases." The administration supported establishment of the Global Fund to Fight AIDS, Tuberculosis and Malaria, once it took the form of a public-private partnership separate from the U.N. that operates more as a corporation and has an independent administrator. And most important, President Bush announced a bold new initiative to triple the amount of funding for AIDS treatment and prevention programs to $15 billion over five years in his State of the Union address in 2003. This U.S.-managed plan calls for the treatment of 2 million AIDS victims and prevention of 7 million new cases in 15 hard-hit countries over five years. Earlier this year, Secretary Powell reiterated that AIDS — not terrorism — poses the greatest threat to the world.

Bush policies are driven by the terrorist threat and a moral desire to square health issues with religious convictions. The 9/11 terrorist attacks and subsequent war on terrorism sensitized administration officials to the need to deal with the roots of state failure and terrorism. That entails ameliorating threats to human security such as HIV/AIDS. Equally important, the administration believes that tackling the HIV/AIDS crisis and its destructive impact on families, women, and children is a moral imperative that cannot be shirked. That includes other conservatives such as ex-Senator Jesse Helms, who lamented that he had done so little to help AIDS victims and subsequently introduced a bill to secure $500 million to prevent mother-to-child transmission of the disease. The upshot is that the United States is clearly in the forefront of the global fight against infectious diseases and HIV/AIDS in particular, contributing more than two-thirds of the funding and much of the sense of urgency.

That has not shielded the administration from criticism by HIV/AIDS activists, health experts, and political opponents alike. First, the administration's budget request for its AIDS plan fell considerably short of its $3 billion annual pledge — ostensibly because designated recipient countries lack the ability to absorb larger amounts — and it was only congressional efforts that pushed the amount up from under $2 billion to $2.4 billion this year and $2.7 in 2005. Second, the administration has de-emphasized support and funding for the Global Fund it formerly backed in favor of the U.S. plan, highlighting its concerns about the accountability of international programs and a preference for unilateral programs, and again compelling Congress to make up the shortfall to some $500 million. Third, the administration appears to be favoring U.S. drug firms rather than much cheaper foreign generic drug manufacturers in the provision of anti-retroviral drugs for the plan's treatment component. Fourth and most controversial, the administration insists that one-third of the funds spent on prevention must be spent on abstinence programs, sparking charges that these are of little or no demonstrated effectiveness and designed mainly to appeal to its evangelical constituency.

A LIKELY DEMOCRATIC HEALTH SECURITY POLICY

Looking forward, the growing linkage between health and national security reflected both in the academic and political worlds is likely to persist with the debate limited more to means over ends. Although a second Bush administration would likely adhere to the international health policies set during its first term, a Kerry administration would face a variety of challenges and choices as it contemplated its responses to the infectious disease threat.

First, a Democratic administration is more likely to incorporate the fight for better health and against infectious diseases into a broader grand strategy that is more personal security- than state security-centric. This may not translate into substantially more funds than the considerable sum the Bush administration has committed, however, since it may want to spend more on health for its gay and other marginalized domestic constituencies. But it may well be more inclined to fund the program fully.

Second, a Democratic administration will want to burnish its more multilateral orientation and credentials. Giving the U.S. effort against infectious diseases a more multilateral cast would be a low-cost and efficacious way to do so, certainly lower than multilateral initiatives on Iraq and other "hard" security issues. This may entail selecting a new global AIDS coordinator not associated with the U.S. pharmaceutical industry (The current coordinator, Randall Tobias, is a former executive officer of Eli Lilly); abandoning the current policy of using only those anti-retroviral drugs approved by the Food and Drug Administration in favor of accepting much cheaper generics approved by the World Health Organization; and, most important, substantially increasing the proportion of U.S. funds allocated to the Global Fund.

Third, a Democratic administration, like its predecessor, will want to maintain a balance between prevention and treatment, but it almost certainly will purge the U.S. program of all influences seen as originating in the Bush administration's evangelical support base. Specifically, the" abstinence" component of the U.S. program that currently receives 33 percent of funding allocated for prevention efforts will be jettisoned in favor of expanded condom and other programs that are seen as more demonstrably effective — and moral in a non-religious sense. This also would appeal to the broader Democratic constituency that supports family planning, choice regarding abortion, and fewer restrictions on stem cell research aimed at finding cures for infectious and non-infectious diseases.

A LIBERAL/CONSERVATIVE NEXUS

In sum, while much may divide liberals and conservatives — and neoconservatives — as they try to gauge the dynamics of the new international system we are in, there is a growing consensus that the concept of security must be expanded to include the types of non-traditional challenges that fuel the despair, anger, and hatred that are at the core of the terrorist and other 21st-century threats we confront. The growing health divide between North and South that will determine who lives and who dies of AIDS and other diseases is one such challenge.

INTELLIGENCE SUPPORT TO REFUGEE OPERATIONS: WHO'S THE EXPERT?

James D. Edwards

(Originally published in Perry L. Pickert's compilation of JMIC theses titled Intelligence for Multilateral Decision and Action, June 1997. Embedded references are retained, but bibliography in the original document is too large for inclusion in this volume.)

INTRODUCTION

Increased U.S. military participation in refugee operations highlights the need for a better understanding of intelligence in these nontraditional missions. While skeptics assert that the Office of the UN High Commissioner for Refugees (UNHCR) does not produce intelligence, it does collect, analyze, and disseminate "information" — a term which has become a euphemism for intelligence within the United Nations. Because the UNHCR is a professional refugee protection and assistance organization with a world-wide presence in the field, its operational elements typically have better intelligence than an *ad hoc*, U.S. military joint task force. Consequently, the U.S. military can improve its intelligence in refugee operations by studying the UNHCR.

The UNHCR's intelligence-gathering system is specifically designed for refugee crises, while U.S. military intelligence organizations focus on an enemy or threat. As a result, operational elements within the UNHCR have more warning that they will be involved in an impending refugee crisis than their counterparts in the U.S. military, and the UNHCR has better intelligence to plan its response. Because of its technical collection capabilities and its emphasis on threats, however, the U.S. military is better at force protection during an ongoing refugee operation.

The lessons the military should draw from the UNHCR include: (1) Non-Governmental Organizations, and other organizations with a presence in the crisis area, are usually the best sources of information in a refugee emergency; (2) an infatuation with "threats" to the relief force should not inhibit the intelligence staff's ability to assess the political, economic, and social aspects of the situation; (3) clandestine human intelligence will probably not be effective; and (4) unclassified intelligence products are essential.

REFUGEES IN THE POST-COLD WAR WORLD

Massive flows of refugees and displaced persons have become the central feature of most humanitarian emergencies (Eliasson: 185).

Jan Eliasson, former Under Secretary-General for Humanitarian Affairs

This essay compares intelligence in U.S. military "refugee operations" with a similar function in the world's leading refugee organization, the Office of the United Nations

High Commissioner for Refugees (UNHCR).[485] After establishing the context for the study, the paper addresses the issues of intelligence in the United Nations (UN) and how intelligence differs from information. Then, it analyzes the intelligence functions of the U.S. military and the UNHCR by comparing strategic warning and the planning and conduct of refugee relief operations in each organization.

The end of the Cold War brought profound changes to the international security environment. Today, there is a paradox that while there is less threat of global war, there is also less peace in the world. Armed conflicts have increased dramatically since 1989, but the fighting is not between states; it is within them.[486] The result has been a proliferation of complex humanitarian emergencies which "combine internal conflicts with large-scale displacements of people, mass famine, and fragile or failing economic, political, and social institutions" (U.S. Mission to the UN *a:* 1). The accompanying map

---

[485] In keeping with common practice, the term UNHCR refers to the institution known as the Office of the UNHCR. The term High Commissioner refers to the individual occupying this office.

[486] According to the UN, "of the 82 armed conflicts in the world between 1989 and 1992, only three flared up between countries. The rest occurred internally..." See Hal Kane, The Hour of Departure: Forces That Create Refugees and Migrants (Washington, DC: Worldwatch Institute, 1995), 21.

depicts areas in which the U.S. Government assesses there is an ongoing complex humanitarian emergency.

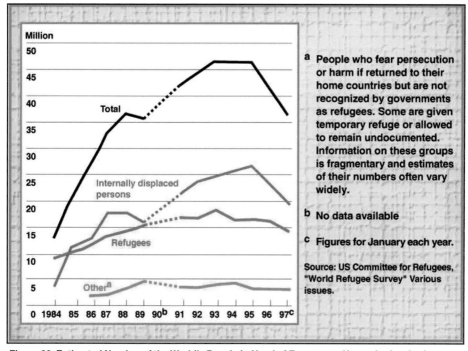

Figure 23. Estimated Number of the World's People in Need of Emergency Humanitarian Assistance, 1984-1997. *source: Central Intelligence Agency.*

International organizations are poorly equipped to handle the victims of these intrastate problems. Their assistance, or intervention, causes the state to assert the prerogatives of sovereignty, limiting the international organizations' capacity to act under international law (Loescher *b:* 141). Taken collectively, the rapid growth of complex humanitarian emergencies has overwhelmed the international community's capability to respond.[487]

While refugee statistics are often a contentious political issue, there is a consensus that the world's refugee population grew rapidly following the end of the Cold War. According to the UNHCR, the number of "persons of concern" to its organization almost doubled during this period.[488]

---

[487] In commenting on the 17 operations the UN was involved in during mid-1994, UN Secretary-General Boutros-Ghali noted the UN was at "system overload." See Hans Binnendijk and Patrick Clawson, eds., *Strategic Assessment 1995: U.S. Security Challenges in Transition* (Washington, DC: Institute for National Strategic Studies, National Defense University, 1995), 164.

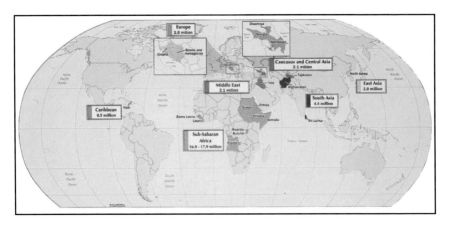

Figure 24. Estimated Number of People in Need by Region *source: Central Intelligence Agency*

Who Is a Refugee?

The difficulty of determining just who is a refugee — and is therefore entitled to protection and assistance under international law — contributes to the international community's dilemma in responding to complex humanitarian emergencies. The most widely accepted definition of a refugee is any person who is outside the country of his nationality . . . because . . . [of a] well-founded fear of persecution by reason of his race, religion, nationality or political opinion (UNHCR *c:* 6, 11).

As a result of intrastate conflict, however, millions of internally displaced persons (IDPs) now find themselves in refugee-like situations without ever having crossed a border. In many cases, the UN has responded by authorizing the UNHCR to assist these IDPs as if they were actually refugees (Boutros-Ghali *c:* 268).

In practice, the lines between refugees, IDPs, and migrants have become increasingly blurred and subject to political manipulation. During the Cold War, Western governments encouraged refugees to flee from repressive regimes because their flight undermined the legitimacy of communist governments. Now, Western governments are tightening their immigration policies and strictly interpreting their obligations to provide asylum to refugees under international law (UNHCR g: 35-37).

---

[488] While most governments and Non-Governmental Organizations (NGOs) accept the UNHCR's refugee statistics as authoritative, UNHCR estimates do not include the vast majority of the internally displaced persons (IDPs) in the world. In 1995, for example, the UNHCR acknowledged there were some 20 million additional IDPs not included in its numbers, placing the total number of people who had fled their homes at almost 50 million. (UNHCR, Brochure, UNHCR by Numbers, January 1995, 2.) A 1996 U.S. Government study reached similar conclusions, noting there were some 16 million refugees and an additional 22-24 million IDPs in the world. U.S. Mission to the UN, Global Humanitarian Emergencies, 1996 (New York: U.S. Mission to the UN, February 1996), 3-4.

This study takes a traditional view of the term refugee (Gorman: 15-20). It considers a **refugee to be any person who has fled persecution or is the victim of forced migration.** This determination facilitates a comparison of UNHCR and U.S. military operations in the field without cluttering the issue with the subtleties of international law. It also recognizes that the distinction between a refugee and an IDP is largely insignificant to an ongoing relief effort because the humanitarian support requirements are the same in either case. Thus, this study uses the term refugee in a much broader sense than most legal definitions of the word.

Refugees, U.S. National Interests, and the Military

Large population movements are inherently destabilizing influences on global and regional security structures. When the populations on the move are refugees, they are also symptomatic of an underlying political crisis that frequently involves U.S. national interests. The U.S. national security strategy implicitly recognizes this connection by stating, "transnational problems . . . like . . . refugee flows . . . have security implications for both present and long term American policy" (U.S. President *b:* 1). While many people view refugee assistance as a humanitarian obligation, the U.S. often has political, economic, or security concerns in a refugee emergency.

Of course population movements have always been a part of the "strategic landscape" (Sarkesian: 549). But the refugee crises of recent years have increasingly involved militaries for two major reasons. First, the suddenness, severity, and frequency of refugee emergencies have strained the international relief community's capability to provide emergency assistance. Militaries have been the only organizations capable of mustering viable relief efforts on short notice. Second, because most refugees are victims of ongoing internal conflicts, there has been a tremendous need for militaries to protect the relief workers laboring in the middle of these wars (Loescher *a:* 363 and McHugh: 10).

U.S. military participation in refugee relief efforts has been widespread. All five of the U.S. unified combatant commands have activated joint task forces (JTFs) to conduct refugee operations in recent years.

U.S. military doctrine classifies these activities as humanitarian assistance operations (U.S. DoD d: III-4). Unfortunately, humanitarian assistance implies tasks as diverse as disaster relief, support to police forces, and fighting forest fires (Siegel: 3-6). In order to compare a group of U.S. military operations with UNHCR activities, it is necessary to define a sub-category of humanitarian assistance as "refugee operations." The distinguishing feature is that a refugee operation has the primary mission of providing assistance to refugees, while other humanitarian assistance operations may treat this objective as an ancillary task.

Procedures for Comparing Intelligence Effectiveness

Having established a common vocabulary for refugees and refugee operations, it is now necessary to describe the nature of the comparison between intelligence in the U.S.

military and the UNHCR. This study begins by establishing the context of intelligence in each organization. It then compares how the UNHCR and the U.S. military conduct the intelligence functions of strategic warning and support to planning and conducting refugee operations.

In making this comparison, this paper examines how each organization intends to conduct intelligence as well as how effectively they have actually conducted intelligence during refugee operations. For the U.S. military, joint doctrine defines the intent, and after-action reviews and press accounts describe what actually happened. Within the UNHCR, the *UNHCR Manual* and an assortment of the organization's internal documents provide the intent, while interviews with UNHCR officials provide a candid assessment of the effectiveness of UNHCR intelligence.

No two refugee operations are the same for the U.S. military or the UNHCR, but general trends are apparent. Each institution has similar intelligence requirements, but organizational culture, intelligence collection methods, and the degree to which intelligence is integrated with operations are among a host of dissimilar features.

INTELLIGENCE IN CONTEXT

We don't call it intelligence, but it's the same thing. We both have a need for accurate and timely information. (Ogata 1996)

Sadako Ogata, High Commissioner for Refugees

Figure 25. Author with UN High Commissioner for Refugees, Sadako Ogata, 1996. *photo used with permission*

People use an intelligence process to analyze information, but many organizations have bureaucratized this concept by assigning intelligence functions to individuals or elements of their organization. The U.S. military has thoroughly bureaucratized the concept of military intelligence by designating personnel, staffs, and even units responsible for collecting and producing intelligence. However, the UNHCR has never really separated its intelligence function from its operational elements. In the UNHCR, even the idea of intelligence is controversial because it connotes activities which an impartial, non-political organization would like to avoid. Nevertheless, the UNHCR needs intelligence for many of the same reasons militaries require intelligence in refugee operations. As Mrs. Ogata indicates, UN organizations frequently cloak their intelligence functions under the euphemism of information.

Information Is Not Intelligence: A U.S. Military View

In joint and service doctrine, the U.S. military considers intelligence to be something much more than just information. Information is raw, uninterpreted data, whereas intelligence is information that has been refined into meaningful knowledge about an area or an adversary. The distinction may not always be clear in practice, but the theoretical separation of intelligence from information is significant because of the value added by analysis.

For example, a story in *Pravda* may contain information of interest to the military. In order for it to become intelligence, however, an analyst must evaluate the story considering a variety of factors, including:

- the paper's editorial bias;
- the motivations and reputation of the author;
- the accuracy of previous stories;
- the possibility of deception (that the author has been duped or deliberately intends to deceive); and
- whether or not the information in the story is consistent with other information available to the analyst.

Based upon this evaluation, the analyst then fuses the information from the story with other available information to form a "product" that meets his consumer's needs.

In comparing these organizations, it is useful to think of intelligence products as the outcome of a process which converts information into intelligence. U.S. military doctrine calls this process the "intelligence cycle," and its most basic functions include collection, analysis, and dissemination. As the next section demonstrates, the UN follows a similar process in its "information" activities.

INTELLIGENCE IN THE UN

According to an authoritative peacekeeper handbook (International Peace Academy *a:* paragraph 140), in UN operations "the use of the word `intelligence' is avoided and 'information' used instead." The reason for this semantic distinction is that the UN's fundamental principles clash with the popular notion of what constitutes intelligence. To most people, intelligence is not just the conversion of "information" into a useful product; rather, intelligence implies clandestine collection techniques, covert operations, and spying on an "enemy" (Hugh Smith: 174). All of these activities are anathema to the UN because it has no enemies and its Charter requires it to respect the sovereignty of member states.

Despite the stigma attached to intelligence, UN leaders have recognized a need for intelligence for decades. Their repeated efforts to create early warning systems to support preventive diplomacy demonstrate this desire. The argument is basically that the UN cannot be effective in maintaining international peace and security — its purpose as stated in the UN Charter — if it does not know when a conflict, famine, or massive refugee flow is likely to occur (Boutros-Ghali *a:* 46-49). The Department of Humanitarian Affairs (DHA) is particularly important to refugee operations because it is responsible for early warning of humanitarian emergencies.

As a semiautonomous UN agency,[489] the UNHCR maintains its own intelligence capability separate from the UN Secretariat. While the bulk of the intelligence work in the UNHCR occurs within the organization's operational elements, the Centre for Documentation and Research (CDR) fulfills a bureaucratic intelligence role. It collects, analyzes, and disseminates "information" on countries where refugees originate (Druke: 186), and it serves as the focal point for UNHCR early warning efforts.

Created in 1986, the CDR originally belonged to the UNHCR's Division of International Protection. The division promotes the UNHCR's traditional mission of "protecting" refugees by promoting international recognition of their legal rights. Consequently, initial CDR databases contained extensive information on refugee law. As the UNHCR has become more heavily involved in international relief efforts, however, the CDR's holdings have expanded to support operational requirements.

A reorganization in January 1996 highlighted the CDR's expanded role by removing the CDR from the Division of International Protection and placing it under the Assistant High Commissioner. This official is the number three position in the UNHCR, and he has responsibility for policy, planning, and operations. As such, he coordinates the activities of the UNHCR's five regional bureaus and its special operations.

INTELLIGENCE IN REFUGEE OPERATIONS

Intelligence requirements vary with each refugee operation, but they generally fall into one of three distinct, chronological groupings. First, intelligence provides the general, background knowledge necessary to interpret a refugee emergency. Then, intelligence performs a warning function, notifying policymakers that a crisis is likely to occur and their organization may need to act. Once a policymaker decides to act, intelligence supports planning processes and field operations. Although these activities frequently overlap in practice, they are conceptually separate.

General Knowledge

General knowledge of an area or situation relevant to a refugee operation includes intelligence on a tremendous variety of topics, including political, societal, economic, environmental, and even military issues. The UNHCR and the U.S. military often have

---

[489] Technically, the UNHCR is a subsidiary organ of the General Assembly. See UN General Assembly Resolution 428(V), 14 December 1950. The UNHCR's autonomy comes from its largely independent sources of funding and from its mandate to be "entirely non-political [in] character." See Yves Beigbeder, The Role and Status of International Humanitarian Volunteers and Organizations: The Right and Duty to Humanitarian Assistance (Dordrecht, Netherlands: Martinus Nijhoff Publishers, 1991), 27.

similar requirements in these areas, and thus, they create many similar intelligence products.

Within the UNHCR, the CDR maintains the organization's general knowledge base. The CDR's databases, known collectively as "REFWORLD,"(for Refugee World) include comprehensive information on a variety of topics related to refugees and countries that are likely to generate them. CDR products turn this information into intelligence by analyzing specific countries, areas, or topics.[490] Detailed analyses are the result of the CDR's Country Information Project (COIP). Begun in 1992, the COIP now includes information on "political, economic, social and legal structures, human rights, cultural and religious norms, minorities, . . . maps and chronologies of relevant events" (Rusu *b:* 2).

Within the U.S. military, a complex array of intelligence organizations have institutional responsibility for providing a similar "base" of knowledge necessary to support refugee operations. The U.S. Army's venerable *Area Handbook* series and the Defense Intelligence Agency's (DIA) Contingency Support Studies are two prime examples of this type of general intelligence (Constantine: 11). The content of these products is somewhat similar to UNHCR products.

General knowledge of an area or situation is the foundation of all intelligence analysis. In the context of refugee operations, it provides the requisite background on a broad variety of topics necessary to warn of an impending crisis and to plan and conduct assistance activities.

Strategic Warning of Refugee Flows

When Rwanda exploded, frankly, we were focused on Bosnia and northern Iraq. (Hayden: 18)

Brigadier General Michael V. Hayden, Intelligence Officer, U.S. European Command

---

We always have warning of refugee emergencies . . . Early warning comes from the field. (Ogata c).

Sadako Ogata, High Commissioner for Refugees

These quotes underline the basic differences between U.S. military and UNHCR concepts of warning in refugee emergencies. The military, with its abundant intelligence resources, is often surprised by refugee crises because of its understandable preoccupation with other issues — namely "enemy" forces. On the other hand, the UNHCR is completely focused on predicting future refugee flows, but it suffers from limited resources, constraints arising from its impartial nature, and an inability to act on the warning in most cases.

---

[490] Many CDR background papers are available on the Internet.

Strategic warning is an intelligence function in both the U.S. military and the UNHCR. Each organization conducts warning activities intended to enable proactive responses to impending refugee crises. However, there are significant differences in the concept of warning and the warning systems found in the U.S. military and the UNHCR. These differences arise from the divergent purposes of each organization. The military exists to fight wars, while the UNHCR is a refugee protection and assistance organization. This section compares the warning systems in the UNHCR and the U.S. military. After first considering the different concepts of warning in each organization, I conclude that the UNHCR's strategic warning is more effective than belated warnings of refugee flows in the U.S. military.

WARNING IS PRIOR KNOWLEDGE OF AN EVENT

There is no universally recognized concept of what constitutes warning of an impending crisis or disaster, but a common definition might be: Warning is knowledge of a future event early enough to allow action to influence events. Within a military context, several respected scholars share a fundamental assumption that the goal of warning is to prevent surprise (Betts: 5; Kam: 22). Within the UN, however, early warning is linked to concepts as diverse as "early notification, urgent action, the good offices of the Secretary-General, crisis control and preventive diplomacy" (Ramcharan: 7-8). In both the U.S. Government and the UN, however, the concepts of warning are inextricably linked to a desire to act to preempt or mitigate a crisis (McCarthy: 5; Dmitrichev: 264).

Warning in the U.S. Military

During most recent refugee operations, the U.S. military has had little warning prior to commencement of its relief efforts.[491] Certainly, the amount of warnings issued to policymakers and the reluctance of the U.S. to act preventively has varied in each instance, but Rwanda represents the worst possible warning failure on the part of the military. The senior military intelligence officer responsible for warning of the crisis admitted his attention was focused on other areas when the crisis erupted (Hayden: 18-19). Furthermore, the commander of the U.S. relief effort noted the difficulty his intelligence staff had "because there was no 'enemy' on which to focus, but rather a "situation"" (USEUCOM *a:* 5). Thus, the military often experiences problems in applying wartime warning techniques to peacetime warning situations.

---

[491] For instance, the U.S. European Command mounted Operation PROVIDE COMFORT-the 1991 mission to assist the Kurds in northern Iraq-less than 24 hours after notification! See U.S. European Command (USEUCOM), Operation PROVIDE COMFORT After-Action Report, 1-4. More recently, in Operation SAFE HAVEN, the commander of the JTF had about 96 hours notice until he was expected to receive and care for 10,000 Haitians. Ultimately, political considerations delayed the JTF's activation and changed the mission from assisting Haitians to Cubans, but there was very little initial warning. James L. Wilson, BG, USA, former commander, JTF SAFE HAVEN, interview by author, 3 April 1996.

Warning in the UNHCR

The UNHCR's warning efforts have the sole purpose of detecting and warning of impending refugee flows, and the UNHCR's recent emphasis on preventive solutions has highlighted the need for more extensive efforts in these areas (UNHCR g: 43). Unfortunately, the UNHCR's mandate poses substantial problems for early warning — problems to which the UNHCR has developed several compromise solutions.

Three characteristics of the UNHCR's mandate reduce the utility of early warning and the UNHCR's capability to provide this warning. First, the UNHCR was originally mandated to act on behalf of refugees already in existence — not potential refugees. Thus, UNHCR warning efforts have little practical effect since the organization is not authorized to take action to avert new refugee flows. Second, all UNHCR actions must have the consent of the government concerned. Because this same government either intends to create the refugee flow or usually does not want to acknowledge its existence, the government generally resents UNHCR warnings (Gordenker: 360). Finally, the UNHCR is limited to "non-political," "humanitarian and social" activities. Strictly interpreted, this constraint restricts explicit warning because the warning itself almost certainly has political implications for the host state (Druke: 181).

Recent changes in the international security environment have demonstrated the inability of traditional solutions to resolve the world's refugee problems (UNHCR *g:* 19-40). By its very nature, prevention requires early warning, and this imperative has caused the UNHCR to intensify its warning efforts during the last five years. There are actually two distinct forms of so-called early warning now used within the UNHCR. The first is a systemic, bureaucratized form of early warning, while the latter involves early notification and emergency preparedness. Each represents a compromise solution to the constraints of the UNHCR's mandate.

The CDR is the focal point for **systemic early warning**, and its early warning systems are intended to identify crises before they occur so that the UNHCR, in cooperation with other UN entities (with appropriate mandates), can take preventive action to avert potential refugee flows. Toward this end, the CDR oversees two "warning systems" — the Country Information Project and the International Refugee Electronic Network (IRENE) (Ruiz: 155) — and it represents the UNHCR at DHA's interagency working group on warning (Dedring: 99).

These warning systems do not produce formal warning products, however, and the High Commissioner relies on early warning from the UNHCR's field offices. Privately, UNHCR officials comment they never receive early warning from DHA because it has no field presence. In fact, DHA relies on UNHCR reports for warning of refugee movements. Mrs. Ogata's comment that early warning comes from the field indicates a second type of UNHCR warning activity which is similar to **early notification**. Early notification does not predict a potential refugee flow; rather, it provides the earliest possible report that a refugee flow has already begun and is likely to escalate into a crisis.

Early notification allows the operational elements of the UNHCR to prepare for a potential emergency. One senior UNHCR official indicated that operational elements of the UNHCR develop their own, informal "early warnings" of impending crises using a variety of information sources that they monitor themselves. In this case, the purpose of early warning is to ensure the UNHCR's emergency response capability is prepared to meet the eventuality of a refugee emergency. Mr. Bernard Doyle of UNHCR likened the UNHCR's mission to that of an ambulance driver. The ambulance driver cannot prevent an accident from occurring, but he can anticipate the conditions (such as a snowstorm) under which accidents are likely to occur and plan accordingly.

Thus, early warning within the UNHCR means different things to different people. There is considerable institutional skepticism over the value of early warning, in its purest form, because of the UNHCR's inability to take preventive action in most situations. Operational elements of the UNHCR consider early warning to be linked to emergency preparedness, and Mrs. Ogata considers most early warning to be early notification. The CDR has institutional responsibility for coordinating early warning efforts with DHA and for overseeing the UNHCR's warning systems, and it is these warning systems which will be considered next.

The UNHCR's warning "systems" do not produce warning messages per se. Rather, they share information and intelligence that can be useful throughout the UNHCR and the international relief community (Ruiz: 155). While the UNHCR considers IRENE and the COIP to be warning systems, they really represent a communications system and a database that can support other early warning efforts.

IRENE. IRENE is a system of electronic bulletin boards that allows refugee agencies around the world to exchange information using electronic mail. It evolved from a project known as the International Refugee Documentation Network (IRDN) which originated following a 1986 conference attended by 25 different relief agencies. Conference participants recommended the UNHCR administer the IRDN, and in June 1987, the High Commissioner agreed to assume a "coordinating function" for the project (IRDN *b:* 10). Unfortunately, IRENE "suffers considerably from lack of participation by other IRDN members" (IRDN *a:* 6).

COIP. The COIP is really just a database with a modicum of intelligence analysis. According to the CDR, the COIP acts as the principal resource within the UNHCR for the provision of "relevant, credible, reliable, and current" information, including political, economic, social and legal structures, and human rights, in likely refugee producing or receiving countries (Ruiz: 155).

The COIP supports early warning efforts solely by making information and intelligence available to a wide variety of users throughout the UNHCR and the international relief community. Neither IRENE nor the COIP routinely produce warning products that are publicly available. However, the intent is eventually to produce warning reports for UN and UNHCR decisionmakers.

HEWS. The UN Department of Humanitarian Affairs does operate a Humanitarian Early Warning System (HEWS) which issues warning messages derived from an indicator-based methodology, but it is still not effective at forecasting future refugee flows. HEWS has never provided the High Commissioner with early warning (Ogata *c*), and HEWS actually relies on the UNHCR to provide most of its data on population movements through interagency coordination meetings. The fact that this working group has not met since May 1995 is symptomatic of how poorly this coordination process actually works.

Other problems which hinder UNHCR warning efforts — such as collecting, transmitting, and analyzing warning information — are related to the UNHCR's need to maintain its impartiality. For example, the UNHCR relies on its field offices in over 100 countries to report information on the situation in these areas, but it has traditionally discouraged its field personnel from attaching analytical comments to these reports. Lack of secure communications channels makes these reports subject to compromise, and any public disclosure of "confidential" information reported by UNHCR field offices could subject the UNHCR to criticism by the local government (Druke: 181).

Thus, although the CDR does receive "confidential" information from the field, the bulk of the useable data assembled under the COIP comes from public sources. Hans Thoolen, a former CDR director, explained the problem this way.

A UNHCR protection officer in Sri Lanka sends in a report on the latest human rights and protection issues in Jaffna. The same day, both the Sri Lanka Monitor and the International Herald Tribune carry a story with precisely the same information. What to do? One is private, the other public. The former, if made public, could be mistaken for UNHCR's own assessment and could provoke immediate diplomatic, if not substantive, challenge. The latter, originating from the public domain, is immediately useable and can withstand challenge due, not so much because of what it is, but how it has been classified. So it is that public information takes on greater weight and authority simply because it can be verified, while the private report, though in the public domain, can be used solely in a controlled context, "for your eyes only" (Rusu *a:* 6).

For these reasons, the CDR's COIP relies almost exclusively on publicly available information obtained from a variety of NGOs, the media, governmental agencies, academics, and other sources. Unfortunately, the necessity of using public information creates its own analytical problems of bias and information overload (Thoolen: 170-175).

INTELLIGENCE SUPPORT TO PLANNING AND CONDUCTING REFUGEE OPERATIONS

Information is not the problem; the problem is analysis.

Senior Emergency Preparedness and Response Officer, UNHCR

The information required to produce intelligence for planning refugee operations is readily available to anyone who has access to a refugee crisis area. Because of its limited access and organizational culture, however, the U.S. military tends to use its traditional, "high-tech" collection assets to gather this information, while the UNHCR often assembles similar data through less costly and more effective use of its field offices.

This section examines the intelligence requirements common to both UNHCR and U.S. military planning and execution of refugee operations.

Both the U.S. military and the UNHCR plan and conduct refugee operations using a form of management by objective (U.S. DoD c; UNHCR *j:* 4/3.2). Intelligence contributes to these efforts by providing the "situational awareness" necessary for planning. The U.S. military product containing this awareness is an intelligence estimate, while the UNHCR dubs it a needs and resources assessment (UNHCR *e:* 16).

Once a refugee operation is underway, intelligence supports the operation by monitoring the general situation in the crisis area and by assessing potential threats to relief providers. The U.S. military calls this latter intelligence function "force protection," (U.S. DoD *a:* III-5) while the UNHCR dubs it "safety and security."

Because intelligence supports similar planning and operational efforts in each organization, the UNHCR and the U.S. military share many similar intelligence requirements. Typical requirements found in both U.S. military and UNHCR publications include:

- political, economic, and social data
- details about the refugees themselves
- specific needs (food, water, shelter, medical)
- cultural and demographic considerations
- future intentions
- maps and physical characteristics of the crisis area
- infrastructure and resources in the host country
- major relief organizations in the crisis area
- threats to relief personnel from
- hostile armed forces
- criminals
- land mines
- civic violence
- health risks (USMC: 159-164; UNHCR *e:*16-19; UNHCR *i:* 4/3-4).

Although they have many similar intelligence requirements, the UNHCR and the U.S. military collect, analyze, and disseminate this intelligence in decidedly different fashions.

UNHCR INTELLIGENCE IN REFUGEE OPERATIONS

While the CDR serves as the UNHCR's institutional intelligence shop, its support to planning and operations is minimal. Executives in the UNHCR's "operational" sections — such as the regional bureaus, its specialoperations/units, and the emergency preparedness and response section — each produce their own intelligence. To do so, they rely heavily on reports which originate from UNHCR field offices, the media, and other UN organizations and NGOs with a presence in the crisis area. Field offices have the primary responsibility for collecting, analyzing, and reporting intelligence to UNHCR headquarters. Then, personnel in the regional bureaus further analyze the intelligence, passing it on to the policy level within the UNHCR as they deem appropriate.

Needs Assessments and Intelligence Reporting

In responding to a refugee crisis, the UNHCR immediately conducts a needs and resources assessment. The country overview is of particular interest from an intelligence perspective. Intelligence topics include summaries of:

information on the general political, economic and social situation in the country . . . [and] major changes reflected in [refugee statistics], with any additional information, as relevant, on gender breakdown, vulnerable cases, sources of information, variances between UNHCR and official figures, group, or individual determination (UNHCR *k:* 1993).

Figure 26. Unsettled scene in Srebrenica, Yugoslavia, 1993. •*photo used with permission*

Principal sources of information are:

- Refugees themselves
- NGOs in the crisis area
- Host Nation governments
- Regional and international organizations
- Other UN organizations with a field presence
- Local media (UNHCR *f:* 215, 225).

NGOs are often the most critical source of information because they generally have broad access to the crisis area. Unfortunately, the NGOs' need to negotiate for access may influence their ability to speak frankly about conditions (DeMars: 395).

Security and Safety

Security has become a major issue for UNHCR field personnel as the world's refugee crises increasingly occur in the midst of violent ethnic and civil conflicts. In 1993 and 1994, 11 UNHCR and other humanitarian staff lost their lives in the field, and although this number represents a smaller fatality rate than that for peacekeeping forces overall, it underscores the need for better tactical intelligence (Ogata *b:* 124; Boutros-Ghali *c:* 161; Browne *b:* 8). In response, the UNHCR has increased security training, added security specialists to UNHCR field missions, and formalized the security responsibility of its relief team leaders (UNHCR *d:* 7-8). However, the UNHCR is still not particularly efficient at assessing threats to its personnel in the field.

Because of its humanitarian nature, the UNHCR finds collection and interpretation of tactical intelligence very difficult. This has led the UNHCR to rely — to some extent — on UN peacekeeping forces in a crisis area. A recent UNHCR training document noted:

Equally important is the use of military information [intelligence]. Commanders and heads of humanitarian missions alike require military information for the purpose of executing tasks in the conflict environment. The collection, collation and dissemination of military information is a skill that UNHCR staff members will most certainly lack . . . The collection and use of military information is obviously a matter of great sensitivity. The parties to the conflict will doubt the neutrality of any party which is in contact with their opponents, especially where the neutral party shows an interest in military matters (UNHCR *h:* 29; UNHCR *a:*36).

Thus, the UNHCR excels at assessing the situation in a refugee crisis based largely on open sources of information, but it has great difficulty in assessing military-style threats which often require secretive methods of intelligence collection. The U.S. military, not surprisingly, has exactly the opposite problem.

INTELLIGENCE IN U.S. MILITARY REFUGEE OPERATIONS

U.S. military intelligence personnel excel at determining traditional "threats" to military forces, but their collection systems are not designed to capture the types of "situational" information necessary to support relief operations. This limitation is greatest during the planning phase of an operation because the military often lacks access to first-hand information on the crisis area, but it continues throughout the operation as the military struggles to assess a refugee situation in which there is no enemy. In cases where there is a hostile threat, however, intelligence personnel can provide useful information for force protection.

These themes were abundantly clear in the 1994 U.S. relief effort in support of Rwandan refugees. In his after-action review, the commander of JTF SUPPORT HOPE noted:

Our intelligence systems initially had some difficulty readjusting from high-tech to low-tech requirements. Their task was made all the more difficult because there was no "enemy" on which to focus, but rather a "situation" with many low-tech angles that had to be developed. My contacts with the UN/NGO community, subordinate commanders, UNAMIR [UN Assistance Mission for Rwanda] and my ability to move around the widely-dispersed RCA [Rwanda Crisis Area] gave me a wide cross-perspective on the true nature of the situation in our area of responsibility that was unavailable to anyone else (USEUCOM *a:* 5).

Similar problems have occurred in other U.S. refugee operations even when there was an extremely permissive environment for intelligence collection. During Operation SAFE HAVEN, for instance, the intelligence staff focused overwhelmingly on its human intelligence collectors while paying minimal attention to other individuals in regular contact with the refugees (Wilson).

Reconnaissance and Planning

Most refugee operations require the military to activate a JTF, which rapidly deploys into a crisis area. JTF activation and deployment are usually concurrent with operational or contingency planning. This leaves little time for reconnaissance, and the intelligence staff frequently lacks the detailed knowledge of the situation required to support deliberate planning. In the case of Rwanda, the senior intelligence officer in USEUCOM noted: "By the time it had become clear that we were to deploy forces to central Africa, we were forced to run very hard to build the needed database" (Hayden: 19).

Imagery and signals intelligence collectors were designed to detect Cold War military forces. They are not well suited to many subtle intelligence requirements. For example, the after-action report for Operation PROVIDE COMFORT noted, "HUMINT [human source intelligence] collection used with tactical reconnaissance produced the key intelligence necessary for operations and security" (USEUCOM *b:* 12).

While human intelligence is ideally suited to collect on non-traditional intelligence requirements, the military's initial lack of access to the crisis area makes collection very difficult. The Defense Attache system offers a limited capability for overt collection, but any new human collection requires extensive amounts of time — to develop sources — that simply does not exist in a crisis scenario (Pelletiere: 11-12).

Force Protection and Intelligence Reporting

Unlike the UNHCR — where a capability to report intelligence information already exists in the crisis area — the U.S. military builds an intelligence architecture to support a new refugee operation. Thus, intelligence reporting from the crisis area tends to begin later and be less incisive than similar reporting by the UNHCR. Analytical reporting is typically called an intelligence summary (INTSUM) or an intelligence report (INTREP), but the formats of these reports vary widely in practice.

Because of the natural inclination for military intelligence personnel to focus on enemy "threats," INTSUMs and INTREPs are dominated by force protection — rather than situational awareness — reporting. In an environment where there is an ongoing or latent conflict, this is certainly appropriate, but these reports do not provide the JTF commander the intelligence necessaryto assess the effectiveness of his relief operations (Wilson). In Rwanda, the JTF commander partially remedied this shortcoming by visiting UN organizations and NGOs (USEUCOM *a:* 5).

In most recent refugee operations, U.S. military commanders have used Civil Military Operations Centers (CMOC) to facilitate information exchange and unity of effort with UN organizations and NGOs. The CMOC holds tremendous potential to provide this situational awareness — or intelligence — to the JTF through a free and frank exchange of "information" with non-military organizations (Wallace: 36-41; U.S. DoD *g:* IV-4 to IV-7).

SUMMARY

As complex humanitarian emergencies proliferate around the world, the global refugee population will probably continue to increase. Simultaneously, traditional countries of asylum, like the U.S., will continue to tighten their immigration policies, interpreting the status of refugees more narrowly. These trends will make strategic warning of refugee flows more important, and they will require intelligence to plan and conduct refugee operations.

Both the UNHCR and the U.S. military collect, analyze, and disseminate intelligence, but the UNHCR has not bureaucratized intelligence to the extent the U.S. military has. In some ways, the comparison of intelligence in the UNHCR and the U.S. military is artificial because neither organization operates in a vacuum and because each organization has different objectives. Nevertheless, the U.S. military and the UNHCR each have a need for strategic warning of refugee emergencies and a need for intelligence to plan and conduct operations.

In the case of strategic warning, the UNHCR is clearly more effective. The UNHCR lacks the capacity to act unilaterally to prevent refugee flows, but it does use early warning to prepare its emergency response personnel and field offices for impending crises. Thus, while there can never be a warning "success" in the sense that U.S. government agencies define the term, early warning allows the UNHCR to respond rapidly to a crisis. Conversely, the U.S. military is often surprised by refugee crises, creating JTFs to conduct refugee operations in a purely reactive manner.

In planning and conducting refugee operations, the effectiveness of intelligence in the U.S. military and the UNHCR is mixed. Because of its earlier warning and access to the crisis area, the UNHCR typically is more effective at planning refugee assistance. However, the UNHCR lacks the capability to conduct military style "force protection" intelligence during a refugee operation, sometimes even relying on militaries to fill this void.

INTELLIGENCE LESSONS FOR FUTURE REFUGEE OPERATIONS

While the UNHCR is not perfect in conducting intelligence activities, the U.S. military can draw some important lessons from the UNHCR's wealth of experience. These include:

1) The best sources of information on an emerging refugee crisis will be the NGOs and other organizations with a presence on the ground. From an economic perspective, these sources are also much more effective than using expensive technical collection assets to obtain information that is already publicly available. Honest and open communication is the key to tapping this resource. Immediately after receiving warning of a refugee emergency, JTF intelligence personnel should conduct liaison with NGOs either using commercial telecommunications equipment or through on-line services. Once the relief force enters the crisis area, the Civil Military Operations Center may prove an excellent place for this liaison to continue to occur.

2) Information is abundant, but analysis (the conversion of relevant information into intelligence) is the problem. Determining the accuracy and biases of major NGOs involved in reporting information on refugees is essential.

3) Force protection will remain an issue, particularly in unstable security environments, but an infatuation with "threats" should not inhibit the intelligence staff's capability to monitor other aspects of the situation. These include political, economic, demographic, and societal factors which affect the overall success of the refugee operation.

4) Clandestine human intelligence is unlikely to be useful because there will be insufficient time to make it operational and because it undermines the humanitarian nature of the operation.

5) Unclassified intelligence products are imperative. In a complex humanitarian emergency, the U.S. military must coordinate with an extensive array of international actors who will need access to U.S. intelligence. Sensitive information should be handled with discretion instead of classification.

6) Military leaders must understand the culture and objectives of other organizations involved in the relief effort. Many NGOs are as suspicious of the UNHCR — and each other — as they are of militaries. It is unrealistic to expect the UNHCR, or any other single organization, to be able to thoroughly coordinate all efforts of the entire range of actors in a refugee operation.

RELIGION AND WAR IN THE 21ST CENTURY

Pauletta Otis

(Originally published as a chapter in Religion: The Missing Dimension of Security, Rowman and Littlefield, 2004.)

The 21st Century will be a time of religious violence and warfare. As religious zealots and opportunists use the power inherent in religious ideology and escalate the forms, levels, and types of violence, there is potential for devastation and destruction unknown in human history.

Although religion has long been a contributing factor in all warfare, providing the parameters of *jus bello* and *jus en bello,* it is emerging (or re-emerging) as the single most important political — ideological default mechanism in global conflict. Yet, the Western world seems reluctant to address this reality. Some scholars maintain that the Western world has been self-blinded to the reality of global religious issues clinging to an illusionary vision of a "secular" state and thereby unable to provide a full explanation of contemporary warfare. Conversely, others contend that the Western world is only too aware of history and shudders at the tragic mistakes of past generations.

Leaders from each major religious tradition vigorously reiterate that the purpose of religion is love and peace, not killing. Nevertheless, each and every religion is, in fact, an ideology that provides comprehensive ideals for life and principles that govern **both** life and death. This is a universal premise that includes all religions in all times and in all places. No longer can any faith-based community afford to compartmentalize its thinking about religion and conflict but must seek sound principles based in systematic investigation and spiritual awareness.

"A man with an idea is more powerful than 100 men with interests," according to John Locke, but when ideas and interests combine, the chemistry may be lethal. The combination of religious ideology and group interests are becoming an increasingly potent force in Africa, Asia, the Middle East, and even the Americas. As the world's hegemonic power, the United States has been involved in these conflicts most notably in the Balkans, Somalia, Afghanistan, and Iraq. In each of these cases, religious factors were a significant part of the enemy's motivation, intent, capabilities, and goals. In addition, global terrorism is increasingly characterized by violence perpetuated by individuals and small groups, with religious motivation, using non-conventional weapons, choosing symbolic targets, and judging success by obedience to God.[492]

As groups fight each other and the US becomes increasingly engaged on a global scale, a grim picture emerges of the largely conventional forces of the single world

---

[492] Douglas Johnston, in *Religion: the Missing Dimension of Statecraft* (Oxford University Press, 1994) and *Faith-Based Diplomacy: Trumping Realpolitik* (Oxford University Press, 2002), makes the point that the religious factor is regularly overlooked in the analysis of both war-making and peace-making.

hegemonic power fighting various groups of global religious *mujahadeen* in asymmetrical wars where the stakes include economic, political, and cultural power. It would be too simple to resign world events to the inevitability of "doom and gloom." It takes courage and commitment to search for balance and perspective that is based in the faith aspect of belief systems. We are in a global competition for "hearts and mind" — our own and those of our "enemy.

In spite of the immediacy of this requirement, both the U.S. government and the faith-based community address religious factors in conflict, war, and terrorism in an *ad hoc*, haphazard, and superficial way. Although numbers of conferences have been held and experts (and 'instant experts') engaged, the level of integrated knowledge and wisdom reflect the marginalized nature accorded to cultural and religion. Given the increasing visibility and seeming importance of religious factors in contemporary conflict situations, this is no longer a preferred or viable option.

No one would seriously suggest that religion is the only explanatory factor in explaining warfare: Religion relates and overlaps other explanatory variables — specifically economic and political factors. But, whether religion is treated as causal in ideological explanations, or as a contributing factor to other variables, it is an integral piece of the security puzzle and as such, deserves focused attention.

WHY HAS THE UNITED STATES NEGLECTED "RELIGION" AS A SPECIALIZED TOPIC IN SECURITY ANALYSIS?

There has been a traditional reluctance on the part of the people of the United States to address religion in relationship to U.S. national security. There are four major reasons: (1) a preference for a "wall of separation," (2) traditional· "realpolitik" analysis, and (3) the inherent level of risk in the topic makes it avoided by risk-adverse or seemingly rigid institutions, and (4) the potential for political backfire given the sensitivities and sensibilities of the American public. [493]

The first reason is fundamental: in the United States, there has been a tradition in support for a "wall of separation" between religion and politics. There are several reasons: The traditional separation of state and church in the U.S. government, albeit not strictly a Constitutional wall, has worked very well for the United States.[494] Throughout U.S. history, the combination of religion and warfare have had frightening overtones. The framers of the Constitution, well versed in European history, were only too aware of the potential for conflict and chaos. Throughout the history of the United States, religious issues and potential conflict situations, even those apparent during the Civil War and Spanish Ameri-

---

[493] In his recent volume, *Terror in the Mind of God: the Global Rise of Religious Violence*, Mark Juergensmeyer provides information and analysis of six terrorist groups. His work provides clear evidence of both the global nature of the violence and the fact that all major "global" religions are somehow implicated.

[494] There is a rich political and historical literature available on this topic. See Julia Mitchell Corbett's *Religion in America* (Prentice Hall, 1990), which provides a nice overview or Franklin Gamwell's *The Meaning of Religious Freedom* (State University Press of New York, 1995), that gives a more theoretical perspective.

can War, were treated rather circumspectly. There seemed to be both an acknowledgement that the United States had "Christian" culture and values, but that institutionalized "Church-State" relationships were inherently problematic. The world's experiences in the 20th century also weigh heavily on this topic. In World War I and World War II, there was an unsavory connection between religion and national fascism. The ugly reality was that religion, this case, the Christian religion, was used for demonic purposes. Religion, albeit universally found as part of culture and society, became to be seen as dangerous when linked to politics (or war) in any way. "Religion," however defined, became suspect and the rules regarding the separation of church and state, somewhat convoluted (or at least confusing).[495]

Secondly, the theoretical approach used by Cold War military analysts was generally that of "realpolitik." It was assumed that ideology such as communism merely masked the reality of state power of countries such as the Soviet Union or China. The study of war became the study of balance of power — replacing an early emphasis on the role of ideas, or ideology, with behavioral analysis and quantification of military power. Security analysts typically measured war-making capabilities on the basis of things that are "countable" — bottom line — weapons systems and uniformed military. Although there were always those who included "strength and will," the scales balanced towards quantification of power.

In the past twenty years, the quest for "security" has replaced war aims resulting in a more nuanced approach to international power. National security is now seen as a complex arrangement of political, economic, social, and military factors. U.S. military power is hegemonic but it is recognized that even overwhelming military power can accomplish only limited security objectives. The nature of "the enemy" in warfare terms, has changed. Along with that change, the nature of the conflict is understood differently. It is no longer conventional force-on-force, but low intensity conflict, asymmetric warfare, and urban warfare. The frame of reference is less about "victory" and more about "prevailing" in a globalized competitive environment.[496]

Thirdly, religion is a delicate and difficult subject. Knowing what the U.S. needs to know and why, takes expertise, balance, attitude, and mature judgment. There is a significant risk of misusing religious information and a significant risk of neglecting religious information. There is a valid perception that religious information could be used in a cynical manipulation of critical human values. There is a related concern: individuals within

---

[495] The United States became a country subsequent to the viscous religious-political European wars of the 17th century. As a result, the Framers of the U.S. Constitution, historically aware and uncommonly prescient, set out new guidelines for the relationship between church and state-commonly referenced as the Establishment Clause and Free Exercise Clause in the First Amendment. The country continues to struggle with the various ramifications of this arrangement and continues to use the courts as a virtual battleground.

[496] An illustration of this concerns the rules that apply to military chaplains. Chaplains are in the uniform of their country and are therefore political "targets," but because they also wear religious insignia in relationship to a religious institution, they are specifically precluded from participating in combat. Chaplains, by law, have two conflicting identities and roles.

the U.S. government have personal and private religious preferences. It is assumed, that given the power of religious belief, personal agendas might interfere with the task at hand and thereby corrupt or misuse information. There is a contention that finding the 'right' people who are balanced, informed, with integrity and evenhandedness would be difficult if not impossible.[497]

The fourth reason that the U.S. government has been reluctant to take on religious issues is the basic sensitivity of religious matters where they overlap politics. There is a wide divergence of views within the United States as to the role of religion, politics, and warfare and anyone taking a visible or strong stand is risking political or professional suicide. There is also a divergence of views in the rest of the world about what U.S. or international military forces "should" and "should not" take on with the use of force. There are some who contend that that the U.S. should take on injustice whenever and wherever it is found — environmental warfare, all systematic abuses of human rights, preemptive strikes against "rogue" states, and elimination of tyrants. Others argue that U.S. military force should be used only in defense of territorial borders. To find anything resembling agreement on engaging in conflict that has a religious component would be ephemeral.

There is a tendency to over-attribution i.e. the tendency to attribute all hostility to the theology, practice, or even cooptation of a major religion.[498] The singular focus on theology has tended to blind many to the complex relationships between religion, culture, politics, and war in global conflict environments: Aum Shinrikyo is found in Australia, New Zealand, and Japan where there is a great divergence in political, cultural, and economic factors. Likewise, these factors are found in different configurations for Akali Dal in India, the Christian militia in the U.S., a new and virulent form of Hindu nationalism in India, Hezbollah and Hamas in the eastern Mediterranean, and millenarian movements throughout Africa and the Pacific. The range of diversity and complexity seems overwhelming. All religions provide reason for living and dying within their respective theologies. How this is applied varies in specific contextual arrangements. The cultural application of religious principles seems to indicate more about violence than basic theology. [499]

Even with these explanations and cautionary notes, the United States is now a mature hegemonic power so it is important to "take the risk" in a self-conscious and systematic manner. The Christian community has no alternative but to think these things through very carefully and understand and hold to basic faith systems, but interpret behaviors in their social, economic, and political context before making spurious judgments.

---

[497] See Barry Buzan, Ole Waever, and Jaap de Wilde's sophisticated treatment of this subject in *Security: a New Framework for Analysis*, published in 1998 by Lynne Rienner.

[498] This does NOT imply that individuals "give up" their own deeply held religious convictions to be of value to U.S. security. It DOES mean that balance, integrity, and objectivity are guiding principles.

[499] For example, violence is assumed to be intrinsic to the theology, practice, and even cooptation of Islam. This basically negates the truth that over 1 billion people are at least nominally Islamic and only a few are also terrorists. It also is in denial of the fact that the major religious wars of history have occurred in the Christian countries of Western Europe.

SECURITY AND "RELIGIOUS CONFLICT"

The traditional U.S. reticence notwithstanding, the country is now a mature hegemonic power and faced with a world that seems increasingly plagued with religious conflict. Religion has emerged, or re-emerged, as a central causal factor in war. It is therefore important to "take the risk" in a self-conscious and systematic manner. The foreign policy and faith communities have no alternative but to think these things through carefully (separately and together). Religious beliefs and behaviors must be seen in their social, economic, and political context before making premature or spurious judgments. If faith leaders and security professionals intent to contribute meaningfully to a positive nexus between religion and security, they must first understand the ways in which many contemporary global conflicts are — and are not — religious.

It is apparent that religion plays a critical role in human security, both in preventing and provoking various forms of conflict — from convention state-state warfare to unconventional forms of political violence carried out by individuals or groups. It is generally acknowledged that: [500]

- Religion is present in all conflict — as it concerns life and death — just war and justice in war
- Religious conflicts tend to have higher levels of intensity, severity, brutality, and lethality than other forms of war
- Wars are longer in duration when religion is a major factor
- Over half of all contemporary conflicts have a significant religious dimension
- Religious leaders emerge as primary authority figures under conditions of state failure
- Religious factors are invariably related to ethnic group identity, language, territory, politics, and economics
- Religious factors are an essential component of effective conflict management and resolution

Currently, religious factors play a role in conflicts on all continents and between all major religions.[501] The Hindu and Muslim strains are apparent in Gujurat. The Shia-Sunni divisions continue to factor in the Iraq conflict. The Lord's Resistance Army in Uganda pits Christians against Christians. In Sudan, the Muslims are said to repress and enslave Christians and animists. In Nigeria, the many ethnic groups have gradually polarized and re-defined the ethnic-tribal conflict as basically religious. The Aum Shinrikyo in Japan, associated with Buddhism, was responsible for the use of chemical weapons in a terrorist

---

[500] These statements represent the author's conclusions and are drawn from a number of different research agendas that include religious, military, historical, and political sources.

[501] There is a paucity of good research data and analysis possibly because scholars tend not to agree on how to define and tabulate statistics on (a) when religion is the primary factor, and/ or (2) when religion plays a role in the escalation and maintenance of conflict. Current research tends to be politically or religiously motivated, thus inherently biased.

attack in a Tokyo subway and continues to be of concern in Australia and New Zealand. The conflict between Israel and Palestine is often held to be a religiously complicated war between Jews and Muslims; Lebanon pits groups identified as religious — Druze, Maronite, Catholic, and Shi'a. In Eastern Europe, various Christian groups, Orthodox, Catholic, Protestant, have evidenced levels of hatred and hostility not seen since the seventeenth century. [502]

Why now? Religion as a critical dimension 21st century warfare is a result of at least three principle factors: (1) the seeming failure of other ideologies and institutions, (2) the power of religion as ideology supporting social justice, and (3) the power of religion in society providing an ideological basis for social coherence and comprehensiveness.

In the 20th century, as the world's problems became more complex and more visible, the solutions available in the ideologies and corresponding programs of Marxism, Communism, Fascism, Nationalism, and Materialism became less able to explain injustice or provide programs to ameliorate suffering. Even capitalism and democracy have had significant problems in explaining the ideal and the reality to peoples of the so-called Third World. Democracy has succeeded in some places; failed in others. The important point is that much of the world believes that democracy will not work *for them.* They believe it works only in the Western context and then is dependent on exploitative world capitalism. More sophisticated analysts also maintain that democracy (even a Constitutional democracy), is the rule of the majority, and consequently not "moral and ethical." They contend that only the guidance and rules provided by a Supreme Being should guide the affairs of man. The Western, Christian world understands this argument only too well.

No one can disagree with the fact that the world remains horribly divided between rich and poor, haves and have-nots. The competing ideologies of the 20th century that promised hope and a quick fix failed much of the world's population. Few who believe in a Supreme Being would disagree that it was meant to be that way hence the entrance of religion as "default" ideology.

As human attempts are deemed inadequate, recourse to the supernatural power of a Supreme Being seems to be the only available strategy to ensure both temporal and spiritual security. Religion provides both rationale and modality for fighting against injustice and provides hope when all else has been "tried and failed." This is more than a passive default mechanism; religion is reemerging in a new, invigorated, and powerful force in global politics.[503]

Religion is an integrated, systematized set of beliefs, behaviors, values, institutions, modes of communication, and leadership. It institutionalizes transcendency and provides

---

[502] See Jonathan Fox's *Ethnoreligious Conflict in the Late Twentieth Century* (Lexington Books, 2002) or his "Do Religious Institutions Support Violence or the Status Quo?" *Studies in Conflict and Terrorism* 22, no. 2 (1999): 119-139.

[503] In *Ambivalence of the Sacred: Religion, Violence, and Reconciliation* (Lanham, MD: Rowman and Littlefield, 2000), Scott R. Appleby coherently and cogently describes religious "power" to be both a factor in violence and in peace-making.

preferred patterns of behavior for human beings in relationship both to a supernatural power and fellow humans. It is both an ideology and a set of appropriate and preferred behaviors reflective of that ideology.

Religion as ideology is derived from an external framework that links individuals to the greater whole and provides formal institutions that help define and organize that whole. It provides a meaningful worldview as well as the rules and standards of behavior that connect individual actions and goals to the worldview. It has the ability to legitimize actions and institutions.

Religion as the codification of individual and group behaviors mirroring religious ideology(s) was institutionalized in Europe during the first century. The church had responsibility for both secular and spiritual realms; religion was the central ordering social device and authority came solely from the church. This was challenged during the Reformation period and the world saw the emergence of the sovereign State. State authority became "official" at the Treaty of Westphalia, 1648. The Church and the State were to share power.[504]

The power of the state limited the authority of religious institutions; prerogatives of the Church were limited by the State. This empowered both while keeping some of their respective, and perhaps negative, aspects at bay. The division of power and authority was codified in legal codes and constitutions that reflected a deep fear of the unlimited power of either. The Western world tried to impose this arrangement on the rest of the world in the form of the "secular state" with mixed success. In Europe and the Americas where it seemed more durable, this arrangement is now undergoing significant challenge as a result of globalization. In other regions, religion and politics had never been really separated. Colonialism and nationalism, to this way of thinking, failed in large part because the Western world did not understand that reality.

Even the scholarly assumptions of the "major powers" concerning the centrality of the state and monopoly control over the use of force, are undergoing significant challenge. There are political challenges emanating from the human rights and environmental communities and challenges to military hegemony from both private military enterprises and global terrorists. The power generally attributed to states, has been undermined and redistributed in terms of economic, political, social-cultural, and military power(s) thereby redefining and enlarging the definition of international security.

Economic, social, and political viability is now dependent on international agreements that go beyond state borders variously connecting individuals, economies, and societies in networks of complex relationships. Another significant challenge to the state system is the contemporary acknowledgement that in some areas, neither the idea nor the reality of the modern state took shape, and in others, the state has "fragmented" or "failed" because it was not compatible with political-economic-social-religious reality.

---

[504] See John D. Carlson and Erik C. Owens, *The Sacred and the Sovereign* (Washington, DC: Georgetown University Press, 2003)

Religion has effectively filled a void and united populations of several states, over state territorial boundaries, and provided social cohesiveness not explainable by any other factor. The emerging cultural fault lines have clear religious boundaries. (Both Samuel Huntington and Robert Kaplan were correct i.e. *global ideas and identities have emerged at the same time as fragmented political-security systems.*)

For the United States, the writing is on the wall: the U.S., although commonly acknowledged as "the world's dominant superpower," may be hegemonic only in terms of sheer catastrophic military capabilities. Human security and state power have been redefined in the new global environment.[505]

As religion, as a social institution has become more important, it has also become less "institutionalized. Decision-making authority is now devolving to the individual or small group. Individuals and groups contest the role of formal religion in favor of a more "democratic" religion. In this context, the individual is directly responsible to God rather than "man-made" traditional institutions. Individual transcendence and responsibility takes the place of group worship and community involvement. Individuals are no longer responsible to a traditional church (mosque, synagogue, temple, church) but encouraged to think and behave for themselves. This is a global phenomenon and examples abound in Africa, North and South America, Europe, South Asia, and the Middle East. The rules that govern warfare, although based in theological *premii* and codified over centuries, are now challenged by individuals who see themselves responsible only to God. [506]

At the same time that the state lost centrality due to globalization of economics, politics, and social factors, both the state and institutionalized religion lost authority and legitimacy in the eyes of the world because they were not able to solve problems of social and economic justice, and individuals and groups on all continents and in all social stratum began constructing a new world religion(s) based on the relationship between a transcendent being and themselves — bypassing or redefining traditional forms of state/ church authority. The new reality is the emergence of particularistic *do-it-yourself religion(s)*, where individuals see themselves as responsible only to God and use a peculiar form of logic to perpetuate violence in order to fulfill what they believe is God's will. Thus, the structure of violence and warfare in the modern world is not that of state against state: rather, it is violence perpetuated by individuals on the global stage in pursuit of transcendent goals — albeit by earthly means.[507]

As Mark Juergensmeyer points out in his book, *Terror in the Mind of God*, the religious terrorist believes that there is a grave social injustice that offends God, that there is

---

[505] The Commission on Human Security (UNHCR, 2003) has published an important global overview of "human" security. The authors take a "human" security approach defining security in terms of people, rather than states. The assumption is that "human beings" are the essential element of any real definition of security.

[506] S. N. Eisenstadt provides an insightful perspective on this topic in *Fundamentalism, Sectarianism, and Revolution: the Jacobin Dimension of Modernity* (Cambridge University Press, 1999).

[507] For a superb treatment of this subject as it relates to Africa, see Kwame Bediako's "Africa and Christianity on the Threshold of the Third Millennium: the Religious Dimension," *African Affairs 99*, no. 395 (April 2002): 303 - 323.

a single enemy responsible for the social injustice, that individuals are required to obey God, and that God will approve of actions taken on His behalf. This is pointedly an individualistic premise as opposed to one supported by a traditional, institutionalized, religious community. The implication is clear: a focus on mainstream religious beliefs and behaviors is not sufficient to explain current instances of religious violence in the emerging global context. This "democratization" of religion is occurring as part of globalization and can be identified as emerging out of traditional, main-stream Christian, Jewish, Islamic, Hindu, Buddhist, and Sikh communities but it not a direct result of the respective theologies.

The United States must come to terms with the reality of "religious warfare." However, if "religious war" means that each of the mainstream religions is pitted against one another, then it is a misleading and alarming term. There must be a rejection of hyperbole. For example: this is not a period in history where the entire *"umma"* of Islam is fighting the entire *"brotherhood"* of Christianity. Islam has 1 billion adherents — very few are engaged in any sort of conflict of any kind at any time. Christians are certainly not united in opposition to all Muslims. Not all Hindus hate all Muslims. Buddhists are not always pacifist.

Yet, it is clear that "religion," however defined, plays a role in all conflict and war. After all, one of the major functions or purposes of religion is to explain the meaning and value of life and the conditions under which it is justifiable to "take" life. A clear analysis of religion's role in international security will have empirical and practical value when it keeps crucial distinctions in focus. The analysis of religion in warfare must not be limited to a simplistic "cause" (*vis a vis* the motivations of individual combatants) but must add a nuanced approach to religion's contributory effects in dynamic relationship to other factors.

There are clear cases in which religion contributes to warfare but is not the primary explanatory factor. In Sri Lanka, the Hindu Tamil and Buddhist Sinhalese have had a tragic civil war that seems particularly intransigent. Religion is used as an identity factor, some religious personages have contributed to the polarization of the communities by use of incendiary language, schools and places of worship have been variously destroyed or used as basis for guerrilla operations, and yet, no one would say that the Sri Lankan conflict is basically about "religion." Ireland is another case in point: the protagonists are separated by religious identity, leaders have been variously contributory to violence and to peace, religious institutions have been used by each as symbols of "the other," and international journalists refer to the parties as "Catholic" and "Protestant." Clearly religion plays a role, but neither can claim that the mandate for violence comes from Scripture. The Lord's Resistance Army (LRA) in Uganda uses and abuses children in religious rites and practices prior to sending them into battle for causes unrelated to religion. In the Sudan, the parties to the conflict are identified, as Muslim and Christian but neither the "causes" nor the "cures" for the conflict will be found exclusively in their respective theologies. Al Qaeda tried to hijack Islam and was condemned by authoritative Islamic clergy. In 1991, Saddam Hussein seemingly became "religious" virtually overnight. And, who would contend that the current situation in Palestine and Israel is simply based in the Talmud and Koran?

Religion is generally seen as a negative contributory variable especially when used in conjunction with other factors. For example, religion can be used to rationalize terrorism primarily undertaken for political goals. It can be used to legitimize the use of weaponry designed to inflict maximum suffering, and it can be a mobilizing factor in genocide by defining the "enemy" in religious terms. Religion is a significant factor in suicide bombing and death squads, providing "cause" and promise of "reward." Religion plays a role in ethnic violence because it typically is one of the major factors of group identification. In some societal contexts, it can undermine the state and thereby contribute to state failure when the leaders of the polity are not seen as "religious enough."[508]

Religion should not be analyzed only in terms of its potential negative effects but must be studied with regard to its "assets."[509] Religion has "power" in war as a direct result of its control of resources, interpersonal relationships, communications, and expertise. The **resources** of religious personages and institutions include control over goods and services, organizational capabilities; social networks that are community based but may also be global in scope, and various types of support for political personages, agendas, and programs. The resources of a particular religion are a direct result of their numbers, reputation, coherence, and willingness to mobilize for political/ religious purposes.

Religion is an important power broker in human **relationships**. Religion helps define the attributes of a good and trustable person, prescribe rules concerning how individuals transact social, political, and economic business, and identify "friend" and "enemy" according to a set of traditional and legitimate factors. When states fail, or particular political personages are de-legitimized, religious personages often help define who, when, and under what conditions a new political leader will emerge. Most importantly, they are also assumed to be in touch with the power of a Supreme Being and therefore have special insight concerning social relations among God's children.

Religion provides for common language and means of **communication** between members of a group. Religious leaders communicate with authority, generally have written and spoken expertise, have access to media, and know significant music, poetry, and art forms of non-verbal, symbolic communication. Religious personages and institutions are often deeply involved in the education of children and the training of future generations. Parents rely on religious educational and medical institutions when the state fails to provide those resources. Historical languages often provide a sense of continuity and may be used to motivate or in symbolic communication. Religious leaders are often accustomed to keeping confidences or secrets and are trusted for their discre-

---

[508] Assassination of religious leaders seen as "not quite religious enough" seems to be a recurring pattern in international affairs. Note the deaths of Anwar Sadat, Mohandas Gandhi and Rajiv Gandhi at the hands of "fanatics."

[509] For an informed and thoughtful treatment of this complex subject, see Marc Gopin's *Between Eden and Armageddon: the Future of World Religions, Violence, and Peacemaking* (Oxford University Press, 2002).

tion. Most importantly, religious leaders are often more believable in failed or fragile states than political leaders and therefore have power above and beyond the sheer strength of numbers or observable resources.

Religious actors have **expertise** in many areas above and beyond that of the general population. They generally have an in depth knowledge of people, places, and communities. They know the sensitivities of the community. They know the personal history of leaders and their families. They move easily in a community and have access to areas off-limits to others. Quite literally, they know where the bodies are buried. In a very real sense, religious personages and communities know more about food, water, and health than others in the community. They are the individuals that people "go to" when all else fails.

Religious leaders, as force multipliers, have significant social-cultural power and are able to effect war and peace more than is commonly recognized. Both on the "U.S" side and the "other" side, religious leaders must engage the topic of peace and use their inherent power to move towards a more peaceful world.

CONCLUSION

Those responsible for U.S. National Security are increasingly convinced that religion and war must be addressed in a new, comprehensive, and focused way. Not only did the events of September 11, 2001, provided a tragic, if clarion call, but the wars in Afghanistan and Iraq were telling instances of the consequences of "not knowing."

The White House and Congress have shown enthusiasm for supporting faith-based non-governmental organizations in aspects of homeland security and peacekeeping operations. The Department of Defense now demonstrates a keen, if belated, interested in religious factors relevant to the Middle East. The Departments of State, Justice, and Homeland Security are engaged in learning about the "religious factor" as it applies to their responsibilities. There have been dozens of conferences in Washington, D.C. that provide a forum for dialogue between government sponsors and faith-based community representatives. Meanwhile, there has been an explosion in the public media and scholarly journals on topics concerned with religion and warfare. The traditional admonition that polite discussion should not include "religion or politics," has been turned up-side-down. In 2004, almost all conversations concerning security include a discussion of religious factors. (The implied caveat is that public attention can be a two-edged sword. It is important to remain sober, thoughtful, and careful stewards of information and insight.)

Military experts and faith-based scholars know that contributing to peace in the world is more than winning against an enemy or even supporting the cessation of hostilities. Peace not "made" only after fighting stops. In all stages along the time dimensions of war, religion plays a crucial role. It is an important element in the process of decision-making that precedes hostilities, exerts influence on behavior during the most intense fighting, and is a resource for setting parameters for peace negotiations and reconciliation.

The relevance of this discussion is not limited to "protecting and defending the homeland" or even global U.S. interests. Rather it extends to a genuinely sound analysis of the global politics of security. The complex configuration and interplay of economic, political, social, and religious factors as they relate to war and peace, is of concern to all. The fear of ethno-religious wars, the incomprehensibility of religiously motivated terrorism, and the shadow of 'clash of civilization' scenarios are on the forefront of world consciousness, and provide motivation for taking the subject of religion very seriously.

There are other immediate and pressing concerns that need serious and prayerful consideration such as the use of non-lethal weapons by police and security forces, the ethical basis of pre-emptive strikes, the use of torture or "torture-lite," issues related to religious refugees, and defining a religious perspective on the appropriate use of hegemonic state power. The ethical, moral, and religious dilemmas presented by these questions are problematic for everyone and go to the heart of the relationship between religion and violence. The answers require deep soul searching, sound theological scholarship, and courageous truth-telling.

Religion and warfare are the two of the most difficult and important topics facing the United States. It is incumbent on all of those concerned to take a serious and systematic approach to how religion impacts contemporary conflict and its role in human security.

COLLABORATION TO MANAGE WMD INFORMATION: INTELLIGENCE SUPPORT TO THE LIFE SCIENCE COMMUNITY TO MITIGATE THREATS FROM BIOTERRORISM

James B. Petro

(Originally published in Studies in Intelligence 48, the Unclassified Edition (2004): 57-68.)

The al-Qa'ida attacks of 11 September 2001 and the delivery of *Bacillus anthracis* (anthrax) via the US Postal Service triggered a significant increase in initiatives to improve defense against biological attacks. They also reinvigorated a decades-old debate about the contributions that openly published scientific research might make to the efforts of bioterrorists and others who may be developing a biological warfare (BW) or other weapons of mass destruction (WMD) capability. Resolution of this debate could be made easier by input from knowledgeable intelligence and other national security professionals. Collaboration involving the national security and bioscience research communities could be key to minimizing the challenges posed by proliferation of research findings that have bioterror and BW applications.

Unfortunately, while there have been recent discussions involving these communities, the relationship between them has been nearly nonexistent. Accordingly, initial approaches and interactions must be planned and carefully carried out to ensure that the bridges built between the two communities are solid and long lasting. A necessary first step is to make sure that national security professionals who enter this collaboration are thoroughly familiar with the current and past debates among scientists about the potential openly published research findings have to enable BW or bioterrorism. This article is an overview of this debate, and it summarizes the most recent discussions among bioscience researchers. In addition, it offers some options the Intelligence Community (IC) can consider to help the life science community continue its work effectively while safeguarding national security. [510]

EARLY DISCUSSIONS OF NATIONAL SECURITY AND SCIENCE

Since the 1940s the US national security community has worked with scientific organizations and research communities to develop a policy for identifying areas of basic and applied research requiring control of information. Such research, historically related either to weapons development or sensitive nuclear technologies, has been designated as

---

[510] For another review of these topics, see D. Shea's "Balancing Scientific Publication and National Security Concerns: Issues for Congress," *CRS 2003 Report for Congress* (Washington, DC: Congressional Research Service, 2003).

classified and is subject to strict dissemination controls. For example, before the United States entered World War II, physicists in the private sector researching nuclear fission voluntarily stopped publishing results in scientific journals for fear of contributing to Germany's nuclear bomb project.[511]

In early 1940 the joint National Academy of Sciences (NAS) — National Research Council (NRC) Advisory Committee on Scientific Publications was established to explore options for restricting publication of information about nuclear fission. After US entry into the war, this committee secured the cooperation of scientific journals in the United States.[512]

Controls of information concerning research into nuclear power have also been instituted. Private industry was permitted to explore limited applications of nuclear power under the Atomic Energy Act of 1954. Before then, the federal government protected nuclear energy activities with security and secrecy programs. The Atomic Energy Act prohibited dissemination of nuclear research information from its creation regardless of who controls it.[513]

Such information, even if developed privately and without federal government aid, is regarded as "born classified." Importantly, when fundamental research is not classified, no other information controls are placed on it.[514]

However, the federal government retains authority over results that relate to atomic weapons, production of special nuclear material (SNM), and use of SNM in the production of energy.[515]

Federal government controls have been relatively successful in mitigating security concerns related to the proliferation of specific nuclear technologies. In large measure this is because federal regulations regarding nuclear research were implemented at a time when the research field was relatively young and expertise was consolidated within a handful of talented minds. This made it possible to, in effect, capture fission research by creating mutually beneficial relationships between key scientists and the federal government, in which Washington supported research and development in a secure environment under classification control.

The same circumstances do not exist in the life sciences, making the challenge of providing protection against threats enabled by the life sciences much greater. With the exception of specific work pertaining to the former U.S. bioweapons program — halted in

---

[511] P. J. Westwick, "In the Beginning: The Origin of Nuclear Secrecy," *Bulletin of the Atomic Scientists* 56 (November/December 2000): 43-49.

[512] R. C. Cochrane, *The National Academies of Sciences: The First Hundred Years, 1863-1963* (Washington, D.C.: National Academy of Sciences, 1978), 385-87 and Shea, 2-6.

[513] See 42 U.S.C.S. 2014(y) (2003)

[514] Shea, 2.

[515] H. Relyea, *Silencing Science: National Security Controls and Scientific Communication* (Norwood, NJ: Ablex Publishing Corporation, 1994), 94-96.

1969 under executive order by Richard Nixon — and a handful of biodefense projects funded by the Department of Defense (DOD), the vast majority of life science research projects over the past 50 years have advanced without any restrictions or controls. Expertise exists in an international network containing tens of thousands of researchers working to address fundamental questions across a broad spectrum of life science fields. Federally mandated containment is not the effective option it was 60 years ago.

Not only is generalized federal restriction of life science research impractical, it could be disastrous. Life science research builds upon multiple findings across a variety of seemingly unrelated fields in a manner not unlike a spider's web. Removing one strand of that web through federal restriction likely would have negative implications for the other fields that are difficult to estimate. Even generalized restriction within fields with greatest application towards bioterrorism or BW could greatly hinder biodefense research efforts to develop medical countermeasures, including new vaccines and therapeutics. Before national security professionals can productively engage the scientific community regarding threats presented by the open publication of some research findings, there must be mutual agreement that the generalized, federally mandated restrictions used to contain nuclear research are not a viable option.

THE LIFE SCIENCE/NATIONAL SECURITY DEBATE BEFORE 2001

Discussions about the impact on national security of discoveries in life science first received major attention in the U.S. research community after major advances were made in recombinant DNA research — specifically the development of reliable techniques to manipulate an organism's genetic material and elicit a novel effect. Genetic engineering and the creation of recombinant species thus became topics of great contention in the 1970s and led to calls for regulation of methods for manipulating DNA and control of experiments containing genetically engineered species.[516]

To find ways to resolve these concerns, a number of leading scientists gathered in 1975 at the Asilomar Conference in Pacific Grove, California, to discuss mechanisms for assessing and managing the risks of such research.[517]

Asilomar Conference participants drafted a consensus statement that called for a voluntary moratorium on certain aspects of recombinant research and an increase in personal security and containment requirements for related research areas. This consensus statement was the starting point for rules later developed by the National Institutes of Health's (NIH) Recombinant DNA Advisory Committee (RAC), which was formed to oversee such research.[518]

---

[516] Shea, 6.

[517] D. S. Fredrickson, "Asilomar and Recombinant DNA: The End of the Beginning" in *Biomedical Politics* (Washington, DC: National Academy Press, 1991), 258-98 and *The Recombinant DNA Controversy, A Memoir: Science, Politics, and the Public Interest 1974-1984* (Washington, DC: ASM Press, 2001).

[518] Shea, 6.

The RAC and its decentralized Institutional Biosafety Committees have remained the basis for oversight of the safe conduct of recombinant DNA research in the United States and have served as models used by other countries to regulate the creation of genetically modified organisms.[519]

In the early 1980s, concern that potentially hostile foreign students and scientists had too easy access to fundamental information across a wide range of scientific disciplines, including information that might be considered to fall under export control regulations, led to an effort by the DOD to restrict information presented in classrooms and conferences. To better understand the risk to national security, DOD helped fund a study through the NAS, which convened a panel of leading researchers to evaluate the situation in which "recent trends, including apparent increases in acquisition efforts by our adversaries, have raised serious concerns that openness may harm US security by providing adversaries with militarily relevant technologies that can be directed against us."[520]

The panel's extensive report offered a set of principles to "resolve the current dilemma." The panel, with the Soviet Union as its prime focus, concluded that potential security benefits derived from restrictive controls were outweighed by the potential that such controls would weaken US security by hampering scientific advancement. The panel identified three categories of information for consideration of security controls:

- Activities and findings in which the benefits of total openness overshadow their possible near-term military benefits to the Soviet Union.
- Areas of research for which classification is clearly indicated.
- A small "gray" area that lies between the first two and for which limited restrictions short of classification are appropriate.
- Furthermore, the panel provided guidelines to assist the federal government in categorizing research activities.
- According to the panel, "no restriction of any kind limiting access or communication should be applied to any area of university research, be it basic or applied, unless it involves a technology meeting all the following criteria:"
- The technology is developing rapidly and the time from basic science to application is short;
- The technology has identifiable direct military applications, or it is dual-use and involves process or production-related techniques;
- Transfer of the technology would give the USSR a significant near-term military benefit;
- The US is the only source of information about the technology, or other friendly nations that could also be a source have control systems.

---

[519] R. M. Atlas, "Public Health: National Security and the Biological Research Community," *Science* 298 (25 October 2002): 753-4.

[520] This and the following three paragraphs are derived from the report of the NAS Panel on Scientific Communication and National Security, *Scientific Communication and National Security* (Washington, DC: National Academy Press, 1982).

The panel suggested that in dealing with gray technologies and federally-funded research, the government could achieve sufficient security by restricting the access of foreign students and researchers to the laboratory undertaking the research and stipulating a policy of federal review of research manuscripts and other products before their publication or open dissemination. The panel's findings appeared to provide sufficient guidance for the federal government at the time to adequately address the issue of Soviet acquisition of dual use technologies. The panel recommended that the federal government take the lead in implementing the suggestions, but it stressed the critical need for partnership between the scientific and national security communities to ensure effective and appropriate implementation.

Following the release of the NAS panel report, President Ronald Reagan issued National Security Decision Directive (NSDD) 189, which reaffirmed US policy regarding the flow of scientific information:

It is the policy of this administration that, to the maximum extent possible, the products of fundamental research remain unrestricted. It is also the policy of this administration that, where the national security requires control, the mechanism for control of information generated during federally-funded fundamental research in science, engineering, technology and engineering at colleges, universities and laboratories is classification. Each federal government agency is responsible for: a) determining whether classification is appropriate prior to the award of a research grant, contract, or cooperative agreement and, if so, controlling the research results through standard classification procedures; b) periodically reviewing all research grants, contracts, or cooperative agreements for potential classification. No restrictions may be placed upon the conduct or reporting of federally-funded fundamental research that has not received national security classification, except as provided in applicable US statutes.[521]

NSDD 189 has not been superseded and remains federal policy concerning the control of federally-funded research. However, throughout the late 1980s and early 1990s, a handful of individuals raised the possibility of increasing security by compartmentalizing research of concern. According to Raymond Zilinskas, "compartmentalization, a less restrictive form of secrecy, allows scientists to exchange data only if they can establish that their colleagues need the data to proceed with their research."[522]

Ultimately, although the Asilomar Conference, NAS panel, and later, but infrequent, discussions into the 1990s provided helpful insights, the efficacy of their proposed resolutions must be considered in a broader political and historical context. In general, the recommendations and findings of these groups have largely been superseded by the fall of the Soviet Union, the emergence of international terrorism, and the advancement of science. For example:

---

[521] White House, Office of the President, National Security Decision Directive 189, 1985.

[522] R.A. Zilinskas, T. Wilson, "The Microbiologist and Biological Defense Research. Ethics, Politics, and International Security," *Annals of the New York Academy of Science* 666 (31 December 1992): xi- xvii. The idea did not develop legs at the time, possibly because so few were concerned about the issue.

Although researchers at Asilomar were able to assuage public concerns at the time through their consensus statement and subsequent work within NIH, the central tenet of the conference's recommendations was that personal integrity and accountability were sufficient to prevent the misuse of genetic engineering technology acquired through scientific exchange. Such principles will not deter the nefarious researcher, and information regarding the former Soviet bioweapons program reveals a concerted effort to incorporate genetic engineering technology to enhance biowarfare threat agents had been occurring.[523]

Close analysis of the subtext of the 1982 NAS panel report on Scientific Communication and National Security reveals that the panel was principally concerned with sciences and technologies other than the life sciences. Discoveries in the life sciences are likely to decrease the amount of time, effort, and expertise needed to develop a biological weapons capability at a rate that will outpace the monitoring ability of the national security community. Thus, people doing security assessments of life science findings need to consider that the applicability of life science findings to BW or terrorism is not as clearly defined as in many of the physical sciences.

The NAS panel report focused exclusively on risks relative to Soviet militarization. The panel itself acknowledged the limitations of their recommendations even as they looked ahead to new challenges: "there are clear problems in scientific communication and national security involving Third World countries. These problems in time might overshadow the Soviet dimension." [524] Clearly, a reevaluation of the findings of the 1982 panel would be prudent.

RESURRECTION OF THE LIFE SCIENCE/SECURITY DEBATE

In the post-9/11 and post-anthrax attack environment of heightened security awareness the public, legislators, and government leaders have increased their scrutiny of potential sources of support for terrorists. The openness of the life science research community is again a subject of discussion. For example, in an effort to curb the flow of potentially valuable information to bioterrorists, the DOD drafted a report "Mandatory Procedures for Research and Technology Protection within the DOD," which outlined plans to provide DOD program managers greater oversight of whether DOD-funded laboratories could publish some of their findings. The proposal drew harsh criticism from the scientific community and was eventually discarded.[525]

In addition, NIH and Congress implemented new restrictions on federally-funded life science research laboratories to try to reduce the potential that bioterrorists would

---

[523] K. Alibek, *Biohazard: The Chilling True Story of the Largest Biological Weapons Program in the World* (New York: Random House, 1999) and I.V. Domaradskij and W. Orent, *Biowarrior: Inside the Soviet/Russian Biological War Machine* (Amherst, NY: Prometheus Books, 2003).

[524] *Scientific Communication and National Security*, 7.

[525] D. Malakoff, "National Security. Pentagon Proposal Worries Researchers," *Science* 296 (3 May 2002): 826.D. Malakoff, "Bioterrorism. Congress Adopts Tough Rules for Labs," *Science* 296 (3 May 2002): 1585-87.

gain access to dual-use technologies. The *Public Health Security and Bioterrorism Preparedness and Response Act* required tighter laboratory security, government registration, and background checks for scientists and others handling any of more than three dozen potential bioterror agents identified on the Center for Disease Control's (CDC) "Select Agent List."[526]

In addition, agencies such as NIH for the first time considered supporting classified research. Following implementation of these regulations, scientists began to express concern that some biologists with government funding were being encouraged to rein in full publication of their own work.[527]

Following similar developments in the United Kingdom, some scientists became concerned that the defensive response was disproportionate to the actual threat.[528]

Growing tension between some leading researchers and the federal government continued to escalate throughout the spring and summer of 2002, largely due to media reports that highlighted the dual-use potential of a number of recent scientific publications.

- In 2000, Australian researchers genetically engineered a strain of mousepox virus in a way that inadvertently increased its virulence.[529] At the time, publication of their findings was met with harsh criticism.[530] This mousepox research and associated criticism were raised again in 2002 during additional debates on science and security.

- In July 2002, researchers at the State University of New York at Stony Brook revealed that they had successfully created infectious poliovirus from artificially engineered DNA sequences.[531]

- Some observers saw open publication of their achievement in the journal Science as enabling the proliferation of a methodology with high BW potential.[532]

- Researchers at the University of Pittsburgh identified key proteins in variola (smallpox) that contribute to the virus' virulence and demonstrated how to synthesize the virulence gene via genetic modification of smallpox's less deadly cousin vaccinia.

---

[526] D. Malakoff, "Bioterrorism. Congress Adopts Tough Rules for Labs," *Science* 296 (3 May 2002): 1585-87.

[527] E. Check, "Biologists Apprehensive over US Moves to Censor Information Flow," *Nature* 415 (21 February 2002): 821.

[528] M. McCarthy and S. Ramsay, "Fears that Security Rules will Impede US and UK Science," *Lancet* 359 (23 February 2002): 679.

[529] R. J. Jackson, A. J. Ramsay, C. D. Christensen, S. Beaton, D. F. Hall, and I. A. Ramshaw, "Expression of Mouse Interleukin-4 by a Recombinant Ectromelia Virus Suppresses Cytolytic Lymphocyte Responses and Overcomes Genetic Resistance to Mousepox," *Journal of Virology* 75 (2001): 1205-10.

[530] J. Stephenson, "Biowarfare Warning," *Journal of the American Medical Association* 285, no. 6 (2001): 725.

[531] J. Cello, A. V. Paul, and E. Wimmer, "Chemical Synthesis of Poliovirus cDNA: Generation of Infectious Virus in the Absence of Natural Template," Science 297 (9 August 2002): 1016-18.

[532] R. Weiss, "Polio-Causing Virus Created in N.Y. Lab: Made-from-Scratch Pathogen Prompts Concerns about Bioethics, Terrorism," *The Washington Post*, 12 July 2002.

The published report was the subject of a highly publicized news article that questioned the value of publishing discoveries that might aid bioterrorists.[533]

■ Researchers at the University of Pennsylvania successfully developed a hybrid virus composed of an HIV core surrounded by the surface proteins of ebola. This new virus was capable of infecting lung tissue, potentially enabling aerosol delivery, and could facilitate the expression of foreign genes in infected cells. The published findings arguably provided a roadmap to engineering of a viral vector capable of efficiently delivering bioregulatory agents.[534]

■ Researchers in Germany reported the creation of a DNA-based system for performing reverse genetics studies on the *ebola* virus. This system introduced the possibility of reconstituting live ebola virus from DNA in the absence of a viral sample. Other researchers expressed concern that this information could lead to the artificial synthesis of the virus, increasing the potential for agent proliferation, as DNA can be more safely transferred than viral samples.[535]

Dana Shea at the Library of Congress has nicely assessed the overall response: "these articles have led some to question the wisdom of openly publishing information that could be used to threaten national security."[536] An editorial in New Scientist stated:

That this mind-boggling quantity of information is going to transform medicine and biology is beyond doubt. But could some of it, in the wrong hands, be a recipe for terror and mayhem?[537]

Maybe so. Bioethicist Arthur Kaplan from the University of Pennsylvania was reported as saying:

We have to get away from the ethos that knowledge is good, knowledge should be publicly available, that information will liberate us. Information will kill us in the techno-terrorist age, and I think it's nuts to put that stuff on websites."[538]

---

[533] A. M. Rosengard, Y. Liu, Z. P. Nie, and R. Jimenez, "Variola Virus Immune Evasion Design: Expression of a Highly Efficient Inhibitor of Human Complement," *Proceedings of the National Academies of Sciences of the United States of America* 99 (25 June 2002): 8808-13 and N. Boyce, "Speak No Evil: Should Biologists Publish Work that Could Be Misused?" *US News and World Report,* 24 June 2002.

[534] G. P. Kobinger, D.J. Weiner, Q. C. Yu, J. M. Wilson. "Filovirus-pseudotyped lentiviral vector can efficiently and stably transduce airway epithelia in vivo," *Nature Biotechnology* 3 (19 March 2001):225-30.

[535] V. E. Volchkov, V. A. Volchkova, E. Muhlberger, L. V. Kolesnikova, M. Weik, O. Dolnik, H. D. Klenk, "Recovery of Infectious Ebola Virus from Complementary DNA: RNA Editing of the GP Gene and Viral Cytotoxicity," Science 291 (9 March 2001): 1965-69; Epub 1 February 2001 and S. P. Westphal, "Ebola Virus Could be Synthesized," *New Scientist,* 17 July 2002.

[536] Shea, 5.

[537] "Surfing for a Satan Bug. Why are we Making Life so Easy for Would-be Terrorists?" *New Scientist,* 20 July 2002: 5.

[538] E. Lichtblau, "Response to Terror; Rising Fears that What We Do Know Can Hurt Us," *Los Angeles Times,* 18 November 2001: A1.

Apparently, a number of members of Congress agreed with Kaplan. After a series of news reports about the prevalence of dual use in scientific journals, a handful of members of Congress filed a resolution that criticized Science's publication of the synthetic creation of a poliovirus and called on journals, scientists, and funding agencies to exercise greater caution before releasing such information. Representative Dave Weldon (R-FL) and seven other congressmen introduced a resolution criticizing Science's publisher, the American Association for the Advancement of Science (AAAS), for publishing "a blueprint that could conceivably enable terrorists to inexpensively create human pathogens."[539] Weldon's resolution called on the executive branch to review current policies and ensure that information that could be useful in the development of WMD is not made accessible to terrorists or countries of proliferation concern.[540]

In addition to congressional interest, the Office for Homeland Security (OHS) announced that it would be considering initiatives to create a category of information that would be "sensitive, but unclassified" for application to a variety of dual-use topics, possibly including life science research of concern[541]

This naturally raised the suspicion and concerns of researchers who feared OHS might seek to make decisions that in their opinion would be more appropriately made by NIH.[542] Separately, the American Society for Microbiology (ASM) sent a letter to NAS requesting a meeting of biomedical publishers to discuss whether and how editors of leading research journals should publish research that might be coopted by terrorists.[543] By fall 2002, the debate on scientific openness and national security had officially been reopened.

THE CURRENT DEBATE

As the federal government initiated informal efforts to develop a strategy for addressing the issue of science and security in late 2002, insights were coming from a variety of highly knowledgeable sources. Mitchel Wallerstein, former deputy assistant secretary of defense for counterproliferation policy (1993-97) offered guiding principles:

- First, open access to scientific knowledge on university campuses remains as important as it was 20 years ago;
- Second, the areas of scientific knowledge and/or technological application that are immediately applicable to the development of WMD are already known;
- Third, carefully conceived restrictions on scientific and technical communications remain necessary but should be applied to substantially fewer areas of scientific inquiry and technology development than during the Cold War;

---

[539] J. Couzin, "A Call for Restraint on Biological Data," *Science* 297 (2 August 2002):749-51.

[540] H.R. 514 107th Congress of the United States of America.

[541] E. Check, "US Prepares Ground for Security Clampdown," *Nature* 418 (29 August 2002): 906.

[542] G. Brumfiel, "Mission Impossible?" *Nature* 419 (5 September 2002): 10-11.

[543] Couzin, 749-51.

■ Fourth, university faculties have a responsibility for imparting values that emphasize the positive role of S&T in addressing human needs and the immorality of their
use to cause mass casualties and human suffering.[544]

Wallerstein's first, third, and fourth recommendations provide a good roadmap to
address many underlying concerns. However, it may be presumptuous to assert that all
"areas of scientific knowledge and/or technological application that are immediately
applicable to the development of WMD are already known." The central issue of the
exponential increase in discoveries in the life sciences and the potential implications of
those discoveries for a revolution in BW fundamentally requires a continuing reevaluation
and identification of research disciplines with application to BW and biodefense.[545]

Ideally, such evaluations should include insights from leading life science researchers
actively engaged in "cutting edge" science, as they will have the clearest insights on the
technical capabilities and limitations of biotechnologies for malevolent purposes.

Partially in response to media frenzy surrounding the Weldon resolution, on 18 October 2002, NAS outlined its recommendations for addressing the issue in its "Background
Paper on Science and Security in an Age of Terrorism." It contained a list of action items
for the life science research community and the federal government, citing the success of
recent collaborations between government and scientists:

> The nation must balance two needs for achieving a safe and secure
> society: 1) the need to restrict access to certain information, and
> 2) the need for a strong research enterprise that improves both our
> general welfare and our security. Clearly, policy-makers must seek
> mechanisms by which both interests can be served.
>
> To this end, we call for a renewed dialogue among scientists,
> engineers, health researchers, and policy-makers. To stimulate such
> a dialogue, we present two "action points": one focused on
> scientists, engineers, and health researchers and the other focused
> on policy-makers.

Scientists quickly voiced support for the highlighted principles, including their distaste
for the concept of creating a category for "sensitive but unclassified" research. Ron Atlas,
the president of ASM, and others testified before the House Science Committee that the
government needs to clarify what constitutes a threat before it can implement protective
guidelines, such as screening foreign graduate students for entry to U.S. laboratories.[546] Moreover, scientists argued that clear distinctions need to be made between classified and unclassified research since "poorly defined third categories of sensitive but
unclassified research that do not provide précise guidance on what information should be

---

[544] M. B. Wallerstein, "Science in an Age of Terrorism," *Science* 297 (27 September 2002): 2169.

[545] J. B. Petro, T. R. Plasse, and J. A. McNulty, "Biotechnology: Impact on Biological Warfare and Biodefense," *Biosecurity and Bioterrorism* 1, no. 3 (2003): 161-68.

[546] D. Malakoff, "Security and Science. Researchers See Progress in Finding the Right Balance," *Science*
298 (18 October 2002): 529.

restricted from public access . . . generate deep uncertainties among both scientists and the officials responsible for enforcing regulations."[547]

Editorials in leading scientific journals expressed concern that many scientists would either deal with the issue of classification by determining that it should be rejected from university laboratories as unsuitable (as was the case at the Massachusetts Institute of Technology) or deem the "sensitive" label as prone to too many interpretations to be accommodated in an academic setting.[548] Despite these views, however, NAS demonstrated its willingness to withhold certain information from general release without a demonstrated "need to know." This option came into play when the academies agreed to remove an entire chapter of the 2002 NAS study on agricultural bioterrorism that the authors and the Department of Agriculture agreed would be of high dual use value to individuals with bad intentions.[549] Also, with some scientists, the concern over research classification was secondary to the potential consequences of misuse of their research. As one such researcher wrote, "scientists need to be aware of the regulatory and ethical implications of bioweapon proliferation."[550]

In addition to lobbying Congress and federal agencies, biologists began to independently discuss new voluntary guidelines on publishing potentially dangerous information, in part to head off possible government rules.[551] On 9 and 10 January 2003 NAS and the Center for Strategic and International Studies (CSIS) hosted a workshop for life science researchers and national security experts to discuss the issue of assessing and mitigating potential threats presented by biological research. Although many of the 200 senior scientists and researchers argued that scientists should be free to publish all unclassified work, some academicians acknowledged that the community needs to reassure the public and the government that it is acting responsibly.[552]

Moreover, statements by senior policymakers reassured scientists but challenged them to take the initiative. According to Dr. Parney Albright, then associate director of homeland security for the president's Office of Homeland Security, "it is the policy of this administration that, to the maximum extent possible, the products of fundamental research remain unrestricted" and that as per NSDD 189, "no restrictions will be placed upon the conduct or reporting of federally-funded fundamental research that has not received national security classification."[553] However, Dr. Albright did not give the

---

[547] B. Alberts, R. M. May, "Scientist Support for Biological Weapons Control," *Science* 298 (8 November 2002): 1135.

[548] D. S. Greenberg, "Homeland Security is Good and Bad News for US Scientists," *Lancet* 360 (21-28 December 2002): 2056.

[549] M. Enserink, "Science and Security. Entering the Twilight Zone of What Material to Censor," *Science* 298 (22 November 2002): 1548.

[550] J. A. Singh, P. A. Singer, "Isolationism is not the Answer to Bioterrorism," *Nature* 420 (12 December 2002): 605.

[551] Malakoff, "Security and Science," 529.

[552] E. Check, "US Officials Urge Biologists to Vet Publications for Bioterror Risk," *Nature* 421 (16 January 2003): 197.

[553] B. Vastag, "Openness in Biomedical Research Collides with Heightened Security Concerns," *Journal of the American Medical Association* 289 (12 February 2003): 686, 689-90.

research community a free pass, making it clear that "the science community ought to come up with a process before the public demands the government do it for them . . . that will be driven by the rate at which controversial papers hit the street."[554]

Ultimately, scientists at the NAS/CSIS meeting agreed that there may be some research that should not be published, although clear guidelines would be helpful in identifying future papers of concern. To help craft a better definition of such "taboo" science, the academies and CSIS announced a plan to convene such meetings in the future. Gerald Epstein, a security expert with the Institute for Defense Analyses, proposed a simple question to aid scientists in deciding whether a paper should be more closely reviewed: "Would you like it to be found in a cave in Afghanistan with sections high-lighted in yellow?"[555]

During the second day of the workshop, a group of editors from leading scientific journals crafted a statement on the publication of research with potential for aiding bioterrorism.[556] An editorial that ran alongside the statement in Science highlighted the need for researchers, editors, and national security professionals to reach a consensus on guidelines for scientific information that should not be published.[557] The editorial did not represent a radical departure from standing policy, but concisely stated the opinions of the editors present at the workshop. It made four points:

- First, the scientific information published in peer-reviewed journals carries special status, and confers unique responsibilities on editors and authors.

- Second, the editors recognize that the prospect of bioterrorism has raised legitimate concerns about the potential misuse of published information, but also recognize that research in the very same fields will be critical to society in meeting the challenges of defense.

- Third, scientists and their journals should consider the appropriate level and design of processes to accomplish effective review of papers that raise such security issues.

- Fourth, on occasion an editor may conclude that the potential harm of publication outweighs the potential societal benefits.[558]

The response of researchers and security experts to the statement was mixed. Some researchers complained that they were not consulted. For example, Steven Block, a biophysicist at Stanford University, was quoted as saying the statement is "more equivocal and less definitive" than he would like to see. Others believe that scientists should go much further to address security concerns about life science research. David Heyman, a science and security expert at CSIS, said that the statement was "only a step" and that sci-

---

[554] Check, "US Officials," 197.

[555] D. Malakoff, "Science and Security. Researchers Urged to Self-Censor Sensitive Data," *Science* 299 (17 January 2003): 321.

[556] Statement on Scientific Publication and Security," *Science* 299 (21 February 2003): 1149.

[557] "D. Kennedy, "Two Cultures," *Science* 299 (21 February 2003): 1148.

[558] "Statement," 1149.

entists should make changes earlier in the research process to reduce the risk of biological research being misused.[559]

By far the sharpest public critic of the statement, respected microbiologist Stanley Falkow, has taken issue with the failure of its authors to elicit more discussion before its publication. Falkow faults the authors for failing "to provide guidelines regarding who exactly would make decisions about publication and what constitutes a potential contribution to the activities of bioterrorists."[560] Falkow's statement suggests that he supports the formation of a committee to provide insight and oversight regarding research of concern. However, it is his opinion that the issue should be "earnestly discussed by the broad community of scientists, together with those whose mission it is to guard national security."[561]

In a further effort to characterize the challenges posed by misuse of biotechnology, the NAS created the Committee on Research Standards and Practices to Prevent the Destructive Application of Biotechnology. It directed the committee to consider ways to minimize threats from BW and bioterrorism without hindering the progress of biotechnology. The committee's report, Biotechnology Research in an Age of Terrorism (commonly referred to as the Fink Report), released in October 2003, proposed a new system for mitigating the potential for the misuse of life science knowledge by establishing "a number of stages at which experiments and eventually their results would be reviewed to provide reassurance that advances in biotechnology with potential applications for BW or bioterrorism receive responsible oversight."

The Fink Report included seven recommendations for the mitigation of the potential for misuse of dual-use knowledge and seven guidelines for identifying "research of concern."[562] The report clearly identified the absence of an "established culture of working with the national security community among life scientists as currently exists in the fields of nuclear physics and cryptography" as a challenge to achieving consensus on the identification of dual use information and mitigation of its potential misuse. In one of its seven recommendations, the NAS committee called for a role for the life sciences in efforts to prevent bioterrorism and biowarfare, recommending that "the national security and law enforcement communities develop new channels of sustained communication with the life sciences community about how to mitigate the risks of bioterrorism." The report suggested that leading scientists believe some guidance from intelligence professionals would assist the scientific community as it seeks to identify information that may be of use to terrorists and to support comparative assessments regarding the cost-benefit ratio of limiting the availability of such information.[563]

[559] E. Check, "Journals Tighten Up on Biosecurity," Nature 421 (20 February 2003): 774 and "Biodefense Plans Earn Luke-warm Response from US Academics," Nature 422 (20 March 2003): 245-6.

[560] S. Falkow, "Science Publishing and Security Concerns," Science 300 (2 May 2003): 737-9.

[561] S. Falkow, 739.

[562] G. Fink and others., Biotechnology Research in an Age of Terrorism (Washington, DC: The National Academies Press, 2004), 3, 111-26.

[563] G. Fink and others, 85, 123.

In response to the recommendations of the report, the Department of Health and Human Services (DHHS) recently announced the creation of a National Scientific Advisory Board for Biosecurity (NSABB).[564] According to the DHHS press statement, the NSABB will "advise the Secretary of HHS, the director of the NIH, and the heads of all federal departments and agencies that conduct or support life sciences research" by "recommending specific strategies for the efficient and effective oversight of federally conducted or supported potential dual-use biological research taking into consideration both national security concerns and the needs of the research community."[565]According to the NSABB Web site, the group will be charged specifically with guiding the development of guidelines for the identification and conduct of research that may require special attention and security surveillance.[566]

Although NSABB members have not yet been publicly identified, the board will consist of voting and ex-officio members from the national security and intelligence communities as well as an abundance of leading life scientists. Thus, the NSABB may serve as one vehicle for consistent and productive interaction between the intelligence and life science communities. Maximum benefit of this relationship could best be realized by ensuring that intelligence and national security professionals assigned to support NSABB efforts possess a strong background in the life sciences; it will do little good for intelligence professionals who do not adequately understand the underlying principles to engage life scientists in discussions on the potential security implications of highly technical research findings.

INTELLIGENCE SUPPORT TO THE SCIENTIFIC COMMUNITY

The life science research community clearly would benefit from insights of the IC and other national security professionals if it is to progress beyond the current state of discussion and develop a coordinated strategy for assessing and mitigating threats enabled by research of concern. Engagement of the scientific community should be of paramount importance to biological warfare and CBRN terrorism analysts in the IC.

In addition to obvious areas in which security experts could contribute, such as providing insights and methodologies for deriving threat assessments and offering national security information to cleared life science experts, there are many less obvious opportunities for IC input. For example, the IC is well positioned to see that life science experts are educated about the activities terrorist groups and foreign states allegedly undertake to support their BW efforts. Also, IC personnel possess access to a wealth of information pertinent to the physical properties and characteristics of biothreat agents. Much of this information, at least that which is unclassified or for official use only (FOUO), would be useful to researchers struggling with the development of novel countermeasures and systems for civilian biodefense.

---

[564] DHHS press release available at: *http://www.biosecurityboard.gov/NSABB_press_release.pdf*.
[565] Ibid., 1.
[566] NSABB Web site: *http://www.biosecurityboard.gov*.

A deeper relationship between the IC and life science communities has the potential to benefit the IC, which has long struggled to maintain an internal core of bioscience expertise. In addition, formulation of a positive view among life science professionals about the IC could lead to an increase in the number of top graduate students and young life science researchers who seek employment in intelligence or national security agencies. Most importantly, closer and continuing contact with life science investigators could yield greater insight regarding suspicious attempts of foreign researchers to acquire from legitimate scientists information, reagents, or technology of high dual-use value. Such insights could enable further targeting of IC resources. In order to develop the potential synergy between the two communities; the national security community will need to take the first steps. Ultimately, none of the potential benefits will be realized until long after IC professionals have sown seeds of goodwill within the life science research community and engaged influential scientists as partners on BW counterproliferation initiatives.

"SALSA FOR CYBER SONICS," EDUCATION AND RESEARCH AT THE JOINT MILITARY INTELLIGENCE COLLEGE

A. Denis Clift

(Originally published as a speech, MASINT Conference, National Reconnaissance Office, February 2, 2005.)

"We pursue the impossible, because our adversaries believe it will never work." These words shaping the mission and the esprit of the Measurement and Signature Intelligence staff here at the National Reconnaissance Office should be adopted and embraced by the Intelligence Community and by leaders in the private sector engaged in the work of intelligence.

We meet at a time when the Intelligence Reform Act of 2004 urges a new Director of National Intelligence, not yet in place, to exercise bold leadership and initiative. It is a time when the initiatives called for by the Homeland Security Act of 2002 are still taking form. It is a time when the nation sits in the center of a crossroads it has been able to steer around before — the crossroads bringing together foreign intelligence and enhanced national — or domestic — intelligence in a manner that strengthens our security at the same time it safeguards the freedoms and rights we cherish in this democracy.

It is a time when intelligence is being called on to understand arms races underway, some of which are only dimly understood — and, a time when there are weapons and components of weapons around the world, which in the hands of either nations or non-nation players can do this nation harm. There are people around the world, who in settings of dictatorship, extremism, and poverty are being led to believe that their one opportunity for glory and martyrdom is to land a blow against this nation and our allies.

At the same time that the probe from the Cassini-Huygens space mission dazzles us with its descent through Titan's ground fog and its first successful transfer of images from this moon of Saturn, we are still staggering against the virulence of contagious disease and against the extreme blows of nature on this planet.

We turn to the challenge of pursuing the impossible in the work of intelligence against the daunting obstacles of bias and mindset. In the book *Wings of Gold,* retired Admiral Noel Gayler, a 1935 Naval Academy graduate and a pioneering, young aviator at the dawn of the 1940s, reflects on the factors contributing to the success of the Japanese attack on Pearl Harbor. Far more than a failure of intelligence or the ins and outs of whether the President wanted war, the failure, to his thinking, was the mindset of the commanders who had been brought up in the big-gun battleship Navy. "I don't think any of them actually imagined than an air attack could be more than a raid... The image of a raid suggests something that may be a nuisance, but that's it. I think it was that failure of imagination."[567]

A failure of imagination ... Sixty-three years later, this past summer, the 9/11 Commissioners would write in their Report: "We believe the 9/11 attacks revealed four kinds of failures: in imagination, policy, capabilities, and management." In a section of the Report titled Institutionalizing Imagination: The Case of Aircraft as Weapons, the Commissioners wrote: "Imagination is not a gift usually associated with bureaucracies ... It is therefore crucial to find a way of routinizing, even bureaucratizing, the exercise of imagination."[568]

If we need to exercise imagination, to pursue the impossible, against an incredibly complex array of challenges, we need to do so at a time of dramatic change in our people. There is a new generation of men and women coming into the intelligence service. As we move on from the baby boomers, we have opened the doors to the cyber sonics.

There is nothing particularly awesome to the cyber sonics about the capabilities of a Predator being flown over Afghanistan from a command center in Nevada. This is the generation of instant, ever-accessible communications, a generation of geospatial video- and computer-game dexterity, a generation pressing for each new information-technology linkage and computer software advance.

This is a generation that thrives on multi-tasking, on accomplishment and recognition, on job change. Life is the expanding cyber universe with its opportunities and its unknowns. Each individual is the key board and the mouse.

What was speed in the intelligence work force just a few years ago is slow to the cyber sonics. What was taken as gospel is open to doubt. A speed reading instructor told a group of Master's candidates at my College: "I'm going to teach you how to read each page in four seconds," and one student said to another "Why not three?" These young men and women understand the importance of career development and growth through expanding opportunities and experience, and do not understand why the departments, agencies, and organizations in the intelligence community make career shifts within the community and sabbaticals in the private sector so monumentally difficult.

This is a generation that is ready to exercise imagination in pursuing the impossible, and it is the responsibility of those leading the implementation of intelligence reform to clear the path. If you think about this community today, if you think about our collective lack of imagination, a lot of clearing lies ahead. You do not have to look far. How about the mind-numbing acronyms we use to label to the major fields of our profession -OSINT, MASINT, IMINT, HUMINT? You would think they had been fed to us by our adversaries to keep us in a perpetual fog.

---

[567] Gerald Astor, *Wings of Gold* Ballantine Books, New York, 2004, p. 19.

[568] *The 9/11 Commission Report,* Final Report of the National Commission on Terrorist Attacks Upon the United States (New York: W.W. Norton & Company, 2004), 339 and 344.

"OSINT?" the cyber sonic asks. Aren't we talking about all the literature, all the language out there, A-L-O-T? Why not say A LOT? MASINT! Is this something George Carlin wouldn't eat as a child, or graveside muttering from an Erskine Caldwell novel? Aren't we talking about the intelligence we can draw from space, the atmosphere, the land, the sea, data out there for intelligence action? Space, atmosphere, land, sea, action— SALSA. Keep your OSINT/MASINT they say. With what's on my plate, I need A LOT of SALSA.

The men and women, military and civilian, officer and enlisted, in the Master's and Bachelor's programs at the Joint Military Intelligence College are among the very finest of the new cyber sonic era. They come from across the Armed Services, the entire Intelligence Community, the FBI and the Department of Homeland Security. Those who have been selected as Intelligence Community Scholars come from colleges and universities across the land — diverse, multilingual, incredibly talented individuals — fresh from the award of their baccalaureate degrees into the ranks of defense intelligence, with their first stop their Master's degree at the College.

In 1962, the Secretary of Defense chartered the College with the dual mission of intelligence education and intelligence research. The College's graduate and undergraduate degree-granting powers for the Master of Science of Strategic Intelligence degree and the Bachelor of Science in Intelligence degree are vested in it by Congress. The College is accredited by the Middle States Commission on Higher Education, and it is a member of the Consortium of Universities of the Washington Metropolitan Area.

The College is educating and guiding research in an era where the formerly dominant challenges of understanding force-on-force foreign military capabilities and intentions have been subsumed in a far-broader spectrum of intelligence challenges and requirements. While it is essential to have expert understanding of each of the world's nuclear and conventional military forces, we are now in an era where it is essential to know something of intelligence value about every subject, every issue of interest to the nation.

The classified and unclassified intelligence- and intelligence-related research conducted by the College's students, faculty, and research fellows not only helps shape the curriculum to the shifting demands of a changing world but also contributes most importantly to the day-to-day work of intelligence. The College's international programs are contributing to better intelligence for coalition operations.

In this cyber- and information-era world marked by failed and failing nation states, religious and cultural conflicts, the proliferation of conventional weapons and weapons of mass destruction, and virulent international terrorism, the future intelligence leaders the College is educating must have an appreciation of regional cultures, religions, and politics as well as the smoldering tinder intentions and the sparks of conflict. In a strategic environment where U.S. forces with their allied and coalition partners are called upon to provide forward deterrence, produce forward stability, and ward off threats to the U.S. homeland, there is virtually no geography, no political, cultural ideological, or religious presence anywhere that is not of relevance to the intelligence professional. The challenge is to educate the mind, to engage the reasoning and to exercise the imagination to crystallize that relevance.

Today's student and today's intelligence researcher recognize that effective strategic warning is the most important component of effective intelligence. Such warning, addressing both threats and opportunities, is what policy-makers and commanders look to intelligence to provide for both the security and the wellbeing of the nation. And here, I am drawing on Cynthia Grabo's work *Anticipating Surprise, Analysis for Strategic Warning* published by the College in 2002. Such strategic warning often flows from mists and vapors. Such warning involves gifted, dedicated analysts using indications methodologies and related techniques. It involves the perception of emerging threats of seeming low probability. It involves exhaustive research. It involves dedicated collection against such threats, to include innovative and imaginative collection plans allowing for penetration of those who would deny and those who would deceive. It involves hearing out analysts whose voices are in the minority. It involves responsibility on the part of the commander and the policy-maker to pay attention to those providing such warning however much it may run counter to the mindset, the cultural bias, the accepted view of the most likely course of future events.[569]

As a contributor and a force for change in the intelligence dynamic of the early 21st century, the College continues to expand its education and research programs out from the key defense core across each of the larger, interlocking rings comprising the national intelligence requirements essential for both the policy-maker and the combatant commander. In the assessment of the College's distinguished Board of Visitors, the Joint Military Intelligence College is today the *de facto* national intelligence university.

Among the nation's federally chartered colleges and universities, the College has the distinction of annually awarding both graduate and undergraduate degrees. The Master's degree has been offered since 1980. In 1997, the Congress authorized the College's new Bachelor of Science in Intelligence degree, the first time such baccalaureate degree granting authority had been given by the Congress to a Federal degree-granting institution since the creation of the Air Force Academy in the mid-1950s. The BSI degree is enabling non-commissioned officers from each of the services to move up into the commissioned ranks. It is enabling civilian clerical personnel, secretaries, and technicians to break glass ceilings and move up into the professional ranks. It is proving a resounding success.

In the year 2000, the Director of Central Intelligence certified the College's Master's degree program, with its leadership and management elective, as meeting all course requirements for Intelligence Community Officer Certification. It is a very rigorous program — 14 courses and the research and writing of a Master's thesis in one year. It is a multi-disciplinary program, with the number of courses expanding as faculty numbers continue to grow. Those courses include the four-course Denial and Deception Program offered in partnership with, and sponsored by, the National Intelligence Council.

---

[569] Cynthia Grabo, *Anticipating Surprise, Analysis for Strategic Warnimg* (Washington, DC: Joint Military Intelligence College, 2002).

As we meet today, the College's advertisement for a senior MASINT faculty member is on the Web. The Master's curriculum includes an elective on Measurement and Signature Intelligence, with the College Catalog advising "The course may be used to lay the groundwork for MSSI theses that will make original contributions to the MASINT field."[570] The theses, both classified and unclassified, that are emerging are receiving awards and being recognized by the Community. Some truly boggle the imagination.

The College offers the Master's degree not only in the one-year fulltime study program, but also in part-time, evening, weekend, and month Reserve formats. In addition to the main campus at Bolling Air Force Base, the College has two satellite campuses: the first in operation since 1990 at the National Security Agency; the second, opened this past summer, at the National Geospatial Intelligence Agency. Through the NGA campus, the College is now also linked with the Air Force Institute of Technology allowing our NGA graduate students to take AFIT's MASINT certificate program and apply the credits earned toward their MSSI degree.

The College's alumni in positions of prominence today include Admiral Bill Studeman, former Deputy Director of Central Intelligence and today a Commissioner on the President's WMD Commission. They include NSA Director Lieutenant General Mike Hayden, INSCOM's Commanding General Major General Jeff Kimmons, CENTCOM's J-2 Brigadier General John Custer, PACOM's J-2 Rear Admiral Jack Dorsett, and the incoming Director of Naval Intelligence Rear Admiral Bob Murrett.

The alumni include Marc Viola, Class of 1995, and today Director of MASINT Review on the President's WMD Commission. Marc was looking to the future with his MSSI thesis on "Verification Implications of Commercial Satellite Imagery." Five years after graduation, when asked if he would recommend the Master's program, he praised the College for allowing its Master's candidates "to think outside the box," for giving them the opportunity to cultivate an in-depth understanding of focused intelligence issues.[571] He would serve as the College's first MASINT instructor. He believes deeply, as do those who have studied under him, that we are living in an age when foreign adversaries are progressively improving their countermeasures, and the agility to effectively employ their countermeasures against our traditional sources and methods. In his words, 'Measurement and Signature Intelligence, as the newest and least understood of the U.S. intelligence disciplines, holds the promise of countering the increasing use and effectiveness of adversarial denial and deception."[572]

In the work of intelligence, imagination, or lack thereof, is not solely an attribute of Government. The Intelligence Community finds itself today — witness this conference — in a rapidly growing, evolving partnership with industry. The ground rules for this partnership differ in many ways from those of the Cold War era, with industry now often in

---

[570] Joint Military Intelligence College, *Catalog, Academic Year 2004-2005* (Washington, DC, 2004), 46.

[571] *Preparing America's Leaders*, Joint Military Intelligence College 40th Anniversary Publication, Joint Military Intelligence College Foundation, McLean, Virginia, 2002, 50-51.

[572] Marc Viola, conversation with author, 18 January 2005.

the lead and with industry and contractors sometimes playing roles not played before. To provide our students, the future leaders, with an appreciation of this dynamic, the College — supported by the private, non-profit Joint Military Intelligence College Foundation — will be offering an Intelligence and Industry elective course, already fully subscribed, this spring quarter.

We will be pushing well beyond this in exercising the 'I' word, with the establishment this year of a Center for Advanced Intelligence Concepts. Our goal with this center will be to advance the state of the intelligence profession and its major disciplines. Our goal will be to promote the development of a network of organizations and individuals in government - at the federal, state, and local levels, in the academic world, and in industry, a network to identify key challenges and opportunities before the intelligence profession, and the pursuit of conceptual and methodological breakthroughs contributing to their realization and their solution.

The Center will serve as a catalyst providing an over-the-horizon capability for the intelligence community, bringing together those best suited to spotting fresh opportunities, best suited to identifying and taking on the challenges — topical, technical, and methodological — of the national security future. It will serve as a forum in which experts from inside and outside government can come together to address current and emerging issues.

This is exciting work, with the prospects for the future more exciting still. As we move from MASINT for the baby boomers to SALSA for the cyber sonics, as the work of intelligence reform moves forward in 2005 and beyond, the College looks forward to expanding its service to the nation as the intelligence community's center of excellence, its premier element, for education and research.

INTELLIGENCE: AN ECONOMIC GOOD

Mark A. Jensen

(Originally published in the Defense Intelligence Journal 10, No. 2 (2001): 67-79.)

Topics that come to mind when one considers the confluence of economics and intelligence typically include: the strength of foreign economies, globalization and international trade, technology transfer, currency exchange, sanctions and embargoes, smuggling and money laundering, and economic espionage. Often excluded from the foregoing litany is intelligence as an economic good. This topic weighs heavily on the U.S. Intelligence Community, not so much on the subjects that intelligence analysts study, research, and write about, but on how intelligence is sought, resourced, produced, and used.

Although intelligence as a product requiring the expenditure of effort should be treated as an economic good, in practice it is not. Consumers invariably ignore the costs associated with the production of intelligence. Intelligence is frequently regarded as a "free good," a commodity for whose delivery they bear no cost. The notion that the availability of intelligence is not infinite rarely enters their minds. Intelligence producers tend to operate with a similar mindset because the cost of collection seldom dawns on them. Non-intelligence consumers have to consider how many cruise missiles, aircraft sorties, or gallons of fuel are available to conduct their operations. The hard reality applies to intelligence as well. Once the Intelligence Community and its consumers understand the value and cost of intelligence, they can make more efficient resource allocation decisions, engendering optimization, an across-the-board objective in economics.

ECONOMIC PRINCIPLES

As a general rule, intelligence personnel and their consumers rarely think about intelligence as an economic good or consider the return on their intelligence "investment." Inattention to economic principles can result in product shortages, waste, and the inefficient use of intelligence assets. Collection managers, for example, wanting to provide producers the necessary input to ultimately satisfy their consumers, often go to great lengths to get intelligence information, sometimes using inefficient methods, such as:

- Disregarding the level of effort required by a collection asset to obtain the desired information
- Initiating new collection rather than taking the time to search archives to determine if existing products would satisfy the need
- Flooding the community with requirements: asking for everything and not distinguishing between needs and nice-to-have wants
- Inflating priorities just to increase the likelihood the requirement will be validated and collection tasked
- Ignoring the concept of tradeoff and the priorities of new, higher priority requirements in relation to existing, lower priority requirements

Blending intelligence with economic principles will foster a more productive Intelligence Community and develop a more educated consumer base that can properly set its expectations for intelligence as a product on which it relies. Henry Rowen maintains that consumers must be empowered to drive intelligence and suggests that they be given "vouchers" with which to "purchase" intelligence products they want.[573] Todd Brethauer argues similarly that unchecked demand for intelligence, coupled with a limited supply of collectors, results in unmet expectations.[574] He focuses on limiting the demand for intelligence by having consumers make hard tradeoff decisions about which questions they want answered. Furthermore, an independent task force of the Council on Foreign Relations has concluded: "Some sort of market constraint, under which intelligence consumers can only receive so much free intelligence before their own agency has to find resources to support a greater intelligence effort, should be introduced."[575]

In the private sector, as prices increase, producers are willing to produce more, while consumers typically lower their demand. If prices decrease, production lags and demand rises. In the intelligence sphere, two significant exceptions alter the usual functioning of supply and demand.

First, competition does not exist in government as it does in the private sector. Intelligence products, for the most part, are produced by the government for use by the government. Some advocate that the various intelligence organizations, such as the CIA, DIA, the State Department's INR, and the service intelligence agencies, compete with each other.[576] Yet, despite some overlapping interests, each organization has been set up to service certain customers. Furthermore, desirable competitive analysis has been instituted to limit the "jump-on-the-bandwagon" syndrome. The recent advent of outsourcing and the growing use of open source intelligence will likewise alter the nature of competition for intelligence products and promote the recognition of intelligence as an economic good.[577]

Second, interference with the supply and demand mechanism causes artificial shortages and surpluses. Since intelligence is all too often treated as a free good, demand by definition will far exceed supply. With the end of the Cold War, the demand for intelligence on a multiplicity of issues has grown exponentially. Nonethe-

---

[573] Henry S. Rowen, *Reforming Intelligence: A Market Approach* (Washington, DC: Consortium for the Study of Intelligence, 1993), 11.

[574] Todd Brethauer, "The Intelligence of Nations: Adam Smith Examines the Intelligence Economy," *Studies in Intelligence* (1996). URL: <http://www.odci.gov/csi/ studies/96unclas/examines.htm>, accessed 14 January 1998.

[575] Maurice R. Greenberg, Chairman, "Making Intelligence Smarter: The Future of U.S. Intelligence," April 1996, Independent Task Force of Council of Foreign Relations, URL: <http://www.copi.com/articles/IntelRpt/cfr.html>, accessed 16 February 1999.

[576] One could even argue that the various organizations specializing in single-discipline intelligence could compete with each other. That, however, is a different argument because each discipline, by definition, has different advantages and disadvantages, and an all-source approach is the best.

[577] Robert Steele, the founder and chief executive officer of Open Source Solutions, Inc., is considered by many the premier champion of open source intelligence.

less, Congress "artificially" limits the supply of intelligence when it establishes the top-line budget for the Intelligence Community. At a fixed resource level, only increased efficiency (hence the oft-quoted maxim "doing more with less") can increase the supply of intelligence.

The government must recognize that economic principles govern resource allocation decisions, including intelligence resources. Accordingly, it must weigh costs and benefits and expend the resources in the most judicious way so that the greatest advantage will accrue, given the resource constraints.

MEASURING VALUE

Today, the Intelligence Community attempts to assign value to intelligence requirements by prioritization. Although helpful, this represents only a rudimentary effort to establish value. Furthermore, no common method for establishing priorities throughout the entire Intelligence Community exists.[578] More importantly, prioritization does not by itself take into account all factors bearing on intelligence value, as will be discussed below. Society places value on goods and services according to their potential benefit. Likewise, intelligence has value to the extent it provides a benefit to its consumers, i.e. the reduction of uncertainty that it provides to these consumers/decisionmakers.[579] True, intelligence can be a subjective commodity whose value is sometimes difficult to measure. Nevertheless, intelligence possessing certain characteristics is innately more valuable. William Brei describes five attributes of intelligence that make it valuable. These are:

- Accuracy: All sources and data must be evaluated for the possibility of technical error, misperception, and hostile efforts to mislead.

- Objectivity: All judgments must be evaluated for the possibility of deliberate distortions and manipulations due to self-interest.

- Usability: All intelligence communication must be in the form that facilitates ready comprehension and immediate application.

- Relevance: Information must be selected and organized for its applicability to a consumer's requirements, with potential consequences and significance of the information made explicit to the consumer's circumstances.

---

[578] Community Management Staff, Briefing Slides, *Community Priority System* (CPS), December 1996, 2. The CMS proposed the CPS as an attempt to synchronize priority systems among national agencies, not the entire Intelligence Community. The CPS is intended to convert the tiers of countries and issues defined by Presidential Decision Directive 35 into numerical priorities that all disciplines will use

[579] William J. Broad, "Spy Satellites' Early Role as 'Floodlight' Coming Clear," *New York Times*, 12 September 1995, C12. The article quotes President Lyndon Johnson as saying: "We've spent $35 billion or $40 billion on the space program and if nothing else had come out of it except the knowledge we've gained from space photography, it would be worth ten times what the whole program has cost. Because tonight we know how many missiles the enemy had and, it turned out, our guesses were way off. We were doing things we didn't need to do. We were building things we didn't need to build. We were harboring fears we didn't need to harbor."

- Timeliness: Intelligence must be delivered while the content is still actionable under the customer's circumstances.[580]

SITUATION DEPENDENCY

Although information can possess attributes contributing to its value, ultimate determination is situation dependent. The same information can have different values at different times and in different situations. Factors impacting the situation and determining intelligence value include the following:

- Degree to which U.S. citizens or allies/friends are physically threatened
- Degree to which interests of the U.S. or allies/friends are threatened
- Impact on foreign policy decisions or relations with foreign countries
- Impact on military operations or plans
- The identity of the requester, for example the president, policymaker, or warfighter

In addition, the nature of the information needed for any of these situations and related specifications such as timeliness or accuracy/resolution contribute to the determination of its value. The information desired may range from critical to simply "nice to know." Composite aspects of relevance, given an acceptable level of reliability, capture the concept of value since these encompass both the importance of the information to the decisionmaker as well as its timeliness. In short, the value of information relates to the degree to which uncertainty for a decisionmaker in a given situation is reduced

Besides the situation, numerous factors impact the determination of value. These include:

- Importance vs. Urgency. Importance relates to intrinsic worth; urgency means action is needed quickly. "Must-have" information with a longer suspense may be more important than gathering "nice-to-have" information with a short suspense.

- Required vs. Desired. Some requirements may indicate both required and desired specifications, such as due dates or levels of accuracy of technical parameters. Desired specifications are typically more stringent.

- Decomposed/Consolidated Requirements. This issue deals with how to modify the values of the new requirement(s), if at all, based on the values of the original requirement(s).

---

[580] William Brei, *Getting Intelligence Right: The Power of Logical Procedure*. Occasional Paper Number Two (Washington, DC: Joint Military Intelligence College, 1996), 6. Joint Pub 2-0, IV-15, lists and describes "Attributes of Intelligence Quality," which include the five Brei attributes plus "completeness." Both lists include an additional attribute "readiness." However, this attribute describes the overall intelligence system and not the information.

- Synergistic Value. Synergy means that the overall value of knowing the answers of multiple requirements is greater than the additive value of having answers to individual requirements.

- Multiple Uses/Customers. This issue is similar to synergy and deals with the issue of whether the satisfaction of a requirement should have a greater value, and if so by how much, if it has multiple uses or satisfies needs of more than one customer.

- Standing vs. Ad Hoc Requirements. The key distinctions between standing and ad hoc requirements are timeliness and the situations, if any, for which the requirements are generated.

- Stated vs. Implied Requirements. Assigning value for stated and implied requirements is the same. However, the risk is that effort will be wasted if the analyst's inference of information need is different from what the customers actually need.[581]

- Internal vs. External Requirements. At issue is how one should relate the value judgments of one organization with those of another.

- Inflation. The issue of inflation is closely related to the internal-vs.-external requirements issue. In order to increase the likelihood of validation and probability of collection, some originators may be tempted to inflate the priority of their requirements. However, prevention of inflated priorities is critical to making a prioritization scheme work.

THE PRICE OF EVERYTHING, THE VALUE OF NOTHING?

Measuring the value of information is difficult for several reasons.[582]

First, the situation, which determines the value of information, is constantly and rapidly changing. In addition, the truth about the current situation is not always nor readily known. Furthermore, perspective will cause observers to discern situations differently.

Second, decisionmakers' perceptions of the situation and their need for information can fluctuate over time. Their emotional state may also play a role. Stress levels affect reactions, thinking and judgment. Furthermore, each individual sets his own subjective

---

[581] Amos Kovacs, "The Nonuse of Intelligence," *International Journal of Intelligence and Counterintelligence* 10, no. 4 (Winter 1997-98): 389. The author notes that situations often change so fast that "it is not uncommon to find valuable collection assets spent and jeopardized to collect intelligence which is no longer required."

[582] Edison Cesar and others, *A New Approach for Measuring the Operational Value of Intelligence for Military Operations: Final Report* (Santa Monica, CA: The Rand Corp., 1994), xvii. Even the Rand Corporation, the well-known military think tank, recognizes the difficulty in determining the value of intelligence. The authors opted not to totally explore the concept of specific information value. They state: "In this report, the value of intelligence does not pertain to the intrinsic value of intelligence to a particular operation, which must always be scenario-dependent, but rather, to the kind of intelligence that is provided by various collection capabilities and its potential effect on decisionmaking." The kinds of information referred to include products resulting from: detecting, locating generally, locating precisely, classifying, identifying, tracking, acquiring (for targeting purposes), and assessing operational status.

standard of relevance, even with a consistent level of reliability.[583] The value of intelligence, like beauty, is in the eye of the beholder.

Third, not all requirements are equal in nature, granularity, importance, or urgency. Some requirements may deal with enemy capabilities and be fairly straightforward, such as: "Does country X have weapon Y?" or "Where is ship Z located?" Other questions may ask for enemy intent and encompass many subordinate questions. Clearly each requirement's specifications can affect its value.

A fourth reason why measuring the value of information is difficult is that no standard unit of measure can assess value. Perhaps the conservation of lives, dollars, time or other measurable attributes could help assign value to intelligence, but these do not adequately capture the concept of information value. Even though these objectively measurable units have absolute countable values, they also have relative values, measured subjectively, which are perhaps more useful in assessing their level of importance. For instance, a single dollar has greater significance to a pauper than a millionaire. Likewise an hour can have greater or lesser importance, depending on its proximity to an absolute deadline, such as a scheduled departure time.

Fifth, the value of information is unrelated to the level of effort required to obtain it. This disconnect is in contrast to the market for economic goods. For instance, the value of a bicycle is derived roughly from the cost of the parts and the level of craftsmanship applied to its manufacture. Intelligence may have tremendous value, yet require little effort to obtain. The converse is also true. Furthermore, the value of intelligence and the associated cost of obtaining it cannot be measured in similar terms. The value of the bicycle and its cost can both be measured in dollars. The value of intelligence has no comparable unit of measure. The cost of intelligence, on the other hand, can be measured in terms of dollars (to build, maintain, and operate assets), but more importantly in terms of minutes of operational asset usage.

Since no absolute basis exists for objectively measuring the value of intelligence information, the only way to assess value is to do so in relative, prioritized terms. Some measure of value is required, even if subjective, in order to determine optimization. The value of intelligence information expected to be derived from a requirement and its subsequent collection, processing, and dissemination is established during the existing prioritization process. It should be based on two major components. The first is the importance of the specific situation for which the information will be used. The second is the criticality of information, which is driven by three primary factors: intrinsic importance, timeliness, and accuracy (or resolution).

---

[583] Glenn Hastedt, "Intelligence and U.S. Foreign Policy: How to Measure Success?" *International Journal of Intelligence and Counterintelligence* 5, no. 1 (Spring 1991): 49-62. Professor Hastedt cautions that the value of intelligence should not be determined by the success or failure of an operation based on the intelligence information.

Granted, because of the subjectivity inherent in the value determination process, the establishment of value can be abused. The difference between the urgency and importance of requirements in given situations should be recognized, and more timely or accurate information invariably has greater value. Automation, particularly if it contains advanced reasoning logic, can assist with the complicated determination of value. Regardless of how value is established, some measure is needed in order to determine whether the Intelligence Community is getting its money's worth.

COST OF INTELLIGENCE

In economics, cost is an amount expended or sacrificed in order to obtain something of value. The concept of cost to obtain intelligence information is the same. It is the amount of intelligence assets "used up," expended, or consumed in order to gain information of value. If a sensor, for instance, can only image six targets per hour, then the asset cost to image each target is ten minutes. For purposes of this article, cost is expressed in terms of asset consumption, not financial expenditure.

Although a comprehensive cost of obtaining valuable information also includes human, equipment, and facility costs associated with processing, exploitation, production, and dissemination, only the costs associated with collection asset use need be considered here. Clearly these other activities are substantial and are often more constrained than the collection assets. In order to simplify the juxtaposition of value and cost, however, this abbreviated approach will be taken. Without collection, the other activities cannot take place. Potential value of the information resides in collected raw data that, after processing, may eventually satisfy the consumer. If the potential value can be maximized while the collection asset cost is minimized, then at least the requirements management function will have been optimized.

FACTORS IMPACTING THE CALCULATION OF ASSET CONSUMPTION

The key component of asset consumption is time. The following factors impact the calculation of asset consumption measured in time.

- Normal Capacity. Not every asset, especially those that require human controllers, operates 24 hours a day. A daily capacity under normal operating conditions must be calculated for these assets.

- Downtime. Some assets can only operate on the move; some assets cannot operate on the move; others can operate under either condition. For those that cannot operate on the move, transit time as well as tear-down and set-up time must be built into cost estimates.

- Accuracy and Timeliness. Typically, greater accuracy implies a greater cost because more sensor dwell time or more assets are needed to achieve the accuracy. Although greater accuracy results in higher costs, increased timeliness generally does not.

- Required vs. Desired. In addition to accuracy, other specifications, such as technical parameters or level of output detail, generally have increased costs as the specifications become more stringent.

- Marginal Cost. Marginal or incremental cost bears a similar relationship to cost as synergy does to value. One or many requirements might be satisfied with a single element of cost, whether measured as a single minute, image, etc.

- Cost Apportionment. The cost of a collection mission must be apportioned among all the requirements against which collection was attempted, not just those for which collection was successful.

The explanation of the impact of the situation on cost follows the discussion on issues, unlike the section on value, for two reasons. First, other elements besides the consumption of an asset's time and the situational impact on consumption contribute to the determination of cost. Second, the actual cost to collect information can vary radically from the expected cost. The situation certainly impacts expected value, but value is determined primarily in pre-collection planning mode. On the other hand, the cost of collection is subject to the pitfalls of reality and the laws of probability during execution.

In addition to the generic factors itemized above, the following situational factors could impact the calculation of an asset's time to collect against a specific requirement. To some degree, the collection requirements manager should be able to estimate the impact of these factors on the *time* calculation.

- Weather. Anticipated adverse weather conditions could cause a deviation in a normal flight path or require a sensor to extend its dwell time in order to adequately sense the target. Weather could also prevent collection from taking place at all.

- Terrain. Like weather, terrain (especially man-made changes such as battle damage or camouflage) could limit sensor access so that greater dwell time is required to sense the target.

- Enemy. The enemy could threaten an asset and hinder access so that fewer targets could be sensed in a single mission. Hence the cost per requirement would be greater.

- Friendlies. Because of the imposition of restrictive rules of engagement, the time required to collect certain information may increase. Flight paths may be curtailed or the availability of certain desirable terrain, such as high ground, may be reserved for operational forces.

- Recent Asset History. The state of the asset, such as maintenance level, or of its operators, including the level of sleep deprivation, will affect the efficiency of the asset and hence time consumption. Overtasking could also result in inefficiencies and human error.

- Use of Marginal Assets. Because of issues related to asset capabilities, accessibilities, and availabilities, in addition to the factors noted above, some assets may only be marginally capable of collecting against a requirement. If marginal assets were selected to execute the collection mission, their anticipated inefficiencies may impact the calculation of time, in addition to potentially impacting other variables such as accuracy or value.

As noted above, additional elements, besides the consumption of an asset's time, impact the potential cost of executing a collection mission. However, unlike the time factors above, which should be relatively simple to estimate, these other elements are subject to the laws of probability. The process of executing collection missions introduces risk that additional costs besides time may be incurred. Examples of these costs include:

- Degradation/malfunction/loss of an asset, either temporarily or permanently, due to enemy action, fratricide, weather, or bad luck
- Loss/degradation of access, either temporary or permanent
- Perception of collected data as genuine, which are made available as part of an enemy's deception plan
- Loss of asset effectiveness due to overuse or rapidly changing missions and associated non-productive time
- Compromise of current/proposed friendly missions/lives
- Compromise to intelligence sources and methods

Although these potential costs are subjective and difficult to measure, both in terms of probabilities and severity of the penalty, an experienced collection requirements manager should be able partially to control or minimize them by choosing effective strategies. The difficult part of assessing the impact of these potential costs is obtaining historical data on which to base judgments.

An important point to remember is that even if a mission is not successful in collecting the data, the cost of its execution has still been incurred and must be accounted for. The issue of cost apportionment then comes into play. This is the same concept as a marketer who expends effort to procure a sale, but is unable to make it. Because actual costs could vary dramatically from anticipated costs, the post-collection assessment phase must include a review of planned vs. actual costs, something critical to future optimization.

CALLED TO ACCOUNT

Cost, like value, is difficult to measure. As noted above, it consists not only of a time element, but other potential expenditures as well. Integrating these factors into an intelligible model is challenging to say the least. The calculation is further complicated because the situation can change so rapidly and because limited data will be available to judge probabilities.

Cost determination is exacerbated by the complicated organizational structure for collection within the Intelligence Community. Because collection requirements managers do not directly control the collection assets, they must rely on asset managers to provide detailed cost data. Some asset managers may consider the provision of detailed cost data as an infringement on their turf. However, without the weighing of values — which collection requirements managers know, against costs — which asset managers know — optimization is impossible. Furthermore, asset managers may seek to optimize the performance of their assets, to the detriment of optimizing the use of all assets. As the importance of optimization increases, the functions of requirements and asset managers may draw closer together or even merge.

The cost of each asset to be considered for a collection problem is determined during the candidate asset development phase. The first step in calculating asset cost is to establish the amount of time necessary to collect the information requested in the specific requirement. The asset managers should make available to the collection requirements manager each asset's generic "capacity." For technical assets, the manufacturer should have estimated the capacity in terms of numbers of channels, numbers of photos per hour, or suchlike. The capacity of human assets can also be estimated based on workload and distances to travel. Costs would typically be greater to collect against a requirement's desired, as opposed to required, specifications. Of course, generic capacities and costs will have to be modified for existing, real-world conditions. The ability to estimate costs will come through experience and by knowing the current requirements set and collection posture.

Other costs cannot be measured in the same manner that time is. These are intangible and can only be "quasi-estimated" in terms of lives, asset capabilities, plans/intentions/ information compromised. Determining whether these other costs are worth the potential benefits of collection is a subjective policy decision. The collection requirements manager, in conjunction with the asset manager, or even the senior decisionmaker in significant cases, will have to determine the tradeoff, perhaps on a requirement-by-requirement basis.

The probability for estimating other costs can be categorized as high, medium, or low. The severity of the impact is likewise estimated in one of three categories. The norm for both estimates will be considered low. If an estimate of the other costs for a given requirement equals the norm, further consideration of the risk of other costs should cease. If the potential risk exceeds the norm, then a human decision is required whether to pursue the collection.

Only after the value and cost of intelligence are understood and quantified to a degree, can efficient resource allocation decisions be made. Efficiency leads to optimization, the ultimate economic state for efficient intelligence operations.[584] For a finite set of collection assets, only a finite set of requirements can be satisfied. Optimization attempts cost-effectively to satisfy the demand for intelligence with a limited supply of assets. During the strategy development phase of the collection requirements management process, values and costs should be compared and adjusted via sensitivity analysis

---

[584] David W. Pearce, editor, *The MIT Dictionary of Modern Economics* (Cambridge, MA: The MIT Press, 1996), under the word "optimum." Optimum is "the 'best' situation or state of affairs. To achieve optimum is to 'optimize.' ... In attempting to attain an optimum we are usually constrained by the fundamental scarcity of goods and resources."

so that an optimal strategy can be devised. During the post-collection assessment phase, the collection requirements manager can determine how close to optimum the just-executed strategy was.

Only when the Intelligence Community plans and executes intelligence operations using economic principles will it provide proficient service to decisionmakers. This approach includes considering the value of intelligence products and the cost of producing them, as well as implementing strategies in optimal ways. Educating consumers about these principles will help the Intelligence Community to become more efficient and effective, the truly "economic" way to do business.

NARCO-MERCANTILISM AND THE WAR ON DRUGS: IS VICTORY AN OPTION?

William H. Drohan

(Originally published in the Defense Intelligence Journal 10, No. 2 (2001), 41-52).

Mercantilism invokes vague images of trading empires, sailing ships carrying the wealth of the New World off to merchant princes in Europe, and perhaps the exploitation of whole populations in that New World. The prefix "narco" augments an already extensive vocabulary of politically charged terminology, and compounding the noun produces such alarming concepts as narco-trafficker, narco-dictator, and narco-terrorist. Each word suggests evil or, as in the cases of narco-insurgent and narco-dictator, something outright sinister. So powerful has the impact of this simple prefix become that even such a sanctified term as democracy, conveys a profoundly vile and corrupt image when it becomes "narco-democracy." That said, before a discussion of narco-mercantilism can be of any practical use in examining potential threats to our national security, we must get beyond the merely reflexive.

STAKEHOLDER CAPITALISM

Mercantilism is a geo-political doctrine emphasizing a nation's economic interests over those of individuals, and promoting the concentration of resources on export production with an aim to maximizing national wealth accumulation. Narco-mercantilism is a concept with the potential to capture the imagination, but it should do so only long enough to dispel the veil draped over the flaws in our understanding of the real threat the international drug trafficking industry poses to U.S. national security and the attendant quandaries national policy makers face.[585] Like its namesake, narco-mercantilism stems from a doctrine focused on the acquisition of great wealth. Subject from top to bottom to the law of supply and demand, narco-mercantilism applies relatively simple agricultural techniques in remote, loosely regulated areas with ready supplies of cheap, semi-skilled labor to produce drugs, and especially in the cases of the cocaine, heroin and marijuana industries, from easily cultivated plants. Illicit products are then shipped, often at great distances to countries of the developed world and sold at an enormous mark-up, with profits accruing to the narco-mercantilists. The salient difference between the narco-mercantilists and many other international business endeavors lies in the illegality of the drug trafficking industry virtually everywhere. Yet, like other businesses, narco-mercantilists seek out secure locations in which to conduct their operation places where the crops upon which the industries depend can be grown" easily and cheaply. These are characteristi-

---

[585] Narco-mercantilism is a term that I coined several years ago, specifically to describe the way that drug trafficking had evolved from its beginnings as a relatively localized crime problem into an enterprise with truly global reach and impact. It is intended both to convey some sense of the magnitude of the drug problem, and to capture the reader's imagination long enough for this sense to become a part of the reader's frame of reference. It is not intended simply to expand the already extensive, frequently frivolous lexicon of similar "narco-" terms.

cally areas which lack significant, legitimate demands for labor, and where drug trafficking offers at least a reasonable expectation of making more money than any other pursuit. In poverty-stricken regions, people need only believe they can acquire more money than any alternative livelihood offers for the drug trafficking industry to gain wide and willing support. Narco-mercantilists enjoy the advantage that their profit margin from the production to consumption area is so great that they can outbid any competitor for labor resources and popular support, and still expect to accumulate the huge personal wealth narco-mercantilism promises.

While some governments in nations where drug traffickers operate have tolerated, or even supported drug trafficking industries, the latter remain privately dominated enterprises?[586] A result of this private wealth has been the steady rise of a select class of international criminal entrepreneurs with resources that permit them to rival, or even surpass, the capabilities of the governments in nominal control over their base areas. History already offers several examples of non-state actors challenging the power governments for their own ends. The wealth and pursuits of the Knights Templars set them at odds with the French king, who reigned, but was chronically short of money. The Hanseatic League, prosperous by dint of its trade empire, exercised sweeping authority over a large region of northern Europe for centuries. In a more recent example, British policy India was largely dominated by the mercantile interests of the British East India Company, a commercial empire that outfitted and deployed its own army and fleet to protect Company interests. Where narco-mercantilists have gained power, they have in some cases established predominance in regions of strategic importance to the security interests of the United States. Such non-governmental competitors for local power often defy failing governments, thereby frustrating regional security goals and keeping large areas mired in chaos and poverty.

At the Dawn of the new millennium, the United States is at war with these drug traffickers. It has, in fact, been involved in a lingering war since 1973, with the intensity of the struggle waxing and waning during its long history. The conflict has entailed war without borders, without clearly identifiable enemies, devoid of well-defined objectives, and ultimately without victory. Such is the "national war on drugs." Vaguely identified by this phrase, the conflict has retained an amorphous quality since its inception during the Nixon administration. Lack of clarity about national objectives and the nature of the task at hand has been a major factor in producing the perpetual climate of failure haunting this critical national effort. While failures in this endeavor are evident, since drug traffickers are still smuggling tons of their products around the world and continue to reap enormous profits, these have been in the areas on which critics gener-

---

[586] Among the best sources for specific information regarding the association of individual nations and drug trafficking over the last twenty years that readers should consult for further data are two unclassified, annual U.S. government reports: The International Narcotics Control Strategy Report (INCSR), published by the Department of State; and the National Narcotics Intelligence Consumers Committee (NNICC) Report, The Supply of illicit Drugs To The United States, published by the Drug Enforcement Administration. These documents are widely employed throughout the Federal counterdrug community and are two of the most important sources for the state of international drug trafficking over time.

ally focus. Illicit drug trade has not been decisively defeated, and drugs remain a major social problem within the United States and in ever expanding areas abroad. Victory is proving to be a long and hard road indeed. But in fairness to all those who have labored, conscientiously if not altogether successfully, to end the American drug problem, lack of success does not spring from want of talent or exertion. The national effort against drugs has *not* produced failure, so much as it has not produced something clearly identifiable and generally accepted as success in a poorly defined and understood task where definitive success may not be attainable.

A new U.S. administration at the threshold of a new century provides an opportunity to re-examine the fundamental questions of what the United States set out to accomplish in the 1970's, and whether more detailed and disciplined examinations of what it has confronted all these years may be useful in charting the future course of national drug policy. One must not belittle the contributions of those officials at all levels who have devoted their careers to combating drugs, many at considerable personal or professional risk, sometimes even at the cost of their lives. Neither should one sit on the ground and sing sad songs, like those dejected Greek warriors outside Troy after Achilles was killed, when it seemed Troy would never be defeated. While victory in the familiar military sense of the term may not be attainable, significant improvement is possible. We can only move forward and accurately assess our progress, though, if we develop a better understanding of the task the United States set for itself in this national "war on drugs." Given the scale the threat from drug trafficking has reached in the last quarter century, the United States has no choice but to confront the drug threat. The alternative to doing so is a rapidly expanding class of new, non-state-based challenges to American national security. The potential harm narco-mercantilism engenders leaves counterdrug (CD) policy-making officials longing for the prosaic days in the late 1970's of multi-ton marijuana loads, slow coastal freighters and "good ol' boy'" smugglers. True, disciplined intelligence assessment of the threat posed by drug trafficking raises serious doubts about the best CD efforts the US car mount; yet, at the same time, analysis can guide policy makers to more effective and realistic policy choices. The gravest error in national drug policy would be failure to confront the true nature of the drug threat and the practical limits of our own capabilities.

WHAT WE ARE ABOUT, AND HOW WE GOT HERE

When President Richard Nixon first declared his national war on drugs, the United States was already deeply involved in another conflict, Viet Nam.[587] There the American military was experiencing severe problems as a result of the ready availability of drugs,

---

[587] *The Politics of Heroin, CIA Complicity in The Global Drug Trade*, Alfred McCoy, Lawrence Hill Books, Brooklyn. New York, 1991 is a good source on the early days of the current drug trafficking problem, and the development of U.S. drug policy. Although I disagree with some of his analyses and details, McCoy provides a useful view of the long history of drug trafficking, set in a broad context of its impact on other major events occurring in the same regions and time periods. This book goes a long way in dispelling the idea that drug trafficking is simply a large collection of individual crimes, lacking a broader significance as a regional security issue.

notably heroin and marijuana, to American troops, as well as from national division over the war more broadly. Domestically, the United States faced a mounting crisis from an expanding variety of illicit drugs then being widely abused by Americans President Nixon's concern for these twin threats, drugs abroad and at home prompted him to identify the national effort to halt the abuse of illicit drug as a major policy goal of his administration. In articulating his intention Nixon echoed the politically successful theme of a "war on poverty" from the preceding Johnson administration. His use of this rhetorical device describing his new initiative as a "war," should not, however, be taken as an indication that the effort lacked sincerity or executive authority. Even a cursory examination of the manner in which the Nixon administration vaulted bureaucratic boundaries, re-ordered major elements of several cabinet departments, and ultimately chartered an entirely new government organization, The United States Drug Enforcement Administration (DEA) reveals Nixon's determination to bring the full weight of the federal government to bear in solving the national drug problem. In truth, the ringing, but inaccurate metaphor of making "war on drugs" served the Nixon administration and its successors in office badly. The war metaphor on offer at the outset of the Nixon initiative and never wholly repudiated though frequently criticized and even ridiculed in subsequent years, has caused a considerable amount of the confusion and lack of focus in America's CD effort ever since.

THEY CRY "WAR, WAR" BUT THERE IS NO WAR

However firm President Nixon and his administration were in their intent to solve America's drug problem, they did not go to war. There was no war on drugs, any more than there was actually a war on poverty, and there had been no such war in any of the years since the Nixon administration enormous yearly appropriations for the national CD effort notwithstanding what those dollars have been supporting cannot be called a war. When nations go to war, they characteristically devote their full power to defeating the enemy, as reflected in the classic U.S. Army phrase of "close with and destroy the enemy by force or violence." Nations at war also suspend many of the customary features of normal international relations. They engage in conduct violating the normal courtesies and relation between nations, although this suspension is applied only to nation recognized as parties to the war, while customary relations with others may continue. Although the effort against drugs was referred to as a war, it was not pursued through traditional military strategies, which provide for such things as direct assaults across national boundaries. The attack, the essence of the offensive, is central to such strategies. When the U.S. launched its CD effort, it employed instead a law enforcement strategy, grounded in such concepts as due process and the rules of evidence, a far more restrictive operating environment than the rules governing the conduct of military operations. Law enforcement is based upon an inherently reactive strategy, a defense, and police action occurs in response to the illegal activity of criminals. Law enforcement organizations are generally denied the benefit of seizing the initiative, and, above all, initiating the attack at a place and time of their own choosing. The task facing law enforcement officers is thus significantly more complicated than the tasks of military commanders who can seek direct confrontation and decisive engagement of the enemy when advantageous circumstances arise. Military officers are also favored by considerably less stringent rules of engagement, not being required, for example, to identify specific individuals as legitimate targets and then to support their conclusions before an open court, as their law enforcement colleagues must. This selection of a law enforcement strategy probably occurred without much conscious thought, the nature of the problem appearing so obvious. Drug trafficking and drug abuse were crimes and criminal activities were the normal province of law enforcement organizations. No enemies were attacking U.S. territory in the classic, military sense, so no targets to assign to military forces presented themselves. There were only lawbreakers, and clearly the task was one for law enforcement organizations. If the existing organizations were not already configured to effectively address the present drug threat, then the solution must be to improve the U.S. law enforcement structure, which is exactly what the Nixon administration did, most notably with the establishment of DEA. Law enforcement became the point of departure for Subsequent approaches. Policyrnakers understood that drug trafficking was an international problem, with much of it being conducted outside the jurisdictions of U.S. law enforcement agencies. If drug criminals operated outside U.S. jurisdiction, the thinking went, then they had to be in somebody's jurisdiction. In consequence, U.S. strategy would come to be based on a variation of the basic law enforcement approach. U.S. agencies would receive increased authority, funding, and encouragement to deal with drug problems within U.S. jurisdiction. Outside that jurisdiction, the cooperation and support of foreign law enforcement agencies would be sought and cultivated. Yet again, the law enforcement effort would be billed as a "war."

No pundit or Congressional committee could legitimately claim to have been deceived about the nature of this new "war" on drugs. DEA was clearly and publicly tasked to lead the national charge, with the bare support from the military elements that would normally be associated with war-making. The military raised no outcry that their preserve had bee violated; in fact, the military adopted a hands-off attitude to which it would cling well into the Reagan administration. There was general agreement and in some quarters probably a considerable amount of relief, that challenging new drug effort would be a law enforcement matter generally: and a DEA endeavor specifically. In spite of this consensus, however, tl contradictions in the rhetoric about a war on drugs were merely superficial indications of the disappointments, the inevitable recriminations, and policy divisions soon to come. Whatever the degree of tacit agreement on the la enforcement approach within the Washington Beltway, the country at large told of a war, expected not just dramatic efforts, but decisive result Despite the rhetoric of war, the US had not made war. Indeed, it had r intention of making war, and the discrepancy would soon become obvious Critics of the Nixon and subsequent administrations could always find fat with the manner in which the war on drugs was being pursued, and, above all, the vigor of the effort at any given point, but opposition was general tempered by a widely shared caution. Sentiments among members of both major parties were against an actual shift from the familiar parameters, an unsuccessful law enforcement CD strategy, to one where they would openly cry havoc and let loose the dogs of war. The only dogs in this war would be sniffing suitcases in the airport, and that was about as much even the most virulent critics would allow. No constituency for adopting a true war footing on the drug issue emerged. Despite a drug problem growing exponentially and the shortcomings of the law enforcement model every administration has nonetheless embraced the latter. The chief inadequacy of this model was that it did not work. The reactive approach to drug trafficking did not and could not produce the kind of prom] decisive resolution to be expected from war. As each subsequent administration assumed power, it found quickly that the drug problem h not gotten any easier, and the answers remained as elusive as they had be for its predecessor, whom it had recently criticized for failing to devise lasting solution to the national drug problem. One after another, each would solemnly take seats beside Hamlet, clinging to a law enforcement strategy, the evil of which they knew, rather than fly to new ones they knew naught of.

I'M NOT A GANGSTER; I'M A BUSINESSMAN[588]

The expanded local law enforcement model that prevailed in law enforcement circles in the late 1970's was clearly inadequate to describe what government agencies were confronting. Drug trafficking was no longer a simple aggregation of individual crimes, each with a relatively localized effect. Drug trafficking had become an industry, generating wealth on such a scale that it did far more than make individuals rich and afford them a lavish lifestyle. It had actually begun to put amounts of money large enough to be accurately described as capital into criminal hands. True, earlier recent instances of criminal capital accumulation, such as the money made on illegal alcohol, gambling and prostitution, which provided the capital to develop the Las Vegas gambling industry, did occur, but these did not match the scope of the international operations being observed in drug trafficking. Among the traffickers, money was being made hand over fist, and was rolling in faster than anything law enforcement had previously experienced. In a single generation, street criminals could hope to amass sufficient money to expand into legitimate enterprises, effectively shielding themselves from the criminal origins of their fortunes. Worse, drug traffickers could become economic forces in the poverty-stricken countries where many of their operations were based. They were developing and cultivating social and political influence, acquiring their own constituencies, and even entering foreign governments themselves. Mario Puzo's "Godfather," Don Vito Corleone, could be speaking about these drug traffickers when he proffers his wry quip that he is not a gangster, but a businessman. To be sure, Don Corleone surpassed the status of common criminal. By the early 1980's, many drug traffickers too had become businessmen of sorts. While they exercise substantial influence on entire countries, their objectives are not political or revolutionary, but economic.

One should regard drug trafficking for what it is: a global, clandestine criminal industry. This description distinguishes it from the widely held view of drug trafficking as simply a large grab bag of individual crimes. Although the phrase "international drug trafficking industry" has since gained general acceptance, the term "global" is a key element of this working definition of drug trafficking. The distinction represents more than just a literary preference. While the term "international" may flow nicely in papers and

---

[588] Comment by Vito Corleone from the Mario Puzo/Francis Ford Coppola "Godfather" book and cinema series.

speeches, it refers to activities that can involve as few as two nations. The term "global," for its part, offers a much more compelling reminder of the vast playing field upon which drug traffickers operate, and of the broad selection of alternative producing and transit countries from which narco-mercantilists can freely choose in planning individual operations. The term "clandestine" reflects one of the two key differences between drug trafficking and any other international business. Drug traffickers must, at least nominally, keep their activities hidden from law enforcement agencies. The term "criminal" reflects the second of these key differences. While drug traffickers may be able to operate in defiance of the governments of many impoverished countries with ineffective internal control of their national territories, or enjoy extensive protection afforded by corrupt officials in other countries, drug trafficking still violates numerous laws in virtually every country. Finally, the tern "industry" reflects the basic nature of drug trafficking. While their activities may be hidden and illegal, drug traffickers produce and sell products to make a profit; they do it for the money. Further, they must continue doing it to achieve and maintain their desired levels of success in the industry. Although drug traffickers are often associated with such other international problems as insurgency and terrorism, the raison d'etre of drug trafficking is money. The intended disposition of this money may be tied to other threats to international stability, but where drug trafficking is a source of capital accumulation, the profit motive is instrumental t narcotics trafficking.

PECUNIA NON OLET: MONEY DOES NOT RETAIN THE SMELL OF ITS ORIGIN

No verifiable estimates of the total amount of money being generated by international drug trafficking exist, but raw figures ranging into the hundreds of billions of dollars are close enough to cause even first world governments serious concerns. Though total drug revenues are wide dispersed among trafficking organizations, the evidence is compelling that drug trafficking is putting huge amounts of unregulated money into the hands of criminals and groups with a penchant for violence. Even unsuccessful aspirants to drug trafficking wealth can benefit from their more successful colleagues. For one thing, an individual drug criminal does not have to make millions in order to feel that he is at least on the way to wealth. He only needs to make more money than he could make doing anything else that may be available to him. For thousands of lower-level participants in poverty-stricken countries where drug crops are raised, shipments transit en route to world markets, amounts as small as a five hundred dollars, minute operating expenses for more important traffickers are sufficient inducement to attract a reliable labor pool for even the most dangerous and demanding jobs in the trafficking industry. Hence, the continuing *anticipation* that anyone can become rich in drug trafficking, confirmed by the relatively smaller number of those who truly succeed proves an irresistible lure for the poor and the desperate whom the industry recruits.

IT ISN'T THE ACQUISITION, BUT THE DISPOSITION

Achievement of even modest wealth can equate to serious influence and power in third world economies, making civic leaders and politicians out of some drug traffickers, and friends of civic leaders and politicians out of many more. Drug criminals attaining political and economic influence in countries where the US has strategic interests inevitably represent a potential challenge to those interests. By way of example, U.S. relations with much of Latin America have been dominated for the last quarter century by considerations of the "three d's" (democracy, development and drugs), with drugs often playing a disproportionate and perhaps inordinate role because of the sheer magnitude of drug trafficking in many Latin American countries. Elsewhere as well, in such areas as southeast Asia and south Asia, U.S. policy makers, even U.S. regional Commanders-in-Chief, have had to confront challenges to U.S. national objectives resulting from the influence of drug trafficking in host country economies. Worse than the international economic influence of drug traffickers is the exploitation of drug trafficking's economic potential to bankroll political movements and military organizations. Some analysts contend that selected insurgents have become drug traffickers in order to finance their wars against established governments. Drug trafficking and insurgency, redoubtable as these are, ultimately have conflicting objectives, but short-term marriages of convenience furnish motivation to cooperate against a third party, the national government. Accordingly, the US is currently on the verge of a greatly expanded effort to prevent the government of Colombia from being overwhelmed by the combined effects of rampant drug trafficking and unbridled insurgency. No resolution to the debate about who is a terrorist or narco-mercantilist, nor answer to the basic question whether major U.S. interests in Colombia are threatened by an alarmingly well capitalized insurgency, is likely to be found. That said, drug trafficking is transferring immense amounts of illicit revenue to individuals actively fighting against this beleaguered friendly government. The destructive potential of the drug shadow economy to produce or to support effective competitors for power within the borders of an existing nation state makes drug trafficking a legitimate U.S. security concern in the Andes, and in other similarly threatened regions.

IDENTIFYING THE KEYS TO SURVIVAL

While the effort against drug trafficking should not be called a war, many concepts and techniques developed for both strategic and tactical intelligence in support of military operations can be readily adapted to the needs of counterdrug operations. First among these is the detailed analysis of opposing forces and the enemy situation. Framing the analysis in military terms usually assists readers with military backgrounds to apply the invaluable experience they can bring to the counterdrug campaign. Further, it provides readers from all sectors of the existing multi-agency environment more common ground to develop the combination of ideas and techniques necessary to achieving progress against the drug target. In such a model, there are attackers and defenders, and an understanding of their differences is critical to everything that follows. At the most basic level, a threat to the national security of the United States from unrestrained, international drug trafficking presents itself. The existence of this threat has even been codified in a National

Security Decision Directive (NSDD 221)[589] signed by the President. While there is no single enemy, neatly defined and identified by international borders and uniforms with fixed insignia, there are attackers and defenders in the broader sense that one side .holds the initiative and other advantages, while the other does not.

The attacker in this model is the narco-mercantilist. As is his wont, the attacker enjoys the advantages of being able to choose the time, place and manner of assault. He can also elect not to attack, at least for some extended period of time. Short-duration law enforcement surge operations supported by temporary assignment of additional law enforcement and military assets, involve long planning and approval cycles, and once it motion, are often difficult to modify because of other, pre-schedule commitments. Favored by their far shorter planning and approval cycle drug traffickers have often frustrated major interdiction operations simply by suspending their activities until the end of the planned interdiction surge. After the additional, temporary assets return to their new assignments, the traffickers resume their own operations, confident of a extended period before the assets will be available to attempt the next law enforcement surge.

The counterdrug elements, both law enforcement and military, are the defenders in this model. As such, they must await the actions of the traffickers and respond as well as they can. Where the customary military model involves one attacker, the multiple, independent organizations that make up the drug trafficking industry present counterdrug elements with multiple attackers, all of which must be defeated separately. The problems of the defender can be summarized as having to defend everywhere against everything, all the time. One is reminded of Frederick the Great's cogent remark that to defend everything is ultimately to defend nothing. Such is the dilemma.

A variant of another military model can be employed to examine the possible approaches around which the U.S. might organize a sound national counterdrug strategy. Military planners often assess enemy vulnerabilities by identifying and evaluating what an opposing force must accomplish or possess to achieve its objectives. A simple example of this method is the maxim that in order to survive on the battlefield, a military force must be able to move, shoot and communicate. Drug traffickers, for all the advantages they have, are also bound by certain critical requirements to succeed or survive on their own battlefield. These broadly defined are:

- the ability to maintain reliable sources of supply,
- the ability to maintain reliable demand,
- the ability to move products and supplies,
- the ability to maintain operational and personal security,
- the ability to safely enjoy the proceeds.

---

[589] National Security Decision Directive (NSDD) 221. Ronald Reagan,. cited in "Strategic Planning and the Drug Threat," William W. Mendel and Murl D. Munger, A Joint Study Initiative by the National Interagency Counterdrug Institute (NICI); The Strategic Studies Institute; US Army War College, and the Fort Military Studies Office, Fort Leavenworth Kansas, August 1997: 11.

Just as military analysts seek enemy vulnerabilities that might disrupt one or more of the key elements of battlefield survival (Move-Shoot-Communicate) to plan military strategies, counterdrug policy makers can evaluate these five requirements for successful drug trafficking for opportunities to attack their targets. The essential idea is to identify factors critical to the success of the enemy. Truth be told, no single point where the drug trafficking industry can be decisively engaged and destroyed presents itself. Yet, there are opportunities to assail all five requirements for successful drug trafficking, and U.S. counterdrug elements are becoming more astute at exploiting such vulnerabilities. Granted, progress has been uneven and success elusive, but no more conclusive outcome appears attainable. Narco-mercantilism is likely to remain a threat to U.S. national security interests and those of other nations for years to corne. The most promising approach to combating this opponent is to focus counterdrug efforts on the five areas, seizing opportunities as they present themselves, and dispelling unrealistic expectations about counterdrug efforts.

About the Contributors

PART I: THE WORK OF INTELLIGENCE

- Most professions have a body of literature that lays out the "doctrine" or the "philosophy" of that profession. Intelligence is no exception. In his article, "Meeting the Intelligence Community's Continuing Need for an Intelligence Literature," **Dr. Russell G. Swenson** discusses a historical foundation for intelligence literature in the work of Sherman Kent, then shows how work being done at the Joint Military Intelligence College is contributing substantially to the contemporary body of literature in the profession. Dr. Swenson is the Director of the Center for Strategic Intelligence Research at the Joint Military Intelligence College, and has been responsible for the publication of scores of books and articles by college students and faculty.

- **James S. Major** came to the Joint Military Intelligence College in 1985 as a Lieutenant Colonel in the United States Army and remained after his retirement as the Director of the College Writing Center. His book *Writing with Intelligence* is a textbook in graduate and undergraduate courses at the College and is widely used throughout the Intelligence Community. The excerpt presented here is chapter 2, "The Basic Tools of Writing with Intelligence," stressing the importance of such basic considerations as clarity, conciseness, and correctness in intelligence writing.

- **Lisa Krizan,** a civilian employee of the Department of Defense, completed her master's thesis at the Joint Military Intelligence College in 1996. Entitled *Benchmarking the Intelligence Process for the Private Sector: A New Role for the Intelligence Community,* it was subsequently adapted as an Occasional Paper, *Intelligence Essentials for Everyone* (Washington, DC: Joint Military Intelligence College, June 1999). In his Preface to that paper, Lieutenant General James A. Williams, U.S. Army (Retired), a former Director of the Defense Intelligence Agency, writes: "[Lisa Krizan] has articulated clearly the fundamentals of sound intelligence practice and has identified some guidelines that can lead toward creation of a solid intelligence infrastructure. These signposts apply both to government intelligence and to business." Excerpted from that paper for this book are the Prologue, Part I, and Part II.

- **Dr. Ronald D. Garst** is the Provost of the Joint Military Intelligence College, and Dr. Max L. Gross, formerly the Dean of the School of Intelligence Studies, is currently serving as a Senior Research Fellow at the College. Their article, "On Becoming an Intelligence Analyst," appeared in the *Defense Intelligence Journal* 6, no. 2 (1997): 47-59. Reprinted here in its entirety, the piece "describes that set of talents, skills and personal characteristics required of the successful all-source intelligence analyst" (page 47). The table referred to in the text, citing the College curriculum for academic years 1988–1998 and 1998–1999, has been updated to reflect the current curriculum at the Joint Military Intelligence College.

- **William S. Brei** was a Captain in the United States Air Force when he wrote his master's thesis at the Joint Military Intelligence College in 1993. Entitled *Assess-*

ing Intelligence by Principles of Quality: Case Study of Imagery Intelligence Support to Operation PROVIDE COMFORT, it was adapted in 1996 as an Occasional Paper, *Getting Intelligence Right: The Power of Logical Procedure* (Washington, DC: Joint Military Intelligence College, January 1996). In his Foreword to that paper, Dr. Russell G. Swenson, Director of the College Center for Strategic Intelligence Research, writes that Captain Brei's "critique of joint intelligence doctrine is constructive, and is informed by his decade of experience in intelligence management. ... [His] argument establishes the value of closely scrutinizing widely used but ill-defined intelligence terms." An excerpt of Brei's Occasional Paper is presented here.

- **Jan Goldman**, a faculty member at the Joint Military Intelligence College, teaches such diverse subjects as ethics in intelligence and indications and warning intelligence. In June 2000, he compiled Occasional Paper Number Eight, *Dangerous Assumption: Preparing the U.S. Intelligence Warning System for the New Millennium* (Washington, DC: Joint Military Intelligence College, June 2000). That work contained condensed versions of 11 course papers written by our students and dealing with the subject of warning. Included in this book of readings are Goldman's introduction to the Occasional Paper and one of the papers from the work: "Opening Windows of Opportunity: The Need for Opportunities-Based Warning" by **Stewart C. Eales**, a civilian employee of the Office of Naval Intelligence.

- In June 1999 the Joint Military Intelligence College hosted a conference on teaching intelligence studies at colleges and universities. Scholars from throughout the intelligence and academic communities participated and presented papers at the conference, held at the Defense Intelligence Analysis Center at Bolling Air Force Base, Washington, DC. Among the presenters was faculty member **Mark G. Marshall,** whose paper, "Teaching Vision," is reprinted in its entirety here. **Marshall** offers a unique perspective, having been an imagery analyst, then a Joint Military Intelligence College student, and now a faculty member in our Department of Intelligence Collection and Technical Operations. All papers from the conference were assembled and published as Occasional Paper Number Five, *A Flourishing Craft: Teaching Intelligence Studies* (Washington, DC: Joint Military Intelligence College, June 1999).

- **Jon A. Wiant**, a career member of the Department of State's Senior Executive Service, now serves as under contract as a faculty member at the Joint Military Intelligence College. His article, "Spy Fiction, Spy Reality," appeared in the Summer 2004 issue of *American Intelligence Journal*. That article, reprinted here in its entirety, reflects some of the key differences between some of the public perceptions of the "spy business" as reflected in popular fiction and the hard, cold reality of true human intelligence work.

- **Francis J. Hughes** is a faculty member at the Joint Military Intelligence College. He teaches courses in thesis research and writing as well as intelligence analysis, focusing on the necessary tasks of gathering evidence and convincing the reader through sound argument. The excerpt reprinted here, dealing with "Evidence Marshaling and Argument Construction," is from the course notes used in his class on *The Art and Science of the Process of Intelligence Analysis*.

- **Thomas Dowling** served from May 2003 until the conclusion of its work as a professional staff member of the National Commission on Terrorist Attacks upon the United States, popularly known as the 9/11 Commission. A 1996 graduate of the Joint Military Intelligence College and currently on the faculty, Dowling had a distinguished 30-year career in the Department of State Foreign Service, focused on the Middle East and South Asia. He brings to bear that expertise in his current teaching and writing. Reproduced here is the text of an address Dowling gave as the keynote speaker at the Third Annual Homecoming of the Joint Military Intelligence College Alumni Association at the United States Naval Academy in October 2004. His speech, rooted in his personal experience, addresses a "profound failure of vision in the Intelligence Community."

- **William C. Spracher** is editor, Center for Strategic Intelligence Research, Joint Military Intelligence College. In addition to teaching a course on Latin American issues at the College, he has taught diverse subjects at NDU's Center for Hemispheric Defense Studies and School for National Security Executive Education, the Inter-American Defense College, as an adjunct for American University, and the USMA Social Sciences Department. A retired Army colonel and doctoral candidate at George Washington University, he presented versions of the article "Homeland Security and Intelligence" at an international defense education seminar in Chile and at an educators conference at the Yale Center for International and Area Studies in 2003. Subsequently published in the journal *Low Intensity Conflict & Law Enforcement*, the article discusses the problems of merging disparate cultures — law enforcement vs. intelligence, civil entities vs. military, federal vs. state and local levels, and domestic vs. international focuses — in responding to the challenges of a post-9/11 world.

PART II: THE HISTORY OF INTELLIGENCE

- **A. Denis Clift** is the President of the Joint Military Intelligence College. Some of his extensive writings and speeches are compiled in a book, *Clift Notes*, 2nd ed. (Washington, DC: Joint Military Intelligence College, 2002). Reprinted here is chapter 3 of that book, "The San Cristobal Trapezoid," an extraordinary account of the Cuban Missile Crisis in 1963, which he co-authored with **John T. Hughes**, the intelligence analyst who briefed the nation on that crisis on 6 February 1963.

- **Eugene L. Zorn**, a Senior Analyst with the Department of Defense, wrote his master's thesis at the Joint Military Intelligence College in 1999. Entitled *Expanding the Horizon: The Origins of Israel's Reconnaissance Satellite Program*, it was condensed in 2001 into a shorter article for *Studies in Intelligence*, the Unclassified Edition, Winter-Spring 2001): 33-38. The article, "Israel's Quest for Satellite Intelligence," is reprinted here in its entirety. It reflects the fact that often vast quantities of information on seemingly the most sensitive subjects are available in open sources.

- Colonel **Thomas W. Shreeve**, United States Marine Corps Reserve, Retired, was a faculty member in the Postgraduate Intelligence Program for Reserves at the Joint Military Intelligence College. In that capacity, he compiled several case studies that could be used to teach intelligence. Those case studies were published by the College as Discussion Paper Number Twelve, *Experiences to Go: Teaching with Intelligence Case Studies* (Washington, DC: Joint Military Intelligence College, September 2004). An extract from that paper is reprinted here.

- **Dr. Anne Daugherty Miles** is a retired U.S. Air Force Lieutenant Colonel who served on the Joint Military Intelligence College faculty and continues to serve as an adjunct faculty member. In 2001 she compiled an overview of the role of congressional oversight in forming a major national agency. That work was published as Occasional Paper Number Nine, *The Creation of the National Imagery and Mapping Agency: Congress's Role as Overseer* (Washington, DC: Joint Military Intelligence College, April 2001). Her paper, reprinted here in its entirety, is instructive for its insights into the importance of congressional oversight in the Intelligence Community.

PART III: THE APPLICATIONS OF INTELLIGENCE

- **George C. Fidas** is a faculty member at the Joint Military Intelligence College. His article, "Health and National Security," first appeared in the book *Divided Diplomacy and the Next Administration: Conservative and Liberal Alternatives* edited by Henry R. Nau and David Shambaugh (Washington, DC: The Elliott School of International Affairs, The George Washington University, 2004). Fidas, a retired CIA analyst, has written extensively on European and transnational security issues. This article clearly shows the importance of the growing infectious disease threat.

- **Dr. Perry L. Pickert**, a faculty member at the Joint Military Intelligence College, compiled a book called *Intelligence for Multilateral Decision and Action* (Washington, DC: Joint Military Intelligence College, June 1997). The book, edited by **Dr. Russell G. Swenson**, contained condensed versions of 23 master's theses written by our students, all dealing with multinational issues of interest to the Intelligence Community. The article presented here, "Intelligence Support to Refugee Operations: Who's the Expert?" was written by United States Army Captain **James D. Edwards** in August 1996.

- **Dr. Pauletta Otis**, an adjunct faculty member at the Joint Military Intelligence College, writes widely on ethnic issues, especially on violence in a religious context. Her article, "Religion and War in the 21st Century," was published as a chapter in *Religion: The Missing Dimension of Security* (Rowman and Littlefield, 2004). The article is a powerful account of one of the most troubling phenomena in our time: the religious basis for violence in contemporary warfare.

- **James B. Petro** wrote his master's thesis at the Joint Military Intelligence College on the important subject of bioterrorism. A condensed version of his article appeared in *Studies in Intelligence* 48, the Unclassified Edition (2004): 57-68. The article, "Intelligence Support to the Life Science Community: Mitigating Threats from Bioterrorism," is reprinted here in its entirety.

■ **A. Denis Clift** is the President of the Joint Military Intelligence College. On 2 February 2005, he spoke to the MASINT Conference at the National Reconnaissance Office about the importance of intelligence in today's fast-moving world. Coining some new terms for this new world, he called his speech " 'SALSA for Cyber Sonics': Education and Research at the Joint Military Intelligence College." The text of that speech is reprinted here.

■ **Mark Jensen** has extensive experience in the Intelligence Community in both MASINT and collection management. A Colonel in the U.S. Army Reserve, he serves on the faculty of the Postgraduate Intelligence Program for Reserves at the Joint Military Intelligence College. The material here has been adapted from the author's thesis written for Joint Military Intelligence College entitled *Knowledge-based Tools: A Solution for Optimizing Collection Requirements Management*. He writes of the importance of economic principles in the Intelligence Community. Often overlooked, even by the most seasoned intelligence professionals, those principles can "help the Intelligence Community to become more efficient and effective," thereby better serving our consumers.

■ **William H. Drohan** works in the Defense Intelligence Agency and has experience in both the Drug Enforcement Administration and the United States Customs Service. A graduate of the Joint Military Intelligence College with the Master of Science of Strategic Intelligence degree, Drohan is a Colonel in the U.S. Army Reserve and serves with the faculty of the Postgraduate Intelligence Program for Reserves. As his article points out, the war on drugs remains important to our national security. That war has been almost "lost in the shuffle" since the nation turned its attention to terrorism after 9/11. Yet illegal drugs remain a threat, and the profits made from their sale and distribution help to finance shadowy terrorist operations. Drohan assesses this problem by looking at the economic roots of what he calls "narco-mercantilism."